GM01548268

READING ROBERT BURNS:
TEXTS, CONTEXTS, TRANSFORMATIONS

Poetry and Song in the Age of Revolution

Series Editors: Michael Brown
Katherine Campbell
John Kirk
Andrew Noble

Titles in this Series

1 United Islands? The Languages of Resistance
John Kirk, Andrew Noble and Michael Brown (eds)

2 Literacy and Orality in Eighteenth-Century Irish Song
Julie Henigan

3 Cultures of Radicalism in Britain and Ireland
John Kirk, Michael Brown and Andrew Noble (eds)

4 The Politics of Song in the Age of Revolution
Kate Horgan

5 James Orr, Poet and Irish Radical
Carol Baraniuk

www.pickeringchatto.com/poetryandsong

READING ROBERT BURNS:
TEXTS, CONTEXTS, TRANSFORMATIONS

BY

Carol McGuirk

PICKERING & CHATTO
2014

Published by Pickering & Chatto (Publishers) Limited
21 Bloomsbury Way, London WC1A 2TH

2252 Ridge Road, Brookfield, Vermont 05036-9704, USA

www.pickeringchatto.com

All rights reserved.
No part of this publication may be reproduced,
stored in a retrieval system, or transmitted in any form or by any means,
electronic, mechanical, photocopying, recording, or otherwise
without prior permission of the publisher.

© Pickering & Chatto (Publishers) Ltd 2014
© Carol McGuirk 2014

To the best of the Publisher's knowledge every effort has been made to contact
relevant copyright holders and to clear any relevant copyright issues.
Any omissions that come to their attention will be remedied in future editions.

BRITISH LIBRARY CATALOGUING IN PUBLICATION DATA

McGuirk, Carol author.
Reading Robert Burns: texts, context, transformations. – (Poetry and song in the age of revolution)
1. Burns, Robert, 1759–1796 – Criticism, Textual. 2. Burns, Robert, 1759–1796 – Language. I. Title II. Series
821.6-dc23

ISBN-13: 9781848935198
e: 9781781444986
ePUB: 9781781444993

This publication is printed on acid-free paper that conforms to the American
National Standard for the Permanence of Paper for Printed Library Materials.

Typeset by Pickering & Chatto (Publishers) Limited
Printed and bound in the United Kingdom by CPI Books

CONTENTS

Acknowledgements vii
List of Figures and Tables ix
Chronology xi

Introduction, with a Brief History of Burns's Relation to Literary Canons 1
1 Robt. Burness to Poet Burns: Bard, Interrupted 29
2 'If Thou Indeed Derive Thy Light from Heaven': Wordsworth Responds to Burns 75
3 Highlands: Burns, Lady Nairne and National Song 109
4 Three Drunk Men: Visionary Midnight in Robert Fergusson, Burns and Hugh MacDiarmid 151
Epilogue: Burns and Aphorism; or Poetry into Proverb 185

Notes 191
Works Cited 233
Index 245

ACKNOWLEDGEMENTS

A 2002–3 Research Fellowship from the National Endowment for the Humanities, allowing a year of study and writing, laid the groundwork for this book. I also thank the Thomas Cooper Library at the University of South Carolina for a W. Ormiston Roy Fellowship in summer 2004. Professors G. Ross Roy and Patrick Scott helped me to make optimal use of the Scottish poetry and Burns collections there. Sabbatical semesters from Florida Atlantic University in 2006 and 2013 enabled completion of several chapters and final revision of the work. The Dorothy F. Schmidt College of Arts and Letters and FAU English Department have provided funding for three research visits to Scotland.

Kenneth Dunn, Senior Curator of the Manuscripts and Maps Collection at the National Library of Scotland, gave crucial help before and during my research visit in 2012. I was able to examine Burns's Glenriddell Manuscript and the settlement agreement with Elizabeth Paton (December 1786). NLS staff were most helpful during an earlier visit as well, assisting me to trace early editions of the songs of Lady Nairne. Jason Sutcliffe, Museums and Development Manager for the East Ayrshire Council, along with Museums Officer Bruce Morgan and community liaison Linda Fairlie, welcomed me to Kilmarnock, which that day was undergoing what a Floridian immediately recognized as a small hurricane, however extratropical. They provided a quiet spot for me to look closely at 'Scotch Poems', otherwise called the Kilmarnock Manuscript in scholarly editions but, as I discovered, not known under that title in Scotland. Finally seeing it before me was a highlight of my research. Although the buffeting winds hindered travel south to view the Stair MS at the Alloway Robert Burns Birthplace Museum, I am most grateful to Amy Miller, Curator of the Museum, for her help in verifying the location and contents of the treasury of manuscripts held there. To the Mitchell Library in Glasgow I owe thanks for years of research support, from my early work on my dissertation (whose unofficial first director was Joe Fisher of the Mitchell) to my most recent visit in 2012. I thank Andrew Noble, John Kirk, Michael Brown and Katherine Campbell, editors of the Pickering & Chatto series Poetry and Song in the Age of Revolution, for their encouragement, their invaluable feedback and their patience.

Patricia Crain has provided perceptive readings of successive drafts, raising larger questions that greatly helped the revision process. I profited greatly from the discerning advice and encouragement of Julia Prewitt Brown and Ellen Pollak, who read the work at different difficult junctures. Parts of Chapter 3 ('Highlands') have been published in a different form in *Studies in Scottish Literature*, 35:1 (2007), pp. 184–201 and in a special issue on ballads, guest edited by Ruth Perry, in *Eighteenth Century: Theory and Interpretation*, 47 (2006), pp. 253–88. The Epilogue reprints in altered form the opening and closing pages of 'Burns and Aphorism', in *Robert Burns and Transatlantic Culture*, ed. Sharon Alker, Leith Davis and Holly Faith Nelson (Farnham, Surrey: Ashgate, 2012), pp. 169–87).

Early Burns editions given to me over the years by my kind brother, Dr Donald L. McGuirk, have allowed me to work productively from my home in South Florida. My coeditors at the journal *Science Fiction Studies* (Arthur B. Evans, Istvan Csicsery-Ronay, Jr, Joan Gordon, Veronica Hollinger, Rob Latham and Sherryl Vint) have generously shouldered more than their share of the editorial work during my sporadic mental absences, especially during the final phases of this project. Finally, I thank all friends, colleagues and family members who have encouraged this work, among them Paul and Ellen Alkon, Henry and Nancy Fulton, Dick Hudson, Thomas Keith, Diana Curry McGuirk, Sean McGuirk and Marsha Gillette, Stuart and Jane McGuirk, Laurie Prencipe, Katherine and Brian Rittershaus, Lucie Roy, Elizabeth (Lisa) Swanstrom and Scott Svatos, Sandra Taylor, Helen Vendler, Simon Walton of the Baltimore Robert Burns Society (NA) and Wenying Xu. I thank the late Kenneth G. Simpson for his gentle friendship, his scholarship and his organization of the annual University of Strathclyde Burns conferences as well as his editing of the ensuing conference volumes. The late G. Ross Roy, mentor of so many Burns scholars over the years, is an important influence on this work.

No book is thrown together as quickly as a fritter, as Cervantes observes in *Don Quixote*; but this one was unusually protracted in the making, which has only multiplied my debt to (and gratitude for) the organizations, institutions, colleagues, family members and steadfast friends who have helped along the way.

LIST OF FIGURES AND TABLES

Figure 3.1: Carolina Oliphant (later Lady Nairne) at the time she was writing many of her songs — 129

Figure 3.2: Carolina Oliphant's sketch of her birthplace, the Old House at Gask, abandoned for a new family house *c.* 1800 — 148

Figure 3.3: Victorian revision of Nairne's original sketch of the Auld House — 149

Table 1.1: *The First Commonplace Book* (April 1783–October 1785). Sequence of texts and verse-forms; frequent use of common measure — 41

Table 1.2: 'Scotch Poems': Sequence of texts and verse-forms; emphasis on standard Habbie and traditional Scottish forms — 51

Table 1.3: *Poems, Chiefly in the Scottish Dialect*: Burness and Burns — 59

Table 2.1: Poems by Wordsworth most strongly linked to Burns — 76

CHRONOLOGY

25 January 1759	Robert Burns (also spelled Burnes or Burness) is born at Alloway in south-west Scotland, first child of William Burnes (as his father spelled the family name) and Agnes Broun (or Brown) Burnes.
1760	Gilbert Burnes is born.
1762	Agnes Burnes is born.
1764	Annabella Burnes is born.
1765	The last parish school having closed in 1752, Alloway has no regular schoolmaster or school building. William Campbell opens a school at Alloway Mill in early 1765 in which William Burnes enrols Robert and Gilbert, but the school closes a few weeks later when Campbell accepts the position of Master of the Workhouse in Ayr. On behalf of several local families, William Burnes conducts an emergency search for a new teacher. He hires John Murdoch (1747–1824). Tuition and boarding of the schoolmaster are shared among the participating families.
1766–77	The Alloway cottage becomes too small for the family and William Burnes, who has failed to profit sufficiently from Alloway's seven-and-a-half acre market garden, is relying for income on work as a gardener at Doonholm, an estate near Ayr. Trying for independence, he rents Mount Oliphant farm, seventy acres leased for twelve years from his generous Ayr employer, William Fergusson, a retired London physician. At Mount Oliphant the family will be able to stay together rather than sending the older children away to work on other farms as paid labourers and helpers. Located on the grounds of Doonholm, Mount Oliphant is far from the main roads. Its soil is poor and the family struggle with unavailing intensity to succeed as tenant farmers. Robert and Gilbert continue at Murdoch's school in Alloway until he leaves the area in 1768.
1767	William Burnes, a third son, is born at Mount Oliphant.
1767 or 1768 (?)	Ashamed of his handwriting, William Burnes dictates to the schoolmaster Murdoch a catechism now known as *A Manual of Religious Belief*, in which salvation (contrary to strict Calvinism) is said to be achieved in part by good works and strenuous personal effort. Original sin is described but there is no mention of Hell or punishment. The strongest proof of the existence of a benevolent Creator, Burnes teaches his small children, is all around them in the perfect beauty of the natural world.
1769	John Burnes is born.
1771	Isabella (or Isobel) Burnes, youngest of the family, is born.

1772	In summer Robert and Gilbert take turns attending a school in Dalrymple in order to improve their handwriting.
1773	Burns lodges in Ayr as a pupil of John Murdoch, newly returned to the region. At William Burnes's behest, they review English grammar, but the poet-to-be also absorbs the rudiments of French (an interest of Murdoch's) well enough to read Fenelon's *Les aventures de Télémaque, fils d' Ulysse* (1699) without help from an English translation. The subject matter is as congenial as the language-study: Fenelon's character Mentor criticises war-mongering kings and narrow nationalism, promoting universal brotherhood and human rights.
1774	Smitten by his partner in the harvest, Burns writes his first song, 'O once I lov'd' ['Handsome Nell']. 'I did not well know … why the tones of her voice made my heartstrings thrill like an Eolian harp … Among her other love-inspiring qualifications, she sung sweetly; and 'twas her favorite reel to which I attempted giving an embodied vehicle in rhyme'.
Mid- or possibly late 1770s	Burns, in his 'seventeenth year', attends a dancing school in Tarbolton in 'absolute defiance' of his father. By the poet's account, their bitter confrontation causes a permanent breach: 'from that instance of rebellion, my father took a kind of dislike to me, which, I believe was one cause of that dissipation which marked my future years. I only say, Dissipation, comparative with the strictness and sobriety of Presbyterean [sic] country life'. In his autobiographical letter to Moore, the poet tells this story before describing his summer studies in Kirkoswald that same year (see the item below), but the quarrel might have happened after Burns's return from school. In the letter to Moore Burns calls this period of his mid-teens his 'climacterick'. Along with the onset of puberty, a great change is Burns's increasing determination to stay connected with young people outside his family. Resigned to tireless and uncomplaining labour alongside his parents and siblings, he rejects with growing vehemence the social isolation of farming life as he has known it.
1775 [July–September?]	He stays several months in Kirkoswald, studying mensuration and trigonometry at Hugh Rodger's locally renowned mathematics school. Kirkoswald is a centre for brandy smuggling, in which sideline Burns's uncle, Samuel Broun (or Brown), with whom the poet lodges on a farm outside the town, is probably active. (Accused of skipping Sabbath worship in order to smuggle, Brown indignantly replies that he never neglects church attendance.) Toward the end of the term, Burns is dazzled by the charms of Margaret Thomson; the couple continue to see each other occasionally until her marriage to John Neilson in 1784. By some accounts, they meet in Tarbolton where they attend the same church; but as Kirkoswald is almost twenty miles from Tarbolton, this seems unlikely unless she sometimes stays with relatives in the area.

Whitsunday (Pentecost) 1777	William Burnes moves the family from Mount Oliphant to Lochlie (or Lochlea) farm. Following the death of William Fergusson late in 1776, management of Doonholm and its farms is delegated to a factor who harasses the family for payment of overdue rent. 'A Novel-Writer might perhaps have viewed these scenes with some satisfaction', Burns later recalls of these threatening visits, 'but so did not I'. Lochlie lies some two and a half miles from Tarbolton; its rent is more than triple that of Mount Oliphant. The family's new landlord, David McLure, requires no written agreement about the terms of the lease. This leads over several years to a protracted legal fight that hinges on whether William Burnes has been promised that McLure will see to (or reimburse Burnes for) the liming of Lochlie's acidic soil. Burnes evidently deducts from the rent the costs of any improvements. He is soon in arrears, for the rent is high: twenty shillings an acre.
11 November 1780	Burns is founder and first President of a monthly debating society, the Tarbolton Bachelors' Club. These were popular in cities but Burns's may be the first debating club established in rural Scotland. One of the early topics is whether a 'young man, bred as a farmer but without any future' should marry 'a girl of large fortune, but neither handsome in person nor agreeable' or 'a girl every way agreeable…without any fortune'. Burns argues the case for the undowered girl.
4 July 1781	Burns is initiated as a Freemason in Tarbolton.
Late summer 1781– January 1782	Probably with help from his father, Burns invests in a business partnership that fails, staying in the town of Irvine to learn flax dressing. After several months of exhausting labour learning to process the harvested flax through three stages – breaking, 'scutching' (scraping) and 'heckling' (combing) – he falls seriously ill. A prayer in verse written around this time is later copied into Burns's *First Commonplace Book* with a description of ominous symptoms: 'fainting fits, & … a Pleurisy, or other dangerous disorder, which indeed still threaten me'. Chest pain and fainting suggest heart disease, although the doctor who treats Burns prescribes drugs (emetics, laxatives and especially quinine) that themselves can cause fainting and an irregular heartbeat. The quinine can indicate treatment for fever but it is also used to treat seizures and muscle cramps. Burns is visited by his alarmed father, who moves him from the loft of the dust-filled flax storage shed, where he has been sleeping, into a clean and quiet rented room. On New Years' Day 1782, the shed catches fire during a holiday celebration and all hopes of profit go up in flames. Deterred by continuing ill health or perhaps by the heavy snows that winter, Burns stays on in Irvine until early March. Dates are uncertain but the year's disasters include a jilting 'under peculiar circumstances of mortification' by 'Dear E' (probably Elizabeth Gebbie).
1783	William Burnes's goods and stock are seized for non-payment of rent at Lochlie farm.

1783–5	Burns begins to transcribe what later generations will call *The First Commonplace Book*. (The delightful but very discursive title page offers a self-introduction that is 137-words long.) The first entries copy early writings and muse on remorse and love. In later entries he begins to add new work, including early versions of his verse-letters to John Lapraik. By the time *The First Commonplace Book* is broken off in September 1785, it has become a lively working notebook.
November 1785	Death of the poet's sixteen-year-old brother, John, from a wasting illness, probably tuberculosis.
Autumn 1783	In their own names, Robert and Gilbert sublease Mossgiel farm, 118 acres at a rent of £90, as a shelter for the family in the event that their father loses the fight over the terms of the lease at Lochlie. Mossgiel is much less isolated than the family's earlier steadings, not quite a mile from the town of Mauchline. Gavin Hamilton has been leasing the former dairy farm from the Earl of Loudon as a summer residence, but his wife dislikes the place and Hamilton wants to help the poet's family. Like Burns, Gavin Hamilton is a Freemason.
Late January 1784	William Burnes wins his legal battle in late January but dies, most likely of tuberculosis, on 13 February. Creditors descend on the family. 'When my father died, his all went among the rapacious hell-hounds that growl in the kennel of justice'. William Burnes is buried according to his wishes in the graveyard of the abandoned church of Alloway, the village in which he and Agnes Broun had set up their first household in December 1757 and where they had welcomed their first four children.
22 May 1785	Burns's first child, Elizabeth (Bess, d. 1817), is born to Elizabeth Paton. The poet and the elder Bess meet when she is employed at Lochlie farm during William Burnes's lingering illness. Burns addresses his newborn daughter in a striking early poem. He never publishes the stanzas but continues to polish them for six years, copying a final version, 'A Poet's Welcome to his love-begotten Daughter', into the Glenriddell Manuscript.
Late 1785	Burns purchases a blank notebook that he titles 'Scotch Poems'. His signature is the same as that for *The First Commonplace Book*: 'Robt. Burness'. The work contains fifteen poems, almost all in Scottish vernacular. 'Scotch Poems' is also the title given on the subscription forms for his proposed first publication (his 'Proposal' is dated 14 April 1786), so this notebook plays a part in his earliest planning for printing his poems. It serves him as a home for fair copies and a place to experiment with how to design an appealing sequence of texts. The first two entries are stanzas 1–18 and part of stanza 20 of 'The Holy Fair', followed by stanzas 18–28 and part of stanza 17 of 'Halloween'. Conserving paper, the poet fills up almost the whole of each page, leaving as little of a margin as possible.
February 1786	Jean Armour tells Burns that she is pregnant, or so the poet hints in a letter of February 17 to his friend John Richmond. The couple have known each other for a year or two (sources differ), having met in 1784 or 1785.

March 1786	Jean Armour tells her parents that she is pregnant and that the father is Burns. James Armour faints away and Mary Smith Armour hastens to a tavern to fetch a cordial. Jean, one of eleven children, is Mr Armour's favourite. When he has revived, their daughter shows her parents a co-signed marriage agreement, but the Armours confiscate it, hiring Robert Aiken, an Ayr attorney (also a friend of Burns's, a fellow Freemason) to void the contract. Even mutual spoken agreement under Scottish law makes up what is called a private or irregular marriage, legitimising any child; but the angry parents repudiate Burns as a prospective son-in-law, seeking a money settlement instead. In mid-April, Aiken cuts the lovers' signatures out of the document, declaring it void. Jean Armour is despatched to relatives in Paisley, not returning until early in June. Because the marriage agreement has been rejected, both lovers will undergo three Sundays of public penance for fornication during the coming summer.
14 April 1786	Burns receives the subscription forms or 'Proposals' for a volume of 'SCOTCH POEMS' (large capitals as on the forms) by 'Robert Burns'. He has settled on the spelling of the name by which posterity will remember him. In a letter to Gavin Hamilton next day, Burns expresses shock over Aiken's destruction of the marriage agreement: 'when [James Armour] told me, the names were all cut out of the paper, my heart died within me, and he cut my very veins'.
April–May 1786	On the rebound following what he sees as Jean Armour's 'broken vow' (a phrase he uses in a poem written during this month), Burns courts Margaret Campbell ('Highland Mary'), a dairymaid who once may have worked in Gavin Hamilton's house as a nursemaid. Myth has entwined itself inexorably round her story, but it is probable that Burns is courting her with marriage in mind. They part on the third Sunday in May so that she can visit her family, an idyllic day in a painful year that Burns memorialises in several famous late songs. At that last meeting, Burns gives her his two-volume Bible.
13 June 1786	Takes his poems to John Wilson of Kilmarnock, at the time the only printer of books in Ayrshire. Avoiding the elder Armours, who have taken out a writ against him, he stays during this summer with his mother's sister, Jean Broun Allan, and her husband; their house is said to be convenient to the printer's office, but its location is no longer known.
19 June 1786	Charles Douglas writes from Jamaica to his brother Patrick, who owns two plantations that Charles manages, that he seeks to employ a young emigrant Scot as a bookkeeper (assistant overseer). This position is offered to Burns later in the summer. The 'bookies' directly supervise and discipline the plantation's groups of enslaved men, women and children.
31 July 1786	*Poems Chiefly in the Scottish Dialect* is published; the price is 3 shillings. Volumes not reserved for subscribers sell out in less than a month. Burns is still in hiding from the Armours. His patrons are urging him to emigrate to Jamaica, a prospect that all but unhinges him.

July or August 1786	Burns pays nine guineas to a shipping agent in Irvine for steerage transport to Jamaica. His first plan is to sail to western Jamaica on the *Nancy* in late summer and travel overland to the Douglas properties but on visiting his prospective employer and hearing advice from Douglas's visiting Jamaican houseguests, he decides on the *Bell* sailing to Kingston, much closer to the Douglas properties. He never goes to Greenock to board this second ship, however, perhaps because Jean Armour (who has resumed seeing Burns without telling her parents) is about to go into labour.
3 September 1786	Burns hears from Jean Armour's brother that she has given birth to twins, Robert and Jean. In another sign of continuing hostilities, infant Robert (d. 1857) is fostered by his grandmother at Mossgiel farm, who also is rearing Burns's daughter Bess; infant Jean (d. October 1787) remains with the Armours.
October 1786	Margaret Campbell ('Highland Mary') dies at Greenock of typhus shortly after nursing her brother safely through the same illness. Burns has sent unanswered letters to her; he learns of her death some weeks after it occurs when her uncle in Greenock informs him by letter.
28 November 1786	Arrives in Edinburgh hoping to find a publisher for a second edition of his writings. Almost his first stop is the Canongate churchyard, where he pauses over an unmarked grave to commune with the spirit of his favourite vernacular predecessor, Robert Fergusson, who had died at the age of twenty-four in 1779 while confined in the Edinburgh madhouse.
9 December 1786	Henry Mackenzie praises Burns's *Poems, Chiefly in the Scottish Dialect* in his periodical paper, *The Lounger*, marvelling 'with what uncommon penetration and sagacity this Heaven-taught ploughman has looked upon men and manners'. A few days after the review appears, William Creech (publisher of *The Lounger* and like Henry Mackenzie a Freemason), offers Burns a new subscription edition. The poet will not have to sail to Jamaica on the *Roselle*; his third prospective ship departs without him in late December.
February 1787	Burns applies to the governors of Edinburgh's Canongate Church for permission to place a stone on Robert Fergusson's unmarked grave.
17 April 1787	Publication of the Edinburgh edition of *Poems, Chiefly in the Scottish Dialect*, which reprints all but two texts from the 1786 edition and adds twenty-two poems.
22 May 1787	The first volume of James Johnson's *The Scots Musical Museum* is published, including two or three songs by Burns (only one, 'Green grow the rashes', is signed). Johnson, a printer, uses pewter plates to cut costs; his plan is for a series of inexpensive songbooks, and from 1786 Burns is in active collaboration with this project, sending 121 songs.
May/June 1787	Burns begins a summer of Scottish travel with a tour of the Borders (a letter of 17 May refers to it as 'a slight pilgrimage to the classic scenes of this country'), collecting song-texts along the way. After going across northern England from Newcastle to Carlisle, he returns through Dumfries and the tour ends around mid-June in Mauchline.
25 June 1787	He sets out on the first of two brief tours of the Highlands, meeting the gentry (he is armed with many letters of introduction) and, mindful of James Johnson's songbook, continuing to learn new songs. Called back to Edinburgh by William Creech on some detail about the 1787 edition of *Poems*, he then resumes his travels. Among his stops are Inverness and (twice) Stirling. In Stonehaven, he meets his Burness relatives. By mid-September he has returned to Edinburgh.

4 December 1787	Burns meets Agnes Craig M'Lehose, exactly Burns's age and the mother of three sons but estranged from her husband, who lives in Jamaica with a second family. They engage in a heated correspondence (6 December 1787–18 March 1788) in which they assume the names 'Sylvander' and 'Clarinda'. 'Nancy' M'Lehose inspires several of Burns's best songs.
14 February 1788	The second volume of *The Scots Musical Museum* is published, including thirty-seven songs by Burns, only one of which is fully signed, although a later reprint puts the poet's full name to sixteen; his other contributions are coded or (especially in the case of Jacobite songs) left unsigned.
3 March 1788	Jean Armour gives birth to twin girls by Burns. One dies seven days later and the other on 28 March.
25 April 1788	Orders a wedding gift, a shawl, for Jean Armour.
4 May 1788 [incorrectly dated 1789 by Burns]	Grandly puts in a bizarre order for 'three or four stones of feathers' for household bedding from his Kirkoswald uncle Samuel Brown (as it is spelled in the letter). To his brandy-smuggling uncle he writes using a smuggling metaphor for his own conduct over the last two years, but he speaks of turning over a new leaf. 'I engaged in the smuggling Trade and God knows if any poor man experienced better returns ... But as freight and Delivery has turned out so D—md Dear I am thinking about takeing [*sic*] out a Licence and beginning a Fair trade'.
25 May 1788	In a calmer letter to Robert Ainslie, Burns speaks of his marriage with Jean Armour as re-established: 'I am truly pleased ... it has indeed added to my anxieties for Futurity but it has given a stability to my mind & resolutions, unknown before'. There is no official record of a new exchange of vows, but the Train Ms. reports that the private marriage takes place in Gavin Hamilton's law office in Mauchline.
May 1788	Having settled accounts with William Creech for the Edinburgh *Poems*, Burns sends £180 (nearly half his profits) to his brother Gilbert to help the struggling Mossgiel family. It is a loan, but for many years Gilbert can repay no part of it, even when pressured by the trustees for Burns's estate. In 1820, he finally reimburses the estate using the proceeds of his own edition of his brother's writings.
11 June 1788	Burns signs a seventy-six-year lease for Ellisland, a farm northwest of Dumfries. Jean Armour and their surviving child Robert join him in December when a house has been built and furnished.
14 July 1788	Having been trained in his various duties, Burns receives his Excise commission. In Burns's day, the Excise collects taxes on many commodities from silks, silver wire and wheeled carriages to vellum and parchment paper; but the imposition of taxes on alcoholic beverages is especially unpopular. Burns does not seem much troubled by the social stigma, perhaps reflecting on his recent narrow escape from the far worse occupation of plantation overseer.
August 1789	Francis Wallace Burns (d. 1803) is born at Ellisland farm.
September 1789	Burns is appointed Excise Officer for Dumfries at an annual salary of £35.
February 1790	The fourth volume of *The Scots Musical Museum* is published, including forty songs by Burns, only six of which are signed with his full name.
24 July 1790	Death of William, the poet's youngest surviving brother, from a fever in London, where has been learning the trade of saddler.

31 March 1791	Birth of a daughter to Helen Ann Park, Burns's second daughter to be named Elizabeth. It is sometimes assumed that 'Anna' dies in childbirth but it may be that she (like Elizabeth Paton) agrees to give her child to Burns while she begins a new life. Jean Armour nurses 'Betty' along with her own son, William Nichol Burns (d. 1872), who is ten days younger. Longest lived of Burns's children, Betty dies in 1873.
10 September 1791	Gives up the lease on Ellisland farm; in November the family move to the town of Dumfries.
6 December 1791	The final meeting of Burns and 'Clarinda', which inspires the song 'Ae Fond Kiss'. Forty years later at age seventy-one, Agnes M'Lehose writes in a journal entry for 6 December 1831 that 'This day I can never forget. Parted with Burns, in the year 1791, never more to meet in this world. Oh, may we meet in Heaven!'
February 1792	Burns is appointed Excise Officer for the Port of Dumfries at an increased salary of £50.
September 1792	Song-editor George Thomson writes to Burns requesting contributions for his songbook series *A Selection Collection of Original Scottish Airs for the Voice* (1793–1845). The two often disagree about the level of gentility to which songs should aspire, which initiates a long correspondence, partly obscured by Thomson having poured ink over some parts of Burns's letters to him. After the poet's death, Thomson attempts to claim copyright for the songs Burns has sent to him despite the poet's insistence in a letter of April 1793 that, as with James Johnson's series, he sends the material gratis to Thomson but is retaining copyright: 'I give Johnson one edition of my songs [but] that does not give away the copy-right'. Burns evidently much regrets having sold the rights to his *Poems*; he never again conveys copyright to a third party.
21 November 1792	His third daughter to be named Elizabeth (d. 1795) is born to Jean Armour.
February 1793	William Creech brings out in two volumes the third and final edition of *Poems, Chiefly in the Scottish Dialect*, with eighteen as yet unpublished writings. 'Tam o'Shanter' makes its first appearance in Burns's *Poems* but has been published earlier (March 1791) in two Scottish newspapers and in April 1791 in Francis Grose's *Antiquities of Scotland* (vol. 2).
12 August 1794	A son, James Glencairn Burns (d. 1865), is born to Jean.
December– April 1794	Burns is appointed Acting Supervisor of the Excise during a serious illness of Alexander Findlater, regular Supervisor in Dumfries.
January 1795	Burns joins the Royal Dumfries Volunteers, formed to repel any future French invasion. The volunteers agree to buy their own uniforms and they serve without pay, training twice a week. They are pledged to serve for town defense only and may not fight outside a five-mile radius of Dumfries. Private Burns attends drill punctually and is never fined for any infraction.
September 1795	Burns is distraught over the sudden death of his youngest daughter, Elizabeth Riddell Burns, shortly before her third birthday.

31 January 1796	Burns writes of hard times and hunger in Dumfries to his elderly friend Anna Wallace Dunlop: 'here, we have famine, & that too in the midst of plenty'. He mentions also his worsening health. He has been suffering from 'a most severe Rheumatic fever ... until after many weeks of a sick-bed I am beginning to crawl across my room'.
12–14 March 1796	Food riots in Dumfries.
3–18 July 1796	Diagnosed by his friend and family physician Dr Maxwell with a 'flying Gout', Burns follows medical advice and tries the waters at Brow Well and bathing in the Solway. His friend Maria Riddell is nearby and invites him to dine with her: 'I was struck with his appearance on entering the room. The stamp of death was imprinted on his features. He seemed already touching the brink of eternity. His first salutation was: 'Well, madam, have you any commands for the other world?'
21 July 1796	Burns dies in Dumfries, most biographers think from complications of infective endocarditis. Jean Armour gives birth to their last child, Maxwell (d. 1799), on the day of Burns's funeral.
December 1796	The fifth volume of Johnson's *Scots Musical Museum* appears with thirty-seven songs by Burns, fifteen of which are fully signed. Johnson's sixth and final volume is delayed until 1803 but includes twenty-six poems identified as by Burns.

Sources

Quotations from Burns are from his letters, most from his 2 August 1787 letter to Dr John Moore, usually referred to as the autobiographical letter. Several other cited letters are listed by date so that they may be easily found. G. R. Roy and J. D. Ferguson (eds), *Letters of Robert Burns*, 2 vols (Oxford: Clarendon, 1985), vol. 1, pp. 133–46.

Information about Burns's elusive signature on his later songs is taken from J. W. Egerer (ed.), *A Bibliography of Robert Burns* (Edinburgh: Oliver & Boyd, 1964), Appendixes 1 and 2, pp. 357–64.

Henry Mackenzie's review of Burns's *Poems* is cited from D. A. Low (ed.), *Robert Burns: The Critical Heritage* (London: Routledge & Kegan Paul, 1974), pp. 67–70.

The quotation from Agnes M'Lehose's journal is from M. Lindsay (ed.), *The Burns Encyclopedia*, 3rd edn (New York: St Martin's Press, 1980), p. 263.

For Maria Riddell's account of her last meeting with Burns, see R. Chambers (ed.) and W. Wallace (rev.), *The Life and Works of Robert Burns*, 4 vols (Edinburgh: W. and R. Chambers, 1896), vol. 4, p. 276.

INTRODUCTION, WITH A SHORT HISTORY OF BURNS'S RELATIONS TO LITERARY CANONS

> I was born a poor dog; and ... I know that a poor dog I must live & die. – But I will induldge [*sic*] the flattering faith that my Poetry will considerably out-live my Poverty.
> Burns, Letter to Mrs Graham of Fintry, 10 June 1790[1]

Burns is famed as a Scottish cultural icon, the source of many phrases and sayings still in lively circulation; but his iconic familiarity has been of little service to critics. The broad brush of myth has only diverted attention from ambiguous and elusive elements in his writings, which often are my topic here. Burns wrote poems and (even more prolifically) songs, with the songs often transmitted anonymously. Critics have tended to focus on one or the other, leaving the relation between his poems and songs unstudied.[2] A further barrier to seeing Burns in total is his literary language, an ever-shifting mixture of vernacular Scots and literary English. During the twentieth-century ascendancy of literary modernism, such influential arbiters as T. S. Eliot rejected Burns's hybrid diction, calling it incompatible with the broad traditions of British poetry. In the same era, specialists in Scottish studies generally preferred to focus on Burns's dialect-intense work, a different way of imposing language consistency on a writer committed to *negotiating* the distance between English and Scots.[3] Another matter that invites further discussion is Burns's creative reconstruction of folk-collected lyrics. He retained copyright for his later songs, suggesting that he thought of them as 'his', but he refused payment and signed very few. He devised a code to identify levels of authorship but sometimes used the code in a spirit of gleeful mischief, a topic of Chapter 3. Jacobite songs often remained unsigned even in code, not necessarily because Burns did not write them, but because if his revival of Jacobitism's seditious commentary on the Hanoverian kings had become generally known, it might have led to his dismissal from the Excise. Finally, any of his writings that contradict elements in the Burns myth tend to be overlooked: posterity prefers that larger-than-life character described by John Berryman in the 1960s as 'drunky, sexy Burns'.[4]

My aim in these pages is not concerned with defining his personality or speculating about his character. I agree with Don Paterson's observation that 'the character of Burns is so complicated as effectively not to exist at all – there is barely a human trait which he did not exhibit, at one time or another, as if it somehow *defined* him'.[5] My focus on providing as full as possible a view of Burns's writings required frequent reconsideration of basic matters and materials, including early manuscripts, preferred verse-forms, habits of revision and biographical and political/cultural contexts insofar as they affected his work. Some of the chapters read comparatively neglected texts ('The Vision'; 'The Whistle'; 'Death and Dr Hornbook') while others approach familiar texts from a new angle: 'Tam o'Shanter' is read in Chapter 4 as a dreamlike montage of scenes from Burns's early life. As in the chapters on Wordsworth's and Nairne's adaptations of Burns, I often read Burns in tandem with other writers.

Myths deal in broad archetypes but the *poet* is in the details. Poets are 'makers' in both Greek and Scottish etymologies; they craft poems by synthesizing disparate elements, from meter, rhyme, verse-form and literary allusion to personal thoughts, political beliefs, current events and literary traditions. One complexity I consider in these pages is far from unique to Burns. This is his link to poets who inspired him and later poets' echoes of his work in their own writings. Both his signed poems and his unattributed songs reached audiences not only in Scotland and the rest of Britain and Ireland but throughout North America. Burns wrote during a time of revolutions which he supported; and post-revolutionary societies in the United States and Canada found his work especially congenial. In the nineteenth century, Walt Whitman argued that Burns is best read not as 'Scottish' but as a 'distinct specimen' of a global 'race': 'the good-natured, warm-blooded, proud-spirited, amative, alimentive, convivial, young and early-mid-aged man ... everywhere and any how'.[6] The Americans Whitman and Ralph Waldo Emerson may have been the first to read Burns as a world poet. Finally, biographical contexts for Burns's writings are sometimes introduced here, particularly close consideration of spring and summer of 1786 in Chapter 1. Several crises he faced then greatly affected the poems that he was revising and readying for publication in the same months. On occasion, later chapters turn briefly to his final years in Dumfries to support my sense that this part of Burns's life, despite deteriorating health, was marked by creative productivity rather than the steep decline emphasized in so many biographies.

My original plan was to consider Burns's writings in contexts both popular and specifically literary; to read him in terms of his development as a writer and his impact on later poets and later audiences. That was expanded, for in early stages of writing and research my study of two early manuscript gatherings – now called *The First Commonplace Book* (1783–5) and *The Kilmarnock Manuscript* (late 1785–early 1786) although these were not Burns's titles – disclosed a distinct variation in his voice. These two alternate personae do not constitute another dyad to be added to those already described: folk versus 'high' culture, poems versus songs, Scots vernacular diction versus 'literary' English. For they are not contraries: one is a dramatic extension of the other.

The poet's default or original voice I call 'Rob Burness', as he signed both those early manuscript collections. Burness channels Scotland without a framing commentary, sometimes using a dialogue format (as in 'The Brigs of Ayr' or 'The Twa Dogs') but more often a dramatic monologue, as in 'The Death and Dying Words of Poor Mailie' or 'The Auld Farmer's New-year-morning Salutation'. Rob Burness is a *bard* whose writings invite readers' full immersion in the here-and-now of the character(s) speaking up. 'Love and Liberty', in which a series of beggars tell their stories, is Burness's masterwork. Poems by the alternate speaker, 'Poet Burns', also often employ dramatic monologue but for a different purpose, as monologue shifts to soliloquy. Poet Burns speaks more urgently and far more personally. If bardic Burness speaks for and as Scotland as it was and is, Poet Burns speaks for himself and for a Scotland yet to be, a nation more equitable and free. This second voicing, more self-conscious (one might as well say more 'Romantic'), can be self-accusing and melodramatic, an element that Wordsworth found compelling, as Chapter 2 discusses.

Neither of the two voicings is restricted by mode, diction or genre. Each speaks in both poems and songs; each sometimes speaks in vernacular, sometimes English but most often in one of Burns's protean blends. One cannot restrict the two even by date, for Rob Burness, the earlier voicing, re-emerges after 1787 in many (though not all) of the hundreds of songs written before Burns's death in 1796. I suggest in Chapter 1 that Poet Burns does have a definite starting point: spring 1786; but *The First Commonplace Book* (begun in 1783) is among other things an attempt to awaken this more personal voicing, although full breakthrough required a few more years and a more confident command of verse-forms beyond the common measure in which most of Burns's earliest work was cast. Breakthrough occurred under intense pressure from the worst crisis that Burns ever faced. From April 1786 to the end of that year, when a second edition of *Poems* was offered and he could cancel a booked voyage to Jamaica where a position as bookkeeper (assistant overseer) on a sugar plantation awaited him, Poet Burns pushed back against forces, as he saw it, that were about to destroy him. He engaged in those months in fierce self-scrutiny; and he buried Rob Burness in the Kilmarnock volume's final poem.

Although Poet Burns emerges in 1786, he coexists with rather than replacing Burness, who soon returns as an alternate persona with a more impersonal way of working. Poet Burns continues to speak in political poems and songs such as 'Is There for Honest Poverty' as well as such *tours de force* as 'Tam o' Shanter' and 'The Whistle', magnificent mock-epics discussed in Chapter 4. Impersonal, bardic Burness and personal, 'I am a poet' Burns offer, among other things, alternative representations of Scottish time. 'Rob Burness' addresses Scotland's past and present, but 'Poet Burns' imagines a future under construction – 'comin' yet', as the refrain of 'Is there for Honest Poverty' puts it. In Poet Burns's imagining, Scotland is not a house in ruins, never to be restored to ancient glory, as in Lady Nairne's belated Jacobitism, a topic of Chapter 3, but an open space – potentially a utopia for 'poor bodies'.

Burns's mixed poetic diction, which intertwines vernacular Scots with standard English, changed literary language forever, in Britain and also in more distant places; and his speakers are as provocative as his distinctive poetic language. The rural tenantry and peasantry were a frequent topic in eighteenth-century poetry, but they had been spoken for by a poet-interpreter in such poems as Oliver Goldsmith's 'The Deserted Village' (1770) and vernacular poet Robert Fergusson's 'The Farmer's Ingle' (1773). In Burns's recasting of this tradition, poor bodies hitherto mute speak for themselves. Burns's mixed poetic diction is precisely calibrated to link these rustic speakers' nonstandard vocabulary to rural struggle but also to shrewd and self-respecting survival. Burns's poor bodies voice thoughts as yet unexpressed (in unfiltered form) in the 'high' poetic tradition, although such voicings were familiar enough to Burns, and to such appreciative early readers of Burns as William and Dorothy Wordsworth, from eighteenth-century popular songs and ballads.

There is a lively current interest in Burns.[7] The pages that follow are intended to expand the discussion beyond specialists in Scottish studies and those familiar with Burns studies to those curious about the figure of Burns and seeking ways to bring his writings into their own reading, research and teaching. I discuss Burns's own literary idol, Robert Fergusson, but also consider his impact as a poet and songwriter on writers in and out of Scotland from his own day to ours: from Wordsworth (Chapter 2), Lady Nairne (Chapter 3) and Hugh MacDiarmid (Chapter 4) to Frederick Douglass (Epilogue).

Chapter Overview

Following this chapter overview, the introduction will sketch critical assumptions that have tended to limit the scope of Burns studies; I also suggest theoretical perspectives useful in challenging some persistent misconceptions. Chapter 1, 'Bard, Interrupted', begins with the poet's signature. 'Robert Burns' is a streamlined version of his family surname, Burness (the poet's father William had spelled it Burnes). The poet signed two important early manuscript collections 'Robt. Burness', and Chapter 1 considers these projects, now known as *The First Commonplace Book* and *The Kilmarnock Manuscript*. The poet does sign his name as 'Robert Burns' in some early letters (seven written before 1783, mainly to Kirkoswald classmates, bear this signature), but for several years he had used only 'Burness' when 'Robert Burns' reappears in April 1786 on subscribers' sheets for *Poems, Chiefly in the Scottish Dialect* (Kilmarnock, 1786). 'Burns' continued as his official signature – by which I mean the name he signed to identify his formally published writings – during the remaining ten years of his life.

Following discussion of the poet's signature(s), Chapter 1 turns to 1786, a year of changes in more than the poet's spelling of the family name. Early in the year, he became entangled in a toxic quarrel with the parents of Jean Armour, who had discovered that she was pregnant. In March, when she told her parents, she showed them a co-signed contract between herself and Burns (the story is complex: for details, see Chapter 1). The Armours pursued legal measures to void this contract (evidently a marriage agreement) and secure a financial settlement instead. At the same time, the poet was advised, perhaps by the Armours' attorney Robert Aiken (also a friend of Burns's, a fellow Freemason) to emigrate to Jamaica. Chapter 1 reconsiders these tangled and intertwining crises and suggests that they strongly coloured the work written or revised that spring. There is a break in Burns's life early in 1786, and the poems and songs completed after March 1786 or polished for publication in May and early June bear its traces and marks. Poet Burns was born in the same months that Rob Burness was undergoing a kind of social death in Mauchline, facing prospective exile and what he saw as a series of betrayals. Chapter 1 analyses, poem by poem, the two handwritten 'Burness' manuscripts and also Burns's first printed volume, *Poems, Chiefly in the Scottish Dialect*. The five poems that open the published volume were finished before April 1786 in fair copy and are redolent of bardic Rob Burness, who speaks for his native region of Kyle in south-west Scotland and also for Scotland at large later in the volume, in 'The Cotter's Saturday Night'. The voice of Poet Burns, after a memorable cameo appearance in the volume's frantic and defensive preface, emerges in the poems printed just before midpoint – specifically, in 'To a Mouse', #14 of the thirty-six items listed on the contents page.

Chapter 2 ("'If thou indeed derive thy Light from Heaven": Wordsworth Responds to Burns') reads the two poets comparatively, emphasizing eleven poems by Wordsworth in which Burns is addressed or invited into the poem; I also closely read Burns's 'The Vision' and several other Burns texts to which Wordsworth frequently alludes. Wordsworth by turns emulates and resists Burns's poetic example. Comparing this group of poems by both writers, a pattern soon emerges that helps to explain why there have been so few comparisons of a detailed nature: the Burns texts that were most important to Wordsworth (and also Coleridge) are among those least regarded today: not only 'The Vision' but 'Despondency, An Ode', 'To a Mountain Daisy' and 'A Bard's Epitaph'. Wordsworth recasts their imagery in 'Resolution and Independence', parts of the 'Immortality' ode, and several other poems. Coleridge works with Burns's 'Despondency' in his own 'Dejection, An

Ode' as well: a speaker's guilty consciousness and lost innocence figures strongly in both odes. A further recurring focus concerns how often Burns's writings transmitted to Wordsworth in a more palatable form eighteenth-century images and tropes that Burns himself had adapted from James Thomson, William Shenstone and (especially) Thomas Gray.

Chapter 3, 'Highlands: Burns, Lady Nairne and National Song', considers Burns's development of what he called 'national song' from the Jacobite song-tradition. The neo-Jacobite lyrics of Carolina Oliphant (later Baroness Nairne (1766–1845)) are also read in some detail. The two writers' opposite viewpoints (Nairne embraces the past; Burns looks to the future) suggest their contrary reshaping of an invitingly fluid tradition, for the Jacobite songs had used circumlocution to avoid sedition charges: their imagery is often tantalizingly oblique. Burns sees the Jacobites as sympathetic revolutionaries although their project of restoring a Stuart monarchy meant little to him. He was attracted to their rejection of the current (Hanoverian) ruling family and to what he saw as a strong lyric tradition: 'The Scotish [sic] Muses were all Jacobites', he marvels.[8] Lady Nairne's link to the rebellions was personal: her grandfather and father had fought in the '45 and after Culloden had wandered homeless through the Highlands. Her husband, however, though descended from a Jacobite lord, was an officer in the British army serving in the garrison at Edinburgh Castle. Nairne never told him that she was a writer of songs, probably because the intense sympathy her lyrics express for the Jacobites' lost heroes would have drawn William Murray Nairne's own loyalties into question at a time when he was attempting to recover his titles and estate. Nairne's chief interest, however, is not in inciting rebellion so much as in summoning beloved ghosts. Her 'auld house' and family seat becomes a symbol for a lost Scotland: Charles Edward Stuart had been sheltered in the house (and the Highlands) after failure of his campaign. Nairne's loyalties were divided between a husband who served the victorious royal family and family members who had been staunch Jacobites. She shows her 'Jacobite' side most clearly in her conspiratorial concealment of authorship. She passed her lyrics to performers and editors in altered handwriting. When forced to visit her publisher, she donned an elaborate disguise. Her authorship of such songs as 'Will Ye No Come Back Again' and 'Caller Herring' became gradually known only after her death in 1845, when her sister published her writings. This long-delayed publication under her own name has encouraged a mistaken idea that she was of a later generation than Burns, but she was just seven years younger. Burns and Nairne both define Scotland as a zone of resistance, and both, although for very different reasons, critique the present political system.

Chapter 4, 'Three Drunk Men: Visionary Midnight in Robert Fergusson, Burns and Hugh MacDiarmid', considers imagery associated with drink in Scottish poetry, especially in the work of two eighteenth-century Scots vernacular poets, Burns and Robert Fergusson, and twentieth-century vernacular modernist poet Hugh MacDiarmid, whose 1926 poem 'A Drunk Man Looks at the Thistle' often refers to Burns and 'Tam o'Shanter'. I begin the chapter with another Burns poem echoed by MacDiarmid, 'Death and Dr. Hornbook' (1785), in which a man encounters Death while returning home following a night of drinking. I turn then to 'The Whistle', a mock-epic/ballad about a drinking contest: Burns's neoclassical stylization is a distinctive innovation to the Scottish 'brawl' tradition. An extended reading of 'Tam o'Shanter', in which a Drunk Man observes a witches' dance encountered on his homeward ride, concludes this part of the chapter. 'Tam' is as deeply rooted in the poet's early life as 'The Cotter's Saturday Night'. 'Cotter' (1785) is notably high-minded and sentimental and 'Tam o' Shanter' (1790) is neither of those things; yet both intensely engage with the formidable spirit of William Burnes, the poet's late father. I emphasize the importance of Tam's destination (Shanter farm is near the village of Kirkoswald): the poet studied mathematics there at sixteen and there he may have experienced his first serious love-affair; his 'Angel' of that period was Margaret Thomson and she is remembered in various ways in 'Tam o'Shanter'. 'Three Drunk Men' also returns to early critics' and biographers' doggedly literal readings of Fergusson's, Burns's and even MacDiarmid's 'Drunk Man' speakers, suggesting that these poems draw on a tradition and cannot be taken as directly autobiographical. Burns himself is not Tam, who according to a Kirkowald classmate of Burns's is based on bibulous Douglas Graham, tenant of Shanter farm; moreover, the biographical element in this poem has more to do with dancing than with drink.

In closing, Chapter 4 considers tavern-life as depicted by Burns. Pleasant mixed gatherings after the close of the market-day express a vision of friendly sharing that for Burns has a utopian political element. His short poem deriding 'Great Folk' and their monopoly of political power was inscribed on a tavern window.

Finally, the Epilogue, 'Burns and Aphorism; or Poetry into Proverb', discusses the disintegration of Burns's distinctive poetic language and characters into scattered phrases and general cultural memory. The chapter opens with discussion of Burns's own use of aphorisms and proverbs, sometimes taken from Scottish folklore, sometimes from Shakespeare, Milton or the eighteenth-century English poets. Walter Benjamin's 'The Storyteller' describes aphorism in elegiac terms as 'a ruin which stands on the site of an old story', a good description of posterity's gradually diminished, fragmentary sense of every poet who lived and worked generations or centuries ago.[9] Cultural memory compresses and digests as it preserves. Nonetheless, Burns's images were transplanted, imported to new continents to become embedded in both everyday and literary language. *Reading Robert Burns* discusses his own writings (and life) and considers predecessors such as Thomas Gray and Robert Fergusson who inspired him. I also consider his impact on later generations, a focus that often leads to consideration of topics associated with Romanticism.

Burns and Literary Canons: A Short History

> [D]ecisions [about literary interpretations and value] are rarely ... arrived at methodically. What happens is rather that the institution requires interpretations to satisfy its tacit knowledge of the permitted range of sense ... But there clearly is a sense in which a professional body *knows* ... There is an institutionalized competence, and what it finds unacceptable is incompetent. It does not, as a rule, have to think hard about individual cases ... [I]t is upon the basis of a corpus of tacit knowledge – shared with whatever qualifications – by the senior ranks of the hierarchy, that we allow or disallow an interpretation.
>
> – Frank Kermode[10]

Any reading of Burns as a poet of broad literary import today is likely to find itself at odds with 'tacit knowledge' that he is significant chiefly as a Scottish writer. Although specialists in Scottish literature have for some time pursued more nuanced approaches, the general consensus on Burns continues to rest on two long-held assumptions: that Burns's poetic diction is 'natural' (i.e., as an untaught farmer, he wrote as he spoke) and, a simpler pre-emptive strike, that the Scots literary tradition itself is wholly separate from the English.

T. S. Eliot had a hand in both presumptions, referring to Burns in 1933 as the 'decadent representative of a great alien tradition',[11] a rich phrase summoning the full semantic range of 'decadent', from 'fallen into decay' to 'ruinously self-indulgent'. Notwithstanding the tempering 'great', 'alien' conveys difference with a strong hint of the grotesque. Eliot had argued in the *Athenaeum* in 1919 under the provocative title 'Was there a Scottish Literature?' that literary culture in Scotland 'was beginning to decay' as early as the Elizabethan era, 'precisely in the years when English literature was acquiring the power of a world literature'.[12] That review-essay ended with a forceful prescription:

> The basis for one literature is one language. The danger of disintegration of English literature and language would arise if the same language were employed by peoples too remote (for geographical or other reasons) to be able to pool their differences in a common metropolis.[13]

In Eliot's view, a mixed poetic language threatened civilization itself, imagined as an empire of consensus emanating out of a central city remote from any distant stirring of (barbaric) diversity. During his lifetime, Burns found himself at odds with the analogous views of Edinburgh's literati, the Scottish capital's cadre of professors and literary lawyers, who had likewise embraced a strict adherence to standard English and pressured him to abandon dialect Scots.

The contrast could not be more marked between Eliot's views and those of such postcolonial critics as Homi K. Bhabha, with his focus on hybridized 'processes' (including language) as 'in-between spaces' that open possible new 'sites of collaboration, and contestation'.[14] Yet in poetry studies modernist preferences still often prevail. Drawing on the formulations of Eliot and others, mid- and late twentieth-century critics continued to prescribe a literary and language homogeneity for poetry antithetical to Burns's poetic practice, encouraging skewed assessments even among specialists in Scottish literature. In *Scott and Scotland* (1936) Edwin Muir wrote that the 'curse' of 'Scottish literature is the lack of a whole language, which finally means the lack of a whole mind'.[15] In John Speirs's *The Scots Literary Tradition* (1940; rpt 1962), the acknowledgements paragraph thanks just two people: F. R. and Queenie D. Leavis, in whose journal, *Scrutiny*, much of the monograph first appeared.[16] Speirs's Leavis-inspired effort was to define a separate canon or 'Great Tradition' for Scotland, and Burns is again a problematic figure because of his dual language-use:

> [Burns's] Scottish verse must first of all be isolated not only from his own English verse (which is so obviously bad that it may at once be dismissed as such) but from English verse. It has no connections with English verse at any point, so that to consider it as a 'reaction' to the English eighteenth-century manner or, along with Wordsworth, the beginning of the nineteenth is (and has been) to breed confusion.[17]

Speirs's survey was influential: in 1969, the headnote in what became for many decades the major anthology of eighteenth-century literature praised *The Scots Tradition* as still 'the context in which Burns is best read'.[18]

Yet there is such a thing as too much streamlined simplicity when considering the complex matrices out of which poetry is spoken, written and circulated. Burns was no bubble-boy encased by the impenetrable force-field of a closed and unitary Scottish culture. Like other Scots of the late eighteenth century, he watched as revolution and counter-revolution turned the world upside down, recontouring the political landscapes of North America and Europe. Moreover, as David Daiches, founder of modern Scottish studies, was among the first to see, literary Scotland was proficient in several languages: in *The Paradox of Scottish Culture*, he noted the importance of Gaelic, Latin and the vernacular (a mixed Scots/English as the poets of the day wrote it) as well as 'standard' English. Most Scottish writers, Burns among them, negotiated among cultures and languages. Speirs was by training a medievalist, but Burns's post-Union Scotland was far less isolated from England (and English) than the Scotland of Robert Henryson or William Dunbar. The extraordinary range of eighteenth-century Scottish writers, from James Boswell and Robert Burns to Tobias Smollett, David Hume, Adam Smith, Joanna Baillie (b. 1760), Lady Nairne and many more, contradicts any notion that Scottish culture, literary or otherwise, was in a state of decline in Burns's day. His poetry tapped into and then itself assisted an exuberant national redefinition and regrouping during his lifetime (1759–96); and his songs were, in their often unattributed origin and mixture of Scots and English, also instrumental in this process.

It is difficult to shift academic consensus, in Kermode's terms to raise doubts about what people '*know*', because its supporting grounds are so often undefined. In her discussion of canon-making, Barbara Herrnstein Smith suggests that long-held tacit assumptions are hardest to see, let alone challenge:

> Those who ... edit anthologies and prepare reading lists ... obviously ... occupy positions of some cultural power; and their acts of evaluation ... constitute not merely recommendations of value but ... also determinants of value ... [T]heir selections not only imply certain 'criteria' of literary value, which may in fact be made explicit, but, more significantly, they produce and maintain certain definitions of 'literature', and therefore certain assumptions ... which are usually not explicit and, for that reason, less likely to be questioned, challenged, or even noticed.[19]

If Burns is best read wholly in Scottish contexts, he does not belong in discussions of wider British literary traditions; yet if he wrote exactly as he spoke, he cannot be taken very seriously as a writer. The undistributed premise in this faulty logic is precisely the dismissal of Burns *as a poet* that goes along with the idea of Burns as a 'natural' Scot. There is no doubt that Scottish traditions are crucially important for Burns, but an overriding focus on national contexts has too often encouraged critics to foreclose any consideration of his relation to other literary cultures, whether in his own day or in ours.

As early as the preface of his debut volume (1786), Burns defined his interests not as descriptive but as palliative: the creation of poetry provided him with 'some kind of counterpoise to the struggles of a world, always an alien scene'.[20] By 'counterpoise', Burns means also counterpose, the projection of a voice that, contrary to expectations, issues dramatically from the silence assumed in Burns's era to be the 'natural' state of Scottish peasants. Prior to Burns, peasants were viewed as good subjects because they made good victims: writers could work elegiac wonders with them precisely because they were mute, inert stereotypes. Peasants are literally part of the rural landscape, a crowd of the dead who sleep in the earth in Thomas Gray's 'Elegy in a Country Churchyard' (1751). Before Burns, there was no sense among eighteenth-century British poets that rural dialect-speakers could function as forceful truth-tellers.

The sympathetic depiction of peasants by Burns's eighteenth-century predecessors, English and Scots, was not at all rare; but it was always others, like Gray's speaker in his 'Elegy', who spoke on behalf of those without land or capital. Gray's cultivated sensibility can only look down with compassion at the inscriptions on the grave-markers, 'uncouth Rhimes and shapeless Sculpture' of the sort inspired by 'th' unletter'd Muse'.[21] (Even Gray's elisions underscore the peasants' contracted prospects.) In Oliver Goldsmith's 'The Deserted Village' (1770), another poem that haunted Burns, peasants are represented as humbly subject to the patriarchal authority of the schoolmaster, the vicar and above all the well-travelled speaker, who has returned in spirit to stage-manage their reconstruction. Wordsworth, in weighing his poetic precursors, objected mainly to their use of a stylized poetic diction. Burns, strongly drawn to all types of stylized language, instead rejects this extra layer of mediation by which the poet is the sole middleman between a mute subject and potentially receptive readers. Sometimes, as in 'The Cotter's Saturday Night', he emulates Gray's and Goldsmith's third-party narrators: it is in a kind of voiceover that 'Cotter' offers tableaux of the family's activities. Only the father speaks and then chiefly to pray, addressing God or his offspring but never the reader. A Patriot Bard flickers into being in the second-last line, but although he is allied with the cotters he remains silent. In other poems, however, Burns's subject *is* a speaker addressing readers more directly, whether as Holy Willie Fisher or the pet sheep Mailie. Even in 'The Cotter's Saturday Night', Burns refuses Gray's view of the rural poor and the peasantry as politically null: his cotters are larger, not smaller, than the social institutions of church and school set in place to manage them. Neither illiterate nor unemployed, Burns's cotters are called a 'wall of fire' (l. 180) repelling from Scotland the vitiating luxury that in Goldsmith's poem has left the idle rich in sole possession of the land.

Burns is not, as might be assumed, following a Scottish tradition when his peasants speak up. The Scottish vernacular poet Robert Fergusson (1750–74), Burns's most important predecessor, was immersed in the city culture of Edinburgh, using Scots dialect predominantly as a cosmopolitan rather than 'peasant' mode of speech. More will be said about this remarkable poet in chapters 1 and 4. Circa 1720, Allan Ramsay had likewise made his reputation as a dialect poet of Edinburgh, the urban backdrop for a number of fine poems, among them 'Lucky Spence's Last Advice' and 'The Last Speech of the Wretched Miser'. Ramsay's popular play *The Gentle Shepherd* (1725) and songbook series *The Tea Table Miscellany* (1724–37) were, as their titles suggest, more Anglicized projects. Ramsay's dramatization of peasants is mixed, much like his dialect: the sympathetic portrait of the elderly peasant woman 'Mause' in the back-story, for instance, is contradicted by the main plot of *The Gentle Shepherd*, in which Ramsay's shepherd-hero is finally revealed (as the title hints) to be the long-lost son of 'Sir William Worthy'. Patie's bride-to-be, Peggy, is discovered to be Patie's cousin: exactly his equal in genteel birth. Mause herself is something other than a simple rustic: once Peggy's nurse and still loyal to the Worthy family, she declares that ignorant peasants such as the farm-servant Bauldy fear her precisely because she is refined in her speech due to her association with the gentry. Even Ramsay's forenames assign a superior grace to the well-born: there is a world of difference between 'Patie' and 'Peggy' and 'Bauldy' and 'Neps', name of the herdsman and his wife-to-be. *The Gentle Shepherd* is a more interesting play than most critics have acknowledged, though Thomas Crawford and Steve Newman have done it justice.[22] But its equivocal dramatization of rustic characters – all the attractive 'peasants' are of gentle birth – shatters no paradigms.

British poets had emerged from the non-owning classes prior to Burns, but these writers tended to suppress the diction of working people. A Scottish example is James Beattie (1735–1803), the son of a struggling tenant and shopkeeper though schooled at a university (gaining his MA from Aberdeen), who became a successful man of letters writing in standard English, with one exception: a fine verse-letter in dialect to Alexander Ross. The thresher-poet Stephen Duck (1705–56) provides an example from England; in his neoclassical *Poems on Several Occasions* (1736) he refers to the rigors of his early life but excludes non-standard spelling or 'rustic' diction. Burns's insistence that he speaks, *as* a poor body, with authority – '*I, Rob, am here*' – is something new in British literature.[23] He positions the most disadvantaged of people as culturally visible subjects, often as forceful speakers. Yet his defence of the unlettered and the dispossessed is to this day often confused with a direct self-portrait.

Poetry and Cultural Ascent

> There are indeed languages of minorities; often of minorities who are in that social situation because their country or place has been annexed or incorporated into a larger political unit. This does not make them 'minority languages', except in the perspective of dominance. In their own place (if they can resist what are often formidable pressures) it is their own language – a specific language like any other.
> – Raymond Williams[24]

In *Distinction*, Pierre Bourdieu describes the 'sacred sphere of culture' as a theatre in which class-assumptions are continually re-enacted:

> The denial of lower, coarse, vulgar, venal, servile – in a word, natural – enjoyment, which constitutes the sacred sphere of culture, implies an affirmation of the superiority of those who can be satisfied with the sublimated, refined, disinterested, gratuitous pleasures forever closed to the profane. That is why art and cultural consumption are predisposed, consciously and deliberately or not, to fulfil a social function of legitimating social differences.[25]

Preconceptions about social class often lurk beneath a priori critical dismissal of Burns's capacities in English. One example is the headnote in an anthology of Romantic literature: 'Almost entirely self-educated, Burns could only modestly compete with university-trained poets, when he attempted writing in English'.[26] Just as often such preconceptions have coloured discussions of the poet's life.

Allegations of sexual misconduct and failure to write up to his talent are often made without evidence. '[H]e had failed in life', wrote Robert Louis Stevenson in 1889, 'had lost his power of work ... He had trifled with life and must pay the penalty'.[27] This myth of 'drink and debauchery' (Stevenson's phrase) is something else critics 'know' about this poet, although these charges largely derive either from misunderstandings about Scottish marriage customs, to be addressed in Chapter 1, or from the reactionary politics, national and literary, of the 1790s and early 1800s. In his introduction to the *Canongate Burns*, Andrew Noble links a persistent emphasis on Burns's 'licentious character flaws' not only to dislike of the poet's politics of the 1790s but also to Francis Jeffrey and the *Edinburgh Review*'s attacks on Wordsworth.[28]

The poet himself complicates efforts at serious reading by declaring in early verse epistles to Jamie Smith and John Lapraik that he writes 'for fun', 'just clean aff-loof' (offhand) or as the spirit moves him. Yet with a dialect writer taken more seriously – Hugh MacDiarmid, for instance – critics would hesitate to take such statements at face value. In my view, Burns's speaker is not so much a spontaneous self-portrait as a by turns defiant and giddy contradiction, printed in boldface, of genteel assumptions about country people. Burns's speaker stood then and stands now as an embodied contradiction of what middle and upper-class people think they know about the 'lower' orders. If a young labourer is supposed to be 'blate' (bashful and sheepish), Burns's speakers will be proud and dangerous, adapting every instance of literary bad-attitude he can remember from his close study of Milton's Satan. If poor bodies are enjoined to a deferential silence, Poet Burns will address the world as a man 'somewhat decided and hard'.[29] If a country boy is presumed to be ignorant, this one will read and study at every meal:

Tho' he was bred to kintra wark,	'country work'
And counted was baith wight and stark,	'both stout and strong'
Yet that was never Robin's mark	
To mak a man;	'make'
But tell him, he was learn'd and clark,	'learned and scholarly'
Ye roos'd him then!	'praised'

'Elegy on the Death of Robert Ruisseaux'[30]

Burns suppressed this poem linking his name not only to the French for brooks (in Scotland 'burns') but also to Rousseau. It might have been too near the simple truth to fit in with the flamboyant hyperbole of his speaker elsewhere in *Poems*. Instant assessments from Henry Mackenzie's 'Heaven-taught ploughman' onward have thrust Burns back into the patronizing assumptions about country people that the poet constructed his persona and his poems to defy and escape.[31] In *Keywords*, Raymond Williams calls 'Nature' 'perhaps the most complex word in the language'.[32]

In truth, farmers and poets alike have little sympathy with a simple state of nature: both cultivate conditions in which nature will yield up more. Throughout his life, the poet's counterpose ('I am not silent, not unlettered; watch me speak powerfully') was dramatized in performances that exaggerated his powers of language. During at least three social gatherings between harvest of 1785 and December of 1786, he recited 'To a Haggis' to general astonishment after having planted a strong impression that he was composing the verses on the spot. In the nineteenth century, Robert Chambers collected evidence that the host was John Morrison, a cabinetmaker in Mauchline. James Hogg was certain it was Andrew Bruce, a merchant in Edinburgh. John Richmond, Burns's close friend in the mid-1780s, reported that the poem was first performed at a meeting of The Haggis Club in the home of David Shaw, a Kilmarnock solicitor. So powerful is Burns's performance as a natural, spontaneous bard that editors are still debating which of the *hosts* was lying about the poem's first performance, when probably all are reporting accurately a characteristic imposture – a studied performance disguised as an offhand improvization.[33]

If Alexander Pope had risen from table and recited forty-eight lines from 'The Rape of the Lock', would anyone present have believed him to be at that moment composing them, whatever he claimed? To be at every moment ready to stand up as a poet is not natural but inconceivable. One cannot imagine Pope, Wordsworth or Milton allowing themselves to feel pressured to do so: Milton spends the early lines of 'Lycidas' complaining of his unreadiness to speak. But we of prosperous posterity cannot for a moment imagine the pressures under which an eighteenth-century Scottish sub-tenant farmer ('lower, coarse, vulgar, venal, servile') rose up to speak as Poet Burns. Far from taking his poetic powers for granted as 'natural', the poet, performing as 'Burns', was intent on exaggerating them. He felt compelled to prove, to men of the owning classes especially, that he was 100 per cent a poet and always ready to speak as such. And because Burns was in other ways so culturally surprising, people took him at his word: their guard was, and is, down.

'To a Haggis' is a mock-epic, intricate in diction. Burns includes an invidious comparison of French with Scottish cuisine and darker imagery of half-starved peasant-soldiers across Europe, obeying orders to cut each other down:

Is there that owre his French *ragout*,	'over'
Or *olio* that wad staw a sow,	'surfeit, stuff'
Or *fricassee* wad mak her spew,	'make'
Wi' perfect sconner,	'revulsion, scorn'
Looks down wi' sneering, scornfu' view	
On sic a dinner?	'such'

Poor devil! see him owre his trash,	'over'
As feckless as a wither'd rash,	'feeble' 'rush (reed)'
His spindle shank a guid whip-lash,	'his skinny leg is whipcord thin'
His nieve a nit;	'his fist [the size of] a nut'
Thro' bluidy flood or field to dash,	'bloody scenes of battle on sea or land'
O how unfit!	
But mark the Rustic, *haggis-fed*,	
The trembling earth resounds his tread,	
Clap in his walie nieve a blade;	
He'll mak it whissle;	'ample fist'
An' legs, an' arms, an' heads will sned,	'make it whistle'
Like taps o' thrissle.³⁴	'cut off, lop, prune'
	'tops of thistle'

Mark the Rustic, indeed, as he conjures images of mayhem as light entertainment for the bourgeoisie, emphasizing the aggressive power, not humility, of fellow country people, at any rate in Scotland. The poem, with comic loftiness, refuses to take seriously the 'feckless' peasantry of other nations, nurtured as they are on culinary and cultural 'trash'.

Burns's wife, Jean Armour, interviewed in later life by Robert Chambers, recalled that 'he was fond of plain things, and hated tarts, pies and puddings'.³⁵ The poem praises haggis as 'Great Chieftan o' the Puddin-race' not because Burns enjoyed the dish but because it has entered his realm of exemplary Scottish props, that inventory of outsized cultural artefacts that Burns takes up to dramatize his counterpose. Burns's 'Scotland' is the sum of these artefacts and dramatizations and is not to be confused with any geographical entity. His imagination of Scotland is hyperbolic, blown-up, like the swelling 'hurdies' (buttocks) and massive 'pin' (penis) of the haggis itself (ll. 8–9).

Burns, magnifying any materials that come to hand, contradicts the presumption that 'poor bodies', owning nothing, are worth nothing and should say nothing. For Lily Briscoe in Virginia Woolf's *To the Lighthouse* (1927) the analogous taunt is: 'Women can't write; women can't paint'.³⁶ Gayatri Spivak has observed that 'A basic technique of representing the subaltern ... is as the object of the gaze "from above"'.³⁷ Not only to meet this appraising stare but to talk back – in italics or small caps, as Burns's speakers often do – is to disturb a serene illusion of safe distance. His poems draw close to readers. Yet direct address in close quarters is just what critics of modernist tastes are unprepared for. Much of Burns's poetry is an effort to reduce social distance that substitutes 'Here I am, speaking to you' for 'There you are, looking at me'. When Burns speaks up, he breaks up what he imagines and resents as the fixed and downward view of privilege.

In 'To a Louse', the verminous creature addressed by the poem is the burlesque object of a moralizing viewpoint that is not allowed to maintain its superior perspective. For the tiny aeronaut is rapidly ascending a balloon bonnet, a new fashion inspired by several well-publicized Scottish balloon ascents by Vincenzo Lunardi. The parasite, impossibly said to have a nose the size of a gooseberry (the total length of a head-louse is less than ⅓ of an inch), looms ridiculously large, being plainly visible to everyone in church:

O *Jenny* dinna toss your head,	'do not'
An' set your beauties a' abroad!	'all abroad'
Ye little ken what cursed speed	'know'
The blastie's makin!	'a term of contempt' (RB)
Thae *winks* and *finger-ends*, I dread,	'people are winking and pointing, I fear'
Are notice takin![38]	

This louse is the poem's hero, a village Hampden liberating all present from the bloodless proprieties of those who would suppress the carnal – especially the minister on his pulpit but also the congregation at large. Jenny is not the only one at church who has put on her newest clothing and her primmest face. Undaunted, 'plump' with blood, the louse on behalf of all present enacts the public return of the repressed, obtruding itself and secretly delighting all who see it.

In 'To a Louse', the disruption of sacred decorum is accomplished merely by the louse's personal appearance at church: to offend, all that he has to do is become visible. This vermin conquest of a higher realm parallels the appearance of Burns himself in 1786, an interloper in the high precincts of poetry whose vernacular language increases the shock of his impudent ascent into cultural prominence. (The ascent of Mount Parnassus by various grotesque means is likewise a frequent image.) '*To see oursels as others see us*!': this italicized phrase in the last stanza of 'To a Louse' suggests the problem posed for Burns by earlier poetry in English, with its dismissive view of people like himself. His mixed poetic language enacts its own cheeky violation of propriety simply by appearing in a didactic context. Hugh Blair, correctly gauging the rage-and-mischief quotient of this nominally comic text, tried to persuade Burns to delete 'To a Louse' from the 1787 edition of *Poems*. In such other early works as the cantata 'Love and Liberty', beggars and vagabonds (like the louse, 'shunned' by 'saunt and sinner' (l. 8)) are not only visible but voluble. Emerson praised Burns's 'secret of genius to draw from the bottom of society the strength of its speech'.[39] The poet's emphasis on language deriving from the social ground, not the hot-air balloon of high literacy, was almost unthinkable in 1786 and may continue to present problems today: keepers of canons scarcely know where to look when Burns's dialect-rich rustics ascend to the pulpit. Far from employing dialect naturally, such poems as 'To a Louse' use it strategically for shock value. The odd words dramatize a speaker who is odd in other ways, too: not only provocative enough, *modern* enough, to embrace his own inner louse but perverse enough to preach a sermon on the matter.

Tartan Ties: Postcolonial Perspectives

[T]he representation of colonial authority depends less on a universal symbol of English identity than on its productivity as a sign of difference.
– Homi K. Bhabha[40]

Well into the nineteenth century, boys in the Scottish Lowlands played at 'English and Scotch', a tug-of-war in which one team tried to draw the other across a line, the victors snatching up the losers' hats and coats in the process.
– Linda Colley[41]

After the Union of Parliaments in 1707, Lowlanders such as Burns were separated from the centre of power neither by vast distances (it is 378 miles from London to Edinburgh, as compared to 4,400 miles from London to Mumbai) nor, unlike Scottish Gaelic speakers, by fundamental differences of language, religion and culture. Yet the variations between Lowland Scots and standard English did generate, in Bhabha's terms, signs of difference that were sometimes anything but slight. Alexander Carlyle, walking with Tobias Smollett in London on the night in 1746 that news of the Jacobite defeat at Culloden spread across the capital, was warned 'against speaking a word, lest the mob should discover my country and become insolent'.[42] Smollett and Carlyle could conceal their Scottishness, but only if they remained silent. Some forty years later, Burns, addressing the world as a poet 'chiefly' in dialect, knew that to speak out, showcasing his differences in language and social class, likewise might attract hostile attention. 'To a Louse' suggests his foreknowledge that some readers would never 'see him' as he 'sees' himself – as a poet. They would see only an encroaching 'ferlie', a Scots word used in line one to describe the louse that Burns's glossary (written to conclude the Kilmarnock edition) defines with marvellous equivocation: 'a wonder ... also a term of contempt'.

Whether the relationship of eighteenth-century Scottish poets to English literary culture may be considered in postcolonial contexts has been much debated.[43] Though an interesting line of inquiry, Scotland must be taken as a special case, for throughout the nineteenth-century Scotland furnished many of the British empire's colonial administrators. Two of Burns's own sons rose from cadet to Lieutenant-Colonel and Colonel in the army in India, retiring to Cheltenham and sharing a house in prosperous middle age. But for a tenant farmer reinventing himself as a poet during the 1780s, there were parallels between Burns's status as a writer in dialect and Gayatri Spivak's account of tensions between vernacular and 'Indo-Anglian' writing:

The relationship between the writer of 'vernacular' and Indo-Anglian literatures is a site of class-cultural struggle ...
The first question to be asked of a piece of Indo-Anglian fiction is the author's relationship to the creative use of his or her native language ... We have not yet seen an Indo-Anglian fiction writer of tribal origin; we are far from seeing one who has gone back to his or her own oral heritage. Indeed, anyone aware of the ruthless history of

the expunging of tribal culture from the so-called Indic heritage, and the erasure of the tribal *paraph* – the authenticating flourish above or below the signature – from Indian identity, will know that the case is difficult to imagine.[44]

The amount of pressure is not commensurate, yet Burns was to some degree pressured to change his language. The pressure originated in a consensus, especially strong in Enlightenment Edinburgh, that English was the language of literary and indeed of literate speakers.[45] Like his vernacular predecessors Allan Ramsay and Robert Fergusson, Burns reclaimed a poetic realm that had been roped off by majority if not universal consent as an 'English' space. In this sense all eighteenth-century Scots vernacular poems and songs are a site of cultural contention. However, only for Burns is there a dimension of what Spivak calls 'class-cultural struggle'.

For while Ramsay and Fergusson used dialect mainly to evoke the city-speech of Edinburgh, Burns's poems of 1786 portray Scots as the language of rural workers, a group as much under slow erasure as their language. Within two generations of Burns's death, a large part of the Scottish tenantry had scattered across the world, not in political exile like the Jacobites but as economic refugees. The Kilmarnock poems address a non-owning farmer's life of unremitting labour – the anxieties, too, over what will happen when age or illness makes labour impossible. There are homeless wanderers in Burns because he saw them often. He knew that this could be his own future.

Unlike Smollett and Carlyle, at any rate, Burns walked as a poet through a crowd of potential English and Anglicizing adversaries not only speaking all the louder in Scots but also, figuratively speaking, dressed in work clothes:

What though on hamely fare we dine,	'plain food'
Wear hoddin grey, and a' that,	'homespun clothing'
Gie fools their silks, and knaves their wine,	'give'
A Man's a Man for a' that.[46]	

This song of 1795 ends with a vision of 'Man to Man the warld o'er' as 'brothers' (l. 40): Burns's idea of brotherhood does not stop at the edges of Scotland. He speaks to working people everywhere, and this is another factor complicating any placement of him as exclusively 'Scottish' or local. Burns never insists on replacing 'their' language with 'our' dialect, or even 'their' leisure with 'our' labour. Instead, cross-dressing English with Scots, he dramatizes a generative interaction of languages and cultures not unlike his emphasis on pleasurable reciprocity ('give and take' as he calls it) in his erotic songs. In a way characteristic of what Benedict Anderson calls first generation nationalism,[47] Burns uses literary English to link his dialect speakers to the English mainstream (including Edinburgh, whose literati joked in Scots but published in the standard language). In this union of

English and Scots Burns is not giving in to English so much as using it to honour Scotland (*working* Scotland; the leisure classes remain nebulous). Like all poets, Burns draws on all traditions available to him, even experimenting with French, Italian and Latin words, usually learned from his close study of other poets.

An interplay between English and Scottish is especially characteristic of Burns's songs. His version of the well-known English song 'Greensleeves', for example, is characteristic in adding to the lady's sleeves a single distinctively Scottish sartorial accent:

> Green sleeves and tartan ties
> Mark my truelove where she lies;
> I'll be at her or she rise,
>   My fiddle and I thegither. –

Be it by the chrystal burn,	'stream, spring'
Be it by the milk-white thorn,	
I shall rouse her in the morn,	
My fiddle and I thegither. –[48]	

The Scottish tartan, set to advantage, laces and re-accentuates the English green.[49] Burns's dialect speaker, even when toned down and de-politicized as in this song, is a new kind of poetic rustic. In Gray's 'Elegy', the one peasant with a speaking part is a hoary-headed Swain who politely directs a visitor to a monument whose inscription he himself cannot read. Burns's swain in 'Greensleeves' is neither grey-headed nor humble: in two brief stanzas, he lives and he loves, delighting in amorous *double-entendre*.

In *Imagined Communities* (1983), Anderson emphasizes the relative ease of movement between Scotland and England during the seventeenth and eighteenth centuries: 'Scottish politicians came south to legislate, and Scottish businessmen had open access to London markets ... *there were no barricades* on all these pilgrims' paths towards the centre'.[50] Anderson cites David Hume, Adam Smith and the Scottish Enlightenment as evidence that the intertwining of English and Scottish cultures after 1707, and even before the Union, precluded the development in Scotland of 'vernacular-specific' nationalism:

> already in the early seventeenth century large parts of what would one day be imagined as Scotland were English-speaking and had immediate access to print-English ... Then in the early eighteenth-century the English-speaking Lowlands collaborated with London in largely exterminating the Gaeltacht. In neither 'northward thrust' was a selfconscious Anglicizing policy pursued – in both cases Anglicization was essentially a byproduct. But combined, they had effectively eliminated, 'before' the age of nationalism, any possibility of a European-style vernacular-specific nationalist movement.[51]

Yet if Burns, never mentioned in Anderson's study, were included in the picture, a counter-argument might emerge. The blaze of attention that greeted *Poems, Chiefly in the Scottish Dialect* suggests that a contemporary audience did exist for a Scottish literature that insisted on points of difference residing in language, although in Burns's poems these differences are co-ordinated, complementary, a tartan ribbon lacing a green sleeve. Burns illustrates Anderson's thesis about first-generation nationalism in seeking not to replace English with dialect but rather to supplement, *connect*, the 'standard' language (and the dominant poetic tradition) with previously inadmissible words, images, subjects and characters.

Burns and Gender

> Are not some female readers *materially* more empowered than others, by virtue of class, race, national, or other criteria? For that matter, are not *some* female readers more empowered than some *male* readers?
>
> – Diana Fuss[52]

Burns at twenty-one co-founded the Tarbolton Bachelor's Club; he joined the Freemasons, who met in the same tavern, a year later. In Edinburgh, invited by his publisher William Creech, he joined the Crochallan Fencibles, a convivial society that met in Dawnie Douglas's tavern at Anchor Close.[53] Members of the Fencibles became the chief audience for his bawdy songs. The club also was probably responsible for the surreptitious publication of *The Merry Muses of Caledonia*, a volume of bawdry in large part written by Burns, in 1799.[54] The fraternal rhetoric of singing and drinking societies (along with the subversive political bent of the Fencibles) often enters Burns's poems, forming one context for his emphasis on universal brotherhood. Yet to say that Burns writes out of a tradition of constructed 'masculinism' does not preclude sensitivity to writings in which he rejects (or re-signifies) that world-view. He refuses the categorical exclusion of women, for instance, in his frequent choice of female speakers, many of whom condemn male aggression:

> O wae upon you, men o' state,
> That brethren rouse in deadly hate!
> As ye make mony a fond heart mourn,
> Sae may it on your heads return!
> Ye mind na, mid your cruel joys,
> The widow's tears, the orphan's cries!
> But soon may peace bring happy days,
> And Willie hame to Logan braes.[55]

In this song of 1793, a mother of young children laments her husband's absence in a foreign (given the date, counter-revolutionary) war; in the final stanza, she curses the 'men o' state' who profit from it. 'Logan Water' was among Burns's favourite songs. He never gave up trying to persuade his hyper-cautious song-editor George Thomson to print it, but it first appeared posthumously in James Currie's *Life and Works* (1800) and was not printed in Thomson's *Select Collection*, set to its dramatic seventeenth-century air, until 1803.

When Burns's speakers do adopt a mock-epic swagger, other male stereotypes may be ridiculed even while love-power is asserted:

> I murder hate by field or flood,
>   Tho' glory's name may screen us;
> In wars at home I'll spend my blood,
>   Life-giving wars of Venus:
> The deities that I adore
>   Are social Peace and Plenty;
> I'm better pleased *to make one more*,
>   Than be the death of twenty. –⁵⁶

'Field or flood' is Burns's metonym for infantry and naval operations: to use the term glory in connection with war is to 'screen' war's violence. Procreation is the opposite of war, murdering hate instead of extending it and creating new life through acts of love. Burns's representations of sexuality, like Blake's, reveal a radical Protestant, Milton-inflected turn of mind. Taking adult consensual heterosexuality as its virtually invariable given (although frequent use of the non-gendered term 'poor bodies' often broadens that emphasis), Burns's representations of sexuality are, like the praise of Scots cuisine in 'To a Haggis', projections that magnify their subject, the poor man. Yet full consent of both parties is central to Burns's imagination of pleasure:

> She is not the fairest, altho' she is fair;
> O' nice education but sma' is her skair;   'share'
> Her parentage humble as humble can be;
> But I loe the dear Lassie because she loes me. –   'love' (rustic pronunciation)

> ... Kindness, sweet Kindness, in the fond-sparkling e'e,
> Has lustre outshining the diamond to me;
> And the heart beating love as I'm clasp'd in her arms,
> O, these are my Lassie's all-conquering charms.⁵⁷

The tune requires the repetition of the song's final disclosure: the woman has conquered the man, whose 'thought and dream', a phrase in stanza one, are of reciprocated passion.

In other songs a male speaker measures the distance between masculine myths and his own sexual life: again, a generous partner makes all the difference:

Young and souple was I, when I lap the dyke;	'nimble' 'leapt over the wall'
Now I'm auld and frail, I douna step a syke.	'dare not cross a ditch'
Buy broom &c.	
Young and souple was I, when in Lautherslack,	
Now I'm auld and frail, and lie at Nansie's back.	'now we turn from each other in bed'
Buy broom &c.	
Had she gien me butter, when she gave me bread,	'had she taken pleasure in our sex'
I wad looked baulder, wi' my beld head.	'look bolder despite my bald head'
Buy broom &c.[58]	

Set to a tune usually adapted to a male conquest song ('I maun hae a wife … '), this song uses double entendre to speak covertly of impotence. 'Old and frail' in the 'now' of his song, the speaker speaks not of power but of vanished youth and strength.

M. M. Bakhtin argues that the language of classic poetry is unitary, 'Ptolemaic', closed to rejoinder.[59] Burns plays with what Bakhtin calls this authoritarian tendency in poetic language; his blend of English and Scots could never be mistaken for a monological utterance. Such expressions as 'a Man's a Man' are at first glance closed off in Bakhtin's negative sense, yet are complicated by their status as counterpoint. This is not complacent masculinism but indignant backtalk. A 'Man's a Man' sets up its tautological circle in order to enclose poverty in terms of dignity, just as virtuous cotters become a circle of fire around Scotland in the final lines of 'The Cotter's Saturday Night'. A circle is not composed of a single point, in geometry or in Burns, who in 'Cotter' imagines a social group collecting itself not to extend its territories but for community support and defence.

Burns's class-perspective sounded like a threat to those among his contemporaries who saw quiescent workers as essential to social stability. 'Is There, for Honest Poverty' was, like 'Logan Water', rejected by George Thomson, who did not print it until nine years after the poet's death, by which time it had spread across Great Britain, Ireland and North America. Of all Burns's songs, that which took 'a Man's a Man' as its refrain may have been the most widely circulated by chapbook and periodicals during the mid- and late 1790s.[60]

Whether female or male, Burns's speakers are always counter-hegemonic: as in the final chorus of 'Love and Liberty', men and women raise their voices to speak *against* power. He was hostile to monarchy, as may be seen from the opening lines of 'Elegy on the Year 1788': 'For Lords or kings I dinna mourn / E'en let them die – For that they're born!'[61] Yet he supported Fox and the Prince of Wales during the Regency Crisis of 1788–9, presumably reasoning that an entrenched king long in power had to be even more corrupt than a younger king-in-waiting. Whether it is the Prince of Wales being slightly preferred to his father, the young man in work clothes talking back to aristocratic 'coofs' – idiots – in 'Is There for Honest Poverty', or the wrathful mother who denounces the Masters of War in 'Logan Water', the further Burns's subjects are from power, the more warmly he admits them into the poem-circle that he calls 'Scotland'. The man in coarse homespun who insists that 'a Man's a Man' is expressing hostility not to women but to the 'fools' and 'knaves', almost all of them men, who governed Britain and Europe.

In short, while Burns's occasional insistence that he speaks specifically as a man needn't be read with admiration, it is best taken in context. Assertions of potency typically contradict what Burns saw as his culture's, including prior poetry's, reduction of the 'poor body' to the status of insignificant non-person. In a letter of late December 1793 to Board of Excise Commissioner Robert Graham of Fintry (the letter is a response to charges of political disaffection), Burns makes a rare admission of the real state of his case: 'Fortune, Sir, has made you powerful, & me impotent; has given you patronage, & me dependance'.[62] Nevertheless, consensus continues to cast Burns as a textbook example of a 'natural' male. Morag Shiach, writing on eighteenth-century women peasant poets, has observed that this 'equation of the manly and the natural' is 'widespread' among figures in popular culture.[63] Shiach quotes Leslie Stephen on Burns: '[he had] strong manly blood coursing through every vein', the kind of vaguely repellent nineteenth-century praise that may be at the back of critics' minds when they think of Burns today as invariably masculinist.[64] Some of his admirers surely have been.

Marlon B. Ross singles out Burns's 'The Rights of Woman' as 'a good "masculine" contrast to [Anna] Barbauld's "feminine" objection to the doctrine of women's rights'.[65] In Ross's view, 'Burns trivializes the subject by treating it humorously. Putting the argument in the mouth of "Miss Fontenelle on her benefit night", Burns humors the woman who speaks as well as the cause that she is made to speak against'.[66] Yet this theatrical prologue of 1792 addresses a political matter linked to the letter just quoted. Burns had been given a subscription for the Dumfries Theatre by his friend Robert Riddell and he occasionally wrote for the company. Louisa Fontenelle (1773–99), a diminutive and childlike actress, was among his favourites, and he wrote two prologues for her. Her benefit night was 28 November 1792. A month earlier, the poet had been at the centre of a riot in the theatre, topic of the letter to Graham of Fintry just quoted. As the poet describes the fracas:

> I was in the playhouse one night, when Çà ira was called for. – I was in the middle of the pit, & from the Pit the clamour arose. – One or two individuals with whom I occasionally associate were of the party, but I neither knew of the Plot, nor joined in the Plot; nor ever opened my lips to hiss, or huzza, that, or any other Political tune whatever ... I never uttered any invectives against the king.[67]

Burns's letter does not reveal that among the 'Political' tunes he had refused to sing was 'God Save the King'. Catherine Carswell's biography describes the chaotic scene in the playhouse:

> It was at the close of the last ... day of blood-sports (loathsome as war to Robert) by the gentlemen of the Caledonian and the Dumfries and Galloway Hunt, which had 'drawn together almost all the genteel families in the three southern counties' [quoting the Dumfries *Weekly Journal*]. And now at night Lord Hopetoun's box ... 'exhibited an assemblage of nobility rarely to be seen in one box in the theatres of the metropolis'.[68]

Those in the boxes had begun the call for 'God Save the King'; the audience in the pit had instead, as Burns reports, begun to sing 'Ça ira' ('it will go [well]', a phrase that originated with Ben Franklin and the colonists' rebellion in America). The *contra danse* air by Bécourt had acquired by 1792 new *sans culottes* lyrics that call for hanging aristocrats from the lamp-posts: '*Les aristocrates à la lanterne!*'

The Caledonian Hunt had subscribed for 100 copies of the 1787 *Poems* and ever since had acted as if they owned Robert Burns. The poet's dislike of the Hunt (or perhaps as Carswell says, their enthusiasm for blood sports) may have played a part in his refusing to sing 'God Save the King' at their demand; but the gentry read political disaffection in his immobility and silence. Recalled Charles Sharpe forty years later:

> The play was 'As you like it', Miss Fontenelle, *Rosalind*, when 'God save the King' was called for and sung; we all stood up uncovered; but Burns sat still in the middle of the pit with his hat on his head. There was a great tumult, with shouts of 'Turn him out! – Shame, Burns!' which continued a good while.[69]

Burns's enemies might have had in mind Thomas Paine, indicted for treason earlier in 1792; he had fled to France following publication of Part 2 of *The Rights of Man*. Paine, too, had been a radical Exciseman.

This event of 28 October was very recent history when Fontenelle spoke the opening lines of Burns's prologue on 28 November 1792:

> While Europe's eye is fixed on mighty things.
> The fate of Empires, and the fall of Kings;
> While quacks of State must each produce his plan,
> And even children lisp The Rights of Man;
> Amid this mighty fuss, just let me mention,
> The Rights of Woman merit some attention.[70]

The poet, masked as 'she', goes on to list among these rights 'Protection', 'Decorum' and 'Admiration', scarcely controversial and apparently trivial, as Ross observes. Yet these lines' bland substitution of 'protection' for liberation mask a political gesture that was evident enough to the poet himself, who never signed or published the poem. The man who sat mute while 'God save the King' was sung in the boxes and the pit called instead for 'Ça ira' concluded 'The Rights of Woman' with a cry of 'ça ira!':

> But truce with kings, and truce with Constitutions,
> With bloody armaments, and Revolutions;
> Let MAJESTY your first attention summon,
> Ah, ça ira! THE MAJESTY OF WOMAN!!![71]

King George's 'majesty' is transferred to the petite woman (and as Rosalind, frequent male-impersonator) speaking on stage. So small and popular a person surely may cry out 'ça ira' in the Dumfries Theatre and Burns by proxy have the last word after all. Burns exchanged letters with Helen Maria Williams and may have corresponded with Mary Wollstonecraft.[72] It is unclear whether his prologue refers her *Vindication of the Rights of Woman* (two editions appeared in 1792) or to Thomas Paine's *The Rights of Man* (1791–2). Neither work is mentioned in Burns's extant letters, but phrases from Paine recur in his later songs.

In his political difficulties of the 1790s, as in his language-usage, Burns walked a tightrope.[73] During 1794 – the letter describing this event is dated only 'Sunday' – Burns was again pressured in public to prove his loyalty, this time to propose a toast in support of the war against France. After a long pause, he responded with 'May our success in the present war be equal to the justice of our cause', causing another uproar: he may have been challenged to a duel by one Captain Dods.[74]

As Cora Kaplan has observed,

> Class and race ideologies are ... steeped in and spoken through the language of sexual differentiation. Class and race meanings are not metaphors for the sexual, or vice versa. It is better to see them reciprocally constituting each other ... a set of associative terms in a chain of meaning.[75]

In Burns's use, this 'language of sexual differentiation' is often used to defend people of his own class and attack the powers-that-be. His assertions of masculinity push back against those of his day for whom people like himself, i.e., those who lacked capital, were non-entities. Speaking not of class but of race, Sojourner Truth performed a similar elision of gender and politics in 1851 when she condemned slavery by insisting on her gender in a speech repeating a simple question: 'Ain't I a woman?'[76]

In Burns's day male poets seeking general applause did not write in rural-inflected dialect; nor did they write ardent love-songs (speaking openly of desire), track the ebb and flow of their emotions in their writings or parade their poverty as a badge of honour. His irrepressible displays of difference did not reside solely in dialect-usage: years of arduous farm labour showed even in his burly physique and pronounced 'ploughman's stoop' – for the genteel paintings lie.[77] He took pains to make any and all differences super-visible. The fact is that in a consciousness of having been born to be dismissed and excluded, Burns had more in common with Felicia Hemans and Anna Aiken Barbauld than with Hugh Blair or Henry Mackenzie. He shared with women writers of his day the advantages (and occasional disadvantages) of a liminal perspective. Even when he publishes, his voice issues forth in an idiom that Hugh Blair, Professor of Rhetoric, speaking from the capital and the centre, can at once recognize and deride as 'words of the stable and the politics of the smithy'.[78]

How then does one read Burns? As a reversal of conventional expectations, a counterpose by which a 'poor body' rose up to speak. Burns's speech engages not in literal description but in contradiction, wishful thinking, resistance. He rewrites experience, cross-dresses English with Scots and responds to calls for 'God Save the King' with an initial tight-lipped silence, followed by a covert 'Ça ira'. He courts, as a speaker poor yet determined, various objects of desire, from Jean Armour to universal brotherhood. Along with motifs of elegy, burial and exile (a particular focus, as Chapter 1 discusses, of the 1786 Kilmarnock *Poems*), infusing his work with another level of contradiction, there is also this poet's unquenchable humour. Burns not only dares to be articulate but also to laugh out loud. He is resolved to be 'merry and free', not doomed and repressed.[79]

For critics to achieve their own counterpoise is necessary, because the merry ebullience of so many of his personae has a tendency, as the critical heritage shows, to disarm the critical impulse. One can mistrust the exuberance of Burns, as William Wordsworth and Jane Austen did, or idolize it, as William Hazlitt and Thomas Carlyle did.[80] Yet once preoccupied with his personality, one is turning from poetic form to myth. One is ignoring, too, many writings that do not fit the myth – the gloomy satires such as 'Address of Beelzebub', never printed in *Poems* though privately circulated among friends. Many neglected poems and songs – another is the fragmentary 'Epistle from Esopus to Maria' – hint of a darker, more complex back-story.[81]

Emphases on nation, class, politics and gender are all useful, yet none by itself can fully illumine the great work of Burns's life, which was to become and to remain a poet. He was no example, in the sense of ordinary sample, of his social class but an extraordinary instance of class-anger, class-denial and class-bargaining on a grand scale. He is also an unlikely candidate for victimhood in that to an unusual degree he got exactly what he wanted from his life: 'Ay routh o' rhymes' or unstinted creative powers.[82] Perhaps at first his goal was mainly to emerge from obscurity – to be 'distinguished', as he puts it in the preface of his Kilmarnock *Poems*.[83] Yet once he achieved fame as Poet Burns, he repudiated him, too. He largely stopped signing his songs unless they were compliments to friends or patrons. By 1791 he was out of farming, trying out a new role as a socially despised Exciseman and uncredited, behind-the-scenes co-editor of *The Scots Musical Museum* (*SMM*). Now considered among the most important of Scottish song collections, *SMM* is Burns's late masterwork, characteristic in its semi-anonymity. 'Let it go to hell', he said, a few years into a seventy-six year lease, of Ellisland farm; and after he left Edinburgh he was in a mood to let the 'ploughman poet' dog-and-pony show go to hell along with it, making sure that his family would be provided for without subjecting himself to the vagaries either of farming without capital or the literary marketplace.[84]

Burns's self-confidence came from his eager reading, his ability to live in and through words and to share with readers the delights of his own escape. Poetry was his personal anti-gravity device, a relief – release – from material subjugation. He positions his speakers and (in many songs his 'Scotland') as 'free', and critics make their best beginning in that free space, a textual and literary more than a literal or geopolitical space. Curiously modern in his double claim to local language yet wide import, Burns invites his audience to see in the free-speaking of a new poetry and song – here is his difference from Karl Marx – full recompense for a life of economic struggle. He saw in poetry also, and here is his similarity to Percy Shelley and William Blake, a force to heal and strengthen, so that all within the circle of songs and poems could ready themselves for new personal freedoms. As a young poet, when Burns tried to imagine a permanent remedy for the ills of life he only could think of death, as in 'Man was Made to Mourn', a song much admired by Wordsworth to be discussed in Chapter 2. Yet in the songs written later in his life, he often dares to hope that those he addresses – those beginning to speak up – will continue to do so. He looks to better days 'comin' yet' despite an oppressive political climate.

A tenant farmer named Rob Burness taught himself in the mid-1780s how to assume the 'public character' of a poet.[85] Then he unlearned that lesson, making a second transformation, through his work with Scottish songs, from famed author to semi-anonymous voice of the people. In the terms of Gilles Deleuze and Félix Guattari, he lost much of his investment in the 'tree' of literary fame and turned to a more rhizomatic way of working. Rhizomes propagate by lateral extension (grassroots proliferating widely) rather than a central top–down taproot. The 'rhizome' metaphor that Deleuze and Guattari use to explain their own work challenges hierarchical assumptions – not only about fame but about writing in a 'non-standard' language. 'There is no mother tongue', they write, in a comment relevant to Burns, 'only a power takeover by a dominant language within a political multiplicity'.[86] In his later years, the poet continued to address the world as 'Burns', the signature and style he had made famous; but he also remained prolific as a song-writer and song-reviser, a matter discussed in Chapter 3. When he turned to cloaked, coded signatures for many of these songs, he ensured that a large portion of his writings would go down to posterity, as Emerson worded it in 1859, not from printed books at all but informally, 'from mouth to mouth'[87] – through performance and recitation. These two modes in which Burns is remembered today, as a famous signature and as a covert maker and transmitter of songs will be the subject of the Epilogue.

1 ROB[T]. BURNESS TO POET BURNS: BARD, INTERRUPTED

[His] copy of Small's Treatise on Ploughs is now before me; not one remark appears in the margins; but on the title page is written, 'Robert Burns, Poet'
Allan Cunningham, 1834[1]

Early in July 1786, Burns wrote briefly to a cousin in Montrose, promising a longer letter as soon as he could also send a surprise, a 'singular curiosity'.[2] He is referring to the 1786 Kilmarnock *Poems, Chiefly in the Scottish Dialect*, published to acclaim later that month. Probably in deference to his kinsman's spelling of the family name, the poet for the last time signed himself 'Burness', the surname his late father had spelled 'Burnes'. 'Robert Burns', the soon-to-be-famous variant selected in March to sign the 1786 *Poems*, has a trochaic lilt all the more poetic for suppression of the final syllable. The streamlining also suggests some shedding of baggage: even before the coming of fame, the poet, 'singular' in his own mind, had begun to distance himself from the close-knit family whose struggle he had taken so much to heart.

Strictly speaking, Robert Burns was not born in 1759: he came into public existence twenty-seven years later specifically as the author of *Poems, Chiefly in the Scottish Dialect*.[3] This chapter describes the convergence of personal crises that marked the months before publication of the 1786 *Poems*; I also discuss the differences between that first volume published at Kilmarnock and two trial, handwritten groupings of early work – each signed 'Rob[t]. Burness' – now known as *The First Commonplace Book* (1783–5) and *The Kilmarnock Manuscript* (late 1785–early 1786). These Burness manuscript projects, the second begun several months after the first was broken off, differ greatly from each other. The first emphasizes English lyrics in common measure that echo the Bible and Shakespeare,[4] while the second, for which Burness's own title is 'Scotch Poems', channels Robert Fergusson's dialect poetry and relies chiefly on Scots verse-forms, among them standard Habbie. This chapter's closing pages will discuss Burns's debut volume, sent to press some six months after 'Scotch Poems' was suspended, as itself, and in more ways than just its signature, a startling departure from either of Rob Burness's early handwritten experiments.

Poems, Chiefly in the Scottish Dialect came from the press of John Wilson of Kilmarnock, the only printer in Ayrshire. The six surviving holograph texts bearing printer's marks include the first five poems printed in the 1786 volume ('The Twa Dogs', 'Scotch Drink', 'The Author's Earnest Cry and Prayer', 'The Holy Fair' and 'Address to the Deil') and the thirteenth, 'The Cotter's Saturday Night', all of which were finished before a period of crisis that marked the works completed in spring. It would have been helpful in writing this chapter if some of these later manuscripts had survived, useful to know whether Wilson worked with polished fair copies like the six texts still extant, or last-minute transcriptions of texts hastily composed or revised under pressure. For during these months, escalating problems contended with the printed *Poems* for Burns's anxious attention. Interlocking miseries – losing Jean Armour, leaving Scotland and violating his personal integrity by agreeing to become assistant overseer on a sugar plantation – suffuse the works revised or completed in spring.

Biographical contexts for the poems written during this period have been much discussed yet remain in some ways poorly understood, perhaps because biographers usually consider in separate chapters events that Burns experienced as a sustained emotional storm on many fronts: the vindictive wrath of Jean Armour's parents; the humiliation of being packed out of the country; the resentment over public penance for fornication; and yet also the faint if fading hope that publishing his *Poems* would change the game.

The next section considers these struggles in close relation with each other follows, not assuming that the poet's responses reveal his character (a matter impossible to determine over two centuries after the fact) but suggesting that they greatly affected the final form of the book then being readied for press. Robt Burness, prior self and lost soul, is explored, analysed, elegized in the Kilmarnock *Poems* – and then, in 'A Bard's Epitaph', the final poem in the volume, symbolically laid to rest.

1786: 'Deep in the Guilt of Being Unfortunate'

In March 1786, Jean Armour, who had met Burns in April 1784 or April 1785, told her parents that she was pregnant. She was twenty-one according to the birthdate entered in the Armour's family Bible.[5] Burns, already father of a child by Elizabeth Paton, knew earlier, perhaps by mid-February judging from hints in letters. For when she told her parents she showed them a signed agreement between herself and her lover. This 'unlucky paper',[6] later destroyed by the Armours' attorney Robert Aiken (also Burns's friend and patron), must have asserted paternity and partnership or there would have been no reason for the

Armours to hire an attorney to quash it. By Scottish custom, mutual consent established an 'irregular' or 'private' marriage.

In Episcopalian England, marriage was a sacrament, but in Presbyterian Scotland it was a contract: mutual verbal agreement before witnesses constituted marriage in Burns's place and time, conferring legitimacy on any children.[7] A written contract presumably marked a more formal commitment than an oral agreement. The Armours, however, rejected Burns as a son-in-law, retaining Aiken to secure instead a financial settlement for 'an enormous sum' according to Burns.[8] Aiken was chief mediator between the Armour family and Burns during these months and most likely a chief promoter of the plan for the poet's emigration to Jamaica. Aiken's subscription for no fewer than 145 copies of Burns's *Poems*, more than twice as many as the next most generous subscriber, Robert Muir, would have made it difficult for the poet to ignore Aiken's guidance on any matter.[9]

The Armours were evidently conservative ('Auld Licht') Calvinists, the group targeted by such early Burns satires as 'Holy Willie's Prayer', then circulating locally in manuscript and making Burns enemies as well as friends. James Armour was a contractor and stone-mason who had built houses for the local gentry and a nearby bridge across the Doon. A townsman whose house near the church stands to this day, he was comparatively well to do, while after the death of Burns's father in 1784, the poet with his brother Gilbert co-headed a numerous family whose scanty farming tools and stock had been seized by creditors several years before in the course of a lawsuit, ultimately successful yet financially disastrous, between the poet's dying father and his landlord. In the view of townspeople in Mauchline, the children of James and Mary Armour had a higher status by some degree than the children of William and Agnes Burnes.

In late March, the Armours sent Jean away to Paisley near Glasgow, where she stayed until early June with her aunt and uncle, receiving visits from Robert Wilson, a weaver in Mauchline.[10] On 2 April, the Session book of Mauchline parish recorded rumours of Jean's pregnancy and removal to Paisley; an official visit to Mary Armour followed ('the Session think it their duty to enquire').[11] In mid-April Burns wrote to his landlord Gavin Hamilton expressing shock that his '*quondam* [i.e., former] friend' Aiken had scissored the couple's signatures out of the 'marriage lines' and declared the document void: 'when [James Armour] … told me, the names were all cut out of the paper, my heart died within me, and he cut my very veins with the news'.[12] The Armours' repudiation of the marriage had consequences: an irregular marriage, while conferring legitimacy on children, called for a rebuke at church, but couples unwilling to marry faced three weeks of public penance.[13] Jean Armour was told to appear at services on 18 June but instead wrote a letter of apology. The poet was upbraided the next week on 25 June, but evidently in acknowledgement of his efforts to establish a marriage, was allowed by the minister to remain with his family rather than seating himself on the stool of repentance. Following two further Sundays of penance on 23 July and 6 August, Burns received a certificate as a single man. The poet saw Jean Armour's retreat from her commitment and her obedience to her parents, as well as her encouragement, or so the story reached Burns, of Robert Wilson's visits to Paisley, as betrayals. He removed complimentary references to her from 'The Vision' in spring 1786, although only to reinstate them for the 1787 Edinburgh edition of *Poems*. Burns wrote distraught new poems, including 'To a Mountain Daisy, On Turning one down, with the Plough' and 'Despondency, An Ode', between April and mid-June, when the manuscript went to the printer.

The first firmly dated references to emigration in Burns's letters likewise occur in June.[14] '[N]ine parts & nine tenths ... stark staring mad',[15] as the poet described his mood in this crisis, he began to make what a later letter calls 'what little preparation was in my power for Jamaica', adding that 'Before leaving my native country forever, I resolved to publish my Poems'.[16] The unusual quantity and quality of the poetry written between August 1785 and January 1786 suggest that Burns was planning his book many months prior to April 1786. But as the emotional storm of early spring broke over his head, publication reshaped itself as a farewell gesture. By January 1786 Burns had begun most of the poems the volume would make famous, but those added or completed that spring broadened and intensified the impact and the range of the collection. By turns giddy, tender, sardonic, elegiac and mortally wounded, the speaker who emerges at mid-volume of *Poems, Chiefly in the Scottish Dialect* is a forceful presence.

Both *The First Commonplace Book* and the *Kilmarnock Manuscript* position their speakers as observers: Rob Burness channels the overheard speeches of all kinds of characters. After the opening poems of the volume, the 1786 *Poems* by contrast becomes histrionic and self-dramatizing. One example is #16, 'The Lament. Ocassion'd by the Unfortunate Issue of a Friend's Amour', written in spring 1786, in which the poet's attempt to displace his own sorrows by disguising them as those of a friend is wholly undermined by inclusion of the word 'Amour' in the title, which all but publishes Jean's surname. 'Unfortunate Issue' likewise conveys more information than the poet probably intended. The stanzas themselves are operatic:

> Oh! can she bear so base a heart,
> So lost to Honor, lost to Truth,
> As from the *fondest lover* part,
> The *plighted husband* of her youth?[17]

A long letter addressed to David Brice, a shoemaker in Glasgow (written the night before the manuscript of *Poems* was delivered to John Wilson), discusses it all: the rupture with Jean Armour, prospective emigration and the publication of his book:

> I just write to let you know that there is such a worthless, rhyming reprobate ... still in the land of the living, tho' I can scarcely say, in the place of hope ... – Poor, ill-advised, ungrateful Armour came home [from Paisley] on friday last ... – What she thinks of her conduct now, I don't know; one thing I know, she has made me compleatly miserable. – ... [I] do still love her to distraction after all, tho' I won't tell her so, tho I see her, which I don't want to do. – My poor, dear, unfortunate Jean! how happy have I been in her arms! ... I can have no nearer idea of the place of eternal punishment than what I have felt in my own breast on her account. – I have tryed often to forget her: I have run into all kinds of dissipation and riot ... but all in vain: and now for a grand cure, the Ship is on her way home that is to take me out to Jamaica, and then, farewel dear old Scotland, and farewel dear, ungrateful Jean, for never, never will I see you more! You will have heard that I am going to commence Poet in print; and tomorrow, my works go to the press ... – It [is ju]st the last foolish action I in[tend]to do; and then turn a wise man as fast as possible.[18]

This letter of 12 June is the poet's first date-stamped reference to emigration. Though framed as a jest, its Calvinist references reveal a bitter train of thought. Burns ventriloquizes local opinion of him as a 'worthless, rhyming reprobate' – worthlessness, rhyme and preterition all coming down to the same thing in the village mentality that damns poetry, damns love and damns him. He admits to a continuing passion for Jean Armour but awaits the 'grand cure' of a voyage to Jamaica. Though technically still in 'the land of the living' (alive and in Scotland), Burns is far from 'the place of hope', having renounced the lodestars of his youth ('Love and Poesy'[19]) for a new life as a 'wise man' – i.e., plantation overseer.

A month later he transferred the copyright of his poems to his brother Gilbert to be held in trust for his first-born child. The document is dated 22 July 1786, nine days before the 1786 *Poems* appeared:

> whereas I intend to leave Scotland and go abroad, and having acknowledged myself the father of a child named Elizabeth ... and whereas Gilbert Burns ... my brother, has become bound, and hereby binds and oblidges himself to aliment clothe and educate my said natural child in a suitable manner as if she was his own, in case her Mother chuse to part with her, and that until she arrives at the age of fifteen years. Therefore, and to enable the said Gilbert Burns to make good his said engagement, Wit ye me to have assigned, disponed, conveyed and made over to ... the said Gilbert Burns ... all ... movable effects ... I shall leave behind me on my departure from the kingdom ... And particularly ... the profits ... from the Publication of my Poems ... And also, I hereby depone and convey to him in trust for behoof of my said natural daughter, the Copyright of said Poems in so far as I can dispose of the same by law, after she arrives at the above age of fifteen years complete.[20]

This July 1786 conveyance of copyright to Elizabeth Paton's child reads as retaliation for the elder Armours' writ *in meditatione fugae* against him – their legal action, that is, to restrain him from emigrating until he met their financial demands. Hugh Barclay, writing in 1832, defined 'Meditatio Fugae' as an old principle of Scots law that if a creditor could make an oath that his debtor was in meditatione fugae to avoid payment of his debt, he may apply to a magistrate who may grant warrant for apprehending the debtor for examination, and subsequently, grant warrant to imprison the debtor until he finds caution judicio sisti [the last phrase meaning posting bail and pledging to stay in the area and appear at trial].[21]

Looking back in 1787, Burns recalled in his autobiographical letter to John Moore that during the same week in late July 1786 that the Kilmarnock *Poems* appeared, he was 'sculking from covert to covert under the terrors of a Jail' because 'some ill-advised, ungrateful people [the Armours] had uncoupled the merciless legal Pack at my heels'.[22] Burns's emphasis on his state of terror during this time is sometimes discounted or dismissed by biographers, but imprisonment did threaten debtors suspected of an intention to leave the jurisdiction and he did not have the resources to post bail.[23]

The immediate and sensational success of Burns's *Poems* made moot the Armours' claim that the poet was fleeing the scene and also made them somewhat more amenable to compromise. Jean Armour gave birth to twins, Robert (d. 1857) and Jean (d. 1787), in early September. Burns's mother fostered infant Robert at Mossgiel farm while infant Jean remained with the Armours. A marriage – still 'irregular', as there was no church ceremony – was not reaffirmed between Burns and Jean Armour until April 1788, following the birth in March and death soon after of two new daughters, a second set of twins.

Burns's brother Gilbert described the events of 1786 in a letter sent in 1797 to Anna Wallace Dunlop and later reprinted in James Currie's peculiar but highly influential biography of Burns (1800). Mrs Dunlop had been a patron and correspondent of the poet. At the time Gilbert sent her his account in 1797, she may already have been hoping to help his family; in the event, she encouraged her son, Captain John Dunlop, to hire Gilbert Burns to manage his estate, a position that Gilbert held from 1800 to 1804. In reading his version, one must bear in mind the tastes of his recipient and patroness: Mrs Dunlop's younger sons had all made their fortunes serving in the army and navy at the outposts of Empire; even her first grandchild, John, was at age twelve put into the army and sent out to India. Gilbert may be addressing her preferences in highlighting zeal for emigration and meek submission to his patrons as his brother's guiding principles during 1786, but in doing so he confuses his timeline and misrepresents the almost unhinged state of mind actually disclosed by the poems and letters written during those months.

Gilbert begins by emphasizing a joint decision with his brother, made early in 1786, to give up the tenancy of Mossgiel farm. He implies a four-year courtship before Jean Armour's pregnancy; the couple had known each other at most half that time. And as Gilbert tells the story, a decision to emigrate not only preceded but indeed caused Burns's publication of his poems, in Gilbert's account a course undertaken in compliance with the advice of his landlord Gavin Hamilton in order 'to provide him more liberally with necessaries for Jamaica':

> Our crops ... were very unprofitable, and notwithstanding our utmost diligence and economy, we found ourselves obliged to give up our bargain, with the loss of a considerable part of our original stock. It was during these four years that Robert formed his connexion with Jean Armour, afterwards Mrs. Burns. This connexion *could no longer be concealed*, about the time we came to a final determination to quit the farm. Robert durst not engage with a family in his poor, unsettled state, but was anxious to shield his partner by every means in his power ... It was agreed therefore between them that they should make a legal acknowledgment of an irregular and private marriage, that he should go to Jamaica to *push his fortune*, and that she should remain with her father till it might please Providence to put the means of supporting a family in his power. Mrs. Burns was a great favorite of her father's. The intimation of a marriage between them was the first suggestion he received of her real situation. He was in the greatest distress, and fainted away. The marriage did not appear to him to make the matter any better. A husband in Jamaica appeared to him and to his wife little better than none, and an effectual bar to any other prospects of a settlement in life that their daughter might have. They therefore expressed a wish to her, that the written papers which respected the marriage should be cancelled and thus the marriage rendered void ... [Robert] felt the deepest anguish of mind. He offered to stay at home and provide for his wife and family in the best manner that his daily labours could provide for them; that being the only means in his power. Even this offer they did not approve of ... In the state of mind which this separation [from Jean Armour] produced, he wished to leave the country as soon as possible, and agreed with Dr. Douglas to go out to Jamaica as an assistant overseer, or as I believe it is called, a book-keeper, on his estate. As he had not sufficient money to pay his passage ... Mr. Hamilton advised him to publish his poems in the mean time by subscription, as a likely way of getting a little money to provide him more liberally in necessaries for Jamaica. Agreeably to this advice, subscription bills were printed immediately[24]

Gilbert uses hints (Jean's 'connexion' with his brother *'could no longer be concealed'*) and equivocations (Jean's pregnancy became visible 'about the time of' a decision to move from Mossgiel) to draw an improbable portrait of his irritable, independent-minded brother as compliant to advice. Or perhaps he has forgotten the sequence of these events from eleven years earlier. Gilbert's order is: (1) looming homelessness for the Burnes clan as the family abandon the lease of their farm; (2) discovery of Jean's pregnancy after long courtship; (3) the elder Armours' rejection of the marriage *because* their son-in-law is going to Jamaica; and finally (4) Burns's practical decision to publish his poems so that he can provide himself with 'necessaries' for his new life.

This timeline places the poet's settled intent to emigrate three months before the position of assistant overseer is mentioned in letters between his prospective employers, Patrick and Charles Douglas. Moreover, the poet's own letters first mention sailing to Jamaica in June, although talk of possible emigration may well have occurred earlier.[25] Breaking the lease for Mossgiel is not discussed in any of Burns's letters during spring 1786 to their landlord, Gavin Hamilton. The poet did resign his share in the tenancy of Mossgiel in 1786 but that was late in July, in the same legal document that provided for his daughter Bess. (The family, supported by £180 from Burns's profits for the 1787 edition of *Poems*, in the event stayed on at Mossgiel until 1798.) There is no epistolary evidence of plans to leave Mossgiel farm early in 1786, and the poet's letters offer evidence contrary to Gilbert's statement that Burns's decision to publish followed from the Armours' declaration of war. Burns received the printed subscription blanks for 'Scotch Poems', ordered on 3 April, on the evening of 14 April, the night *before* Robert Aiken cut the couple's signatures out of the agreement they had co-signed.[26] That the chief subscribers took dozens of copies (Gilbert Burns himself subscribing for seventy) does suggest a link between the Armours' pending lawsuit and the financing of Burns's volume: a distribution subscription diminished the author's role by dispersing copies to close friends and well-wishers for sale among their own contacts.[27] Nonetheless, two intense years of writing and revision preceded 1786, and Burns's experiments with the sequence in which readers would encounter his poems date back at least to January 1786, when he began to transcribe *The Kilmarnock Manuscript*. Arguably they could be traced to *The First Commonplace Book*, which begins with his earliest poem but then arranges its entries according to other protocols.

Burness had gone through his earlier trials as part of a close-knit family, but in 1786 he stood alone. Publicly jilted, he looked into the future and by June foresaw that he would live and die in Jamaica as a 'poor Negro-driver'.[28] This ambiguous phrase ('poor', modifying both 'Negro' and 'driver', is at once self-condemning and self-pitying) is used in 1787 by Burns in his autobiographical letter to John Moore, a friend of Mrs Dunlop's and, as Moore's novel *Zeluco* (1786) suggests, no supporter of slavery. It was a tacit admission of guilt to bring up slave-driving to the author of *Zeluco*, in which several chapters decry Zeluco's murderous greed as a planter in Cuba, especially in the context of Burns's prefatory excuse that his conflict with the Armours had all but driven him insane:

> 'Twas a shocking affair, which I cannot yet bear to recollect; and had very nearly given [me] one or two of the principal qualifications for a place among those who have lost the chart and mistake the reckoning of Rationality.[29]

Yet in mid-1786, Burns's letters and poems never mention slavery. Many of the Ayrshire gentry derived income from plantations or had relatives prospering in Virginia or Jamaica; Burns may have felt constrained by his patrons' simultaneous promotion both of the subscriptions for *Poems* and the Jamaica plan. As in Burns's political statements of the 1790s, whose wording sometimes recalls his brother Gilbert's embarrassed obliquity of style, the poet tiptoes around his preceptors' probable opinions. In a letter of October 1786 to Robert Aiken (a painstaking father, or so the first stanza of 'The Cotter's Saturday Night' implies),[30] the poet expresses revulsion for emigration but for reasons unrelated to the slave trade, posing instead an incoherent question. If he abandons his three children in infancy, how will he answer to God? How will he meet their reproachful gazes on his day of judgement, for he imagines Jean's newborn twins and Bess as all predeceasing him:

> how should I, in the presence of that tremendous Being, the Author of existence, how should I meet the reproaches of those who stand to me in the dear relation of children, whom I deserted in the smiling innocence of helpless infancy? ... Since I wrote the foregoing sheet, I have seen something of the storm of mischief thickening over my folly-devoted head. Should you, my friends, my benefactors, be successful in your applications for me, perhaps it may not be in my power in that way to reap the fruit of your friendly efforts. What I have written in the preceding pages is the settled tenor of my present resolution; but should inimical circumstances forbid me closing with your kind offer, or enjoying it only, threaten to entail further misery[31]

Far from revealing a frank embrace of expedience, this letter suggests a person struggling to complete his sentences, unable to follow through on a torrent of conditionals: 'should', 'may be', 'perhaps'.

On 19 June Charles Douglas likewise wrote rather incoherently from Port Antonio, Jamaica to his elder brother Patrick in Ayr describing 'The young fellow I want' as someone who 'can write & read so as to be able to answer a letter I ought write to him whether I am abroad'; he mentions a salary of '10 or 12 pound a year or less', although that figure was evidently later negotiated to £30.[32] Patrick Douglas, trained as a surgeon, had purchased the properties and his brother Charles managed them. A November 1788 census sent to England from Spanishtown listed the population of the parish of Portland, location of the two plantations – named with incongruous lyricism 'Ayr Mount' and 'Nightingale Grove'[33] – as 5,510, among whom 4,960 were slaves. 'White' people numbered 375.[34] A bookkeeper would soon learn the catastrophic mortality rate for sugarcane workers, whether from labour in the fields or the extremes of the tropical climate. He would also learn of mortality rates for Europeans, which were high: 'Of indentured servants arriving in the island between 1719–1758, 36% died within five years. White mortality was so high that it even surpassed that of brutally exploited African slaves'.[35] By the end of the eighteenth century, the population of slaves in Jamaica was around 300,000; but the tiny European population constituted the wealthiest group in the British Americas. Even leaving the sugar planters aside, by the 1770s the merchants of Kingston had established it as populous and wealthy, the 'third most important [British] colonial town, behind Philadelphia and New York'.[36]

The plantation position was sometimes defended by early biographers as having little direct involvement with the slave trade, but a narrative written in post-slavery Jamaica for a newspaper in 1906 (reprinted in the *Burns Chronicle* in 1911) sets the record straight:

> The ... book-keeping portion of the duties of even a modern book-keeper in Jamaica form far and away the least part of these duties, and the work, with extended license, was similar in the slavery days. The 'bookie' had control of the gangs of negroes in the field, in the boiling house, and in the still-house ... In addition to a liberality of whip-cord the Jamaican slave-laws of the period admitted of such attentions for misdemeanours as branding, dismemberment, and other mutilations, and with such cases the book-keepers were more or less directly associated ... The book-keepers did not reside with the 'squire' or his representative 'the busha'. Their residence was the wretched 'barracks' situated somewhere near the factory set in the heart of the malarial influences which always hang around a sugar estate ... Rum could be procured ad lib., and it was drunk in the corresponding ratio ... There were no restrictions on life or living – society offered none, government pressed none, the moral tone of the period dictated none. Thus it is not surprising to learn from authentic records that no fewer than ninety per cent, of the white book-keepers who came to Jamaica died from the effects of imprudent courses.[37]

If, contrary to Gilbert's account, it was not the poet himself who was eager to '*push his fortune*' by sailing into this nightmare, what patrons or friends had urged the plan for Jamaica? Robert Aiken is a possibility: with the attorney's wide acquaintance and residence in Ayr, he would have known Patrick Douglas. Burns respected Aiken: 'The Cotter's Saturday Night' is dedicated to him and 'Orator Bob' is one of the heroes of 'Holy Willie's Prayer'. During the same week that he destroyed the 'marriage lines' on instruction from the Armours, Aiken re-ingratiated himself with Burns by becoming the Kilmarnock edition's most generous subscriber. Another possible advocate of emigration to Jamaica is John Ballantine, also of Ayr. During that autumn, Burns sent Ballantine, a banker and dedicatee of 'The Brigs of Ayr', a hurried request for a print of the old 'Cross of Ayr' that the poet wished to take to Jamaica. Perhaps the two men jointly promoted emigration: a letter Burns addressed to Aiken in late September opens 'I never end a letter to you of late but I think of Mr. Ballantine', implying a recent meeting.[38] Aiken and Ballantine were Freemasons, a group with a mixed reaction to slavery. His Masonic friends would not necessarily have deterred Burns. The membership of Merchant's Lodge in Liverpool at the end of the eighteenth century, for instance, included the owners of slave ships but also active abolitionists.[39] One eighteenth-century Freemason, James Boswell, defended slavery as a 'very important and necessary ... branch of commercial interest' in his *Life of Johnson*,[40] while another, former slave-holder Ben Franklin, became active in the abolition movement in the 1770s.

For Burns, especially around late July, emigration meant the end of harassment by the elder Armours but also the end of everything else. On 30 July he sent a farewell message to his friend John Richmond in Edinburgh worded as if from a deathbed: 'My hour is now come – You and I will never meet in Scotland more'.[41] During a visit to Patrick Douglas in Ayr in mid-August, however (the first mention of Douglas in Burns's own correspondence), the poet was advised to defer his voyage.[42] Charles Douglas was reluctant to prepay the £50 required for an overland journey between Savanna-la-Mar, where the ship *Nancy* would land, and the plantations themselves, which lay some 140 miles to the east. Douglas recommended *The Bell* as a better choice in calling at Kingston; it was to sail from Greenock on 1 September, though in the event its departure was delayed until 20 September.[43] Later still, the poet rescheduled for the *Roselle*, due to sail at the end of December from Edinburgh's port of Leith.[44]

Following the success of his Kilmarnock *Poems*, Burns hoped from about August that a new edition would allow him to stay in Scotland. Successive deferrals of his voyage do not constitute evidence of an irresolute temperament, for Burns never intended to sail unless compelled by legal or financial pressures. A settlement with Elizabeth Paton signed on 1 December 1786 providing somewhat differently for Bess (pledging support but not mentioning copyright or reappointing Gilbert as trustee), suggests that Burns, despite having paid for his passage,[45] was at that point arranging to stay in Scotland, where if any future crisis arose with his daughter or her mother he would be near enough to respond himself. On 9 December, a favourable review of his *Poems* by the novelist Henry Mackenzie appeared in the *Lounger*. It closes by berating the Ayrshire gentry for doing nothing to prevent the poet's departure, or perhaps for too zealously promoting it: 'I have learnt from some of his countrymen that he has been obliged to form the resolution of leaving his native land, to seek under a West Indian clime that shelter and support which Scotland has denied him'.[46] This appeared three weeks before the *Roselle* was to sail, but Burns had only four more days of suspense, at which point he wrote to John Ballantine that William Creech, who published the *Lounger*, had offered him a second edition of *Poems*. He wrote also to Aiken on 16 December in the flattering strain always used with this tricky patron: 'I have found in Mr Creech, who is my agent forsooth, and Mr Smellie who is to be my printer, that honor and goodness of heart which I always expect in Mr Aiken's friends'.[47] The last of Burns's prospective ships sailed without the poet. In the same letter to Aiken, Burns confesses that he still looks 'down on the future as I would into the bottomless pit',[48] but the letter is at least written in complete sentences, not the disoriented fragments of midsummer and autumn.

I have only sketched events about which biographers have often differed: the many gaps can be filled in differently. Yet the main points should serve to convey the panic-stricken intensity of the months prior to and just after the publication of the 1786 *Poems* as well as how much depended on the volume's success. Unmentioned as yet is Burns's possible new betrothal, during Jean Armour's absence in Paisley in April and May, to Margaret Campbell ('Highland Mary'). Evidence is scanty and contradictory, but Burns's emigration plans at one point probably included some hope of leaving with her.[49] The year 1786, a wild ride, saw the birth of Poet Burns from the ashes of Robt. Burness. The latter explored national language, music and character, and his voicings are quieter, more elusive, than 'Burns's' performances. I turn now to the two 'Burness' manuscript projects predating 1786 before closing this chapter with the mixed messages of the 1786 *Poems*.

'Soft Image of our Youthful Mind': *The First Commonplace Book*

> Pleasing when youth is long expir'd to trace,
> The forms our pencil, or our pen design'd!
> Such was our youthful air and shape and face!
> Such the soft image of our youthful mind.
>
> Shenstone, 'Elegy 1'[50]

Burns created what is now called *The First Commonplace Book* (April 1783–October 1785) from eleven folio sheets folded to form a book-like object of some 12 by 8 inches. Forty-three pages are numbered in the poet's hand. Originally 'broached with a coarse thread' (most likely by Burns himself), the work was later 'handsomely bound in morocco', not a bad emblem of the distance between posterity's showy repackaging of Burns and the person writing poems during the mid-1780s.[51] The title page displays one of the poet's chatty early titles, just short of 140 words. As in a printed book, page two is left blank. The poet transcribes twenty-five early poems and songs, the majority written in standard English, with the first entries embedded in prose commentary.

With its focus on meditations, prayers and love songs fitted to Scottish airs, *The First Commonplace Book* is less a precursor to the 1786 *Poems* than a shadow volume by 'not-Burns', an alternate debut of a contrary kind. The work is less descriptive, less vernacular in diction, and far less adventurous metrically than the 1786 *Poems*. It is more intensely lyrical, however: a majority of the texts are songs. 'Robt. Burness' speaks in a quieter register, yet this voicing is in its own way compelling. After the first item, he writes that 'Lest my works should be thought below Criticism ... I am determined to criticise them myself'.[52] *The First Commonplace Book* not only transcribes but in some detail assesses the value of the texts included. Only nine poems appear both in *The First Commonplace Book*, broken off in October 1785, and *Poems*, sent to the printer eight months later in June 1786, meaning that only about 25 per cent of the Kilmarnock poems had been copied from *The First Commonplace Book*, itself selective in excluding many works that existed in some form by that time, among them 'Address to the Unco Guid', 'Epistle to Davie', 'Holy Willie's Prayer', 'Death and Dr. Hornbook' and 'A Poet's Welcome to his Love-Begotten Daughter'. In this first undertaking, 'Robt. Burness' chiefly dramatizes his speaker's shifting states of mind: 'how a ploughman thinks, and feels', he says on his title page, 'under the pressure of Love, Ambition, Anxiety, Grief'.[53] Fifteen of the twenty-five texts are songs in near-standard English that retain just 'a dash of our native tongue', to use the poet's description of his song-diction in a later letter.[54] The melodies to which the poet fits his words are mostly Scots, however. Identification of the tunes often provides the only token of a title. The poet himself composed the music for the final song in the volume, but he did not know how to transcribe it, so the musical composition was lost.

Table 1.1: *The First Commonplace Book* (April 1783–October 1785). Sequence of texts and verse-forms; frequent use of common measure.

The numbers below refer to James Kinsley's conjectural dating and sequence for Burns's writings in his Clarendon edition of Burns. Comparing the twenty-five texts Burns copies into *The First Commonplace Book* (*FCB*) to the several dozen (now more famous) that were well underway by 1783, it becomes clear that Burns's editorial principle even when preparing transcriptions is highly selective and thematic rather than chronological. He is focussed on nearly completed material. As early as *FCB*, he is selecting clusters of finished texts that play off each other, a practice that will lead to the dazzling interplay of the texts in *Poems, Chiefly in the Scottish Dialect*.

(1) Dated 'April–83': #1 in Kinsley; *FCB* title: 'Song – (Tune – I am a man unmarried')', usually titled 'Handsome Nell'. In common measure; see rhyme variants below. The spelling is more 'English' than that of Burns's later transcriptions:

O once I lov'd a bonny lass	(8A)
Ay and I love her still	(6B)
And whilst that virtue warms my breast	(8C)
I'll love my handsome Nell	(6B)
Fal lal de dal &c.	

[Rhyme-scheme in third line below changes to common hymnal measure:]

As bonny lasses I hae seen,	(8A)
And mony full as braw;	(6B)
But for a modest gracefu' mien,	(8A)
The like I never saw.	(6B)

(2) Dated 'Sept. [1783]': #26 in Kinsley, where it is titled '[Remorse]'. Headed in *FCB* not with a title but praise of Adam Smith: 'I intirely agree with that judicious Philosopher Mr Smith in his excellent Theory of Moral Sentiments, that Remorse is the most painful sentiment that can embitter the human bosom'. The metre is unrhymed iambic pentameter (blank verse): 'Of all the numerous ills that hurt our peace'.

(3) Dated 'March–84': #5 in Kinsley; *FCB* title is 'A penitential thought, in the hour of Remorse[–]'. In English blank verse: 'All devil as I am, a damned wretch'.

(4) Dated 'March - 84': Untitled in *FCB*; #15 in Kinsley, where it is titled 'A Prayer, Under the Pressure of violent Anguish' ('O Thou great Being! what Thou art / Surpasses me to know'); in common hymnal measure; the rhyme is abab.

(5) Dated 'April' [1784]: [Untitled;] #10 in Kinsley; *FCB* title is 'Song – (Tune McPherson's Farewell)'; printed in the 1786 *Poems* as 'Winter, A Dirge' ('The Wintry West extends his blast'). In double common measure (two common-measure quatrains printed as an octave).

(6) Dated 'April–' [1784]: #21 in Kinsley; the title in *FCB* is 'Song – (Tune 'The weaver & his shuttle O'). First line is 'My father was a farmer upon the Carrick border O'; variable metre following the cadences of the tune.

(7) Dated 'April–' [1784]: #4 in Kinsley; *FCB* title 'Song – (Tune As I came in by London O)' ('Behind yon hills where Stincher flows'); in common hymnal measure. A song the poet's father, William Burnes, is on record as approving.

(8) Dated 'April–}' [1784]: #32 in Kinsley; *FCB* title is 'Epitaph on Wm Hood Senr in Tarbolton –'; published in 1786 *Poems* as 'On a Celebrated Ruling Elder' ('Here Sowter Hood in death does sleep'); in common hymnal measure.

(9) Dated 'April–}' [1784]: #28 in Kinsley; *FCB* title is 'On Ja^s Grieve, Laird of Boghead, Tarbolton' ('Here lies Boghead amang the dead'); in common measure.

(10) Dated 'April–}' [1784]: #31 in Kinsley; *FCB* title is 'Epitaph on my own friend, & my father's friend, Wm Muir in Tarbolton Miln. –' ('Here lies a cheerful, honest breast'). In octosyllabic couplets (8A8A8B8B).

(11) Dated April–}' [1784]: #35 in Kinsley; *FCB* title is 'Epitaph on my ever honor'd Father–' ('O ye! Who sympathize with Virtue's pains!'). Iambic pentameter (rhyme is abab; final line is lifted from Goldsmith's 'The Deserted Village'). Published, much improved, in 1786 *Poems*.

(12) Dated 'Aug^t. [1784]': #45 in Kinsley; untitled in *FCB* ('Green grow the rashes – O'); variable metre matched to the tune.

(13) Dated 'Aug: }' [1784]: #13 in Kinsley; *FCB* title is 'A Prayer, when fainting fits, & other alarming symptoms of a Pleurisy or some other dangerous disorder, which indeed still threaten me, first put Nature on the alarm. – ' ('O thou, Unknown, Almighty Cause / Of all my hope & fear'); in common measure.

(14) Dated 'Aug:}' [1784]: #14 in Kinsley; *FCB* title is 'Misgivings in the hour of Despondency – and prospect of Death'. ('Why am I loth to leave this earthly scene'). Published in the Edinburgh 1787 *Poems* with the subtitle 'in the manner of Beattie's Minstrel'; in English blank verse.

(15) Dated 'Sept.:}' [1784]: #6 in Kinsley; *FCB* title is 'Song – Tune, Invercauld's reel – Strathspey' ('Tibby I hae seen the day'); in common measure but a variant rhyme (8A6A8A6B).

(16) Dated 'Sept:' [1784]: #46 in Kinsley; *FCB* title is 'Song – Tune: Black Joke' ('My girl she's airy, she's buxom and gay'); variable metre matched to the tune.

(*A break between September 1784 and 1 June 1785 coincides with the lingering illness and death of the poet's father on 13 February 1785 following a successful conclusion in January of the lawsuit with his landlord. The time period also marks the months of Elizabeth Paton's pregnancy: Bess was born 22 May 1785.*)

(17) Dated '1785 June': #23 in Kinsley; *FCB* title is 'John Barley corn. – A Song, to its own Tune'. ('There was three kings into the east'); in common measure.

(18) Dated 'June}': #24 in Kinsley; *1CPB* title is 'The Death an' dyin' words o' poor Mailie – my ain pet ewe – an unco mournfu' Tale. –' ('As Mailie and her lambs the gither'). Published with a slightly different title in the 1786 *Poems*. In octosyllabic couplets.

(19) Dated 'June }': #57 in Kinsley; *1CPB* title is 'A letter sent to John Lapraik near Muirkirk, a true, genuine, Scottish Bard. – April 1785' ('While breers & woodbines buding green'). Published in the 1786 *Poems*; in standard Habbie metre (8A8A8A4B8A4B).

(20) #58 in Kinsley ('To the Same') ('While new ca't ky rowt at the stake'); the *FCB* version is prefaced with this sentence: 'On receiving an answer to the above, I wrote the following April 21st 1785'. Published in revised form in the 1786 *Poems*; in standard Habbie. 'A Stanza forgot ...' from 'Misgivings in the hour of DESPONDENCY' (#14) is inserted here, with a direction of the reader back to 'the foot of page 19th'.

(21) Dated 'August}' [1785]: #64 in Kinsley; *FCB* title is 'A Song – Tune Peggy Bawn' ('When chill November's surly blast'). Published in the 1786 *Poems* as 'Man Was Made to Mourn, A Dirge'; in double common measure. On p. 34 is inserted the direction 'A Verse wanting here – See page 40'. Another note ('The last verse of John Barley corn Page 24th') is inserted after the end of 'When chill November's'.

   [??]. By Burns or admired by Burns
      Dated 'Aug}':
         'And if there is no other scene of Being
         Where my insatiate wish may have its fill; –
         This something at my heart that heaves for room
         My best, my dearest part was made in vain. –'

The lines, uncollected by Kinsley, are introduced by this comment: 'Obscure I am, & obscure I must be, though no young Poet, nor young Soldier's heart ever beat more fondly for fame than mine. –'

(22) Dated 'Aug: }' [1785]: #44 in Kinsley; *FCB* title is 'A Fragment – ' ('When first I came to Stewart Kyle / My mind it was nae steady'); in common measure.

(23) #2 in Kinsley; the *1CPB* title is 'HAR'STE – A Fragment – Tune – Foregoing' [same tune and possibly the same date as #22]. A variant of the first eight lines of 'Song, Composed in August', printed in revised form in the 1786 *Poems*. ('When breezy win's, and slaughtering guns'); in common measure.

(24.) Dated 'Sept }' [1785]: #22 in Kinsley; *FCB* title is 'Fragment – Tune – Galla Water – ('Altho' my bed were in yon muir' ['Montgomery's Peggy']). More or less octosyllabic, with a variable cadence matched to the tune.
'A verse of a Song forgot' is inserted, with the direction 'Vide Page 34' ('Man Was Made to Mourn').

(??) 'When clouds in skies do come together'; a three-stanza song not collected in Kinsley's edition. Burns calls the transcription 'a Debt I owe to the Author, as the repeating of that verse has lighted up my flame a thousand times'. Yet after introducing the song as if by another hand, he adds after the stanzas a remark that identifies the stanzas as his own: 'The above was an extempore under the pressure of a heavy train of misfortunes which, indeed, threatened to undo me altogether'. Form and rhyme are rather irregular.

(25) Dated 'Sept.}': #17 in Kinsley; first published in Cromek's *Reliques of Robert Burns* (1808); no title in *FCB*. First line is 'O raging Fortune's withering blast'. Note in *FCB*: 'I set about composing an air in the old Scotch style ... the following were the verses I composed to suit it'. Kinsley mentions a later note in which Burns says he never published the verses because they were ill-matched to the tune, which 'consisted of three parts, so that the above verses just went through the whole Air'. This is the poet's only reference to 'composing an air'; not being taught to read music, he was unable to transcribe it (to 'prick down my tune properly', as he puts it in his *FCB* note to the lines.) In common measure in stanza two; the opening and closing stanzas are choruses.

Sources: J. C. Ewing and D. Cook (eds), *Robert Burns's Commonplace Book. 1783–85, Reproduced in Facsimile from the Poet's Manuscript and the Original Introduction and Notes of James Cameron Ewing and Davidson Cook; This Edition Introduced by David Daiches* (Carbondale, IL: Southern Illinois University Press, 1965). J. Kinsley (ed.), 'Textual Introduction', in *The Poems and Songs of Robert Burns*, 3 vols (Oxford: Clarendon, 1968), vol. 3, pp. 963–94.

The poet's first song, written *c.* 1773 for his partner in the harvest, is given pride of place in this first prototype book, but after entry #1 the principle of inclusion is not chronological. The contents of *The First Commonplace Book* vary greatly from the probable chronology of composition given by James Kinsley in his Clarendon edition of Burns. Kinsley orders the sequence of *1CPB* as follows: #1 ('Handsome Nell') but then #26, #5, #15, #10, #21, #4, #32, #28, #31, #35, #45, #13, #14, #6, #46, #23, #24, #57, #58, #64, #44, #2, #22 and #17.[55] Determining exact dates for the poet's earliest writings is seldom possible and transcription in *The First Commonplace Book* establishes only a latest possible date of composition. Yet it is clear that while Burns copied some texts soon after completion, including the epistles to Lapraik, most date back to the poet's adolescence, although Burns most likely revised these youthful efforts for *The First Commonplace Book* – just as the works also chosen for the 1786 *Poems* were further revised for the press between winter 1785 and mid-1786.

The mixture of sententious commentary, songs and fragmentary verses establishes not a historical record so much as a sketch or 'soft image' of a bard looking back on his earliest writings. To page 18, Burness inserts thirteen poetic texts among passages of literary critique and musings on life. From pages 19–35, however, he copies seven splendid poems without comment except a short note for 'John Barleycorn'. Some of the seven are in English, including the songs later known as 'Man Was Made to Mourn' and 'John Barleycorn', but others are in Scots, among them the burlesque 'Dying Words' of his pet sheep Mailie and the first two epistles to John Lapraik: in the second letter to Lapraik (21 April 1785), the poet spells his name as in his 1783 signature for *The First Commonplace Book*: 'LAPRAIK, & BURNESS then may rise'.[56] Comments in prose resume (pp. 36–44), but in contrast to the earlier mix of critique and sentimental reverie, these offer technical remarks on fitting lyric stanzas to Scottish airs. In this way, the showplace for early work gradually becomes more of a working notebook, although the poet continues throughout to hand-draw 'typographical' effects, including names in small capitals, superscripts, dashes and symbols such as '}'. Although his 1786 preface to *Poems* asserts that his early work was not 'composed with a view to the press',[57] by the time he transcribed *The First Commonplace Book* he was laboriously simulating a printed work as he made trial arrangements of his writings and experimented with placement and presentation.

Many of the songs in *The First Commonplace Book* are irregular to the eye, phrased to highlight what Burns called the 'feature notes' or stresses in the music, as in 'Montgomerie's Peggy', the twenty-fourth item; the title given is 'Fragment – Tune – Galla Water –':

Altho' my bed were in yon muir,	'moor'
Amang the heather, in my plaidie,	
Yet happy happy would I be	
Had I my dear Montgomerie's Peggy. –	
[Dear Montgomerie's Peggy]	

...

Were I a Baron proud and high,	
And horse and servants waiting ready,	
Then a' 'twad gie o' joy to me,	'Then all 'twould give of joy to me'
The sharin't with Montgomerie's Peggy. –	
[Dear Montgomerie's Peggy][58]	

This is one example of a song so lovingly matched to its upbeat tune that its effect is 'Scots' despite its predominantly English diction. In the entry preceding this song, the poet comments that

> There is a certain irregularity in the old Scotch Songs, a redundancy of syllables with respect to that exactness of accent & measure that the English Poetry requires, but which glides in, most melodiously with the respective tunes to which they are set ... This particularly is the case with all those airs which end with a hypermetrical syllable ... This has made me sometimes imagine that ... it might be possible for a Scotch Poet, with a nice, judicious ear, to set compositions to many of our most favourite airs ... independent of rhyme altogether.

He adds in his next entry, dated the same month ('Sept'.) that 'I have even tryed to imitate, in this extempore thing, ['Montgomerie's Peggy'] that irregularity in the rhyme [such as 'ready' / 'Peggy' / 'plaidie'] which, when judiciously done, has such a fine effect on the ear'.[59]

Fully 60 per cent of the texts in *The First Commonplace Book* are stanzas for songs, only one of which, 'Green Grow the Rashes', is strongly spiced with Scots vernacular. Although several dramatic soliloquies in standard-English blank verse and also several dialect poems in the 'standard Habbie' stanza are included, the majority of the texts, likewise iambic, alternate lines of eight and six syllables in either the rhyme abcb (common measure or metre, frequent in ballads) or abab (common hymnal metre). As Table 1.1 shows, the young poet sometimes alternates between the two in a single song, such as 'O Once I lov'd' or 'Handsome Nell', the first song transcribed for *The First Commonplace Book*. The poet was familiar with common measure through popular songs and ballads, through Presbyterian metrical psalms and through his elementary schooling, which consisted, at the poet's father's insistence, of instruction in English grammar and style, often inculcated through study of prayers by well-known English authors. Among the poet's first favourites was a poem by Joseph Addison in *Arthur Masson's Collection of Prose and Verse, from the Best English Authors*. 'On Gratitude to the Deity for his favours' (first printed in the *Spectator*, 7 August 1712) is among the early items in Masson's fourth edition, which Liam McIlvanney has identified as the edition probably studied by the poet as a small boy.[60] It is in common measure:

> When all thy mercies, O my God,   (8A)
> My rising soul surveys,   (6B)
> Transported with the view, I'm lost (8C)
> In wonder, love, and praise.   (6B)[61]

Here is a doxology in the same measure taken from a mid-nineteenth-century Presbyterian Psalter:

> Let God the Father and the Son,
> And Spirit, be adored,
> Where there are works to make Him known
> Or Saints to love the Lord.[62]

Several of Burns's juvenile writings preserved in *The First Commonplace Book* (they may have originated as home-school exercises) are likewise psalm paraphrases or prayers using this metre:

> O Thou, Unknown, Almighty Cause
> Of all my hope & fear,
> In whose dread presence ere an hour
> Perhaps I must appear.[63]

Throughout his life, the poet favoured tunes compatible with this measure (sometimes, as in 'Man was Made to Mourn', doubled into an octave stanza) for a wide range of songs. Here is a stanza from the unpolished early version of 'Man

Was Made to Mourn' transcribed in *The First Commonplace Book*, where it is titled 'A Song – Tune, Peggy Bawn':

Many the Ills that Nature's hand	(A)
Has woven with our frame;	(B)
More pointed still we make ourselves	(C)
Regret, remorse, & shame:	(B)
And Man, whose heaven-erected face,	(D) [(A), if this line began a new quatrain]
The smiles of love adorn,	(E); (B)
Man's inhumanity to man	(F); (C)
Makes countless thousands mourn.[64]	(E); (B)

Six years later, the same measure was used for a famous love song:

Ye flowery banks o' bonie Doon,	
How can ye blume sae fair;	'bloom'
How can ye chant, ye little birds,	
And I sae fu' o' care![65]	'full'

Five years later still, Burns sent 'Tam Lin', a ballad in this measure, to James Johnson among the final songs for *Scots Musical Museum*:

They'll turn me in your arms, lady,	
Into an ask and adder,	'eft' (lizard)
But hald me fast and fear me not,	'hold'
I am your bairn's father.[66]	'baby's'

'The Cotter's Saturday Night', itself completed after *The First Commonplace Book* was broken off and written not in common metre but in Spenserian stanzas, describes a scene in which the family sing psalms in common measure:

> They chant their artless notes in simple guise;
> They tune their hearts, by far the noblest aim:
> Perhaps *Dundee*'s wild-warbling measures rise,
> Or plaintive *Martyrs*, worthy of the name;
> Or noble *Elgin* beets the heaven-ward flame,
> The sweetest far of SCOTIA's holy lays ... [67]

The passage recalls the sacred songs in common hymnal measure that marked the poet as deeply as Scottish song's more lighthearted traditions. 'Dundee', 'Elgin' and 'Martyrs', mentioned in 'Cotter', are among the Covenanters' traditional 'twelve old tunes'. These were sung slowly, with each beat held two seconds. Out of respect for the biblical source of these 'holy lays', practice verses were often substituted in teaching these tunes, reserving the psalm-texts strictly for worship. The Church of Scotland had no official prayer book but did mandate its own psalms, hymns and tunes, and these settings were an important part of the poet's early experience of Scottish song.

Common measure and a focus on setting stanzas to pre-existing music predominate in every phase of this poet's career except the Kilmarnock *Poems* and its later editions (1787 and 1793), which is why I see those publications as an 'interruption' of his default poetic voice – 'not-Burns'; 'Burness' – a more secretive (often anonymous) and also more lyric, bardic, recessed speaker than Poet Burns. Yet some early writings are pliant enough to convey the voices of both 'Burness' and 'Burns'. Two stanzas and the chorus of an early song – Kinsley placed it among the juvenilia as text #10; it is #5 among the contents of the *First Commonplace Book* and #19 in the Kilmarnock *Poems*, where it is titled 'Winter, A Dirge' – share the devotional cast as well as the common measure of so many texts in the *First Commonplace Book*:

The wintry West extends his blast	
And hail & rain does blaw;	'blow'
Or the stormy North sends driving forth	
The blinding sleet & snaw ...	'snow'
...	
'The sweeping blast, the sky o'ercast,'*	*Dr. Young [RB's note in *Poems*]
The joyless winter day;	
Let others fear, to me more dear	
Than all the pride of May: –	
The tempest's howl, it sooths my soul,	
My griefs it seems to join;	
The leafless trees my fancy please,	
Their fate resembles mine. –	
Thou Power Supreme whose mighty scheme,	
These *woes* of mine fulfil:	
Here firm, I rest, they must [be] best,	
Because they are thy will:	
Then all I want – (O do thou grant	
This one request of mine;)	
Since to enjoy, Thou dost deny,	
Assist me to resign.[68]	

In measure and devoutness the stanzas are suited to *The First Commonplace Book*; yet in their projection of the speaker's anxious emotions onto the regional landscape they also fit well into the Kilmarnock volume.

In this first self-assembled, self-edited work, twenty-one of twenty-five texts, among them fourteen of fifteen songs, are largely in English although the rhymes require a Scots pronunciation. (Those who find Burns's 'English' songs insipid are not hearing the Scottish pronunciation of vowel sounds that he was hearing as he wrote, or the interplay of words and music that from his youngest days drew him to fitting his stanzas to tunes.) The poet includes only three poems in vernacular Scots – all superb, however. And if this first collection does not share the Kilmarnock volume's emphasis 'chiefly' on Scots, the 1786 *Poems* minimizes song, titling only three texts as such, along with two 'dirges' that fit Scots airs and one poem, 'The Farewell', listing a suggested tune. With the exception of the obscene 'My girl she's airy', the songs and poems in *The First Commonplace Book* all were publishable, although a few awaited posthumous appearances in James Currie's *Life and Works of Burns* (1800) or Robert Cromek's *Reliques of Robert Burns* (1808). The poet also selected some of these early writings for transcription in the manuscript volumes that he sometimes put together as gifts for patrons, including the Stair Manuscript (autumn 1786) and Glenriddell Manuscript (1791–3), which among other things offers a much-condensed version of *The First Commonplace Book* (chiefly the prose sections; Burns had already published many of *The First Commonplace Book*'s poems and songs by the 1790s). The poet never printed 'My father was a farmer' despite identifying it in *The First Commonplace Book* as an important early milestone: the song first appeared in Cromek's *Reliques*. In *The First Commonplace Book*, Burns calls the verses a poor match for the music, and the words do crowd up against a busy, lively tune.

This poised, handmade volume is a breakthrough in its own right, recording the creation of a speaker by turns meditative yet, with the volume's wealth of dashes, also abrupt, serious yet whimsical, as in the title-page's rash pledge of 'unbounded good will to every creature rational or irrational'. This elusive bard-in-training is quite different from the Type-A speaker of the Kilmarnock *Poems* who takes centre stage around mid-volume, with a preview in the preface. ('Burns didn't fish for compliments', muses Don Paterson of the preface, 'he went after them with an elephant gun.'[69]) Burness, selecting the standard English of Presbyterian songs and prayers as an appropriate idiom for his devout yet melancholy speakers, does not exclude but de-emphasizes vernacular diction. In *The First Commonplace Book*, 'Robt. Burness' mainly explores how to fit standard-English stanzas to existing songs. The one bawdy item (of many completed by 1785) that the poet copied into *The First Commonplace Book* – predominantly a sober gathering – may have earned its admission because of its conclusion:

Song - Tune: Black Joke [*sic*] –
My girl she's airy, she's buxom and gay;
Her breath is as sweet as the blossoms in may;
   A touch of her lips it ravishes quite.
She's always good natur'd, good humor'd and free;
She dances, she glances, she smiles upon me
   I never am happy when out of her sight.
Her slender neck her handsome waist

> Her hair well-curl'd her stays well lac'd
> Her taper white leg with an et and a c,
> For her a, b, c and her c,? t,
>   And O for the joys of a long winter night.[70]

The author exhibits his proficiency in the standard language by this parodic spelling exercise and recitation of the alphabet.

The First Commonplace Book breaks off on p. 43 after a first sentence starts a fresh paragraph: 'In the first place, let my Pupil, as he tenders his own peace, keep up a regular, warm intercourse with the Deity'.[71] This last entry is dated 'Oct: 85', the month that the poet's youngest brother, sixteen-year-old John, died. When Burns began a new notebook and a new transcription project a few months later, his emphasis had shifted.

'Scotch Poems': The Kilmarnock Manuscript

> Be so good as send me Ferguson ['s *Poems*] by Connel and I will remit you the money.
>   Letter to John Richmond, then in Edinburgh, dated 17 February 1786[72]

The group of early poems that editors refer to as the *Kilmarnock Manuscript* (the poet's own title was 'Scotch Poems', an accurate preview) was most likely begun in January 1786 and is linked to the published volume of late July, for the subscribers' sheets for the 1786 *Poems* (circulated beginning in April 1786) are likewise titled 'Scotch Poems'. Fourteen of the fifteen texts in the *Kilmarnock Manuscript* reappear in the 1786 *Poems* but in a different sequence.

In 1889 David Sneddon compiled *Burns Holograph Manuscripts in the Kilmarnock Monument Museum*, in his words a '*verbatim et literatim*' transcription of the 'Scotch Poems' notebook, which had been taken apart for separate display in the Burns Monument Museum in Kay Park, Kilmarnock. He dates the notebook from 'Autumn of 1785'[73] but this is incorrect: 'Composed in Autumn of 1785' is indeed a notation on page one as Sneddon says, but this is written under the title of the first entry, 'The Holy Fair', and most likely pertains to the date the poet began that poem. The notebook was probably purchased in late 1785, months of feverish composition for the poet, who had by that time evidently decided to prepare his poems for publication. In discussing the *Kilmarnock Manuscript*, I have relied on Sneddon, checked against the original manuscript, now held by the East Ayrshire Council. Sneddon's transcription is meticulous, although he omits Burns's frequent long dashes.

In Sneddon's account, the notebook contained sixty-six pages transcribing fifteen poems, followed by thirteen blank pages, with some revisions entered on the final page. The title page is headed 'Scotch Poems by Robt Burness'. The contents are as follows in Table 1.2.

Table 1.2: 'Scotch Poems': Sequence of texts and verse-forms; emphasis on standard Habbie and traditional Scottish forms.

The notebook titled 'Scotch Poems by Rob Burness'
(1) The first 18 stanzas and part of stanza 20 of 'The Holy Fair'; stanza form is that of 'Chrystis Kirk of the Green':

Upon a simmer Sunday morn	A	'summer'
When Nature's face is fair,	B	
I walked forth to view the corn,	A	
An' snuff the callor air;	B	'sniff the fresh'
The rising sun o'er Galston muirs	C	'moors'
Wi' glorious light was glentin,	D	'glinting'
The hares were hirplan down the furs,	C	'creeping down the furrows'
The lav'rocks they were chantin	D	'larks'
Fu' sweet that day.	E	'full'

(2) Burns transcribes the final 7 lines of stanza 17 and eleven concluding stanzas (18–28) of 'Halloween' as well as his extensive annotations; the poem is in 'Chrystis kirk' stanza-form.

(3.) 'Address to the Deil'; in standard Habbie:

O thou, whatever title suit thee!	(8A)	
Auld Hornie, Satan, Nick, or Clootie,	(8A)	
Wha in yon cavern grim an' sooty,	(8A)	
Clos'd under hatches,	(6B)	
Spairges about the brunstane cootie	(8A)	'flings around the tub of brimstone'
To scaud poor wretches.	(6B)	'scald'

Two stanzas (11 and 15) are struck out by the poet and offered in revised form after the concluding stanza and the flourish of 'Le fin', a phrase that concludes many of the texts.

(4) 'THE AULD FARMER'S New year morning salutation to his auld Meere, on givin her the accustom'd ripp o' corn to Hansel in the New year'; in standard Habbie.

(5) 'John Barleycorn. – A Ballad'; in common measure.

(6) 'Scotch Drink'; in standard Habbie.

(7) 'A Ballad' (the song now usually called 'Man was Made to Mourn'); in double common measure.

(8) 'The Twa Dogs: A Tale'; in octosyllabic couplets.

(9) Two titles are given: 'The Cotter's Saturday Night', with four line epigraph from Thomas Gray's 'Elegy in a Country Churchyard' and then on the next page, 'The Cotter's Saturday-Teen. Inscribed to Mr. Robert Aitken, Ayr' and the same epigraph from Gray. Spenserian stanza-form (10A10B10A10B10C10B10C12C). This is also the stanza-form used by Robert Fergusson in 'The Farmer's Ingle' (1773), one inspiration for 'Cotter'.

(10) 'The Author's Earnest Cry and Prayer to the Rt. Hon[ble] and Hon[ble] The Scotch Representatives in the House of Commons'; in standard Habbie. After stanza 14, there is a stanza marked for excision.

(11) 'Address to J. Smith'; standard Habbie. The second stanza is missing: 'A verse wanting here' and 'Vide last page of the book' are inserted. Those lines are entered on the notebook's last page.

(12) 'Winter, A Dirge' [cancelled title: 'Compos'd in Winter']; in common measure.
(13) 'An Epistle to Davy: A Brother Poet'; stanza-form and rhyme are that of 'The Cherry and the Slae', a poem by Alexander Montgomerie first printed in 1597. Here is a stanza from Burns's adaptation of this stanza:

It's no in titles, nor in rank,	(8A)
It' [sic] no in wealth like Lon'on bank,	(8A)
To purchase peace an' rest;	(6B)
It's no in makin muckle mair,	(8C) 'making much into more'
It's no in books, it's no in lear,	(8C) 'lore, learning'
To mak us truly blest:	(6B)
If happiness hae not her seat	(8d)
An' center in the breast,	(6B)
We may be wise, or rich, or great,	(8d)
But never can be blesst.	(6B)
Nae treasures, nor pleasures,	(6E / E) ('treasures' / 'pleasures')
Could mak us happy lang:	(6F)
The heart ay's the part ay,	(6G / G) ('heart ay's' / 'part ay')
That maks us right or wrang.	(6f)

(14) 'The Death, an' Dyin' Words o' Poor Mailie – My Ain Pet Yowe – An Unco Mournfu' Tale'; in octosyllabic couplets.
(15) 'Poor Mailie's Elegy'; in standard Habbie.

Source: D. Sneddon (ed.), *Burns Holograph Manuscripts in the Kilmarnock Monument Museum, With Notes* (Kilmarnock: D. Brown & Co, 1889).

Opening and closing with two partial transcriptions (presumably the fair copies of the stanzas completed to date), the *Kilmarnock Manuscript* is a working notebook rather than a personal memento like the opening pages of *The First Commonplace Book*. In range of metres it is very diverse. Only three texts are ballads in common measure. Among the poems, one is written in the intricate 'Cherry and the Slae' stanza, two (the first two copied) in the equally complex 'Chrystis Kirk' stanza, and six first-rate performances are in standard Habbie, a verse-form so associated with Burns that it is now often called the 'Burns stanza'. The manuscript ends, as Table 1.2 above describes, with a draft of 'Poor Mailie's Elegy', a new poem in standard Habbie written as a postscript to the octosyllabic 'Dying Words' of the poet's pet sheep Mailie, itself completed by 1782. (Mailie's last words, the poet's earliest surviving and probably his first poem in dialect, had also been copied into *The First Commonplace Book*.) Three favourite largely English songs likewise appear in both early manuscripts: 'Winter: A Dirge', 'John Barleycorn. A Ballad', and 'Man Was Made to Mourn, A Dirge'. ('Mailie', 'Winter' and 'Man Was Made to Mourn' are printed in the 1786 *Poems* as well; 'John Barleycorn' was printed in 1787 in the expanded Edinburgh edition of *Poems*.)

It may be that the poet was considering opening a volume to be titled 'Scotch Poems' with 'The Holy Fair' and 'Halloween', both in dense vernacular and both in the 'Chrystis Kirk' stanza-form traditional in Scotland for satiric accounts of local festivities and brawls; there will be more on this tradition in Chapter 4. The next pairing of poems in the *Kilmarnock Manuscript* shows the poet's even broader extension of Fergusson's much-expanded vision of standard Habbie's possibilities.[74] 'Address to the Deil', an early masterwork, considers 'Auld Hornie, Satan, Nick, or Clootie' ['Hoofie'] in alternate lights, from the ridiculous folk superstitions echoed by its credulous narrator to Satan's central roles in the Book of Job, Milton's *Paradise Lost* and Calvinist theology. The text that follows 'Address to the Deil', likewise in standard Habbie, is sentimental rather than satiric: 'The Auld Farmer's New Year Morning Salutation' pays indirect tribute to the poet's late father and more broadly looks back at the tenantry's vanishing way of life. The two poems that follow form a contrast, too, celebrating whisky in standard English ('John Barleycorn') and then in Scots ('Scotch Drink'). A key stanza in 'Man Was Made to Mourn' describes a rich man arrogantly spurning a poor man's request for work; in the poem that follows it, 'The Twa Dogs', Scottish life (privileged and non-) is likewise seen in a dual perspective in this cordial dialogue between a rich man's Newfoundland dog and a poor man's mongrel collie. 'The Cotter's Saturday Night' celebrates the self-reliant domestic virtue of Scottish tenants and sub-tenants, while 'The Author's Earnest Cry and Prayer' addresses London's less admirable and in several senses more remote power elite, who nonetheless make laws for Mother Scotland. The poet celebrates the joys of friendship and the risks of writing poetry in the epistle to Jamie Smith, a text followed by 'Winter, A Dirge', also transcribed in *The First Commonplace Book*, which describes the pleasure of a long solitary walk through a winter storm. 'Epistle to Davy, A Brother Poet. Jan. 1785' (the spelling in the notebook differs from 'Davie', used in the Kilmarnock *Poems*) warmly addresses another close friend but adds a serious glance ahead at their fate when older and perhaps disabled or homeless.

Edwin Morgan, quoting a couplet from 'Epistle to Davie' – 'To lye in kilns and barns at e'en, / When banes are craz'd, and bluid is thin' (ll. 29–30) – sees such passages as a change from the 'extrovert Burns' of myth, a different voice

> more strange, more mysterious, more secret, often associated with images or settings of twilight or darkness, not so much a matter of whole poems as a few lines which reverberate in your mind and make you wonder where the impact came from[75]

Morgan describes 'Burness', the intuitive, bardic vision or impulse that grounds the more calculated (if nonetheless powerful) performances of Poet Burns. The 'extrovert' speaker, the basis of the Burns myth, does take over the 1786 *Poems* around midpoint of the volume but recedes in such later projects as the poet's collaboration with James Johnson on Scottish song; and at the time he was filling in the pages of the blank notebook that became 'Scotch Poems', the bardic was likewise ascendant, even though this project is not primarily intent on fitting lyrics to music. In the notebook he uses his speakers to represent characteristic parts of the Scottish community, tending to withhold outside commentary by a specifically 'poetic' sensibility. 'The Holy Fair', a fragment of which opens 'Scotch Poems', not only speaks for but sometimes *as* the gathered congregation of conservative ('Auld Licht') Calvinists, channelling *their* scorn for the sermon of New Licht moderate George Smith, who has the temerity to urge good works and moral behaviour as well as faith. The congregation's rejection of this advice as outlandish and poisoned (l. 137) was certainly not shared by Rob Burness himself.

In this early notebook that suggests the poet's initial conceptualization of the 1786 Kilmarnock volume, Burness uses his speakers-in-Scots to evoke regional and (in 'The Cotter's Saturday Night') national character as opposed to his own opinions. Even in 'The Cotter's Saturday Night', something of a hybrid poem, the patriarch's injunctions to his children to 'mind their labours ... and never jauk [joke] or play' (ll. 48–9) receive no speaker's counter-comment. In its portrait of Scottish life, 'Scotch Poems' embraces varying viewpoints as well as the newly acquired 'Cherry and the Slae' and 'Chrystis Kirk' stanza-forms. Burness here emulates Fergusson in both technique and bardic tact, recognizing in his predecessor's poems, as Morgan sensed in Burns's, the visionary power of the *impersonal* poetic voice. To speak outside one's own preferences, to capture and convey the voices of others, is in bardic terms to come closer to speaking for all. Bardic permeability in no way precludes satire, instead allowing full expression to contrary views. As a bard Burns only channels various voices, refraining from explicit judgement and leaving readers to interpret and judge – or not.

The notebook's last pairing links Burness's first poem in Scots, which offers the dying words of his pet sheep Mailie after her fall into a ditch *c.* 1781 (in real life, incidentally, a non-fatal accident),[76] with a new pendant in standard Habbie. Mailie, a 'yowe o' sense',[77] entrusts the herd-boy Huoc with her last words to her son and daughter. Her advice centres on prudent breeding: she warns her daughter especially to be choosy and consort only with 'sheep o' credit'[78] – credit at the bank possibly, as well as in the studbook. Mailie is no poet and wee Huoc (Hugh Wilson, a youngster employed at Lochlie farm; he had run to the family in horror after Mailie's fall) is not yet Burns's later rustic, standing close and speaking up. Mailie's words are exclusively maternal and practical, reflecting a kind of national archetype: the canny, managing Scotswoman.

The first 'Mailie' poem derives from a sly Scots tradition of recording the dying words of individuals still in perfect health. To her own words in the first poem, the 'Elegy' adds a tribute by '*Robin*' Burns (l. 82; emphasis is added in the 1786 *Poems*) that is more official, not to say officious, in ordering pipers all along the rivers Doon and Ayr to tune up for her dirge. The second Mailie poem may also be aimed at English poets such as Thomas Gray, whose grief-stricken speakers are, like Robin here, restless souls overborne by ceaseless reminders of their loss. The word 'bleating', while not applied to sentimental elegists per se, comes into probably mischievous play:

> At times he wanders up the howe,
> Her living image in her yowe
> Comes bleating till him owre the knowe
>   For bits o' bread;
> An' doun the briny pearls rowe
>   For Mailie dead.[79]

In the *Kilmarnock Manuscript* Rob Burness implies a series of contrasts, including Scots mock-elegy versus English sentimental elegy. Among the oppositions in other poems are piety versus superstition, solitude versus convivial glee, landed prosperity versus homeless destitution, and rural Scotland ('The Holy Fair', 'Halloween', 'The Auld Farmer's New Year Salutation') versus an imperfectly articulated Great Britain ('The Author's Earnest Cry and Prayer'). Juxtaposition of opposing quantities further intensifies in the 1786 *Poems*, with its placement in close proximity of further works in English with further works in Scots. Yet even though all but one of the Kilmarnock notebook's texts reappear in the printed volume, Burness's bardic hospitality to a range of voices in his 'Scotch' notebook is in the 1786 *Poems* eventually upstaged by more self-allusive poems, among them 'To a Mouse', 'To a Louse' and 'To a Mountain Daisy', that evidently took their final form during spring and early summer of 1786. ('To a Mouse' bears the date November 1785 but most likely that commemorates, like the dating of 'The Holy Fair', the encounter that inspired the poem. There survives no early working manuscript or fair-copy for 'To a Mouse', first seen by readers near mid-volume (#14) of the printed 1786 *Poems*.[80])

After looking over the material he had copied into the *Kilmarnock Manuscript*, the poet might have decided that 'The Holy Fair', with its serial portraits of local ministers, was too parish-specific to open his book. The printed 1786 *Poems* begins instead with 'The Twa Dogs', probably the poet's least embittered survey of the two worlds, the idle wealthy and the working (or out-of-work) poor, that contend in his imagination of Scotland. As in *The First Commonplace Book*, the bard does not transcribe the texts in their order of composition but experiments with sequencing. Kinsley's edition assigns this chronological sequence to the notebook's fifteen texts: #70, #73, #76, #75, #23, #77, #64, #71, #72, #81, #79, #10, #51, #24, #25.[81] Although most of the poems in the *Kilmarnock Manuscript* are Scots in diction, Burness also transcribes for the first time 'The Cotter's Saturday Night', of a mixed diction but concluding in elevated English: this poem too is both bardic and 'Scotch', however, in its exploration of national character and culture. And like the other poems in this notebook, 'Cotter' is suffused with Robert Fergusson's presence, for 'The Farmer's Ingle', one of

Fergusson's rare vernacular poems set in the country, is likewise a celebration in Spenserian stanzas of the Scottish peasantry.[82]

'The Public Character of an Author': *Poems, Chiefly in the Scottish Dialect*

> ... had a July sun risen on a December morning, the unwonted light could not have given greater surprise.
> Allan Cunningham (1834) recalling the sensation caused by the Kilmarnock 1786 edition[83]

Burns's 1786 *Poems*, showcasing thirty-six texts (if counting, as the poet did, nine short epitaphs as one item), opens with eight Scots poems addressing life in Burns's region (here called Coila or Kyle); the ninth, 'A Dream', glances at wider British culture in its parody of Thomas Warton's 4 June laureate poem for George III's forty-eighth birthday. Warton was entering the second year of his laureateship; in 'The Vision', the poem that follows the parody of Warton, the regional muse Coila crowns Burns with native holly, establishing him as her own laureate. From that point, Burns juggles and juxtaposes Scots with standard English diction: 'The Vision' (mainly English) is followed by 'Halloween' (densely Scots) and 'The Farmer's New Year Morning Salutation' (densely Scots) by 'The Cotter's Saturday Night' (mainly English).

Of the 612 copies printed by John Wilson, some 428 went to subscribers. The remaining volumes, priced at three shillings each, had sold within a month of publication. Burns ordered a copy to send to his cousin James Burness in Montrose and, a few days later, purchased two more to give to friends from younger days: newly married Margaret Thomson, courted in 1775 while he studied mathematics and surveying in Kirkoswald, and Richard Brown, the friend he made while living in Irvine, who had suggested as early as 1781 that Burns should publish his poems.[84] Had Burns sailed to Jamaica in autumn 1786, he might have carried no copy of his book, for none remained. His subscription sales (£64 4s) allowed the poet to repay Wilson in three instalments for paper and costs of production, which totalled £35 17s in all, minus 10 guineas for the seventy copies Wilson himself had reserved to sell in his shop. The biographers have calculated Burns's total profit for the Kilmarnock *Poems* (including the volumes not reserved in advance) at about £54. James Mackay cites tavern bills, an expense Burns ruefully mentions in his long autobiographical letter to Dr Moore, as having reduced this profit to 'near twenty pounds', the amount the poet himself mentions.[85] Yet among expenses against the Kilmarnock income were the 9 guineas Burns paid for steerage transport to Jamaica (mentioned in his 1787 letter to John Moore) and the 'certain sum' – perhaps £20; see above, note 20 – provided in the settlement with Elizabeth Paton on 1 December. There must have been travel expenses as well as he made his way to Edinburgh from Ayrshire in late November 1786, although they would not have included tavern bills, as Burns was much fêted and treated by new admirers on his way to the capital city. Deductions for his passage to Jamaica and Elizabeth Paton's settlement reduce his profit to around £25, and two months after he arrived in Edinburgh Burns applied for permission to place a tombstone on Robert Fergusson's unmarked grave, which he had visited in the first day or two of his visit to the capital. Presumably the stone-worker required a deposit, which also would have reduced Burns's Kilmarnock edition profits. If the final payment of £5 10 (not made until 1792) represented half, Burns's down payment to 'Robert Burn', the man he engaged to erect the stone, would have reduced Burns's Kilmarnock profits to his own estimate of 'near twenty pounds'.[86]

Turning from the modest financial success of the volume, which kept the poet in Scotland, to its framing and presentation of his writings, one is struck at once by the 1786 preface, which bristles with caveats. In 1783 on the title page of *The First Commonplace Book*, Rob Burness daydreams that his transcribed works might provide 'some entertainment to a curious observer of human-nature'; but the preface of the 1786 *Poems* presumes an icily adverse reception, opening with a disclaimer: 'The following trifles are not the production' of a poet who can read the classics 'in their original languages'[87] – hardly the first concern of any reasonable reader, but Burns is talking past ordinary people to scornful critics. The concluding sentence commands those disappointed by his poems to 'condemn' the volume 'without mercy, to contempt and oblivion', wording that has an air, especially if read rapidly, of itself damning any and all discontented readers.[88]

'Unacquainted with the necessary requisites for commencing Poet by rule', he writes in a relatively calm passage in his first paragraph, 'he sings the sentiments and manners, he felt and saw in himself and his rustic compeers around him, in his and their native language'; yet the next paragraph introduces the voice of a scolding critic who insults Burns as an 'impertinent blockhead, obtruding his nonsense on the world'.[89] Burns has chosen to emphasize 'the various feelings, the loves, the griefs, the hopes, the fears in his own breast',[90] but as he sends the volume to press he clearly is having second thoughts. He confides to his by now alarmed readers that as an 'obscure, nameless Bard' he 'shrinks aghast' at impending critical anathema.[91] In one sense, what the preface chiefly conveys is some idea of the poet's lacerated spirit in mid-1786.

The magnificently discursive title page of *The First Commonplace Book* likewise emphasizes a lack of conventional schooling, defining poetry as a kind of self-exploration. Indeed, *The First Commonplace Book*, like the preface of the 1786 *Poems*, employs the formal third-person in introducing the author:

> As he was but little indebted to scholastic education, and bred at a plough tail, his performances must be strongly tinctured with his unpolished, rustic way of life ... [yet] it may be some entertainment ... to see how a plough-man thinks and feels, under the pressure of Love, Ambition, Anxiety, Grief.

The difference is that in late spring 1786, Burns, already humiliated by recent events, can foresee only another storm of invective rolling in on a new front, as the critics ('men ... [with] Greek and Latin')[92] issue their verdict on his long meditated writings.

In this way the curtain rises in 1786 not on a poet's accomplishment so much as an audience's doubts and even grievances. Readers susceptible to the preface's anxious rhetorical strategies will at any rate be on his side; but in the event none of this self-defence was needed. For as the poems themselves begin, a rosy summer dawn, as Allan Cunningham puts it in this section's epigraph, breaks over the opening lines of 'The Twa Dogs', whose companionable spirit at once draws readers into a friendly space. (Though that poem is written in a dialect daunting even for some of Burns's Scottish readers, in another welcoming gesture, Burns wrote a careful and detailed glossary for his volume.) The preface's standoffish formality must have only increased the eventual pleasure in 1786 of a reader's encounter with the first entries in the 1786 *Poems*, which exude confidence, freedom and grace – a seemingly effortless lightness.

The volume had an immediate impact. Wordsworth, a schoolboy at Hawkshead, was loaned a copy by his headmaster within weeks of its publication.[93] Burns's reception in the district his poems celebrate was almost fanatic. His early biographer Robert Heron reports that during the late summer of 1786, everyone in Ayrshire was reading Burns: 'Old and young, high and low, grave and gay, learned or ignorant, all were alike delighted, agitated, transported'.[94] Table 1.3 lists the poems printed at Kilmarnock in July 1786.

Table 1.3: *Poems, Chiefly in the Scottish Dialect*: **Burness and Burns's sequence of texts and verse forms.**

Burns stayed near the printer's office while his book was in press and most likely had some say in the printing format. The amount of emphasis added to the printed titles is characteristic also of Burns's early manuscripts and fair copies, often marked by caps, underlined expressions, and asterisks and dashes. To give some sense of how his poems were encountered by readers in 1786, I have retained below emphases added in the title above the printed poem, not attempting to match font-size exactly but including titles in capitals (small and large), italics, bolded, etc.

(1) 'THE TWA DOGS, A TALE'; 238-line dialogue poem in octosyllabic couplets.
(2) 'SCOTCH DRINK'; 126 lines (21 stanzas); in standard Habbie.
(3) 'THE AUTHOR'S EARNEST CRY AND PRAYER, TO THE RIGHT HONORABLE AND HONORABLE, THE SCOTCH REPRESENTATIVES IN THE HOUSE OF COMMONS'; 186 lines (31 stanzas) in standard Habbie
(4) 'THE HOLY FAIR'; 243 lines [27 stanzas] in nine-line 'Chrystis Kirk' stanza-form.
(5) 'ADDRESS TO THE DEIL'; 126 lines (21 stanzas) in standard Habbie.
(6) 'THE DEATH AND DYING WORDS OF POOR MAILIE, THE AUTHOR'S ONLY PET YOWE,
AN UNCO MOURNFU' TALE'; 66 lines in octosyllabic couplets.
(7) 'POOR MAILIE'S ELEGY'; 48 lines (6 stanzas) in standard Habbie.
(8) 'To J. S****' [James Smith]; 174 lines (29 stanzas) in standard Habbie.
(9) 'A DREAM'; 135 lines (15 stanzas) in Burns's modified 'Chrystis kirk' stanza.
(10) 'THE VISION'; 228 lines (38 stanzas) in the Kilmarnock *Poems*; it was expanded for the 1787 edition. In standard Habbie.
(11) 'HALLOWEEN', 252 lines (28 stanzas). Kinsley notes that this is a 'manners-painting' poem of the sort commended to Burns by the Muse Coila in the previous poem, 'The Vision'. In Burns's modified 'Chrystis kirk' stanza.
(12) 'THE AULD FARMER'S NEW-YEAR-MORNING SALUTATION TO HIS AULD MARE, MAGGIE, ON GIVING HER THE ACCUSTOMED RIPP OF CORN TO HANSEL IN THE NEW-YEAR'; 108 lines (18 stanzas) in standard Habbie.
(13) 'THE COTTER'S SATURDAY NIGHT'; 189 lines (21 stanzas) in Spenserian stanzas.
(14) 'TO A MOUSE, *On turning her up in her Nest, with the Plough, November, 1785*'; 48 lines (8 stanzas) in standard Habbie.
(15) 'EPISTLE TO DAVIE. **A BROTHER POET**'; 190 lines (11 stanzas in 'Cherry and the Slae' verse-form).
(16) 'THE LAMENT, OCCASIONED BY THE UNFORTUNATE ISSUE OF A FRIEND'S AMOUR' Written just after 'To a Mountain Daisy', this poem likewise mourns the loss of Jean Armour. 80 lines (10 stanzas: 8A8B8A8B8B8C8B8C) identified by James Kinsley as a medieval stanza-form known to Burns through Ramsay's *Ever Green* or Watson's *Choice Collection*.
(17) 'DESPONDENCY, **AN ODE**'; 70 lines (5 stanzas) in 'Cherry and the Slae' stanza-form.
(18) 'MAN WAS MADE TO MOURN, A DIRGE'; 88 lines (11 stanzas) in double common measure.
(19) 'WINTER, **A DIRGE**'; 24 lines (3 stanzas in octaves) in double common measure.
(20) 'A **PRAYER**, IN THE PROSPECT OF DEATH'; 20 lines (5 stanzas) in common measure.
(21) 'To A **MOUNTAIN-DAISY**, *On turning one down, with the Plough, in April — 1786*'; 54 lines (9 stanzas) in standard Habbie.
(22) '**TO RUIN**'; 28 lines (2 stanzas) in 'Cherry and the Slae' stanza-form.
(23) 'Epistle TO A **YOUNG FRIEND**'; 88 lines or 11 octaves of what Kinsley calls 'double-stanza, with abundant feminine rhyme'.

(24) 'On a **Scotch Bard** gone to the West Indies'; 60 lines (10 stanzas) in standard Habbie.
(25) 'A **Dedication** to G**** H*******, Esq.'; 134 lines (16 stanzas of irregular length). Placement of the 'Dedication' on pp. 185–191 near the end of the volume may reflect Burns's admiration for Laurence Sterne's novel *Tristram Shandy*. In octosyllabic couplets. a
(26) 'To a LOUSE, *On seeing one on a Lady's Bonnet at Church*'; 48 lines (8 stanzas) in standard Habbie.
(27) 'Epistle to J. L*****k [John Lapraik], an old Scotch Bard'; 132 lines (22 stanzas) in standard Habbie.
(28) 'To the Same'; 108 lines (18 stanzas) in standard Habbie.
(29) 'To W. S*****n, Ochiltree' [William Simson; Burns spelled it 'Simpson']; May 1785; 186 lines (31 stanzas) in standard Habbie.
(30) 'Epistle to J. R*****e [John Rankine] enclosing some Poems'; 78 lines (13 stanzas) in standard Habbie.
(31) 'Song' [It was upon a Lammas Night']; 36 lines (6 octave stanzas and a four line chorus) in double common measure.
(32) 'Song, Composed in August' ['Now westlin winds, and slaught'ring guns']; 40 lines (5 octave stanzas) in double common measure.
(33) 'Song' ['From thee, Eliza, I must go']; 16 lines (2 octave stanzas) in double common measure.
(34) 'The Farewell. To the Brethren of St. James's Lodge, Tarbolton'. Full title with the text [pp. 228–229] distinguishes this 'Farewell' from another poem, not published until 1819, written the same month and bearing the same title. 32 lines (4 octaves); in double long or double hymnal measure (8A8B8A8B8C8D8C8D).
(35) Eight 'Epitaphs and Epigrams' of various dates of composition; mostly in common measure. Burns cuts three from subsequent editions of poems.
(36) 'A Bard's Epitaph', 30 lines (5 stanzas); in standard Habbie.

Sources: Titles are taken from a facsimile edition of *Poems, Chiefly in the Scottish Dialect* (1786): *Robert Burns: Poems 1786–87* (Menston: Scolar Press, 1971). Editors often number the 1786 contents as forty-four texts. In the volume's Contents page, thirty-six titles are given. 'Poor Mailie's Elegy' is numbered separately from her 'Death and Dying Words' but nine short 'Epitaphs and Epigrams' are listed as one item.

This sequence is notable for its late crescendo of parting shots: 'On a Scotch Bard Gone to the West-Indies', 'From Thee, Eliza, I Must Go', 'The Farewell' and a group of epitaphs, including the Bard's own, which concludes the volume. Burns's lifelong reconstruction of nation and community debuts on an appropriately contradictory note, as Scotland, in the poet's personal experience a cheerless setting of defunct relationships and unremitting labour, is poetically transformed at the moment of parting into something luminous. Many a later love song would use the same dynamic.

Burns had completed the opening poems in the volume before the crisis of spring 1786, and all these early entries emulate Robert Fergusson. 'The Twa Dogs' recalls Fergusson's 'Hame Content' – both poems are in octosyllabic couplets and both attack the Grand Tour, urging that landholders look to the proper management of their own property.⁹⁵ Burns diverges from Fergusson in an intensification of vernacular diction, which becomes not merely vivid but conspicuously non-genteel: the dogs Cesar and Luath greet each other with a thorough canine sniffing of hindquarters ('Wi' social nose whyles snuff'd and snowket') before settling down 'on their arse' to discuss men, rich and poor, as '*lords o' the creation*', for an ironic echo of Milton is brought into the earthy mix (ll. 39, 44, 46).⁹⁶ 'Scotch Drink', the second poem printed, emulates Fergusson's 'Caller Water':

> The fuddlin' Bardies now-a-days
> Rin *maukin*-mad in Bacchus' praise,   'hare-mad' (as in 'mad as a March hare')
> And limp and stoiter thro' their lays   'stagger'
>   *Anacreontic*,
> While each his sea of wine displays
>   As big's the Pontic.⁹⁷

Burns's 'Scotch Drink', likewise in standard Habbie, similarly mixes classical allusion with dialect Scots:

> Let other Poets raise a fracas
> 'Bout vines, an' wines, and druken *Bacchus*,
> An' crabbed names an' stories wrack us,
>   An' grate our lug,   'ear'
> I sing the juice *Scotch bear* can mak us,
>   In glass or jug.⁹⁸

Homely vernacular mixes with foreign-derived rhymes ('raise a fracas' / 'druken *Bacchus*'). Burns later rhymes 'verses' with 'arses', pulling lofty poetic inspiration down to earth while making it more vivid, less of a cliché:

> When wanting thee, what tuneless cranks
>   Are my poor Verses!
> Thou comes - they rattle i' their ranks
>   At ither's arses! (ll. 105–8)

After 'Scotch Drink' is a maiden address to Parliament, 'The Author's Earnest Cry and Prayer', whose speaker protests an increase in the cost of whisky. Readers, however, are invited to separate themselves from this bellicose individual, who ends by proclaiming that drunkenness is an act of patriotic zeal: 'FREEDOM and WHISKY gang thegither' (l. 185). The third 'arse' in the Kilmarnock volume – for poems 1, 2 and 3 all use the word – is that of Mother Scotland in 'The Author's Earnest Cry' ('To see her sittan on her arse / Low i' the dust' (ll. 9–10)). By the concluding lines she is so impaired by drink that she 'tines her dam' or loses control of her bladder.⁹⁹

Dogs, poetic imagery, mother-nations: all are robustly incarnated. 'The Holy Fair' (the term 'Fair' conveys a hint of showmanship and huckstering; it may also echo Fergusson's title 'Hallow-Fair') is the next poem printed. Here Burns emulates Fergusson's 'Leith Races': the speakers in both accompany an allegorical figure (Mirth in Fergusson; Fun in Burns) for a day of carnivalesque misrule. Work in Edinburgh was all but suspended during the July horse races along the sands of the port of Leith. Fergusson's poem documents breaches of the law: assaults on the City guardsmen, prostitution, gambling, brawling, public drunkenness. Burns again revisits but boldly revises, choosing as his topic Mauchline's outdoor communion service, or 'occasion'. Burns's cheeky re-naming of the annual event, like his introduction of 'arse' into the first three poems, evidently caused offence, for the Edinburgh edition disavows it as the poet's invention: '*Holy Fair* is a common phrase in the West of Scotland for a sacramental occasion'.[100] In fact the title bears all the signs of a Burns coinage in its irrepressible glee, and the sardonic colouration of the title suits a poem rich in oxymoron, syllepsis and other ironic tropes. While Fergusson, much inclined to gloomy medical advice, concludes 'Leith Races' with a warning about hangovers, Burns's speaker ends 'The Holy Fair' with a look ahead to 'houghmagandie' (fornication) as the probable sequel of the flirting he has witnessed that day.

While emulating Fergusson's diction and verse-forms in these first-printed Kilmarnock poems, then, Burns differs in his more intense focus on body parts and bodily functions. Burns mixes literary allusions to Fergusson, Ossian, Milton, Gray, Young, Goldsmith (and others) with much coarser imagery, infusing poetic insight with real-world immediacy. In 'The Twa Dogs', for example, Burns praises the rich man's pet Cesar for his friendliness and lack of pride, but then instantiates this gregarious spirit by describing Cesar as always happy to stand and piss ('stan't ... and stroan't' (ll. 21–2)) with any chance-met mutt or cur.

In the volume's fifth poem, 'Address to the Deil', Burns returns to Fergusson's preferred standard Habbie verse-form and again echoes 'Caller Water' in his stanza on Adam and Eve (ll. 85–96) but in other ways the poem highlights Burns's differences from Fergusson, who never debated religious doctrine, by intensifying Burns's covert assault on the theological tenets of the Auld Licht. His speaker, lecturing the devil in a friendly manner, advises that Satan 'tak a thought an' men' or repent (l. 122), thereby escaping hell. The doctrine of predestination as interpreted by Auld Licht preachers saw sinners as helpless to change, but in this poem rehabilitation of devils and even poets remains theoretically possible. The dying words of the sheep Mailie follow the speech to the Devil: the two texts may have been linked in Burns's mind by an association of ideas between the rigid doctrine that would condemn 90 per cent of human beings to Hell (as in 'Holy Willie's Prayer' (l. 3)) and the tether or rope intended to protect Mailie that strangles her instead. An emphasis on free-will, freer movement is shared in these adjacent poems.

The first works printed in the Kilmarnock volume, from the 'ance upon a time' fable of two dogs (l. 6) to Mailie's last request that her lambs never be tied up as she was, are bardic in considering national character using a range of views not limited to those of the poet himself. Yet they are Burnsian-bardic in imagery that is not so much down-to-earth as in-your-face: he introduces language banished from late eighteenth-century printed poetry though never, in Scotland, from song. Having worked all his life as a tenant farmer, Burns had easy access to a trove of words derived from farming and husbandry, but he also drew on demotic speech across a range that varied from the plain-spoken to the scatological. Whether speaking as Burns or as Burness, his version of Scots vernacular is *edgy*, more so than Fergusson's, whose diction is vivid and visual yet never pointedly visceral: Fergusson more often uses Scots to paint a picture than to cross a line or to provoke. The interaction of 'proper' and 'improper' language-choices is especially daring in Burns's religious satires which are, like the acrobatic preaching of Black Jock Russell in 'The Holy Fair', by turns riveting, amusing and grotesque. For all his technical emulation of Fergusson, Burns pushes back more vigorously against the cult of a 'standard' language. (Fergusson generally uses thicker dialect for local colour, as when his satires turn to Gaelic speakers residing in Edinburgh: their words place them in context. While he does moralize using Scots in 'The Farmer's Ingle', more often he uses standard English when addressing readers specifically as a poet: one example is 'The Canongate Playhouse in Ruins', with its apostrophes to Shakespeare.)

Burns's provocative mix of earthy Scots and fancy English had never before been seen (until there it was) as admissible in a book of printed poems. Neither Ramsay nor Fergusson had used the words 'Scots' or 'Scottish' in their main titles: Fergusson's *Poems* (1773) hides its selection of his Scots poems in the back of the book, opening with poems in neoclassical English.[101] The title *Poems, Chiefly in the Scottish Dialect*, by contrast, flings down a gauntlet: no wonder Burns's preface is anxious. The capital's literati (many of them clergymen who may have disliked the flippant tone of the religious satires), recognized Burns's extraordinary gifts but rejected his evident resolve to infiltrate the poetic canon, abolishing the standard-English monopoly of literary diction. There is a tone almost of resentment in some of the Edinburgh reactions to Burns's achievement. That resistance to Burns broke out most strongly following his premature death in 1796, but even in 1787 Hugh Blair, who advised Burns on the second edition of *Poems*, evidently insisted on genteel counterbalances: all those asterisked disclaimers at the head and foot of Burns's pages. (This is not to mention Blair's rejection in 1787 of 'Love and Liberty' as 'by much too licentious' to be included in the volume.[102]) By ranging free of an uniformly 'poetic' English diction, Burns did his part in creating a more modern poetry, closer to daily life.

Burns links Mailie's dying words and elegy to the poem that follows them by a vivid shared image: Mailie rebukes her feckless 'son an' heir' for wearing out his hoofs in pursuit of ewes (l. 49), while the second stanza of the epistle to Jamie Smith exaggerates the cost in footwear – 'twenty pair o' shoon' (l. 9) – of the speaker's frequent visits to his new friend. 'To J. S****' considers the disasters that await poets; in part, I have argued elsewhere, Burns echoes Milton's 'Lycidas'.[103] The letter to Smith turns again to the vexed matter of poets 'Far seen in *Greek, deep men o' letters*' who look down on dialect (l. 44) – or perhaps the crux of the charge is that their loyalty to dead languages makes them hostile to living speech. Here Burns foretells victory over his 'betters' (l. 43) in a poem whose predominantly sunny mood may have led to its placement early in the volume: other verse-epistles appear near the end. The next poem, 'A Dream', as mentioned parodies Thomas Warton's 4 June laureate poem, while in the text that follows, 'The Vision', Burns is himself crowned by Coila as laureate of Kyle. Warton, a bard on retainer, received an annual pension of £100 but the resentful opening stanzas of 'The Vision' emphasize the speaker's non-existent '*Cash-Account*' (line of credit; see line 28]), his own fate as a bard.

'Halloween', printed after 'The Vision', bears a headnote in the 1787 Edinburgh edition that identifies the folk-superstitions in the poem as current among the 'unenlightened'.[104] The note in the Kilmarnock *Poems* is more neutral, explaining that in rural Scotland Halloween is a festival of 'Witches, Devils' and 'aerial people' such as fairies; to access these spirits on Hallow's eve, country people use charms and spells.[105] Burns's notes explain the charms more fully.[106] Fergusson's 'Hallow-Fair', which inspired Burns's poem (and title) but is very different in tone,[107] again chiefly describes drunkenness while Burns again changes the subject to rural courtship: his young people all are intent on conjuring images of their future partners.[108] Jamie Fleck goes outdoors to sow hempseed, inviting a portent of his future wife, but encounters only a snorting creature that he later learns is the wandering sow '*Grumphie*' (l. 179). Meg, hoping for a spirit-assisted vision of her lover Tam Kipples, instead startles a rat in the barn and flees, having taken its rustling patter as a sign of Satan's nearby presence (l. 194). The wanton widow Leezie fearlessly goes out into the dark to try dipping her sleeve in water (the local belief is that the dripping sleeve will draw a lover to her) but falls into the brook when surprised by the nearby 'croon' (sound) either of Satan or a young cow (ll. 228–9). As in 'The Holy Fair', in 'Halloween' Burns infuses the supernatural with the carnal, with youthful desire.

The next poem printed brings into a country setting another holiday important in Scotland: New Year's Day. The 'hansel' of the full title of 'The Auld Farmer's new-year-morning Salutation' is the gift brought to closest friends at the start of the New Year. The farmer who speaks here makes his first visit to his old plough horse, Maggie, who chews his gift of grain as he looks back on their years together. Evidently a tribute to the poet's late father, this poem precedes 'The Cotter's Saturday Night', which also remembers William Burnes even as it begins the volume's turn from bardic Burness to Poet Burns in the '*Patriot-bard*' who silently stands behind and endorses the prayer for Scotland's future that closes the poem. (A Patriot-bard is not only a thoughtful reader like the cotter-patriarch but also a powerful *writer*.)

'To a Mouse' is printed next, using the standard Habbie verse-form but otherwise marking a sharp turn from Burness, bawdy renovator of Fergusson's bibulous celebrations of Edinburgh and bardic chronicler of Scottish language, customs and characters. Fourteenth text in the volume, 'To a Mouse' is a tale of November homelessness notable for its proliferation of personal pronouns. If man and beast are all but interchangeable in 'Halloween' and best of friends in the old farmer's 'Salutation' poem, they are estranged in 'To a Mouse' by the speaker's self-consciousness. This speaker laments his unwitting destruction of the mouse's nest, and the last stanzas turn to human cares, especially the speaker's own uncertain future: he envies the mouse's 'blest' insensitivity, her consciousness only of present woe. In November few leaves remain to build a new nest, but the speaker reflects in closing that at least the suddenly homeless mouse need not look desperately ahead, as people do, guessing and fearing (l. 43).

Poet Burns, as he emerges fully in 'To a Mouse', considers a future to be accessed not by rustic charms and spells, as in 'Halloween', but by looking into 'his own breast', as he says in his preface.[109] As a bard Burness channels Scotland's past and also the characters, speech and cultures of his own moment; but Poet Burns seeks intimations of what lies within him and what lies ahead. He feels all the terror of his placement between a social niche no longer viable – life as the sub-tenant of Mossgiel farm – and a poetic aspiration evidently far out of his reach. 'To a Mouse' dramatizes this dissonance; the speaker stops ploughing to compose a poem addressed to a creature who cannot understand it and who already has run offstage. The poem moves from the mouse's crisis to human guesses and fears. Letters of the 1780s show that Burns knew he could not live as his father and grandfather had, not without capital. They had failed despite their constant labour and so would he. Searching himself, he also detects little of his upright father's capacity for self-denial or even any keen desire to live a blameless life.

In poems that deeply struck Wordsworth, as Chapter 2 discusses more fully, Poet Burns mistrusts his overly-receptive nature: will the absolute openness that makes him a poet end by destroying him? In 'The Vision', a poem in two parts that combines the bardic celebration of Kyle, past and present, with reflections on the poet's own life, one stanza breaks through in what will later in the volume be the voice of Poet Burns, though in this text, four poems before 'To a

Mouse', the speaker is Coila, Muse of Kyle, who comforts the despondent poet just before she crowns him with native holly:

> I saw thy pulse's maddening play,
> Wild-send thee Pleasure's devious way,
> Misled by Fancy's meteor-ray,
>   By Passion driven;
> But yet the light that led astray,
>   Was light from Heaven. (ll. 235–40)

Just a few poems later, such self-assessing texts as 'To a Mouse' imagine no such light from heaven. They predict neither the ultimate poetic victory foreseen in the epistle to Jamie Smith nor the last-minute averting of damnation half-promised to Satan in 'Address to the Deil'. The poems of mid-volume worry as they showcase speakers who clearly differ in world-view and vocabulary from 'men' with 'Greek and Latin' yet just as clearly differ from successful subtenant farmers.[110] What sort of ploughman invites a mouse to help herself to some barley now and then?

'The great Misfortune of my life', he wrote to John Moore in 1787 in the long autobiographical letter that is one of his greatest performances as Poet Burns, 'was never to have AN AIM'.[111] The poet has no plan. Yet 'To a Mouse' implies a self-defence in showing the futility of foresight. What avails careful planning when every mortal being is just one random plough-blade away from calamity? Those with scanty resources should lay them out wisely, no doubt; but what of those – like the mouse, like the poet's own father – who lose everything despite all their 'weary' work? Their probable fate is no mystery. The speaker and the displaced mouse must get through winter somehow and the man here, ploughing in November, is probably readying the land for a term he uses in the poem, 'foggage', a coarse grass that reduces winter costs by extending the period of grazing. Foggage is still sown in November in south-west Scotland. The farmer needs grass for his beasts and the mouse needs it for a new nest, but there is 'naething' as yet, and all the diligent planting in the world will not produce the foggage if '*December's winds*' destroy the growing sprouts. When the speaker gently informs the mouse in line 38 that 'foresight may be vain', readers feel all the force of litotes (an understatement trope), for the line suggests the in fact infinite vulnerability of mice and men in a setting where storms are 'snell and keen' and reserves may dwindle in an instant to 'naething, now' (l. 21). As a farmer, the speaker knows how to plan but knows how often the even 'best laid' plans fall through (l. 39). As a poet he likewise guesses and fears, but using his right brain, as the modern phrase puts it, he looks ahead associatively, intuitively.

Still, while seeking within, Poet Burns retains a strong element of the social: in these poems so often specifically identified as speech-acts (addresses, prayers, earnest cries), his speakers' inner searchings are directed to others, ranging from rural friends (the verse-epistles to Willie Simson, John Lapraik, Davie Sillar, Jamie Smith, John Rankine) to the non-human 'Others' he so often hails as 'fellow mortals': the mouse, the louse, the mountain daisy.

In several of these poems Burns considers the strange wildcard he has been dealt: that he can write. One ('On a Scotch Bard') admits that his gift for words is the only thing he takes 'pride in' (l. 47). Yet to write is to risk a further fall, as he says in 'Epistle to Davie', which follows 'To a Mouse' and takes place deeper in winter, 'January' of no specified year. This verse-letter wonders whether it might not be a relief after all to plunge all the way to the bottom and wander as a homeless person:

> To lye in kilns and barns at e'en,　　'evening'
> When bones are craz'd and bluid is thin,　'bones are cracked, stiff'
> 　Is, doubtless, great distress!
> Yet then *content* could make us blest;
> E'en then, sometimes we'd catch a taste
> 　Of truest happiness ...
> 　　And mind still, you'll find still,
> 　　　A comfort this nae sma';
> 　　Nae mair then, we'll care then,
> 　　　Nae *farther* we can fa'. (ll. 29–42)

Because to think oneself anew, apart from social or family expectations, is a challenge not posed by traditional cultures, we see in Burns a non-traditional figure, modern in his apprehensive singularity. From the cycle of traditions and holidays celebrated in the Kilmarnock volume's opening, then, bardic Burness turns approximately at midpoint to consider, as Poet Burns, intuitions that are personal yet not wholly self-centred in their extension outward – to fellow Scots poets, for instance, in his verse-letters to Sillar and Lapraik, the latter a stranger jailed in Ayr for debt in 1785 when Burns heard of his plight and initiated the correspondence.

The volume's early-printed bardic poems address readers through a variety of speakers, some of whom, like the conservative preachers of 'The Holy Fair', express opinions from which Burns himself vigorously dissented. At mid-volume, by contrast, Poet Burns, having measured his own experiences, looks out at his readers from centre-stage to suggest that a hardscrabble struggle for survival without resources is 'Scotland', too, and that it does not call for celebration. Some songs of the 1790s propose or imply remedies as well, but the political dimension in Burns's writing, running against the grain of his bardic hospitality to all voices, developed late.

The poems printed just after 'To a Mouse' in the Kilmarnock *Poems* take up its keynotes: anxiety, homelessness, contingency. All do not date from April 1786: some derive from the poet's other crisis year of 1781, though the poet most likely reworked these earlier writings during late spring of 1786. Burns revised by making existing lines more image-dense but also by adding new stanzas: 'Song, Composed in August', for example, is eight lines long in *The First Commonplace Book* (August 1785) but forty lines in the 1786 *Poems*. It is likely that 'To a Mouse', begun in November 1785, was filled out or reshaped during spring of 1786. Following 'To a Mouse' is 'Epistle to Davie', whose speaker warns against any sour 'pining at our state' while wondering aloud whether a homeless old age awaits them both. Jean Armour, temporarily written out of 'The Vision', is twice lovingly named in 'Epistle to Davie' (ll. 108, 140), only to be roundly scolded in the poem that follows, 'The Lament', where the poet imperfectly disguises his voice as that of a concerned friend.

Printed at midpoint (numbers 17 and 18 of thirty-six texts listed in the contents), 'Despondency, An Ode' and 'Man Was Made to Mourn' became touchstones for later poets in and out of Scotland. Like so many of this mid-book grouping, 'Despondency' looks sadly ahead, asking 'What Sorrows yet may pierce me thro'' (l. 9); its concluding lines echo Thomas Gray's 'Eton College' ode and impressed many contemporaries.[112] Wordsworth, writing in 1799 to Coleridge, praised Burns's 'Despondency' as inspiring and 'solemn'.[113] Wordsworth also admired 'Man Was Made to Mourn, A Dirge', which offers the advice of an eighty-year-old wanderer to a youth whom the older man has stopped to question, the sort of poetic encounter at which Wordsworth himself excelled. In this poem appears Burns's lament for 'Man's inhumanity to Man' (l. 55). 'Winter, A Dirge' and 'A Prayer in the Prospect of Death' follow 'Man Was made to Mourn, A Dirge': all had been copied as early as *The First Commonplace Book* and all enter here as part of the armature for Poet Burns. In their mood of deep unease these poems of his late adolescence accord well with the febrile work completed between April and early June 1786.

'To a Mountain Daisy' is one such feverish new text; it follows 'A Prayer in the Prospect of Death'. The poet sent what was then titled 'The Gowan' to John Kennedy, who had subscribed for twenty copies of *Poems*, on 20 April. The plough has cut the daisy's 'slender stem' and she has died. The image of cutting may hint also at the 'cut' to 'my very veins' the poet felt – 'my heart died within me' – when James Armour told Burns about the destruction of the marriage paper.[114] For the most part an elegy for Jean Armour, the text more briefly 'mourns' (l. 49) Burns's father ('*suff'ring worth*', l. 42) and in a move typical of Poet Burns, the speaker himself. Like the daisy, he was born in an inclement season and briefly flourished, only to be suddenly 'crush'd beneath the *furrows* weight' (l. 53). The lines lamenting the 'simple Bard' who 'mourn'st the *Daisy's* fate' (l. 48) recall in phrasing (and their position in the last stanza) Alexander Pope's 'Elegy to the Memory of an Unfortunate Lady'.[115] But whereas Pope's lady had drowned herself when her parents forbade her to marry her suitor, Jean Armour obeyed her parents, rejected her lover and still she has been cut down. Yet it is the bard of stanza seven, driven abroad on a 'luckless ocean' (l. 38), who will drown: unable to escape his doom and buffeted by gales, he too will be swept away.

With 'To Ruin', which follows 'To a Mountain-Daisy', the volume's downward spiral reaches its lowest point as the speaker hails death, as he had in concluding 'Man Was Made to Mourn', as the best friend of a wounded spirit: 'No more I shrink appall'd, afraid; / I court, I beg thy friendly aid, / To close this scene of care!' (ll. 18–20). Not a favourite of the poet's or at least not copied into *The First Commonplace Book*, 'To Ruin' probably dates from 1781, a year of incapacitating illness and depression, family economic struggle, decline in his father's health and rejection by Eliza Gebbie, who (Burns wrote to John Moore) had, in a preview of his later betrothal to Jean Armour, 'jilted him with peculiar circumstances of mortification'.[116]

Poems (1786) then to some degree eases the pressure, returning to revised early verse-letters and a mixture of recent and early songs. 'Epistle to a Young Friend' addresses Andrew Aiken, Robert's son, soon to leave home for Liverpool to seek his fortune; this is followed by 'On a Scotch Bard Gone to the West Indies', which is as much a eulogy as a valediction:

> Auld, cantie KYLE may weepers wear,
>   An' stain them wi' the saut, saut tear:
> 'Twill mak her poor, auld heart, I fear,
>   In flinders flee:
> He was her *Laureat* monie a year,
>   That's owre the Sea!
>   ...
> He ne'er was gien to great misguidin,
> Yet coin his pouches wad na bide in;
> Wi' him it ne'er was *under hiden*;
>   He dealt it free;
> The *Muse* was a' that he took pride in,
>   That's owre the Sea.   (ll. 25–30 and ll. 43–8)

Line 49 bids '*Jamaica bodies*' to 'use him weel', but the speaker mentions no poetic future, sailing as a former bard. Just as Jean has jilted him (l. 33), he will abandon Kyle and be her beloved laureate no more.

The late-arriving dedication of the Kilmarnock volume (it is displaced in apparent homage to Sterne's *Tristram Shandy* to page 185 near the end of the book), honours Burns's landlord Gavin Hamilton, who receives an affectionate parting tribute. May Hamilton, says the speaker in his closing blessing, live long enough to be buried by the great-grandchild of his son John. And should poet and patron meet again in future as homeless vagrants (ll. 127–34) – an imagined encounter no longer startling given similar imagery in the surrounding poems – at least they will finally meet as equals, clasping hands as 'FRIEND and BROTHER' (l. 134).

'To a Louse', which makes a fleeting reference to Burns's projected voyage, follows the dedication to Hamilton. Its speaker orders the despised creature to emigrate from Jenny's bonnet. '[G]ae somewhere else' (l. 11), he commands, and stop scandalizing the worthy people assembled at church. The best place for a louse is the hair of a beggar, where the louse can join thriving 'plantations' (l. 18) of other parasites, feasting on the blood of their human victims and enjoying their louse-utopia. Burns's reference to the slavery-based prosperity of colonists updates Fergusson's English poem 'The BUGS', whose speaker envies the more progressive 'commonwealth' established by the bedbugs who nightly feed on 'CLOE':

> ... midst the lillies of fair CLOE's breast
> Implant the deep carnation, and enjoy
> Those sweets which angel modesty hath seal'd
> From eyes profane ...
> Even so, befalls it to this creeping race,
> This envy'd commonwealth ... [117]

After 'To a Louse', Burns prints the epistles to John Lapraik, Willie Simson and John Rankine, that last a coarse-tongued neighbour much loved by Burns. Three early, very tender songs ensue, a jolt after the cocky double-entendre of the verse-letter to Rankine but perhaps explicable in terms of an association of ideas: for the heroine of 'Corn Rigs', first in this late-volume group of songs, was most likely John Rankine's daughter Anne (d. 1843).[118] The leave-takings that conclude the volume, then, begin with his vernacular correspondents and proceed to sweethearts of earliest days – Annie Rankine, Peggy Thomson ('Song, Composed in August') and Elizabeth Gebbie ('From Thee, Eliza, I Must Go'), who considered his offer of marriage *c.* 1781 but then accepted the proposal of a hosier who later grew wealthy in Glasgow.[119] The 'Farewell' addresses male friends, the Masons of Tarbolton Lodge, after which a group of epigrams and epitaphs memorialize a variety of people, from a 'Henpeck'd Country Squire' to Queen Artemisa of Helicarnassus and Mrs Campbell of Netherplace: those last two are wives who devour their husbands. Burns offers mock elegies for a 'bleth'ran *bitch*', Jamie, and 'wee Johnie', who had no soul; there follow, however, three respectful epitaphs: for the poet's father, R. A. (Robert Aikin) and G. H. (Gavin Hamilton).[120]

The closing poem looks down on the grave of the bard himself, who, like the speaker of Thomas Gray's 'Elegy in a Country Churchyard', retires underground. 'The poor Inhabitant below' has finally found a home. 'A Bard's Epitaph' also shares Gray's focus on literacy, for as in Gray the speaker specifically addresses an onlooking 'Reader' in the closing lines:

Reader attend – whether thy soul
Soars fancy's flights beyond the pole,
Or darkling grubs this earthly hole,
    In low pursuit,
Know, prudent, cautious, *self-controul*
    Is Wisdom's root.   (ll. 25–30)

This final poem buries the blighted hopes of Rob Burness and bids farewell to his youthful indiscretions, including his poems. The preface began by calling the volume's contents 'trifles' as the poet anticipates his life in exile; it ends with another telling choice, a single word, centred, widely spaced and in small caps, followed by a period: F I N I S.[121]

Rob Burness and Poet Burns

'Tis not the surging billow's roar,
'Tis not that fatal, deadly shore;   Jamaica
Tho' Death in ev'ry shape appear,
The Wretched have no more to fear:
But round my heart the ties are bound,
That heart transpierc'd with many a wound;
These bleed afresh, those ties I tear,
To leave the bonie banks of *Ayr*.[122]

Burns wrote 'Song' ('The Gloomy Night is Gath'ring Fast') in late summer 1786, when he thought his voyage was imminent. He intended it to stand as 'my last song I should ever measure in Caledonia'.[123] Not printed until the Edinburgh edition of 1787, the song is beautifully matched to its tune and offers a reprise of the same conflicting emotions that split the Kilmarnock volume, the same deep place-bound bond ending in the portrayal of rending and rupture of 'those ties' (l. 24).

As the various sub-groupings in the 1786 *Poems* unfold to a reader, a deeply equivocal vision emerges: Scotland as a site of near-starvation and rich family affection, hard-luck and sweet harmony. Slightly before midpoint, with the final stanzas of 'The Cotter's Saturday Night' and 'To a Mouse', the poems adopt the hyper-dramatic voice of 'Poet Burns', briefly glimpsed in the preface. 'The Gloomy Night' shares that afflicted voice and its dual concern with surveying the landscape around him and within him:

Farewell, old *Coila*'s hills and dales,
Her heathy moors and winding vales;
The scenes where wretched Fancy roves,
Pursuing past, unhappy loves!
Farewell, my friends! Farewell, my foes!
My peace with these, my love with those –

> The bursting tears my heart declare,
> Farewell, the bonie banks of *Ayr*!¹²⁴

The speaker's multiple goodbyes are bound to the melody in performance (unlike the words, the air is restrained and spare, yet each four lines flow down to a low note).¹²⁵ The four farewells serve to highlight – punctuate – the speaker's faltering effort to take in (and convey) the idea of exile and what it will mean for him. He will lose everyone, and every place, that he has ever known. With his 'wretched Fancy' roving over Scottish scenes and personal memories one last time, he proves himself to be Coila's bard to the last, for he embraces it all, good and bad, in parting. He blesses it repeatedly.

It is no wonder that the poems printed in 1786 exert to this day such an attraction for expatriated Scotsmen: Burns expected to live out his own life in exile. The poems and songs written or revised between April and December 1786 do not record the passing scene so much as call it back in parting; from mid-volume on, when they look ahead it is in sorrowful apprehension. Edwin Morgan wondered at the mysterious imagery in Burns's poems that so often travel between Burness (cultural memory) and Burns (personal disclosure). Burns's first volume is likewise mysterious in its dissonant staging as a simultaneous arrival and departure. The old Groucho Marx song 'Hello, I Must Be Going' would perfectly capture the contradictory voicings – except that this is no absurd non-sequitur but a seismic imprint on the volume from the poet's 1786 mood of bewildered disorientation, the mood also of 'The Gloomy Night' and the letters of midsummer 1786, with their tangled syntax and proliferating sentence fragments.

The confident debut of Poet Burns at mid-volume of the 1786 *Poems*, followed so dramatically by the burial and eulogy of 'A Bard's Epitaph', led me to the idea of 'interruption', introduced in the chapter's subtitle. For the poet's early handwritten collections, despite themselves greatly differing in diction and verse-forms, share a fundamentally bardic voicing from which, in the process of being torn out of his own life, the new voice of Poet Burns emerged, 'Robert Burns', who so signs this first and only printed book (later editions add to the original core) and who inhabits that book most intensely at midpoint.

As a bard, Burness is a receiver, picking up signals from all over, including places and people as yet inadmissible in books, or so Hugh Blair told the poet in recommending the suppression of 'Love and Liberty', Burness's early bardic masterpiece. In contrast, Poet Burns is a transmitter, ascending the podium as a 'public character' who constantly calibrates his relationship to readers and posterity. Turning from the exuberant bardic celebration of Scotland in the poems printed early in the volume, at mid-point he moves on to consider (the lines from 'Epistle to Davie' admired by Edwin Morgan are one example) the near-impossibility of surviving there – of surviving anywhere without capital, whether he stays or goes.

To document the differences in the poet's voice between *The First Commonplace Book*, *Kilmarnock Manuscript* and the 1786 *Poems* is not merely to show development to a more mature poetic expression, although that is part of the story. Yet much refined and condensed, the bardic and lyric voicings of the earlier two manuscripts return during the years after 1787, as Burness re-surfaces in some poems and hundreds of songs, often circulated anonymously, that spread across Great Britain and around the anglophone world as they accompanied succeeding waves of emigrant Scots. Although there are exceptions to be discussed in later chapters, these later songs often bypass the poet-on-exhibition in the Kilmarnock volume. Poet Burns continues to speak in some signed songs, prose letters and virtually all his later mock-epics, including 'Tam o'Shanter', considered in Chapter 4. For the most part, however, during the last ten years of his life Burns was more absorbed in capturing the nuances of national culture and character than on securing or defending his place in any literary canon. He had tasted personal and literary fame, perhaps, and had discovered that he disliked the taste. He chiefly worked on songs in simple measures, ending where he had begun at age fifteen, although the later songs range more widely through history ('Scots Wha Hae') and across cultures ('The Slave's Lament'). Many are unforgettable even without music, merely read on a printed page.

In *The Frenzy of Renown* (1997), Leo Braudy sees the Poet Burnsian speaker of 'To a Louse' as a prototype for the modern celebrity; Braudy interprets lines 43–4 ('O wad some Pow'r the giftie gie us / *To see ourselis as ithers see us*') as expressing a 'desire to ... regulate one's image before the world'.[126] This hypersensitivity to the view of others, seen also in Burns's preface to the Kilmarnock edition and many of his letters, feels modern, while in their broader and often quieter voicings, Burns's bardic writings, early and late, feel timeless: the Poet-Burnsian 'To a Mouse' bears the date 'November 1785', while the bardic 'The Twa Dogs' is set 'ance upon a time'. Some critics (it might be fair to say most critics) have seen the poet's return to near-anonymous songs as evidence of a decline in poetic power, but the chapters that follow consider the impact of all his writings on later generations. Wordsworth and Hugh MacDiarmid mainly looked to that public character Poet Burns; but others, including Carolina Oliphant (Lady Nairne), responded to his bardic openness to any and all speakers. And while, as I shall argue in the Epilogue, most readers outside Scotland by the late nineteenth century recalled Poet Burns only as a group of half-remembered phrases, in his less acclaimed guise as a bard (that is, through his often unattributed songs), not-Burns, or Burness, flourished throughout the nineteenth century and continues to flourish today. After 1786, creating and revising stanzas for songs was a joyous way to keep writing that did not require the terrified gaze into an abyss of displacement that had wrenched out of him some (not all) of the best things he ever wrote. The threat of exile receded after he began work with the Excise, for one thing; but the poet also came to realize that the Poet Burns persona was unsustainable – too intense to live with or (habitually) to speak from.

2 'IF THOU INDEED DERIVE THY LIGHT FROM HEAVEN': WORDSWORTH RESPONDS TO BURNS

> What is a Poet? ... He ... rejoices more than others in the spirit of life that is in him; delighted to contemplate similar volitions and passions ... and [is] habitually impelled to create them where he does not find them. To these qualities he has added a disposition to be affected more than other men by absent things as if they were present.
> Wordsworth, Preface to *Lyrical Ballads* (1802)[1]

Burnsworth

Wordsworth's feelings about Burns, always intense, were also changeable. He read Burns's Kilmarnock 1786 *Poems* within a few weeks of its publication, so that from age sixteen to his mid-twenties (Burns died at thirty-seven in July 1796) he knew of Burns as a comparatively young poet still publishing work that in subject matter, speaker and in some ways diction anticipated Wordsworth's own experiments in *Lyrical Ballads*. Both poets sought to discover, as Wordsworth puts it in the Advertisement for the first *Lyrical Ballads* (1798), 'how far the language of conversation in the middle and lower classes of society is adapted to the purposes of poetic pleasure'.[2] Burns, eleven years older, was a contemporary of Wordsworth and his sister Dorothy in the days when they were reading and discussing *Poems, Chiefly in the Scottish Dialect*;[3] moreover, Burns's poetry, not his myth, was predominant in the ten years after Wordsworth encountered the Scottish poet's writings. The two never met or corresponded, as Wordsworth never stopped regretting; but they had much in common, including their debut as published poets within the decade 1786–96, Burns with the Kilmarnock *Poems* and Wordsworth with *An Evening Walk* and *Poetical Sketches* in 1793.

In some of his poems Wordsworth echoes Burns so closely that I think of the speaker as 'Burnsworth'. Aside from a shared tendency to link rustic speakers and characters to a poet's concerns, there are biographical overlaps: both fathered a first child, a daughter, out of wedlock and both served in their later years, although at different bureaus and levels, as collectors of taxes. My discussion here will consider in tandem a group of poems by each. Significant differences, from divergent views on rhyme and style to incompatible political views in maturity, preclude any insistence on universal similarities; moreover, John Milton and Samuel Taylor Coleridge were much more frequent sources of inspiration for Wordsworth. Nonetheless, among twenty-nine Wordsworth poems that either directly address Burns or covertly introduce his imagery,[4] the eleven listed below in Table 2.1 show with special clarity elements in his 'Burnsworth' voicing. Wordsworth, who made five pilgrimages to Scotland in his lifetime, regularly returns to Burns as well, re-evaluating his adolescent embrace of the Kilmarnock *Poems*.

Table 2.1: Poems by Wordsworth most strongly linked to Burns.
Wordsworth's date of composition for each title is given; the date following the Burns poems is that of its publication in the various editions of *Poems, Chiefly in the Scottish Dialect*.

Poems by Wordsworth	Alluding to these Burns poems
'Lines in Early Spring' (1798)	'Man was Made to Mourn A Dirge' (1786)
'Simon Lee, the Old Huntsman' (1798)	'Tam Samson's Elegy' (1787)
'A Poet's Epitaph' (1799)	'A Bard's Epitaph' (1786)
'Resolution and Independence' (1802)	'Man Was Made to Mourn', 'The Vision' (1786)
At the Grave of Burns 1803: Seven Years After His Death' (1807–42)	'To a Mountain Daisy'; 'A Bard's Epitaph' (1786)
'Thoughts Suggested The Day Following […]' (completed 1839; published in 1842)	'The Vision' (1786)
'To the Sons of Burns After Visiting the Grave of Their Father' (1805–06; published 1807)	'Epistle to James Smith' (1786); 'The Vision' (1786)
'Benjamin the Waggoner' (1805)	'Tam o'Shanter' (1793)
stanzas 4 and 8, 'Immortality' ode (1803)	'The Vision'/'Despondency, An Ode' (1786)
'If thou indeed derive thy light from Heaven' (written 'after 1813'; published in 1827)	'The Vision' (1786)
'"There!" said a Stripling' (1833)	'To a Mountain Daisy' (1786)

Wordsworth's attraction to Burns partly lay in the sound, the play of words, the sumptuous feast of vowels and diphthongs, the hyperactive rhyming, although all were so different from his own poetic practice.[5] Like Spenser and Chaucer, whom Wordsworth also often reread, Burns appealed most when his diction was most elaborately wrought, suggesting a taste for poetic special effects that few would suspect lurked in the heart of the author of successively austere prefaces to *Lyrical Ballads*. Wordsworth wrote to Allan Cunningham in 1825 that '[f]amiliarity with the dialect of the counties of Cumberland and Westmorland made it easy for me not only to understand [Burns's poems] but to feel them'.[6] In his notes for his Burns edition, Cunningham writes of having heard Wordsworth recite, with relish and from memory, most of Burns's second verse-letter to John Lapraik (which is 108-lines long) and two stanzas of 'On a Scotch Bard Gone to the West Indies', 'pointing out as he went along', says Cunningham, 'the all but inimitable happiness of thought and language'.[7] In his early days, Wordsworth may have considered Burns much as Burns considered his Scots predecessor Robert Fergusson during his own early poetic experiments: as an 'elder Brother in the muse' gifted, perhaps unwise (at least according to myth) and certainly unfortunate.[8] These were fellow-poets to be publically championed (as in Burns's commission of a stone to mark Fergusson's grave or Wordsworth's well-intentioned if maladroit 'Letter to a Friend of Robert Burns') but poetically contended with, revised, adjusted.[9] As late as 1841, Wordsworth spoke of Burns to James Patrick Muirhead with such fierce, and on that day negative, emotion that the young Scottish journalist wondered at his intensity: '[it was] as if [Burns] ... was his own brother'.[10]

Burns's 'The Vision' and Wordsworth's reconsideration of it in 'If thou indeed derive thy light' open my analysis. Each repays a careful reading and deserves one, for both are comparatively neglected, 'The Vision' despite defences by Thomas Crawford, Nigel Leask, Fiona Stafford and Christopher Ricks – and the later sonnets of Wordsworth by consensus.[11] As seen in Table 2.1 above, 'The Vision' was a very important text for Wordsworth. 'If thou indeed derive thy light', his sonnet in colloquy with Burns's poem, so well expressed for him his own poetic concerns that in 1845 he selected it to stand as the epigraph for his collected poems. Burns's poem describes 'Coila', the muse of his region of Kyle in south-west Scotland; in the poem's final lines she crowns Burns's speaker as her laureate. Burns probably took his idea for 'Coila' from 'Scota', a Scottish muse celebrated by vernacular poet Alexander Ross (1699–1784).

Stephen Gill reports a story of 1841: Wordsworth, helping Elizabeth Fletcher and her daughter to plant holly berries at Lancrigg, 'every now and then' repeated aloud 'in his low solemn tone' the holly-crowning stanza that concludes 'The Vision'.[12] If a touchstone for Wordsworth, 'The Vision' was a transitional text for Burns that oscillates, like the better-known 'The Cotter's Saturday Night', between bardic stanzas that remember and celebrate and Poet Burnsian stanzas that look inward to the poet's feelings and ahead to the future.[13] Its partitioning into two duans or parts (it is the only text in the 1786 *Poems* divided in this way) suggests its dissonant concerns, which range from patriotic scenic description to bitter soul-searching. Can a weary thresher (the speaker's activity that day) aspire to poetry? Even if he succeeds in reaching an audience of non-fools (l. 24), what will he live on? The opening and closing stanzas consider links between the speaker's literary aspirations and his troubles in life; but bardic stanzas conclude duan one, which ends with descriptions of Kyle's rivers, mountains and the nearby borough of Ayr in tableaux that scroll across Coila's mantle. This bardic section contains only three stanzas in the version printed in 1786 but in the Stair MS (September 1786) is augmented by nineteen further stanzas that address local heroes: seven of those were eventually printed in the Edinburgh edition of *Poems* (1787). Burns told Anna Wallace Dunlop in January 1787 that the extra stanzas were not recently composed but remnants of earlier drafts.[14] So when editing 'The Vision' for the Kilmarnock 1786 *Poems*, Burns sharply cut back the fluid bardic stanzas.

It was begun as early as 1783 ('long ago', he told Mrs Dunlop in the letter enclosing the 1787 expansion of the text),[15] but reworked in spring 1786 beyond the excision of early bardic stanzas, for Jean Armour's name was removed from line 63 and 'Bess' (Elizabeth Paton) evidently restored. Other revisions were no doubt made but cannot be documented, because as with 'To a Louse' and 'To a Mouse', no extant manuscript predates the truncated version first printed in the Kilmarnock 1786 *Poems*,[16] where it follows a poem with a similar title, 'A Dream', although the two much differ in tone, 'A Dream' being a giddy send-up of Poet Laureate Thomas Warton's customary birthday ode for George III.[17]

Both 'A Dream' and 'The Vision' are covert addresses from Kyle's laureate to Great Britain's, but 'The Vision' differs in being long-meditated and much more serious. Not an improvised burlesque like 'A Dream' but a rival ode, it addresses a region rather than a United Kingdom and crowns a peasant, not a king and most definitely not a laurelled literatus, one of those envied 'men with Greek and Latin' like Thomas Warton, a gifted Oxford literary historian if less than memorable as a crafter of odes.[18] Warton's 1786 birthday ode advises British poets to emulate Pindar and the ancient Greeks, but 'The Vision' looks to the speaker's own traditions, landscapes and patriots (Burns alludes in line 103, for instance, to locally reared though far-famed William Wallace). Its most famous stanza is not bardic, however, but Poet Burnsian, as Coila tells the speaker that the passion that has driven him so far off-course (this stanza was most likely written or recast in spring 1786) also drives his poems:

> I saw thy pulse's maddening play
> Wild-send thee Pleasure's devious way,
> Misled by Fancy's *meteor-ray*,
>   By Passion driven;
> But yet the *light* that led astray,
>   Was *light* from Heaven. (ll. 235–40)[19]

'Light' is twice italicized and in its second appearance as '*light* from Heaven' uses a frequent Calvinist image for grace, although Coila here certifies, 'justifies', not the speaker's soul but his calling as a poet. Passion, pleasure and fancy, however problematic, are ineluctable gifts from a higher power whose bounties cannot be refused. The stanza articulates the double-bind that would haunt Wordsworth's speaker in 'Resolution and Independence': the same energies that make the poet creative and joyful are strong enough to tear him apart.

While earlier in the Kilmarnock sequence 'Poor Mailie's Elegy' (#7) and 'A Dream' (#9) make light of poets and their soul-searchings, 'The Vision' portrays its impoverished yet Heaven-inspired poet-speaker with sympathy. Despite the reduced number of descriptive stanzas in the 1786 printing, 'The Vision' preserves the voice and interests of young Rob Burness in Coila's restriction to the locale of Kyle: unlike 'The Cotter's Saturday Night', this poem never turns even in closing to address Scotland (or the world) at large. Coila of Kyle is 'some' Scottish muse, not *the* Scottish muse, although Burns's choice to print SCOTTISH MUSE in large capitals honours her at the same time (l. 51). Kyle extends some 422 square miles, about ⅟₇ of the total area of Scotland (30,265 square miles). To this 'district-space' (one hears 'strict space', constriction, in the very phrase) the muse and her votary are 'bounded' (l. 193), at least until the '*light* from Heaven' stanza asserts a different, transcendent, origin for a poet's impulses. Coila in fact offers the speaker incompatible 'visions' of poetry, and her corresponding map of her protégé's psychic terrain (from the day of his birth she has been assigned to 'mark' the 'embryonic traces' of his talent and temperament; ll. 147–48) has become so contradictory by the end of the poem as to be illegible.

Poetry arises from local description; poetry descends from heaven like the grace of God. It comes from the poet's consciousness; it comes from the poet's bond with a particular landscape and culture. This pattern of contradiction might be read as a kind of mistake in the poem, Rob Burness and Poet Burns talking over each other, but could also be seen as an aporia in the Derridean sense, an impasse or paradox that speaks, with some exactitude, to the conflicting impulses, the cross fire, inherent in creative endeavour. The muse's answer to the poem's implied question – Can a rural farm-tenant *c*. 1783–86 hope for breakthrough as a writer? – is by turns reassuring and discomforting, for the speaker is first gladdened by Coila's account of a *reasonable* degree of *modest* impact as a *regional* bard but then shudders in agreement when she depicts the terrors of an authentic poetic calling, for he will never know where that light from heaven is leading him, whether to joyous creation or death by meteor strike (l. 237). Just as the winding rivers of Ayr set the scene for the pictorial stanzas that conclude part one, shifting aspirations intersect the emotional landscape of its closing stanzas. The poem gradually unfolds, then, as a dual portrait of Burness/Burns during the period (late spring 1786) that they were separating into two specialized personae. As tenth text in the Kilmarnock volume, 'The Vision' takes Rob Burness as its baseline or starting point but also gave readers of 1786 (Wordsworth among them) a glimpse of the candid, curious consciousness of Poet Burns, soon to take over at mid-volume. Both speakers address readers indirectly through their proxy Coila, who is not a higher power so much as the alternating echo of their contending voices.

At some point before 1827, when the poem was printed, Wordsworth reused '*light* from Heaven' in the starting line of an extended (at sixteen lines) yet simplified (unrhymed) sonnet.[20] Rather than engaging with Burns's standard Habbie stanza, Wordsworth chose blank verse, as did he for his *Prelude*, whose original version (1798–9) was in two parts like Burns's 'The Vision' and also like 'The Vision' considers a poet's life from infancy to his mid-twenties. In the sonnet printed in 1827, Wordsworth's strongest lines (10–12) are enjambed, avoiding the dramatic pause at line-ending so often seen in Burns. Having sufficiently converted metre and diction for his own purposes, the poet sets himself the task of reworking Burns's doubly metonymic original phrase, in which neither 'light' nor 'Heaven' can be taken literally. For in his lines, heavenly light comes from the stars and forms only the top-note in a night landscape of harmonious beauty:

> If thou indeed derive thy light from Heaven,
> Then, to the measure of that heaven-born light,
> Shine, Poet! in thy place, and be content: –
> The stars pre-eminent in magnitude,
> And they that from the zenith dart their beams,
> (Visible though they be to half the earth,
> Though half a sphere be conscious of their brightness)
> Are yet of no diviner origin,
> No purer essence, than the one that burns,
> Like an untended watch-fire, on the ridge
> Of some dark mountain; or than those which seem
> Humbly to hang, like twinkling winter lamps,
> Among the branches of the leafless trees;
> All are the undying offspring of one Sire:
> Then, to the measure of the light vouchsafed,
> Shine, Poet! in thy place, and be content.[21]

To Burns's expostulations in 'The Vision', Wordsworth returns a reply across the decades. He also may be recalling Milton, whose youthful breakthrough sonnet *c*. 1631 conveys some of the young Burns's anxieties in 'The Vision' as well as anticipating Wordsworth's dignity of cadence: 'It shall be still in strictest measure ev'n / To that same lot ... Toward which Time leads me, and the will of Heav'n'.[22] Both Wordsworth and Milton gravely pun on poetic versus practical senses of the word 'measure'.

Wordsworth's lines do not mention any poet by name, as is often the case when Burns is somewhere in the picture. Still, that class of star likened to an 'untended watch-fire' 'burns' suggestively. In 'At the Grave of Burns', begun in 1803 but finished in the 1840s, Wordsworth uses a similar image in praising Burns's first volume of poems, which in 1786 'Rose like a star that touching earth ... doth glorify its humble birth / With matchless beams'.[23] In a note about 'If thou indeed', Wordsworth never mentions his opening echo of what was at the time among Burns's most famous phrases; he passes in silence over the bonding between poets and their well-loved landscapes that is a central concern of 'The Vision' and implicit in his own lines, where a poet shines 'in place'. The note describes only the winter prospects around Rydal Mount, where Wordsworth and his family moved in May 1813:

> These verses were written some time after ... and I will take occasion from them to observe upon the beauty of that situation, as being backed and flanked by lofty fells, which bring the heavenly bodies to touch, as it were, the earth upon the mountain-tops, while the prospect in front lies open to a length of level valley, the extended lake, and a terminating ridge of low hills; so that it gives an opportunity to the inhabitants of the place of noticing the stars in both the positions here alluded to, namely, on the tops of the mountains, and as winter-lamps at a distance among the leafless trees.[24]

These different prospects (valleys, mountains, extended lake) are linked in Wordsworth's sonnet to varying perspectives on poetry and poets.

Wordsworth's sonnet administers a check to worried poets, chiding them for discontent rather than dramatizing their mood-swings as he does in 'Resolution and Independence' and as Burns does in 'The Vision'. The zigzag of emotions in 'The Vision', the 'soaring and grovelling', as Byron memorably described the volatility of tone in Burns,[25] is expunged from Wordsworth's ruminative, anti-dramatic lines, which take their extended metaphor from the night sky. Like the stars seen from Rydal Mount, some poets seem to shine more brightly due to a prominent position in the (literary) firmament. Yet 'zenith' stars do not necessarily possess more appeal than those seen closer to the horizon, some of which appear to touch the mountain ridge like watch-fires or shine through the trees like winter-lamps. The watch-fire stars and lamp-stars seem less lofty as well as more approachable, but this has nothing to do with intrinsic worth: they merely strike the eye at a different angle. Even the sublime zenith stars are not visible to all on earth: 'half a globe' is as large an audience as can be secured by any one star, for the Northern and Southern hemispheres display different constellations (ll. 4–7). So too with poetic light: its effects are variegated, like the night sky or a striking landscape. Human eyes see what they *can* see of starlight, looking up from the earth; but no one sees all the stars, and no one can tell just by looking either the true magnitude of a star or the exact value (to the poet or to others) of a calling to write.

'The Vision' begins with questions of value as its speaker takes inventory. In line 38 of the shorter Kilmarnock version, he broods about his 'empty *Cash-Account*': the financial term is italicized as if a word in a foreign tongue. He laments what poetry has brought him to: there he sits, 'half-mad, half-fed, half-sarket' (l. 29), and that is 'a' the amount' (l. 30). Coila materializes to reassure him about one of his worries, the authenticity of his calling: at the hour of his birth, she says, she 'mark'd' him an 'embryotic' bard (lls. 147–8). Poets play a valuable part in the culture and vitality of Kyle, she says: 'Trust me' (l. 213). Yet her equivocal advice would be difficult to put into practice. 'Strive in thy humble sphere to shine' (l. 212), she tells him. Yet striving and shining typically indicate a resolve to transcend a humble sphere. Coila's verbs ('strive'; 'shine') seem almost to spurn her adjective and noun ('humble sphere').

In his sonnet Wordsworth retains the imperative mood of Coila's verbs, reusing one of them ('shine'). Yet he resists Coila's assumption that Burns's bond with Kyle necessarily cuts him off from wider achievement, and he rejects her exclusion of Burns's speaker from the ranks of the zenith poets in this later stanza:

> Thou canst not learn, nor can I show,
> To paint with *Thomson*'s landscape-glow;
> Or wake the bosom-melting throe,
>   With *Shenstone*'s art;
> Or pour, with *Gray*, the moving flow,
>   Warm on the heart. (ll. 199–204)

Here Coila is not addressing the topography and history of Kyle but pointing out the limitations of local colour. A district muse, she cannot teach her protégé to write in the cosmopolitan mode of James Thomson, William Shenstone and Thomas Gray. Wordsworth is drawn to Coila's linking of poets to specific districts but his sonnet refutes her assertion that an allegiance to place necessarily limits a poet's scope and audience. Indeed, while Burns himself offers no direct rebuttal, he too resists Coila's prohibition. For the same stanza in which the Scottish muse forbids him to dream of success beyond Kyle is written in 'zenith' diction that parodies Thomson, Shenstone and Gray and their neoclassical epithets (e.g., 'bosom-melting throe' for emotion in l. 249). Coila warns that she cannot 'teach' him neoclassicism, but the concluding stanzas of 'The Vision' are at pains to show that Kyle's bard has managed to acquire this knowledge on his own, of which more below.

Wordsworth's sonnet contradicts Coila in a different way, using that extended metaphor that shows his knowledge of stars.[26] Although not strictly speaking fixed, a star does not carom through space like a meteor (Burns's image for 'Fancy' in l. 237). The sonnet suggests that a poet is like a star, a poem like that star's light. Stargazers on earth see not the star itself but only the afterimage of its far-away and long-ago light.[27] So too poets: inhabiting their own place and time, they are moved to write by prospects both outside and within them. The ensuing poems, light the poet has received as an instinct/inspiration and shaped into verse, travel (still in analogy with starlight) across time and space to far places and future generations to be received by observers, whether just a few or a multitude. The degree of perceived brilliance seen in poets (judging them by their light) is nonetheless subject to tricks of perspective, atmospheric distortion and topographical anomalies. Yet the ultimate destination of all poets' work is in the minds of those who will see their light and remember their words. To both Burns in 'The Vision' and Wordsworth in 'If thou indeed derive thy light', success in this enterprise requires a bond with specific places and people as well as skills to shape impulses into poems. Those factors are theirs to work with but beyond that there is no telling. In 'The Vision' Burns's speaker tries to see ahead: what will become of him? He has neglected his material interests for his writing and foresees no material benefit in return. When Wordsworth wrote his sonnet sometime between 1813 and 1827, he was oppressed by a sense of diminished poetic vision: he too looked ahead in fear. The sonnet gently chides all such doubting poets, for they cannot know how their work will be seen by observers, whether they will be seen, to invert a phrase from Burns, as they see themselves. Starlight shines steadily over the earth and across the centuries; Wordsworth's sonnet refutes Coila's hint in 'The Vision' that the 'meteor ray' of poetic inspiration (l. 237) is a passing impulse. The implied view of the sonnet also differs from 'Resolution and Independence', whose speaker, like Burns's in 'The Vision', dramatizes how difficult it can be to serve as a transmitter of 'undying' light. Always to stand and wait, as Milton puts the matter in one of his own sonnets, takes its toll on a poet's equilibrium.[28] The sheer uncertainty could drive a person half-mad.

In the most famous stanza of 'The Vision' Coila tells the speaker that the same passion that has 'driven' him to write drives him also to transgression. For Wordsworth this passage held the key to Burns's character: a puppet of uncontrollable impulses and powerless to change, he had destroyed his early promise. Yet that stanza is best read not as a gauge of Burns's psyche but as an artefact of spring 1786. Grief almost engulfed Burns in the months he reworked 'The Vision' and other not-quite finished poems for printing in the Kilmarnock edition. Wordsworth happened to love these hyper-dramatic poems best but they are not accurate reflections of Burns's usual state of mind. The records suggest that he *was* half-crazy by mid-1786, but not that he continued in that state. Coila refers to his current crisis in the 'light from Heaven' stanza but only to reassure him, not to admonish vice. She warns him only against the seductive lure of Thomson, Shenstone and Gray. Burns's health was fragile but there is no evidence that he brought ill-health on himself, nor is his later work predominantly sad. The late songs sometimes have a political edge tinged with anger but they generally point forward to a better world. There is nothing abject about 'Tam o'Shanter', 'Ae Fond Kiss' or 'Scots Wha Hae'.

In decided contrast to Burns's anxious speaker in 'The Vision', Wordsworth's in his sonnet is ultra-serene, as if he has now become the Leech-Gatherer of 'Resolution and Independence' and stands as a living rebuke to volatility. Poets, he says, should be content. Whatever their 'undying' essence or light, whether they are received as zenith-stars, watch-fire stars or lamp-stars, poets must write as they will: that is their calling. All else is out of their hands. 'The Vision' likewise ends calmly as Coila sets a wreath of holly berries on the speaker's brow. He is the bard of Kyle at any rate; he *is* a poet. On a winter evening, dejected and discouraged, the speaker has seen his Muse, who has reminded him of his long apprenticeship and recalled him to poetry with the authority not of a goddess but a family member, addressing him with something of an 'elder Sister's air' (l. 95). For both Burns and Wordsworth, poetry makes siblings even of demi-goddesses or the ghosts of predecessors.

Wordsworth's extended metaphor of stars may recall an early scene in 'The Vision' in which the speaker, discouraged at his perceived failure, begins to swear an oath by 'yon starry roof' (l. 33) that he will never write another poem. Before the words are fully out, Coila walks into the speaker's house (and poem) to intervene. Wordsworth's lines likewise take up the idea of a starry roof and have the air of an intervention, and like Coila his speaker advises a curb on poetic aspirations for fame and recognition yet also offers consolation and partial validation. 'The Vision' opens on a list of cold-weather discomforts, from snow in the yard and rats in the thatch to cough-inducing reek from the smoking fire. Wordsworth uses a cold-weather image too, but the prospect is anything but bleak: to his speaker's eye, even the leafless boughs are hung with stars.

'Shine, Poet! in thy place, and be content': the command is twice repeated (ll. 3, 16). One imagines Wordsworth reciting the line aloud not petulantly but seriously, in the 'low, solemn tone' remembered by Elizabeth Fletcher's daughter. Yet on one level the lines reprove the discontented speaker of 'The Vision', just as the conditional phrasing of Wordsworth's first line ('*If* thou indeed derive thy light from heaven') sounds a note of scepticism. Still, as a brother-poet (l. 13) Wordsworth accepts his own share of any critique of excessive sensibility. By using the intimate form of the second-person pronoun ('thy light') he can simultaneously address the author of the phrase he is quoting and take the opportunity to think these things over with himself. The sleight-of-pronoun here ('thy' being addressed both to Burns and to Wordsworth himself) allows Burnsworth to speak as (and for) both. 'Resolution and Independence' offers a similar conjunction; 'He' refers to the speaker in line 40 but five lines later 'Him' refers to Burns:

> My whole life I have liv'd in pleasant thought,
> As if life's business were a summer mood:
> As if all needful things would come unsought
> To genial faith, still rich in genial good;
> But how can He expect that others should
> Build for him, sow for him, and at his call
> Love him, who for himself will take no heed at all?
>
> I thought of Chatterton, the marvellous Boy,
> The sleepless Soul that perish'd in its pride;

> Of Him who walk'd in glory and in joy
> Behind his plough, upon the mountain-side:
> By our own spirits are we deified;
> We Poets in our youth begin in gladness;
> But thereof comes in the end despondency and madness.²⁹

This passage is striking in many ways, including its emphasis on 'despondency', a word that he and Coleridge associated with the Burns ode of that title.. The association of Burns with Chatterton, who died at seventeen of an arsenic overdose, is curious, for the speaker of 'The Vision' is far from being self-destructive: his concern is how to survive. Burns does paint his speaker as 'half-mad, half-fed, half-sarket' (l. 29) but near-insanity only begins a series that moves on to more material concerns, hardships that Burns and his family intermittently faced for eleven years (1766–77) at Mount Oliphant: chronic hunger, ragged clothing, exhaustion, the state of the speaker as 'The Vision' opens.

Perhaps Chatterton and Burns converge in Wordsworth's mind not only because he (wrongly, in the case of Burns) saw both as self-destroyers but because both had such an inimitable, idiosyncratic poetic language. He may have associated stylistic ornamentation with instability. Wordsworth's own strong work takes its chances in the other direction, its diction almost puritanically purged of ornament. In emphasizing the speaker's veering moods, 'Resolution and Independence' is like 'The Vision'; it is Wordsworthian, however, in its ruthless simplicity. The passage quoted above conjoins three poets from different milieux and in very different circumstances merely by insisting on their fatal vulnerabilities. They are treated as full peers in sensibility and suffering. Chatterton and Burns, long dead – Chatterton in 1770, the year Wordsworth was born – become ghostly witnesses as Wordsworth's speaker runs headlong from 'blind thoughts' (l. 28) of unspecified future anguish. As a 'resolution' to his speaker's tempest of emotions, the poem offers the opposite of poetic tempests: the self-respecting stoic endurance of the Leech Gatherer, who is at first compared to an impervious 'huge stone' (l. 57) by the agitated speaker.

Although 'Resolution and Independence' was in part inspired by an encounter with a Scottish leech-gatherer recorded in Dorothy Wordsworth's journal entry for 3 October 1800, the poem also recalls Burns's early song 'Man Was Made to Mourn, A Dirge', in which a 'rev'rend sage' 'whose aged step seem'd weary, worn with care' addresses a wandering young man. He comments on the ills of life, the injustices that he has witnessed in every one of his eighty years. While hoping that there is 'some recompense / To comfort those that mourn', the sage mentions only death:

> O Death! the poor man's dearest friend,
>   The kindest and the best!

> Welcome the hour, my aged limbs
>   Are laid with thee at rest!
> The Great, the Wealthy fear thy blow,
>   From pomp and pleasure torn;
> But Oh! A blest relief for those
>   That weary-laden mourn![30]

'Resolution and Independence' adopts the plot of Burns's song (the chance meeting of an elderly and a young wanderer) but omits the bitter social commentary of the sage, instead using his Leech-Gatherer to teach a lesson in forbearance. As elsewhere, Wordsworth draws on his detailed memory of Burns's writings chiefly to open a route inward to his own concerns.

'Man was Made to Mourn', like many of Burns's poems and songs, combines social critique with oblique self-analysis (as in lines 3–4 of stanza 7, quoted below) and expressions of what might be called human solidarity:

> Many and sharp the num'rous Ills
>   Inwoven with our frame!
> More pointed still we make ourselves
>   Regret, Remorse, and Shame!
> And Man, whose heav'n-erected face,
>   The smiles of love adorn,
> Man's inhumanity to Man
>   Makes countless thousands mourn! (ll. 59–66)

Several of the Kilmarnock poems imply or express 'regret, remorse, and shame' for past transgressions. Such passages Wordsworth took fully to heart, along with those expressing good wishes for the well-being of all, as in Coila's description of the speaker's delight in observing nature's rebirth in spring:

> ... [With] joy and music pouring forth,
>   In ev'ry grove,
> I saw thee eye the gen'ral mirth
>   With boundless love. (ll. 69–74)

In scenario though not style, the stanza above from 'The Vision' may form one literary context for the springtime setting of stanzas in Wordsworth's 'Ode: Intimations of Immortality from Recollections of Early Childhood' in which the speaker observes with sympathy the 'jubilee' of 'Creatures':

> Ye blessèd Creatures, I have heard the call
> Ye to each other make; I see
> The heavens laugh with you in your jubilee;
>   My heart is at your festival,
>   My head hath its coronal,
> The fullness of your bliss, I feel – I feel it all![31]

In 'The Vision' Burns's stanzas move from description of spring through to the other seasons in a compressed homage to James Thomson; but the springtime stanza was for Wordsworth evidently the most striking in showing Burns's innate sympathy with childlike joy and nature's annual rebirth.

While Wordsworth is drawn to the Burns who opens his heart, confesses his failings and turns to the world in a spirit of generous affirmation, he is unresponsive to Burns's expressions of grief and outrage over preventable suffering and the inequities of the class structure of his day. When Burns considers social ills, his perspective is outwardly focussed and looks to the future; Wordsworth's meditations are more likely to turn inward and look back, so bringing Burns into alignment required adjustment. Burnsworth, Wordsworth's Burns-facing speaker, is a dual entity like Ulysses/Diomedes in Dante's hell, twin souls who share a single but divided flame; and one element that divides them is the English poet's suppression of the Scottish poet's calls for change. In 'Lines Written in Early Spring' (1798) Wordsworth *almost* proceeds to social critique in a stanza that alludes to Burns. As later revisions change the concluding stanza, two versions are provided below, one printed in 1798 and one printed in the 1840s:

If I these thoughts may not prevent,	If this belief from heaven be sent,
If such be of my creed the plan,	If such be Nature's holy plan,
Have I not reason to lament	Have I not reason to lament
What man has made of man?	What man has made of man?[32]

There is a half-echo of Burns's 'Man's inhumanity to Man' in the last line of each stanza quoted above; and in both versions Wordsworth's second line may remember a late scene in 'The Vision' in which Coila instructs the speaker to uphold the 'dignity of Man' in full assurance that his efforts in that matter are supported by 'the UNIVERSAL PLAN':

> ... Preserve *the dignity of Man*,
>   With Soul erect;
> And trust, the UNIVERSAL PLAN
>   Will all protect. (ll. 267–70)[33]

The speaker of 'Lines in Early Spring' delights in the 'thousand blended notes' of the season, but the disparity between this harmony and the suffering world that human beings have constructed brings 'sad thoughts' to his mind (l. 4). Wordsworth's short lyric implies a more sympathetic view of poetic social critique than is seen in 'Resolution and Independence'; for although the conditions that distress the speaker are not condemned or even named, at least he does not scold himself, as he does in 'Resolution and Independence', for allowing sad thoughts of human suffering to spoil his mood and his day. This poem's not-quite-spoken indictment of social ills has its own power.

Political and social commentaries are no less poetic than confessional meditations, as Wordsworth knew well: revering Milton, he knew that *Paradise Lost* was infused with Milton's vision of contemporary political upheavals. Dante's 'Inferno' would likewise be much diminished by a reading indifferent to what Florentine politics and exile had meant to the poet. Even in the post-epic, post-Romantic era, Walt Whitman and Adrienne Rich would be poorly served by readers determined to tune out the political element in their poetry. Burns, although not of a systematically political bent (in the sense that he draws on assorted ideologies as needed – Chapter 3 will discuss alternating Jacobite and Jacobin allusions in his songs), is consistent in his nuanced portrayal of social strata previously subject to poetic stereotyping and his introduction into poetry of plain-spoken yet eloquent peasant speakers. He seems personally to solicit the sympathy of readers in a few of the Kilmarnock poems ('The Vision' and 'To a Mountain Daisy' most notably) but much more often speaks on behalf of groups and people more oppressed than he. The sage in 'Man Was Made to Mourn' mourns the 'hundreds', the 'crouds in ev'ry land', the 'countless thousands' (ll. 19, 45, 56) treated as subhuman by those whose social rank is higher (stanza 8 was especially admired by Wordsworth).

To observe that Wordsworth suppresses the social dimension in Burns, portraying him as a figure of lonely splendour and misery rather than as a member of a community, is not to diminish these extraordinary poems that Burns helped to inspire. Wordsworth revises to his own purposes as he adapts, just as all poets do. Yet the degree of cutting and pasting involved in his de-socialization of an intensely social imagination is worth pointing out. Wordsworth's cut-down Burns served him well, becoming the core of many poems he cherished, including that sonnet he chose to stand at the front of his collected poems. Yet Burns is far from being the only writer with whom Wordsworth communes in this proprietary, revisionary way. One thinks of his close study of his sister Dorothy's journal entries and adaptation of her images or his intense creative bond with Coleridge, which persisted years after their close friendship had ended: *The Prelude*'s working title through to 1850 was 'Poem (title not yet fixed upon) to Coleridge'. He is most successful when tracing psychic ties with the Scottish poet – both those 'perceived' and those 'half-created', as Wordsworth muses of the mind's conversion of received sense-impressions in l. 106 of 'Tintern Abbey'. Burnsworth is less successful when experimenting with Burns's intricate rhyme and metre: for example, in the stilted standard Habbie of 'To the Sons of Burns' or the incredibly slow-moving 'Benjamin the Waggoner', a poem that emulates 'Tam o' Shanter' in metre and plot (it too is written in couplets – seven syllables rather than Burns's eight – and describes a drunk man's strange encounters on a stormy night) without once breaking into a gallop like Burns's ever-accelerating tale. Wordsworth's story-in-verse has its own fey charm yet could scarcely be more unlike Burns in narrative pacing that, like Benjamin's horses, just steadily plods ahead.[34]

Growth of a (Scottish) Poet's Mind

To pursue the matter of Burns's predecessors and return to Coila's prohibition to Burns's speaker of Thomson, Shenstone and Gray, it is safe to assume that Wordsworth himself would never have set those three poets at the zenith of literary heaven as Coila does.[35] Although Wordsworth's first published poem, *An Evening Walk*, was written in heroic couplets, in maturity he rejected most of the Augustan poetic forms and he deplored periphrasis, personification and other classical techniques of amplification and abstraction. The preface to the second edition of *Lyrical Ballads* (1800) attacks stylized language:

> a language arising out of repeated experience and regular feelings is a more permanent and a far more philosophical language than that which is frequently substituted for it by Poets, who think they are conferring Honour upon themselves and their art in proportion as they separate themselves from the sympathies of men.[36]

The 1802 preface sharpens that point:

> There will ... be found in these volumes little of what is usually called poetic diction; I have taken as much pains to avoid it as others ordinarily take to produce it; this I have done for the reason already alleged, to bring my language near to the language of men.[37]

Burns died in 1796 of heart disease whose symptoms had troubled him at least since 1781; infection following a tooth extraction in 1795 might have hastened his death. If he had lived a few more years, he could have read Wordsworth's thoughts on modern poetic diction in the successive editions of *Lyrical Ballads* and perhaps seen their implication for his own writings. Even without knowledge of Wordsworth's ideas, however, both Burns's early verse-epistles and many of his later songs (1787–96) for James Johnson's *Scots Musical Museum* use just such an unadorned and conversational style.

As a young poet Burns was drawn to James Thomson as a Scot who had achieved critical success and intermittent financial security as a poet in London; he admired Thomas Gray and William Shenstone as writers of high reputation who had described country settings without airbrushing out all the country people. Yet these poets piqued him, too. He often mimics their style in a way that is deliberately over-the-top: 'Tho' large the forest's Monarch throws / His army shade' ('The Vision, ll. 255–6) is an elaborate way to remind readers that the boughs of the oak extend its shade. In 'Tam o'Shanter', Burns's narrator turns out epithets in little series in the vein of Thomson. A curious 'swain' in Thomson's 'Summer' chases a rainbow; the boy sees by turns 'a white mingling maze', a 'falling glory' and an 'amusive arch' before the image vanishes 'quite away'.[38] In 'Elegy Written in a Country Church-yard' Gray's speaker sees a grave as a 'mouldering heap' (l. 14), 'narrow cell' (l. 15) and 'lowly bed' (l. 20); education or 'Knowledge' is a scroll displaying 'the spoils of time' (ll. 49–50). The swallow twitters not from its nest but from a 'straw-built shed' (l. 18).[39] Shenstone's elegies are written with simplicity but his early poem 'The Schoolmistress', a Spenserian parody, showcases a burlesque mixture of archaic and classical diction. A recently whipped schoolboy's cheek is 'besprent' with 'liquid crystal' (l. 217); the willow switch that brings him to tears is a 'baleful sprig' (l. 149).[40] This is ponderous play for Shenstone, but Burns learned from such tricky language ways to bring Kyle, the district space of his vernacular diction, into close and not always submissive contact with 'zenith' poetry and wider British culture. For all is not emulation, particularly in 'The Vision' and 'The Cotter's Saturday Night', both of which use a mixed Scots/English diction not to capitulate to English culture but to push back against poetry's stereotyped portrayal of country people. Burns alternates between Scottish diction that brings his characters vividly to life and loftier passages that frame them with respect; his standard-English stanzas adopt the style of earlier poets including Oliver Goldsmith and Thomas Gray.[41] Burns's hybrid diction challenges earlier poets' portrayal of 'rustic' characters, though Burns loves these earlier poets too for writing about rural people at all. There is homage in the epigraph taken from Gray's 'Elegy' for 'The Cotter's Saturday Night', but there is critique in its centrepiece scene of family worship led by a 'priestlike' father who reads with quiet dignity – indeed, with eloquent authority – from the family Bible (l. 73), contradicting Gray's sad certainty that country folk, however bright, are fated to live and die in ignorance, their souls' genial current frozen by poverty and their talents buried by illiteracy.

Burns himself was no product of 'th' unletter'd Muse' (see l. 81 in Gray's 'Elegy'). After 1768, when his schoolmaster John Murdoch left the area, Burns was vigorously home-schooled. Even during the years of struggle at Mount Oliphant, his father, well aware of his oldest child's unusual brightness, gave painstaking attention to Robert's education. Though money was very scant (as John Weston has established, the family all but starved at Mount Oliphant),[42] William Burnes found some way to gain access to the books of the Ayr Library Society[43] and also borrowed books from friends and neighbours. He arranged for tutoring in French and a refresher course in English grammar during 1773 for short periods when his eldest son, aged fourteen yet chief labourer on the farm, was not needed for farm work and could study and board with his old schoolmaster Murdoch, who had returned to the area as an English teacher in Ayr. He sent Robert in 1775 to Kirkoswald to take a summer course in trigonometry and surveying taught by a renowned local teacher, Hugh Rodgers, a momentous time away for Burns, as discussed in Chapter 4. His brother Gilbert remembered with a touch of resentment that their father was 'proud of Robert's genius, which he bestowed more expense in cultivating, than on the rest of the family'.[44] Burns found mathematics a struggle, although his study that summer in 1775 probably assisted his application to the Excise some dozen years later. But during the earlier sessions with Murdoch in 1773 he had picked up enough of the rudiments of French to read Fénelon's *Les Adventures de Télémache* (1699) without a back-up English translation. 'This was considered a sort of prodigy,'[45] wrote Gilbert in the later 1790s, and Burns was then given by a Mr Robinson, a friend of Murdoch's, a Latin textbook to study on his own. With Latin, however, Robert made little progress, as Gilbert notes with a certain satisfaction. That he never advanced sufficiently to study classical poets 'in their original languages' troubled Burns enough that he mentions the matter in the second sentence of his preface to the Kilmarnock *Poems*, referring to Virgil and 'Theocrites'.[46] (Theocritus was often hailed as a kindred classical spirit by Allan Ramsay and other Scots vernacular poets because he wrote in Doric dialect.) Of Burns's disclaimer of classical learning in the preface, Jeffrey Skoblow has pointed out that it is two-sided, for at the same time Burns apologizes for not knowing the ancient poets 'in their original languages' he is informing readers that he has read them in translation.[47]

Burns did learn classical schemes and tropes, but at second hand through study of such poets as James Thomson, liberally represented (excerpts from 'Summer' and long extracts from 'Autumn') in Burns's first reader, most likely the 1764 edition of Arthur Masson's *A Collection of English Prose and Verse, for the Use of Schools*, which also included extended passages from Milton's *Paradise Lost*, Dryden's *Alexander's Feast* and Pope's *The Messiah* as well as generous samplings of the more conversational style of the London periodicals, from Addison and Steele's *Spectator* to Hawkesworth's *Adventurer* to Johnson's *Rambler*.[48] In Burns's early years, the teaching methods used by the poet's father and the schoolmaster Murdoch (in 1766, an eighteen-year-old university student privately retained by several Alloway families),[49] emphasized memorization, recitation and paraphrase of poems. In the 1790s, Murdoch looked back on the lessons he and William Burnes devised for Robert (age six) and Gilbert (age five):

> The method pursued by their father and me in instructing them ... was, to make them thoroughly acquainted with the meaning of every word in each sentence, that was to be committed to memory. Bye the bye, this may be easier done, and at an earlier period, than is generally thought. As soon as they were capable of it, I taught them to turn verse into its natural prose order; sometimes to substitute synonymous expressions for poetical words, and to supply all the ellipses. These, you know, are the means of knowing that the pupil understands his author. These are excellent helps to the arrangement of words in sentences, as well as to a variety of expression.[50]

At an age not much older than six (for Murdoch worked with the Alloway children for only three years in all), Burns studied a variety of classic English texts. He was tasked to memorize passages from *Paradise Lost* and in adulthood frequently paraphrases and quotes from Milton, especially from the parts of book 4 describing Adam and Eve's happiness in their bower. The first English poem he remembered loving at school was by Joseph Addison and had appeared in 1712 in the *Spectator*. If he could not read the classics in Latin or Greek, he knew from childhood the sophisticated transpositions and word-play of the neoclassics and Augustans. Some of the scenic descriptions in 'The Vision' derive from the luscious imagery of Thomson's *Seasons*, and the free-floating misanthropy of Burns's fretting speaker in 'The Vision' had models in the speakers both of Gray's 'Eton College' ode and 'Elegy in a Country Churchyard' (1742–51). While Shenstone's importance to Burns is typically deplored, Gray himself had learned from him, for Gray's resonant image of mute inglorious Miltons in line 59 of his 'Elegy' evidently recasts in elegiac terms a passage in the 1742 version of 'The Schoolmistress' that assesses, in a joking context, the future potential of the little scholars:

> Even now sagacious foresight points to show
> A little bench of heedless bishops here,
> And there a chancellor in embryo,
> Or bard sublime ...   (ll. 244–8)[51]

Gray and Shenstone were not represented in Masson's textbook until editions later than the one Burns studied. He found them somewhere, however, and pored over their poems, adapting their style and diction in his own writings in order to respectfully evoke people in humble circumstances. He liked to set 'high' and 'low' (Robert Crawford says 'little' and 'large') in interactive motion.[52] All poets are sensitive to shifting levels of language, but as a speaker of Scots vernacular who all his life had read a Bible, sung hymns and studied textbooks in formal and conversational English, Burns was unusually sensitive to the link between levels of address and social status, language-choices that conveyed respectful acknowledgement or (as in satire) its contrary. 'The Vision' describes Kyle vividly in a mixture of Scots passages and more ceremonious stanzas that honour the region by using the elevated English diction 'standard' for serious poetry. It is probably in mock-epic's tightly choreographed clashes of conversational and embellished style that Burns most effectively showcased his command of standard English, his close and productive study of eighteenth-century Augustan precursors.

Burns's Years in Dumfries versus Wordsworth's Elegiac Recasting with an Account of Two Men who Eluded their Elegists

> Too frail to keep the lofty vow
> That must have followed when his brow
> Was wreathed – 'The Vision' tells us how –
>   With holly spray,
> He faltered, drifted to and fro,
>   And passed away.[53]
>
> Wordsworth, 'Thoughts Suggested the Day Following, on the Banks of Nith,
> Near the Poet's Residence'

The fervid poems inspired by Wordsworth's first visit to Dumfries in 1803 position Wordsworth on virtue's side of a gulf created by what he saw as Burns's wilful self-destruction. Christopher Ricks observes of one such poem that 'Never does one feel more sympathy with Burns than when one sets him beside Wordsworth on Burns'.[54] I have wondered whether the ferocity of remonstration in some of Wordsworth's comments on Burns draws on a perceived analogy between what he knew of Coleridge's struggles and what he therefore assumed about Burns's later life. In 'Thoughts Suggested the Day Following' he grieves that Burns was 'too frail to keep the lofty vow' he 'must have' made when Coila crowned him with holly, as if Coila's visit had concerned a proposed regimen for Burns's personal reform. Poems in this vein dismiss Burns's last years as aimless, marked by 'rueful conflict, the heart riven / With vain endeavour' (ll. 51–2). In his certainty that Burns was preoccupied with hurtling to disaster in the 1790s, Wordsworth all but ignores the treasury of Burns's later songs ('the major part of the published repertory of Scottish song' according to *The Grove Dictionary of Music*).[55] He passes in silence over Burns's determined struggle against chronic illness and his in fact moderately successful efforts to support his family without relying either on farming or on the sale of his poems and songs.[56] Burns did his work well for the Excise. A letter discovered in 2010, written by the Dumfries Excise Collector John Mitchell, mentions Burns's visit to the Excise office to collect his salary a week before he died; it records a comment that expresses the poet's own view of his later life. After joking about his wraithlike appearance, Burns observed (shaving a year off his age) that he was 'only 36, 10 of which only I have been in the world, &, in that time, all I shall say, My good sir, I have not been idle'.[57]

Wordsworth saw the Kilmarnock *Poems* as the beginning of the end of Burns, but the poet himself viewed that hard-won achievement as day one of being 'in the world'. A week before his death he could say truthfully that he had not wasted his time. Shortly before his final illness, he served for four months as Acting Supervisor at Dumfries during an illness of the regular Excise supervisor Alexander Findlater. According to his across-the-street neighbour Jessie Lewars, he gave to his wife Jean Armour one of the first gowns of gingham cloth (favoured by the gentry ladies) seen on a townswoman of Dumfries.[58] The poet's son Robert, interviewed during the 1830s, described his family's life in Dumfries, recalling 'much rough comfort in the house'. 'When good company assembled, which was often the case, the hospitable board which they surrounded was of a patrician mahogany'. The 'many presents of jam and country produce from the rural gentlefolk, besides occasional barrels of oysters from Hill, Cunningham, and other friends in town' resulted in his father's being 'possibly ... as much envied by some of his neighbours as he has since been pitied by the general body of his countrymen'.[59] In a book kept by Findlater that records his evaluations of twelve officers, Burns is among five who receive a top rating, while others are classified more critically: 'does his best', 'indifferent', 'doubtful'.[60] Dorothy Wordsworth much disliked the bustle of Dumfries: 'We were glad to leave'. During their visit the Wordsworths 'could think of little except poor Burns, and his moving about on that unpoetic ground'.[61] But Burns enjoyed his town life. Transferring the lease on his last farm in September 1791 had been a relief: 'Tis, as a Farmer, paying dear unconscionable rent, *a cursed life*! ... devil take the life of reaping the fruits that another must eat'.[62]

In the group of poems inspired by the Wordsworths' visit of 1803 (though most remained unfinished for decades), Wordsworth repeatedly deplores Burns's later years. During the 1790s Burns was often ill; he quarrelled with some friends and offended some associates, often because of political differences; but he was held in affection by many (including Jean Armour's parents, with whom he was reconciled). James Currie, Burns's biographer, never forgot that Burns and he had differed 'rather vehemently', perhaps politically, during their one chance meeting in a Dumfries street.[63] In contrast, Maria Riddell, occasional target of Burns's satiric pen, told Currie years after Burns's death that her own recent illness had led her to think about one compensation when she died: enjoying eternity with Burns while 'riding about the spheres on a comet's tail together'.[64] During the 1790s, there was civil unrest in Dumfries, one of the sites of the bread riots that spread across Britain in 1795. Also in 1795, Burns was devastated by the sudden death of his youngest daughter shortly before her third birthday. No more uniformly merry than any other person's life, Burns's nonetheless was neither dysfunctional nor pitiable. There is no evidence of dereliction of responsibility such as that alleged by Currie – or, following Currie, Francis Jeffrey, whose 1809 review of Cromek's *Reliques* depicted the poet as nightly carousing at taverns while his children were 'famishing' and his 'wife's heart ... breaking at her cheerless fireside'.[65] Currie was well-meaning but obtuse as a reader of character; and as a recovering alcoholic he saw the frequenting of taverns as a sign of weak character. He never concedes that measuring the contents of ale barrels, part of Burns's duties as an Exciseman, necessarily brought him into taverns.[66] Wordsworth is on record in his 'Letter to a Friend of Robert Burns' (1816) as distrusting Currie's series of circumstantial innuendos (for example, 'He who suffers the pollution of inebriation, how shall he escape other pollution? But let us refrain from the mention of errors over which delicacy and humanity draw the veil'[67]). Yet Wordsworth did not pull his own version of an out-of-control poet out of thin air. He simply read the most overwrought Kilmarnock poems as representations of Burns's customary state of mind rather than as reflections of the crisis of early and mid-1786.

'To a Mountain Daisy', for instance, written in April 1786, mourns all those crushed by the hazards and difficulties of life. The modest daisy has been cut down by the ploughshare in her first bloom; 'suffering worth' has 'striven' against 'woes and wants' only to be ruined at last (this stanza may refer to Burns's excellent but finally defeated and embittered father). The 'artless Maid' is betrayed and abandoned; the 'luckless Bard' is drowned in 'Life's rough ocean'. In several stanzas Burns uses anaphoric repetition of initial phrases to create a kind of anti-Beatitudes, a list of the unblessed and the ruined:

> ... Such is the fate of artless Maid
> ... Such is the fate of simple Bard
> ... Such fate to suffering worth is giv'n ...

The final stanza envisions not only the daisy but the speaker as 'crush'd' by 'Stern Ruin':

> Ev'n thou who mourn'st the *Daisy*'s fate,
> *That fate is thine* – no distant date;
> Stern Ruin's *plough-share* drives, elate,
>   Full on thy bloom,
> Till crush'd beneath the *furrows* weight,
>   Shall be thy doom![68]

'To a Mountain Daisy' was a favourite poem of Dorothy Wordsworth and is among those most often mentioned by Wordsworth. In the sonnet 'There! said a stripling' (1833), a boy points out to the visiting speaker the field in which Burns's daisy was cut down. Following the cue provided in Burns's original, where poet and daisy both encounter the ploughshare of sudden ruin, Wordsworth ends with a hint of double victims by using one of his distinctively multidirectional pronouns. 'One' points (as in Burns's original) to two implied referents, a martyred flower and a martyred poet:

> Myriads of daisies have shone forth in flower
> Near the lark's nest, and in their natural hour
> Have passed away; less happy than the One
> That, by the unwilling ploughshare, died to prove
> The tender charm of poetry and love.[69]

The ploughshare of 'Ruin' is 'elate' in Burns's poem but 'unwilling' in Wordsworth's, who (along with implying that the ploughman intended the daisy no harm) may be hinting that Burns himself rushed forward at least half way to meet his doom. Wordsworth takes his imagery directly from Burns's poem, a lament and elegy mourning what he feared would be the ruin of Jean Armour; he grieves over her loss as he begins to contemplate a hazardous voyage and life in Jamaica. Yet although Wordsworth does hint that a stronger-willed poet would not have perished like a daisy, these gentle lines at least do not scold.

In 1786 Burns faced exile, a prospect that filled him with horror. In 1781, another epicentre of sorrowful poems, health and family difficulties plagued him as did the failure of a business venture in flax-dressing. A serious courtship ended that year with what Burns refers to as a 'jilting with peculiar circumstances of mortification', linking his disappointed courtship in 1781 to the disastrous marriage agreement with Jean Armour five years later: evidently his lack of means to support a wife in a separate household caused both ruptures.[70] Early in life Burns wrote and dreamed but he also fretted, seeing no workable way of entering 'the world'. In heightened poetic style 'The Vision' portrays his hopes and fears in those years before he published; these same issues are addressed more informally in his verse-letters to Smith, Siller, Lapraik and others.

Wordsworth both admired and in part objected to 'The Vision'. 'To the Sons of Burns' warns the boys specifically against the 'light from Heaven' stanza as a 'seductive lay' (ll. 39–42). Burns's surviving sons (Robert, the eldest, was then seventeen) are instructed to 'think and fear' (half-echoing the last line of 'To a Mouse'), to 'be admonished' (l. 47) by thoughts of their father's premature death. Drawing the sons' attention to the gravesite is all but cruel in context, for the family's second son, fourteen-year-old Francis Wallace, had died only three weeks before the Wordsworths' visit. The expensive Burns mausoleum was years in the future; Jean Armour had not yet placed even the small white stone that briefly marked the grave. In 1803 nothing as yet identified the burial place not only of Burns but two of his sons, neither of whom had deliberately provoked his own untimely death any more than their father had. Wordsworth's poem to Burns's sons nonetheless conveys his fraternal feelings for Burns, as his speaker assumes the role of surrogate father, advising them with all a parent's stern authority.

Burns too could have a heavy hand with elegy. His neo-Ossianic 'On the Death of Sir J. Hunter Blair' becomes monotonous because it is pitched wholly on the level of abstraction (the opening phrase calls the sun 'the lamp of day' and a chain of similar periphrases, some taken from Macpherson, continues throughout).[71] Yet his elegy for 'Tam Samson' is excellent, written in lively Scottish vernacular but neoclassic in its much inverted diction: 'Now safe the stately Saumont sail' (l. 31). Burns's mock-elegy is a call, like the elegy for Hunter Blair, for universal mourning, but here the world mourns not the loss of a civic-minded baronet but of a popular nurseryman and, more relevant to the elegy, Kilmarnock's keenest sportsman. In 1786, Thomas Samson of Kilmarnock was elderly and ailing but far from being deceased, living for another nine years. According to anecdote, at the Kilmarnock tavern where Burns performed this mock-elegy Samson, who was present, became agitated by the phrase 'Tam Samson's dead!', repeated at the end of each stanza, at one point interrupting to protest that 'I'm no dead yet! I'm worth ten dead fowk!'[72] Amused, Burns produced a new final stanza whose last line informs the world that '*Tam Samson's livin*!' (l. 100).

Before setting out for his last day of bird-shooting at the end of what he thought would be his last hunting season, Tam Samson had remarked that he would choose to die that day while out on the moors and be buried on the spot. Burns kindled at the thought of this continuing zeal for old pursuits. Ordinarily caustic on the topic of hunters or hunting, he confines any critique of Tam's beloved pastime to a fantasy of a 'spitefu' muirfowl' avenging herself by incubating her young on his lonely grave (l. 75) and two stanzas in which the salmon, trout, eels and pike celebrate Tam's disappearance into 'Death's *fish creel*' while the partridges, moorcock and hares 'rejoice', strut about in the open and make as much noise as they please (ll. 31–42). The poem, probably written during the summer of 1786 when Burns was staying near his printer's office in Kilmarnock while eluding the Armours, is the cheeriest of those written that summer, although like all Scots mock-elegies it is grim around the edges, as Tam's own reaction suggests.

This is a Burns poem one would not expect Wordsworth to admire, yet he was drawn to it, adapting certain elements in 'Simon Lee, the Old Huntsman', one of his more elusive *Lyrical Ballads*. As with 'Resolution and Independence', the poem about Simon Lee refers to a real-life encounter: the huntsman had lived nearby in 1798 when Wordsworth had stayed with his sister at Alfoxton house in Somerset to be close to Coleridge. Simon Lee shares several traits with Tam Samson, for both enter poetic tradition as men who in different ways ward off their elegists. Both also share an unusual capacity for vehement emotion and a continuing enthusiasm for the sporting pursuits of their younger days. Thomas Samson's real-life protest says it all: they're 'no dead yet', far from it. Tam, a physical wreck, limps out joyously to hunt. No matter that 'Auld-age his body batters / [and] ... the Gout his ancles fetters' (ll. 49–50). Lee, who as huntsman ran behind the hounds during the hunt but by the 1790s could hardly walk, told Wordsworth in 1798 that he still 'dearly loved to hear' the 'voices' of the hounds, a line that Wordsworth worked verbatim into the poem (l. 48). Simon is too feeble to work his plot of land on the common but he daily perseveres. His 'ancles' are swollen, a matter mentioned twice by Wordsworth. Tam Samson's swollen 'ancles' that make hunting on foot difficult are likewise mentioned by Burns. Yet the spirits of these two have not been muted by ailments or age. In a note written in 1845, Wordsworth marvels at his detailed memory of the old huntsman who had thanked him with tears for assistance in clearing a tree root and who had confided to the poet that he still loved to hear baying hounds. Tam Samson is as zealous as ever to fish and shoot: with grotesque glee Burns imagines Death felling Tam just as Tam, dying happy, slays five birds with one shot (l. 65). Simon Lee's gratitude for the speaker's help – 'The tears into his eyes were brought, / And thanks and praises seemed to run / So fast out of his heart, I thought / They never would have done' (ll. 97–100) – infuses the simple anecdote with a potential, says the speaker, to become 'a tale' to enlighten readers. Wordsworth tried to rework 'Simon Lee' towards some clearer message, but what his lines convey is how Simon looked and felt that day. The poem is like a snapshot dating back to 1798, like one of those representations of the human countenance in early photographs that Walter Benjamin said retained 'aura' despite being secondary and a reproduction.[73] Simon Lee turns readers away from mourning and elegy; they admire his persistence and ponder his gratitude for a small kindness. Both Burns and Wordsworth begin by emphasizing their characters' advancing years and failing health; but both heroes prove resistant, refusing to go away. Burns blithely concedes elegiac failure: his original design must be abandoned, for this man is '*livin*'' (l. 100). In his late note on 'Simon Lee', written when Wordsworth himself was seventy-five, the poet marvels that 'after an interval of 45 years, [I have] the image of the old man as fresh before my eyes as if it was yesterday'.[74] Both poets bring their subjects fresh before readers' eyes.

'Simon Lee' is among Wordsworth's most striking adaptations of Burns. In Wordsworth's poems addressing Burns's premature death, however, Burns the elegiac subject (unlike Simon Lee) never escapes from Wordsworth's mournful grip. Continuing to respond to 'The Vision', Wordsworth also cites other self-accusing Kilmarnock texts that remain to be discussed, including 'Despondency, An Ode' and 'A Bard's Epitaph'. These poems in which Burns reveals his failings and fears supplied Wordsworth with what he took as proof of the fatal weakness of poets. In his own presumptive self-elegies in 1786, Burns did see himself as a doomed and drowned man; yet in fact (like Tam Samson) he was not dead yet. He recovered from the tribulations of 1786 and survived another ten years as a poet and writer of songs. Yet the Burns that Wordsworth loved and remembered was that lost-boy Burns of 1786.

Dejected Visions

Wordsworth's 'Written in a Blank Leaf of Macpherson's Ossian' (1824) offers a likely allusion to a doomed Burns. The best poets, this poem argues, are those such as Orpheus about whom nothing at all is known or those such as Ossian whose writing survives only in fragments. Strangely, given this topic, Wordsworth includes John Milton among his unknowns, perhaps because nothing scandalous is known of him. Orpheus, Musaeus, Maeonides, Milton and Ossian are summoned as a contrast to modern poets who are unnamed but described in ways that bring to mind both Burns and Coleridge:

> When thousands, by severer doom,
> Full early to the silent tomb
> Have sunk, at Nature's call; or strayed
> From hope and promise, self-betrayed;
> The garland withering on their brows;
> Stung with remorse for broken vows;
> Frantic – else how might they rejoice?
> And friendless, by their own sad choice! (ll. 45–52)[75]

The withered 'garland' suggests the joyous but in Wordsworth's view false epiphany of 'The Vision'. Wordsworth may also be associating transgressive poets with Eve in *Paradise Lost*: the 'garland' Adam has gathered for her drops from his 'slack hand' as she cheerfully tells him her sin.[76] Wordsworth's 'Stung with remorse for broken vows' remembers the last line of the Kilmarnock poem 'The Lament', although in Burns the broken promise is Jean Armour's (l. 78): Burns's speaker sees a 'hopeless, comfortless' life ahead and all because of a '*A faithless woman's broken vow*'.[77]

'Despondency, An Ode' follows 'The Lament' in the Kilmarnock volume. There is no surviving manuscript for either; both appeared for the first time as printed in 1786 and both speak to events of that spring. Kinsley's note reads them both as commentaries on Jean Armour's retreat from the marriage agreement, but blame is actually redistributed in 'Despondency' as the speaker points chiefly to himself. 'Listless, yet restless', he labours without an 'aim' and without 'hope'. He is not like other men, taking examples from two wildly disparate groups, hermits ('blest' Solitaries) and men of business:

> Happy! Ye sons of Busy-life,
> Who, equal to the bustling strife,
>   No other view regard!
> Ev'n when the wished *end's* deny'd,
> Yet while the busy *means* are ply'd,
>   They bring their own reward:
> Whilst I, a hope-abandon'd wight,
>   Unfitted with an *aim*,
> Meet ev'ry sad-returning night,
>   And joyless morn the same.
>   You, bustling and justling,
>   Forget each grief and pain;
>   I, listless, yet restless,
>   Find ev'ry prospect vain.   (ll. 15–28)[78]

James Kinsley traces echoes in 'Despondency' of Pope's 'Eloisa to Abelard', Edward Young's 'Night Thoughts', Thomas Parnell's 'The Hermit' and most importantly Gray's 'Ode on a Distant Prospect of Eton College'.[79]

Gray's speaker takes a 'distant' view of the playing fields of his old school from the terrace of Windsor Castle – also from the distancing perspectives of middle age and chronic mourning, the mood of so many of Gray's poems. The children's shouts are as far away as childhood, happiness and long-departed friends. Gray's elegiac thoughts have a bitter tinge. Unlike Wordsworth in the 'Immortality' ode or Burns in 'The Vision', he ponders the 'gen'ral mirth' not with 'boundless love' ('The Vision') or measured sympathy (Wordsworth's 'Immortality' ode) but grim irony: what those poor children don't know. Unlike Wordsworth in his poem to the sons of Burns, Gray's speaker does not warn the boys themselves, for adult consciousness ('thought') would 'destroy' their 'paradise': 'No more; where ignorance is bliss, / 'Tis folly to be wise' (ll. 99–100). Still, he cannot help but think of what lies in store:

> Alas, regardless of their doom,
> The little victims play!
> No sense have they of ills to come,
> Nor care beyond to-day!
> Yet see how all around 'em, wait
> The ministers of human fate,
> And black Misfortune's baleful train!
> Ah, show them where in ambush stand
> To seize their prey the murderous band!
> Ah! Tell them they are men! (ll. 51–60)[80]

All adults feel sadness according to their temperaments: 'The tender for another's pain / The unfeeling for his own' (ll. 93–4). In mirror-lines Burns's 'Despondency' speaks of inevitable grief for 'the follies or the crimes / Of others, or my own!' (ll. 61–2). As in Gray, in Burns's ode the misery that follows not only from 'hate' but even from 'human love' makes a sad change from childish play:

> Ye tiny elves that guiltless sport,
>   Like linnets in the bush,
> Ye little know what ills ye court,
>   When Manhood is your wish!
>   The losses, the crosses,
>   That *active man* engage;
>   The fears all, the tears all,
>   Of dim, declining *Age*!   (ll. 63–70)

Gray's speaker is a solitary grown-up linked to the playing boys only by line of sight and distant memories; Burns draws the children at play closer yet likewise uses them to contrast with his despondency: the children are unlike him because they are 'guiltless'. Wordsworth's ode turns the tables: children do not lack something ('thought' in Gray; guilt in Burns) but have something that adults have lost: philosophers (l. 110) and prophets (l. 114), they can teach adults how to reconnect with joy. Wordsworth either knew Gray's 'Eton College' ode well or had rediscovered its images through Burns's 'Despondency', which receives high praise in a letter to Coleridge of February 1799: 'Burns is ... energetic solemn and sublime in sentiment, and profound in feeling. His 'Ode to Despondency' I can never read without the deepest agitation.'[81]

As suggested even by their similar titles, Coleridge's 'Dejection: An Ode', written in response to the early-completed stanzas of Wordsworth's 'Immortality' ode, bears some kinship to Burns's 'Despondency'.[82] The epigraph for 'Dejection' is taken from a Scots ballad that tells of the fatal voyage to fetch Margaret, child-inheritor of Scotland's throne, from Norway in 1290.[83] Coleridge's speaker, like the sailor-hero of the ballad, sees an omen in the appearance of the moon, watching a gathering storm through his window and associating it with a poet's turbulent moods and, as in the ballad, with looming disaster. The wind, not the small child, becomes a 'mighty poet, ev'n to frenzy bold' (l. 109) but like Gray, Burns and Wordsworth, Coleridge looks back on *former* joy: 'There was a time', the first phrase in his stanza four, echoes the first phrase in Wordsworth's ode. Coleridge is closest to Burns in mood in ascribing his speaker's 'afflictions' to his own impurity: and as in Burns's 'Despondency', joy is for others, not for such as he. It visits only 'the pure and in their purest hours' (l. 65). Wordsworth and Coleridge take up Burns's technique, derived from Gray's 'Eton College' ode, of suggesting his own state of mind by contrast to the happiness of others. Burns's speaker looks about and sees self-respecting businessmen, patient hermits and laughing children but can join none of those groups. Wordsworth's ode, in contrast to both Burns's and Coleridge's, refuses a stance of distance, painstakingly constructing a thoughtful connection to the playful young creatures around him.

Burns's intricately rhymed fourteen-line stanza in 'Despondency' is that of Ayrshire-born Alexander Montgomerie in 'The Cherry and the Slae' (*c.* 1584). Like Pindar's original odes, Montgomerie's stanza was designed to be performed to music; Douglas Dunn observes that his 'elaborate structure, this stanza-form, looks ... like the vehicle of High Culture (the property of "Great Folk")'.[84] As a court poet, Montgomerie did address the great folk of his day. His complex new Scottish form, with its plentiful rhyme and alternating line lengths, is a fine homegrown equivalent to a classical ode. Yet while Burns used this stanza memorably for other purposes, his two ode-like adaptations of Montgomerie are uneven, rich though they are in suggesting Burns's chaotic emotions at the time he conceived and wrote each of them ('To Ruin' in 1781–2 and 'Despondency' in late spring 1786). Only in stanza four of 'Despondency' does Burns bring together his multiple topics – the pursuit of money, adult desire, purity of conduct, grown-up sorrow, childlike play and, in closing, a brief flash of anger at the Armours:

> Than [sic] I, no *lonely Hermit* plac'd
> Where never human footstep trac'd,
> Less fit to play the part,
> The *lucky moment* to improve;
> And *just* to stop, and *just* to move,
> With *self-respecting* art:
> But ah! those pleasures, Loves and Joys,
> Which I too keenly taste,
> The *Solitary* can despise,
> Can want, and yet be blest!
> He needs not, he heeds not,
> Or human love or hate;
> Whilst I here, must cry here,
> At perfidy ingrate! (ll. 43–57)

The speaker admits that he would make a poor sort of hermit but is even 'less fit' to calculate profit-or-loss before all else, to control his every impulse. He cannot 'improve the lucky moment', strategizing his behaviour. He cannot like a hermit 'despise' 'human love' but admits that pleasure often turns to sadness and socializing to 'hate'. The sinuous footprint of the Montgomerie stanza here is matched by a successful interweaving of disparate topics and multiple rhymes.

In other stanzas Montgomerie's demanding rhyme scheme is executed without flaw but not with Burns's usual adventurous novelty: rhyme in the first stanza is wholly masculine even in the case of the two-syllable word: 'care', 'bear', 'sigh', 'load', 'road' 'I', 'view', 'appear'. Only the last four lines of stanza two employ Burns's trademark feminine rhymes and slant rhymes ('bustling and justling'; 'listless, yet restless'). At seventy lines the poem is also shorter than most odes. In 'Epistle to Davie', by contrast, Montgomerie's stanza meanders through a variety of topics in one of Burns's most striking verse-letters, which touches on friendship, love, poetry and fear of an uncertain future – or rather a homeless future seen as all too likely. Also written in Montgomerie's measure are all the 'recitativo' sections of the cantata 'Love and Liberty' (Burns takes the term recitativo from Fergusson's 'The Canongate Playhouse in Ruins'), which frame the simple, largely English songs of the beggars. 'Love and Liberty' is disjected rather than dejected. The recitativo shows the gritty details omitted from the beggars' happy songs: the cold November setting, the rags and oatmeal being traded for drink, the cheerful soldier's amputated limbs, the urgent, furtive sex behind the chicken coop. In 'Love and Liberty', Montgomerie's form serves as a grim reality-check that contradicts the drunken beggars' repeated assertion in their songs that they alone are 'free' and 'happy'.

The short, simple poem written just after 'Despondency' was finished shows a different side of Burns's mood in spring 1786 – not dejection but poetic wrath. It is titled from the verse of the Book of Jeremiah that it paraphrases: 'Jeremiah 15.th Ch. 10 V'. In his travails Burns had evidently been studying the Bible and he here accesses a prophet's denunciations of his faithless community. In the Bible verse Jeremiah complains that God's curse has fallen on him unfairly, for he has never broken faith. Scolded by God, the prophet scolds back:

> Woe is mee, my mother, that that thou hast borne me a man of strife, and a man of contention to the whole earth: I haue neither lent on vsurie, nor men haue lent to me on vsurie, yet euery one of them doeth curse me. (King James Version).

Burns liked the short paraphrase (below) well enough to copy the lines into his volume of Robert Fergusson's poems and, years later, into the Glenriddell Manuscript:

> Ah, woe is me, my Mother dear!
>   A man of strife ye've born me!
> For sair contention I maun bear,
>   They hate, revile and scorn me. –
>
> I ne'er could lend on bill or band,
>   That five per cent might blest me;
> And borrowing, on the tither hand,
>   The de'il a ane wad trust me. –
>
> Yet I, a coin-denied wight,
>   By Fortune quite discarded,
> Ye see how I am, day and night,
>   By lad and lass blackguarded. –[85]

Wordsworth could not have read this self-defensive poem, which offers some counterbalance to such self-elegizing poems as 'The Lament', for like 'Love and Liberty' it was not printed during Burns's lifetime.

Burns sees in the Bible text many parallels with his present miseries: the Armours are pressing him for money they must know he does not possess; he has been scorned by Jean Armour despite their vow (she has not kept faith from his perspective). All in Kyle revile him (Burns's public penances extended for several weeks that summer) although he has never hurt them. They serve mammon while he has remained faithful to a higher calling – not indeed as God's prophet but as Scotland's '*Patriot-Bard*' ('The Cotter's Saturday Night', l. 188). In the Bible the Lord relents, telling Jeremiah that those who continue faithless 'shall fight against thee, but they shall not preuaille ... And I will deliuer thee out of the hand of the wicked, and I will redeeme thee out of the hand of the terrible' (Jeremiah 15:20). Not only will the prophet be blessed, but his enemies will be destroyed by various gruesome means described in detail. In inscribing this paraphrase (which, as with other entries in the Glenriddell Manuscript, he did not intend to publish) into his copy of Fergusson's poems, Burns transfers his own situation during the worst crisis of his life to his favourite poet, who had died in terror and poverty at twenty-four in the Edinburgh madhouse, abandoned, like Jeremiah, by all but a few loyal friends.

Or Build Your House Upon This Grave

'A Bard's Epitaph' was expressly written to conclude *Poems, Chiefly in the Scottish Dialect*. Kinsley lists it as #104 of Burns's poems, printing it just before 'Epistle to a Young Friend' for which there is a manuscript copy dated 15 May 1786.[86] The epitaph invites the sigh of a kindred spirit over the bard's grave, and in 1799 Wordsworth offers that tribute in a mirror-poem, 'A Poet's Epitaph'. In stanza 4, Burns describes the Bard's temperament:

> The poor Inhabitant below
> Was quick to learn and wise to know,
> And keenly felt the friendly glow,
>   And *softer flame*;
> But thoughtless follies laid him low,
>   And stain'd his name![87]

The final stanza draws a moral: 'prudent, cautious, *self-controul* / Is Wisdom's root' (ll. 25–30). Wordsworth reads the epitaph literally, as a 'confession', a 'history in the shape of a prophecy! What more was required of the biographer, than to have put his seal to the writing, testifying that the foreboding had been realized and that the record was authentic?'[88]

Burns's opening stanzas invite, as kindred spirits to the deceased, three mourners to the gravesite: a 'whim-inspired fool', 'a bard of rustic song' and 'a man of judgment clear' who nonetheless sometimes runs 'wild' (ll. 1, 7, 15, 18). Wordsworth's poem likewise begins with a list of prospective mourners – 'statists', lawyers, 'men of rosy cheer', and physicians and moralists – but they are excluded as being incapable of understanding the departed poet. The Soldier is welcome but only if he lays down his sword. A truly cordial greeting goes out only to one mourner: an approaching ghost who looks like Burns, for he appears in a peasant's russet coat such as Burns describes himself wearing in l. 37 of 'Epistle to James Smith'. This Burns-apparition never speaks but is spoken for in such a way that both poets are evoked, for 'A Poet's Epitaph' is among Wordsworth's most Burnsworthian writings. As in 'Resolution and Independence' Burns is introduced only as 'He'. Wordsworth's octosyllabic cadence and series of questions partly answer Burns's rhetorical questions in standard Habbie: 'Is there a Bard of rustic song' (Burns); 'Art thou a statist in the van' (Wordsworth). Yet if Burns's epitaph warns readers away from emulation of the departed bard, Wordsworth's ends with an enigma:

> But who is He, with modest looks,
> And clad in homely russet brown?
> He murmurs near the running brooks
> A music sweeter than their own.

... In common things that round us lie,
Some random truths he can impart, –
The harvest of a quiet eye
That broods and sleeps on his own heart.

But he is weak; both man and boy,
Hath been an idler in the land;
Contented if he might enjoy
The things which others understand.

– Come hither in thy hour of strength;
Come, weak as is a breaking wave!
Here stretch thy body at full length;
Or build thy house upon this grave.[89]

These last stanzas (including two not quoted) flicker in and out of an eerie dual portrait. The quiet eye that broods on its own heart sounds most like Wordsworth, although it applies to Burns in some moods; while the reference to a poet who is weak sounds like Wordsworth's version of Burns but nonetheless is like Wordsworth's speaker too in certain poems including 'Resolution and Independence'. Both epitaphs raise the same question as the epitaph that ends Gray's 'Elegy': how does one 'read' a poet's life? Who can be trusted to approach, ponder the grave (and the poems) and interpret the inscriptions with any kind of sympathetic comprehension?

Wordsworth's inscrutable last line only raises further questions. How can the grave of a poet serve as the foundation of a house? What sort of house is built on a grave? (In films at any rate, such houses always are haunted.) His speaker cannot be saying literally that the house of Wordsworth, his whole career, has been built on the grave of a russet-coated bard. Too many other people similarly inspired Wordsworth: Coleridge, Dorothy Wordsworth, many others. It could be, however, that Wordsworth first dreamed of or glimpsed his poetic house in late boyhood when he read Burns at the age of sixteen, so that his encounter with *Poems, Chiefly in the Scottish Dialect* marked day one of his own poetic life. Such a reading is supported by imagery in a different poem, 'At the Grave of Burns', which describes two shocks that came to Wordsworth from Burns – his astonishment during his first encounter with Burns's *Poems* and his grief ten years later when he learned of Burns's death:

I mourned with thousands, but as one
More deeply grieved, for He was gone
Whose light I hailed when first it shone,
    And showed my youth
How Verse may build a princely throne
    On humble truth.[90]

Poets build on what they value, including what they find or half-create in the writings of other poets. In homage to Burns, Wordsworth even writes this poem in Burns's standard-Habbie form.

Throughout his career, Burns shows that 'exquisite regard for common things' that Wordsworth describes as the fertile ground of poetry.[91] Burns's imagery of birds, flowers and streams is shared by Wordsworth, who adds to these larger-scaled images of mountains and cataracts. Burns uses place names in the Kilmarnock poems to situate his poems geographically, to tie them to beloved places within Kyle. The later editions of *Lyrical Ballads* include a group of poems on 'the naming of places'; many more poems, among them 'Tintern Abbey', 'Hart Leap Well' and 'There was a boy' closely link the particularities of a local setting to the events or mood of the poem. Both poets love to describe the murmur of rivers: the Doon, the Afton, the Nith, the Wye and the Derwent. Both celebrate what Wordsworth calls 'The bond of union between life and joy'[92] and both distrust book learning, although in this matter Wordsworth is more consistent than Burns. Wordsworth writes of his university studies that 'I did not love / Judging not ill perhaps, the timid course / Of our scholastic studies'.[93] Burns writes 'gie me ae spark o' Nature's fire, / That's a' the learning I desire', but in another poem asserts that if you want to delight him, tell him that he is 'learned and clerk'.[94]

In a letter of 1818, John Keats speaks of Wordsworth's 'egotistical sublime': as a poet, Keats writes, Wordsworth is 'a thing *per se* and stands alone'.[95] Standing alone in the residue or afterglow of recollected emotion, Wordsworth's speaker repeatedly creates a poem by establishing a thoughtful connection between his subjects and his readers. Burns accesses multiple voices from Scottish history and various classes of Scotsmen and Scotswomen in order to speak personally but also collectively – which is to say that after 1786 Burns often reassumed a bardic role. The difference is that by then Rob Burness, the bard in Burns, was buried – not in his grave to be sure, but in codes that disclosed only single initials (R, B, X, Z) to identify most of his printed songs.[96] In contrast, Robert Burns (July 1786–July 1796) *is* a name, a famous signature. Wordsworth loved the self-conscious poet in Burns far more than the self-effacing bard: that his rejoinder to 'A Bard's Epitaph' is titled 'A Poet's Epitaph' in itself suggests his partly obstructed view of Burns's total achievement. For Wordsworth, the spirit of Burns was enshrined in a number of closely studied poems, mostly those printed in the Kilmarnock volume. In those he recognized a spirit both local and global, like his own. The Scottish poet's writings offered Wordsworth support and solace in moods both of strength and weakness; Burns's was a body of work against which he could measure himself, 'stretch' himself at full length.[97]

Keats sees the loftiness of Wordsworth as a potential limitation: 'What shocks the virtuous philosopher delights the chameleon poet'.[98] But although

Wordsworth was not always in sympathy with Burns's chameleon bardic voicings, there is no question that the English poet drew inspiration from his long contemplation of Burns. In 'At the Grave of Burns' he reflects that if Burns had lived longer, they could have been friends:

> True friends though diversely inclined;
> But heart with heart and mind with mind,
> Where the main fibres are entwined,
>   Through Nature's skill,
> May even by contraries be joined
>   More closely still. (ll. 43–8)

Geographically, the poem says, the two were almost 'neighbours' (l. 41); and even in heart and mind their diverse inclinations could well have drawn them all the more closely together, as Wordsworth and Coleridge had been for a time. Wordsworth could not prolong the Scottish poet's life and indeed seems annoyed at Burns for dying so young; but he does renew and extend Burns's voice, bringing back his imagery and (in a few poems including 'A Poet's Epitaph' and 'Resolution and Independence') even his ghost in poems that also reveal Wordsworth's own inmost heart and hopes for his poetry. In these poems of Burnsworthian conjunction, there truly is close friendship, a bond felt deeply despite all differences.

3 HIGHLANDS: BURNS, LADY NAIRNE AND NATIONAL SONG

> Well, my heart's in the Highlands
> Only place left to go.
>
> Bob Dylan, 'Highlands' (1997)[1]

Burns's idealizing vision of the Highlands did not stem from a favourable first impression. In June 1787, during the first of two brief Highland tours, he wrote from Arrochar to Robert Ainslie describing a forbidding scene: 'savage streams tumble over savage mountains, thinly overspread with savage flocks, which starvingly support as savage inhabitants'.[2] Yet three years later, this most iconic of Burns's Highland songs was sent to James Johnson's *Scots Musical Museuem*, the songbook series of which Burns was virtual co-editor:

> My heart's in the Highlands, my heart is not here;
> My heart's in the Highlands a chasing the deer;
> Chasing the wild deer, and following the roe;
> My heart's in the Highlands, wherever I go. –
> Farewell to the Highlands, farewell to the North;
> The birth-place of Valour, the country of Worth:
> Wherever I wander, wherever I rove,
> The hills of the Highlands for ever I love. –[3]

The song, among Burns's most popular, remembers the Highlands on behalf of all homesick exiles. It was especially popular during the nineteenth century but changed perceptions of the region even in Burns's own day, when many outside the area still thought of the Highlands chiefly as a centre for former insurgency. Burns's song sees the Highlands instead as a place of heroic resistance and natural beauty. This was among Sir Walter Scott's favourite Scottish songs. He quotes from it in *Waverley* (1814) and *Redgauntlet* (1824) and he sometimes performed it at festive gatherings.[4] The song and others like it helped to redefine the region as Scotland's high ground in more than a topographical sense. Scott himself, who divided his time between Edinburgh and Selkirk in the Border district, went on to develop Burns's idealizing vision of the Highlands in his first novel *Waverley*, which uses Highland settings and a Highland cast to explore Romantic aspects of Scottish character.

Imagery of this region as a place of astonishing beauty and noble resistance certainly did not begin with Burns, but he sent such imagery around the world through the ultra-portable (today we might call it viral) medium of songs, which he sometimes wrote but sometimes reconstructed from popular material. He culled eloquent phrases and haunting images from lyrics of prior generations: one example will soon be discussed, a song referring to the rising of 1689 that inspired 'Farewell to the Highlands'. Burns's portrait of the Highlands as a free space still haunts bardically inclined imaginations, as may be seen in Bob Dylan's song 'Highlands', which like Burns's Jacobite songs of the 1780s and 1790s is belated in its mood of balked desire. Dylan's speaker, like many of Burns's, 'talks to' himself 'in a monologue', imagining the Highlands as a place far from the tedium of 'life in the same old cage'.[5] He looks back, wishing 'someone would come / And push back the clock for me' (ll. 14–15). I will return to Dylan's song at several points in this chapter.

Burns's title is '*Farewell* to The Highlands': this song, like the later poems in the Kilmarnock edition, reflects on emigration and exile as facts of Scottish (and personal) history. Its speaker is transfixed by images of his past; here and now do not matter. The Highlands invite Burns's expression of various political viewpoints, just as Ayrshire's religious controversies had inspired Burns to explore its different factions in his early satires. Burns's later songs are not the break from his early work that is sometimes perceived, but among these later writings, the Jacobite and Highland songs turn from manners-painting (as the Muse of Kyle, Coila, calls Burns's sketches of local customs in 'The Vision') to lyrics with a more dreamlike quality.

Although some are edited down (or built up) from surviving Jacobite stanzas, Burns's songs do not support Jacobitism per se; he repurposes this material to address current events in an indirect way. He celebrates this new (to him) region of Scotland, just as in 'The Vision' he had honoured his homeland of Kyle; but his Highland songs also connect Scotland to other places – the North American colonies during the 1770s and 1780s; Western Europe in the 1780s and 1790s – that were struggling not to restore a dynasty but to overturn monarchy altogether. In addition, Jacobite song-revision allowed Burns to revisit his personal struggle in 1786, when he was forced to plan his own emigration. A somewhat muffled Poet Burns does emerge at times in these songs spoken by people so different from himself, historical figures including Charles Edward Stuart ('The small birds rejoice') and James Drummond, son of the fourth Viscount Strathallan ('Strathallan's Lament'). In those soliloquy songs, the poet dramatizes famous personages by channelling his own misery in 1786 as he booked and rebooked, three times, a voyage to Jamaica where he faced a future life as an overseer of slaves.

During his visit to Edinburgh (29 November 1786–June 1788) Burns sang almost nightly with new acquaintances whose sympathies ranged from Jacobite to Jacobin. Jacobites thought that the wrong dynasty had succeeded to power after the succession crises of 1688 and 1714; many also accepted the Stuarts' view of a monarch's total power, the idea that the providence of God, not consent of the governed, made them kings. The Jacobins of Burns's own day (the name derives from a club in France at different times associated with both the French Constitution and the Reign of Terror) were complex and their agenda shifted in response to the revolution as it unfolded, but it can be safely said that they were opposed to monarchy's assumption of hereditary privilege and prerogatives.

Probably it was in Edinburgh that Burns began to collect and seriously think about tunes and lyrics celebrating the Jacobite risings. The last of these rebellions had been suppressed in 1746, at which point the Highlands were further fortified – literally, by rebuilding one fort on a new site and extending the network of military roads. The fortification process had begun in 1724 but ended with the reconstruction of Fort George outside Inverness (the original was blown up by Jacobites in the rising of 1746) and completion of the last military road in the late 1750s. The Dress Act of 1746 prohibited the wearing of tartan; the law was rescinded as late as 1782, the year Burns turned twenty-three. In the eighteenth century the Highlands were already being cleared of people through cultivation of sheep over crops, a policy that dispossessed small farmers.[6]

Burns revised existing lyrics (Highland and Lowland songs as well, which he continued to write) to create a tapestry of *his* Scotland, his implied version of national character and history. He often speaks in these songs as a bard, that is, impersonally; his more self-dramatizing voice as Poet Burns on occasion almost emerges, as mentioned, softened by filtration through long-ago heroic speakers, sometimes historical and sometimes anonymous. When in bardic mode, he does not assume a mask to ponder his own emotions (as the Poet Burns persona does) but instead provides a showcase for speakers with whose opinions he may or may not agree, as in the bloodthirsty lullaby of a Highland mother soon to be discussed.

Burns saw the Highlands as 'savage' ground on his first visit. His response to its wild landscape, very different from Wordsworth's, suggests a farmer's instinctive disapproval of uncultivated spaces.[7] Yet he came to see the region both as a symbol of Scotland's past and a key to its soul. In Edinburgh he met Allan Masterton, a writing master with Jacobite sympathies who later taught in the High School and was a gifted amateur composer. Masterton wrote the music for several songs to which Burns fitted stanzas, notably 'Strathallan's Lament', a soliloquy recast in alternating eight- and seven-syllable lines whose tone is reminiscent of Shakespeare's and Milton's blank-verse solo speeches by Hamlet and Satan:

> In the cause of Right engaged,
>   Wrongs injurious to redress,
> Honor's war we strongly waged,
>   But the heavens deny'd success:
> Ruin's wheel has driven o'er us,
>   Not a hope that dare attend,
> The wide world is all before us -
>   But a world without a friend![8]

Burns's last two lines invert Milton's closing passage in *Paradise Lost*, for Strathallan has no partner in exile, no chance of redemption like that promised to Adam and Eve.[9] Wretched and fatherless after Culloden, he has no friend. As here, Burns often looks to the Highlands to evoke rebellion in a setting of unspoiled wildness: the first stanza of 'Strathallan's Lament' situates the refugee-speaker in a remote Highland cave. He is engulfed by sorrow and also by violent weather, the din of swollen 'torrents' (nearby streams) and the howling of a 'wintry' tempest.

After 1786, Burns shifted from the district of Kyle, to which he bids farewell in 'The Gloomy Night is Gath'ring Fast'. He lived near or in the town of Dumfries after 1788, and his later songs often celebrate nearby rivers, local people and regional archetypes, from his kind-hearted neighbour Jessie Lewars to roguish Galloway Tam.[10] Yet the Highlands became his site for songs of elegy and sorrow. One non-Jacobite example is his group of famous lyrics mourning Margaret Campbell (d. 1786) as 'Highland Mary'. He wrote the first two of these ('Flow Gently, Sweet Afton' and 'Thou Lingering Star') in 1789 within a year of beginning his work with Jacobite songs.

In printing 'Farewell to the Highlands' Burns used his Z code for folk-collected material but wrote in his specially interleaved copy of *Scots Musical Museum* that 'the first half-stanza of this song is old; the rest is mine'.[11] Those borrowed four lines are taken from an earlier source and they centre his song. His Gaelic tune was most likely associated with martial stanzas ('Failte na miosg' means 'the musket salute'). It can be difficult to assess levels of authorship in Burns's later songs. For example, he added to the Law MS (a list of titles he sent to James Johnson, printer of *The Scots Musical Museum*) a tantalizing note next to 'Farewell to the Highlands': 'Mr. Burns's old words'.[12] In withholding the exact nature of Mr Burns's dealings with the old words, the note could be hinting at anything from verbatim transmittal (which Burns's use of his Z code supports but does not necessarily prove) to original composition in an antique style.[13] Clearly the possessive ('Burns's') claims the lines in some fashion. The mystery is somewhat clarified by the existence of 'The Strong Walls of Derry', evidently Burns's source-text. 'Derry' was reprinted in volume 4 of *The Scots Musical Museum* in 1792, two years after 'Farewell to the Highlands' had appeared in volume 3.[14] From this song, which alludes to the Jacobite rising of 1689, Burns took four beautiful lines hidden towards the end. He greatly improves one of those four with small changes (adding one word and exchanging one consonant by changing 'doe' to 'roe'). As printed in *The Scots Musical Museum*, the quatrain in 'Strong Walls of Derry' reads as follows:

> My heart's in the Highlands, my heart is not here,
> My heart's in the Highlands, a chasing the deer;
> A chasing the deer, and following the doe;
> My heart's in the Highlands, wherever I go.[15]

In *Scots Musical Museum*, 'Strong Walls of Derry' is forty-eight-lines long (counting the choruses). Late placement at line 33 obscures its most famous stanza. The song's opening lines and chorus indicate its loose assortment of popular memes:

> The first day I landed, it was on Irish ground,
> The tidings came to me from fair Derry town,
> That my love was married, and to my sad woe;
> And I lost my first love, by courting too slow.
>   Chorus
>   Let us drink and go home, drink and go home,
>   If we stay any longer we'll get a bad name;
>   We'll get a bad name, and we'll fill ourselves fou,   'full'
>   And the strong walls of Derry it's ill to go through.[16]

That Burns focussed solely on stanza eight attests to his editorial acumen. Yet to know his source is to make his use of the possessive in describing the song in some ways more puzzling, for his best lines come almost verbatim from 'Strong Walls of Derry' and in that sense the *old* words are not his. Yet he did write twelve of the song's sixteen lines, which frame and enhance the captured Jacobite stanza, expanding the topic by exalting the Highlands as birthplace of valour and country of worth. In 'Strong Walls of Derry' the speaker begins on a note of woe but his sorrow is private and concerns his sweetheart's marriage to another; he does not speak as a man banished from his home. The speaker of 'Derry' never mentions defeat in battle; it is possible that the moment the song celebrates is a gathering before the Jacobite defeat at the Battle of the Boyne in July 1690.[17] Thus for his own version Burns harvested a small fraction of a popular lyric that had collected some detritus over the years since 1689–90. He simplifies and concentrates the imagery. A single sorrow, loss of the Highlands, preoccupies his speaker, who is alone, talking to himself (as Bob Dylan puts it in 'Highlands') in a monologue. He is not one among a happy group of boon companions, as in 'Strong Walls of Derry', but an outcast who cannot recover from his defeat, for he cannot go home: he will pine 'for ever'. Beyond personal loss of his homeland, he mourns an era when two old words, valour and worth, meant more.

In Jorge Luis Borges's story 'Pierre Menard, Author of the *Quixote*' (1939), a twentieth-century French author succeeds in replicating a small part of Cervantes's seventeenth-century Spanish masterwork without looking at the original.[18] The unreliable narrator insists that Menard's identical fragments nonetheless possess more depth and complexity than Cervantes's novel owing to the dissonance introduced by more than three centuries of intervening history. Burns's re-use yet thorough re-signification of 'old words' is curiously analogous in that his Jacobite songs, with their selective recycling of popular texts, preserve the old lyrics' vehemently adversarial spirit in the context of a greatly changed national and political landscape. Burns may present a partisan Jacobite speaker, as in 'O'er the Water to Charlie' or 'Strathallan's Lament', to express sympathy for Jacobite defeat and dispossession. He was always ready to commiserate with people in distress. Yet he might be inculcating a spirit of insurgency in his own day. In either case, Burns's temporal and ideological separation from Jacobite source-material – he was born sixty-nine years after the Battle of the Boyne – can be felt in his songs' belated and elegiac mood. In 'Farewell to the Highlands' his speaker is not carousing at a tavern in the epicentre of looming battle but surviving in grief-stricken exile. Burns changes jovially diffuse stanzas into what sounds exactly like an old fragment, a neo-Ossianic scrap of intense lyric emotion. Burns's version is short: the music he chose extends through the two octaves, with no refrain or return, no chorus.[19] The tune runs its course and stops; the performance is soon over.

If Burns's shifts in context and temporal perspective are considered, the oracular 'Mr. Burns's old words' begins to make more sense. He gave his song a Z code and in this case he meant it: the heart of the lyric comes from old words. Yet he has transplanted these words into a different type of song, elegiac and timeless rather than dizzy and in-the-moment. (The repeated chorus in 'Strong Walls of Derry' ponders only whether the assembled group should drink some more or go home now.) Burns's chief repetition is the name of a lost but never-to-be-forgotten homeland. His love songs often convey passion by similarly dwelling on the name of the beloved: Anna, Clarinda, Peggy, Mary, Jean. Here his sixteen-line song repeats 'Highlands' eleven times. The source-song, in contrast, repeats the word four times in forty-eight lines, with no mention of the Highlands in the chorus. 'Strong Walls of Derry' brings in the region almost in passing while Burns's revision sets the Highlands stanza as if it were a rare gem, both through placement (it goes first) and reiteration. Burns's speaker remembers a dreamlike landscape with a haunted quality, for it calls up tragic memories. Only in its last line does 'Derry' reprise the lines mentioning the Highlands. Otherwise it ends with a scattering of proverbs:

> There's many a word spoken, but few of the best,
> And he that speaks fairest is longest at rest;
> I speak by experience – my mind serves me so,
> But my heart's in the Highlands wherever I go.[20]

Printed just above this is that perfect quatrain. To become aware of Burns's keen eye for good lyric material is to learn how well his editorial sense served his broader poetic vision. Reconstructing and deconstructing existing songs brought him into close contact with the treasure house of traditional and popular Scottish lyrics; but he was forced to be selective, not only because of the profusion of songs being sung but the mixture of discursive and lyrically concentrated stanzas, especially within the older songs.

In 'Farewell to the Highlands' the speaker's heart is 'not here' (from whatever place he speaks) but forever looks back to a place he will never see again. The 'hills of the Highlands' stand in for everything else he has left behind. Pictorial vignettes such as this song's 'green vallies' and 'wild-hanging woods' are not mere conventions. Half-remembered vistas, blurred by time and distance, lead his speakers down a road to recollection.[21] The deer and the roe are not being described but *remembered*: Burns's Highland songs are chiefly concerned not with landscape but with memory. His Highland songs revive Jacobite speakers some forty years after the last of the risings, and his audience is invited to see dissent and political intransigence as heroic. Burns refurbishes the old lyrics in (and for) an altered political climate, yet one that shared with the Jacobite days a vehement and divisive debate over whether to adjust or abandon existing institutions. Burns's songs of tearful parting and solitary exile must have called to mind for some among his older audience (for whom these events had occurred within living memory) the national cataclysm of 1745–6. Burns's own-age peers, however, often entertained political visions of a different kind inspired by events of the 1770s to 1790s. That younger part of his audience may well have taken these songs, with their portrayal of heroic rebels, as friendly to current revolutionary movements.

Yet there is a third way to take these songs: as warnings against renewed rebellion. In Burns's Jacobite songs, with their far displacement back to prior generations, the revolution is always already over. His heroes have risked all but they have lost. During the 1790s Burns developed strong political opinions, yet crafted his songs in such a way that almost always they remain open to interpretation. It is usually possible to read them simply as nostalgic. Burns's neo-Jacobite songs blur sectarian and historical specifics, often by dwelling not on ideologies but emotions of longing and Romantic vistas, as in 'Farewell to the Highlands'.

The Highlands served Burns's imagination as a repository (once rich; now depopulated and almost emptied) of national cultural memory. The title *Scots Musical Museum*, the songbook series where he printed most of his post-1787 writing, suggests not only the recovery of artefacts that would otherwise be lost but their redefinition and display as cultural treasures.[22] Museum collections must be curated, thoughtfully chosen and displayed, or their cultural import is lost in an impression of randomness and disorder. Most museums preserve the remnants of social and aesthetic movements now belonging wholly to the past; and the

Highland-inflected songs that Burns sent to *Scots Musical Museum* likewise seem to emerge from the long-ago history of a primal, more authentic Scotland.

Bob Dylan's 'Highlands', in part a homage to Burns, likewise looks to the Highlands as a site that speaks to lost freedom and former happiness. Meditating on these now much diminished ideals reveals the insufficiency of the here-and-now. Dylan's speaker cannot turn up the sound on his audio equipment without complaint, cannot have a friendly conversation with a feminist waitress. He cannot 'trade places' (l. 85) with the carefree young people he sees dancing in the park. Nor will his purchase of a 'full-length leather coat' (l. 88) compensate for more pressing and authentic desires, as the sardonic speaker well knows. Dylan's 'Highlands', like Burns's 'Farewell to the Highlands', recognizes joy and spontaneity but they are far away and recovering them may no longer be possible. This motif is not necessarily age-related: the speaker in 'Bob Dylan's Dream', written when he was twenty-two, similarly yearns for a less compromised past existence:

> I wish, I wish, I wish in vain,
> That we could sit simply in that room again.
> Ten thousand dollars at the drop of a hat,
> I'd give it all gladly if our lives could be like that.[23]

The speaker of both songs feels unhappily severed from his ontological ground or spiritual home-place – the same forlorn position as Burns's in 'Farewell to the Highlands'. Dylan's 'Highlands' song imagines travelling there one day; but even though for him the way back is not barred by political exile, he intends to proceed with caution, to 'go there' only when he 'feels good enough' (l. 5) taking 'one step at a time' (l. 20). Burns's speaker in 'Farewell to the Highlands' is in a similar place of diminished agency. He can recall the 'country of Worth' but never can call it back. Burns and his bardic successor Baroness Nairne converted the Highlands into a simple but broad and timeless Romantic trope that speaks to personal memory and reflection as much as to national narrative. In our day, imagery of the Highlands still conveys exile (or its modern equivalent, alienation) as well as remembered (i.e., former) wildness, freedom and beauty. Burns's revival (but partial recasting) of Jacobite songs began the Highlands' gradual literary transformation from smouldering site of insurgency into the Scottish imaginary's lost paradise.

Highlanders and 'Law-landers'

Burns's early cantata 'Love and Liberty', written (and suppressed) long before he saw the Highlands, shares some traits with his Highland lyrics. Burns uses Gaelic-derived words ('usquebae' (l. 19) and 'kebars' (l. 49)) even before the 'Carlin' performs her toast for her beloved John Highlandman. The song arrives at midpoint of six songs comprising the musical part of the cantata. Following the cheery songs of the soldier and his doxy – they are bizarrely upbeat considering the disability and homelessness they describe – the Carlin's song is the first to defy the law:

> A HIGHLAND lad my Love was born,
> The lalland laws he held in scorn;
> But he still was faithfu' to his clan,
> My gallant, braw JOHN HIGHLANDMAN.[24]

A carlin is an old or rough-mannered woman, a crone: a secondary meaning is witch. Thieving and hard-drinking, the Carlin, object of desire both for the crippled Fiddler and the brawling Tinker, may be a Highlander like her hanged lover; in any case she still follows his wandering Highland ways. Her song employs the Gaelic-derived 'philibeg', 'plaid', 'claymore' and 'Och', although (like the other beggars in their songs) she speaks chiefly in standard English:

> We ranged a' from Tweed to Spey,
> An' liv'd like lords an' ladies gay:
> For a lalland face he feared none,
> My gallant, braw John Highlandman.[25]

Highlanders like John do not acknowledge British law, remaining loyal to clan customs that are a mandate to mobility.

The Carlin's view of her lost lover is entirely retrospective. Once upon a time, John Highlandman *held* the Lowland laws in scorn; then the properly constituted authorities hanged him. The crone's memories of her Highland rover/lover not only scorn place-bound Lowland tenants but also speak to the difference between 'then' and 'now': separated from the Highland culture, the destitute crone tells her story in Mauchline's seediest tavern.[26] A similar superimposed contrast (Highland versus Lowland, past versus present) may be seen in 'The Highland Balou', a lullaby in which a love-child's future life as a daring raider is fondly predicted:

> Hee-balou, my sweet, wee Donald,
> Picture o' the great Clanronald;   (he looks just like his father, chief of
> Brawlie kens our wanton Chief   Clanranald)
> Who got my wee Highland thief. –   'begot'
>
> ... Thro' the Lawlands, o'er the Border,
> Weel, my babie, may thou furder: 'farther'
> Herry the louns o' the laigh Countrie,   'plunder the rogues of the low country'
> Syne to the Highlands hame to me.[27]   'Then'

This plainspoken mother is carlin-like in her roughness of speech and, despite her youth, crone-like in serving as a conduit for long cultural memory, for the power of the Highland chiefs had been crushed some forty years before Burns wrote these stanzas. Burns's song refers to the mid-century Jacobite rising when his speaker names the chief of the Clanranald (Clanronald is Burns's spelling) as father of her child. Burns's Scottish audience may have remembered, hearing this name, that this clan had been first to raise forces in support of Charles Edward Stuart and that they were active in smuggling Charles Edward out of the country: Flora MacDonald was of that clan. Burns's late eighteenth-century audience knows of the clan's mid-century defeat and the near-extermination of Highland culture; the song's speaker, however, knows nothing of what is to come, expressing a serene if antisocial confidence about what the future holds for her infant son. She is typical of Burns's Highland speakers in commending activities reprehensible to cautious, place-bound Lowlanders, from the acquisition of livestock through raids to a fluid, restless mobility across borders. In Burns, Scotland's law-abiding Presbyterian precincts, literally spelled 'Law-lands' in this song, find their counterpart in the Highlands, viewed by many Lowlanders as a realm of outlaws. He draws this motif from ballads and popular songs, but his updating and deft simplification of the popular tradition made the material more portable, not only more easily remembered (he tended to shorten his source material), but more memorable, more intense.

Like Burns's other Jacobite songs, 'The Highland balou' has a complex relationship to its audience(s). Those who heard it in the late 1790s lived in a Scotland very different from the 'now' of this Highlander's joyously subversive lullaby. The year 1794 saw the suspension of Habeas corpus for the first time since the 1740s; the Treasonable Practices and Seditious Meetings acts became law in 1795; and 'The Highland balou' was printed in *Scots Musical Museum* some months after the poet's death in July 1796. Like many of Burns's late songs, this edgy lullaby manoeuvres poetic time in order to allow the past – the culture from which the mother speaks – to address the future. What to make of his speaker's words (and the memories they evoke of a fiercely independent but by the 1790s decimated Highland culture) is left open.

Sir Walter Scott likewise juxtaposes Highland and Lowland cultures in *Waverley*, but unlike Burns leaves no possibility for open interpretation. Scott sees the eighteenth-century suppression of the clans as a desirable 'innovation':

> There is no European nation which, in the course of half a century, or little more, has undergone so complete a change as this kingdom of Scotland. The effects of the insurrection of 1745, – the destruction of the patriarchal power of the Highland chiefs ... the total eradication of the Jacobite party, which, averse to intermingle with the English, or adopt their customs, long continued to pride themselves upon maintaining ancient Scottish manners and customs, commenced this innovation.[28]

'Insurrection' is eradicated in Scott's novel, as it was in history. Yet Scott goes further in viewing the 'destruction' of the Highland chiefs and 'eradication' of the

Jacobites as providential, for the defeat of these forces led to 'improvements'. In the final chapters of *Waverley*, Baron Bradwardine's estate is saved (repurchased and extensively renovated) by Edward Waverley's English wealth; and it is through the exertions of the Englishman Colonel Talbot that the Bear of Bradwardine, a drinking cup and the Baron's favourite heirloom, is restored to the Bradwardine family. In *Waverley*, Scott suggests that the ascendency of pro-union sectors in Scottish culture (not to mention what Jacobite songs customarily refer to as English gold) was a blessing even for the defeated Jacobite families.

There is no such voice-over in Burns's Highland songs, no instructions on how to take his speakers. When Burns's rough-mannered women speak, no editorial voice is raised to contradict them. In foregrounding these women's voices of rebellion and resistance, Burns actually evokes a Scottish history all the more haunting because (like his Highland landscapes) somewhat blurred: unlike chiefs and princes, proud Highland mothers or grieving 'widows' such as the Carlin in 'Love and Liberty' speak to their private joys and grievances, translating Scottish historical experience into personal narrative. In contrast to these songs of Highland women, Burns's reconstructed songs of the Prince introduce historical topics and/or speakers. Yet even in more historically specific songs, Burns leaves to his audience whether to admire or reject his speakers' words.

A bard's use of time can be much more fluid than that of a historical novelist. In *Love and Liberty*, up to forty years might have passed since the Carlin's lover John Highlandman was hanged (it depends on how long he stayed out of Scotland before illegally returning from transportation). The longer time-range is possible, for in their early days together she reports that raiding was easy and profitable. Whatever the specific dates of her youthful union with John, the Carlin's song soon enough must move on to its grim conclusion: the 'Law'-landers hang her lover after ever-mobile John Highlandman returns to Scotland from afar. In the bleak later season and setting of the cantata – Mauchline, November, 1785 – she is happily drinking punch in a tavern and choosing a partner for the night, but next day she will be forced to resume her wanderings. While the beggars' songs in 'Love and Liberty' insist that freedom (of movement, actions and speaking) is a benefit of homelessness, the 'recitativo' portion, as mentioned in Chapter 2, undercuts these songs' boozy optimism with a contrary emphasis on the bitter storm outside. The beggars will face a Novemberish reality next morning without the blankets, clothing and food that they have traded for punch.

As Thomas Crawford has pointed out, song-tradition remembers two kinds of Scottish beggars: 'gaberlunzies' or blue-gown beggars, licensed to beg in their own parish, and thieving 'sorners' like the Carlin, '*déracinés*' forced to move perpetually because no parish would maintain them.[29] Burns's beggars belong to this second group, so the mobility of the Carlin in 1785 is not freely chosen. Compelled by law, she walks from parish to parish in all seasons in a grim parody of her free-ranging life with John Highlandman. Though so different in style from 'My heart's in the Highlands', the Carlin's song also remembers a lost world. In *Love and Liberty*, Burns invites his audience to consider the distance between a free-spoken, free-moving Highland-inflected 'then' and the bleak here-and-now of Scotland in their own day.

Some critics have irritably contested Burns's right to leave his heart in the Highlands at all, since he was there only twice, and briefly. Yet Burns needs this malleable, depopulated space. In order to address Scotland in total he must himself become a kind of raider, travelling 'the country 'thro' and thro' like the Carlin and John Highlandman. After his early success with *Poems, Chiefly in the Scottish Dialect*, he sought, especially in songs sent to *Scots Musical Museum*, to seek the high land or higher ground of a more comprehensive lyric speech. If the parish and its people are Burns's 'now' (and he continued to the end to write memorably of local courtships and scandals, sending the sprightly 'Last May a braw wooer' to George Thomson in 1795), his songs addressing the Highlands engage with 'then' – a mistier, nobler Scotland-that-was.

Burns's stanzas for 'O an ye were dead gudeman' use the same tune as the Carlin's song in *Love and Liberty* and draw a similar Highland/Lowland contrast. Recalling a song in David Herd's collection, Burns's revised stanzas feature a speaker who curses her Lowland husband:

> O an ye were dead gudeman,
> A green turf on your head, gudeman,
> I wad bestow my widowhood
> Upon a rantin Highlandman.[30]

Between the settled husbandman and the roving Highland thief, the link in Burns's poems and songs is often a plain-spoken, pleasure-seeking crone: embraced by both, she favours the Highlander.[31] From his earliest writings, poems as well as songs, Burns's crones serve as foils to male speakers. 'The Author's Earnest Cry And Prayer', written in 1785 or 1786, is a burlesque address to Parliament whose speaker (an Ayrshire farmer, judging by the politicians he addresses most particularly) draws the lawmakers' attention to the desperate thirst of his 'auld, respectit' parent, 'Mither Scotland'. She is a crone and, like the Carlin in 'Love and Liberty', a Highlander at heart, for she wears a tartan petticoat and carries on her person a small arsenal of concealed weaponry. The speaker accuses the recently passed Wash Act, which has raised the price of whisky, of creating a national emergency by depriving Mother Scotland of her last comfort:

> An' L—d! if ance they pit her till't,   'put her to it' (force her)
> Her tartan petticoat she'll kilt   'tuck up'
> An' durk an' pistol at her belt,
>   She'll tak the streets,

An' rin her whittle to the hilt, I' th' first she meets!	'knife'
For G–d-sake, Sirs! then speak her fair, An' straik her cannie wi' the hair, An' to the *muckle house* repair, Wi' instant speed, An' strive, wi' a' your Wit and Lear, To get remead.³²	'address her kindly' 'gently stroke her hair' (Parliament) 'learning; lore' 'remedy'

Burns's speaker stands between ferocious Mother Scotland (the Highland crone who stands for *all* of Scotland) and the pusillanimous consensus-forgers of the House of Commons. As in so many other poems, Burns's crone is grotesque and comical yet formidable. The Parliament is inclined to think lightly of her capacity in the mid-1780s to redress her grievances, but the speaker reminds them that she is nonetheless still up in the Highlands nursing them.

The Prince is a second Highland-inflected figure who recurs in Burns, often as a subject and at least once as a speaker. His full name was Charles Edward Louis John Casimir Sylvester Severino Maria Stuart (1720–88), and to call him 'Prince' was in itself a gesture of disaffection. After the death of his father in 1766, Jacobites called him King Charles III; cautious people referred to him as the Chevalier. Burns's tributes to the difficult Charles Edward have little to do with documentary fact. The poet may have heard some of the negative stories – the long estrangement from his father, the beating and abuse of his mistress and his wife – but these songs memorialize an idealized figure associated, like the landscape of the Highlands, with a lost 'then' superior to a repressive 'now'. Like Burns's crone speaker in 'Love and Liberty', Bonnie Charlie, a once-hopeful Prince, has survived into the 1780s but as a much-reduced figure. Burns's songs of 'Charlie and his men' might be intended to suggest that a spirit of Scottish resistance survives, too, its fire banked but having the potential to blaze up again. If so, a spirit of potential change is paradoxically strong in these tributes to the fallen Prince – though the poet was well aware that any insurgency of the late 1780s and 1790s was likelier to overthrow monarchy than to change one dynasty for another.

Even considered just as elegies and not as covert invitations to renewed risings, these songs are powerful, 'remembering' a lost Prince for a diminished Scotland. It could well be because of Burns's reconstruction of Jacobite song tradition through his contributions to *Scots Musical Museum* that so many songs of the '45 are performed to this day, persisting in Scottish national lyric (i.e., Scottish national memory) despite the depopulation of the Highlands in the eighteenth and nineteenth centuries. As William Donaldson has observed, 'Burns ... singlehandedly invented the Jacobite song as an independent type ... [He] was creating a myth, and must have been aware that he was doing so.'³³

Among those who follow Burns's lead are Carolina Oliphant (Lady Nairne), soon to be discussed, and James Hogg, who posed as 'editor' while producing superlative neo-Jacobite songs.[34]

Sometimes Burns incorporates an implied self-portrait in his tributes to the defeated Prince. 'Scots Ballad –', written about a year before 'O'er the water to Charlie' and perhaps similarly inspired by stories of sixty-eight-year-old Charles Edward's failing health, also conveys the poet's defensive love for his own first child, Bess, born out of wedlock in 1785. From 1783, Charlotte Stuart, Charles Edward's daughter by his mistress Clementina Walkinshaw, was known in Europe as the Duchess of Albany. Following France's refusal to continue to support his claims, Charles Edward had been styling himself Count of Albany since 1774; and rather late in her life – born in 1752, she died in 1789 – Charlotte was declared to be his heir, allowing her to inherit some of his estates in France. Yet her status as her father's legitimate child did not supersede the dynastic claims of her uncle Henry Benedict, a Cardinal in Rome. Burns most likely knew that she was not in the line of succession; several of his friends in Edinburgh were fully versed in such matters. Yet his song hails the Duchess not only as rightful heir to Scotland (Albany is a title in the Scottish peerage) but as in every way superior to that 'witless' child of wedlock, the Prince of Wales:

> My heart is wae and unco wae,
>   To think upon the raging sea,
> That roars between her gardens green,
>   And th' bonie lass of ALBANIE. –
>
> This lovely maid's of noble blood,
>   That ruled Albion's kingdoms three;
> But Oh! Alas! for her bonie face!
>   They hae wrang'd the lass of ALBANIE! –
>
> ... But there is a youth, a witless youth,
>   That fills the place where she should be,
> We'll send him o'er to his native shore,
>   And bring our ain sweet ALBANIE.[35]

Burns stands up for 'love-begotten daughters', implicitly including his own, while offering a dig at the official heir to the throne of Great Britain. The poet liked these stanzas well enough to fair-copy them into his *Second Commonplace Book* (1787–90) but they were suppressed as politically offensive until the 1850s.

In another song transcribed in *The Second Commonplace Book* but not printed until three years after Burns's death, Charles Edward himself speaks:

> The small birds rejoice in the green leaves returning,
>   The murmuring streamlet winds clear thro' the vale;
> The primroses blow in the dew of the morning,

And wild-scattered cowslips bedeck the green dale:
But what can give pleasure, or what can seem fair,
   When the lingering moments are numbered by Care?
No birds sweetly singing, nor flowers gayly springing,
   Can sooth the sad bosom of joyless Despair. –

The deed that I dared, could it merit their malice,
   A KING and a FATHER to place on his throne;
His right are these hills, and his right are these vallies,
   Where wild beasts find shelter but I can find none:
But 'tis not my sufferings, thus wretched, forlorn,
   My brave, gallant friends, 'tis your ruin I mourn;
Your faith proved so loyal in hot, bloody trial,
   Alas, can I make it no sweeter return![36]

Burns's title is noncommittal ('Song'); he suppresses the speaker's identity until the second stanza, a lovely surprise that Burns's editor James Currie spoiled in 1800 by creating the title 'The Chevalier's Lament', still often used. The first stanza's generalized landscape (set artfully to music with a 'murmuring' quality) conveys that mixture of blurred natural beauty and chronic grief characteristic of Burns's Highland songs. Charles Edward speaks as a fugitive still in Scotland, for the hills and valleys he surveys are, he says bitterly, his father's by 'right'.

A late song by Burns, 'Charlie is My Darling', was adapted from a street ballad dating back (in printed form) to about 1775. Like 'Strong Walls of Derry', his source wanders in later stanzas: the speaker leaves Edinburgh (having donned all her finery) to visit her lover in Aberdeen and witness the Battle of Culloden.[37] Burns's version takes just four stanzas (of fourteen) from the broadside. He adds one new quatrain, the second stanza quoted below; and he keeps the lively chorus, which views 'Charlie and his men' through the eyes of the dazzled young women of Edinburgh. The song is set during several months in autumn of 1745 when the Jacobite army occupied the capital (all but the Castle, still held by government forces and remaining on lockdown):

… As he was walking up the street,
   The city for to view,
O there he spied a bonie lass
   The window looking thro'. –
      Chorus
An' Charlie he's my darling, my darling, my darling,
Charlie he's my darling, the young Chevalier. –

Sae light he's jimped up the stair,
   And tirled at the pin;
And wha sae ready as hersel
   To let the laddie in. –
An Charlie &c.

> He set his Jenny on his knee,
>   All in his Highland dress;
> For brawlie weel he ken'd the way   'very well he knew'
>   To please a bonie lass. –
> An Charlie &c.
>
> It's up yon hethery mountain,
>   And down yon scroggy glen,   'scrubby'
> We daur na gang a milking,   'dare not'
>   For Charlie and his men. –
> An Charlie &c.[38]

These stanzas, written late in Burns's life, in part may look back on his own brief conquest of Edinburgh in 1787–8. He was not only fêted by the literati, the aristocrats of the Caledonian Hunt and the roisterers of the Crochallan Fencibles but found women friends such as Margaret Chalmers and lovers including May (or Meg) Cameron, Jenny Clow and Agnes Craig M'Lehose ('Clarinda').

Another frequent Highland-inflected image in Burns is the exiled heart, a trope appearing in Burns's songs even more often than dispossessed princes and indomitable crones. This frame of reference is not exclusively Highland or Jacobite. Dispossession in Burns is common to Highlanders and Lowlanders, afflicting not only Jacobite noblemen who have forfeited their estates but Lowland cotters who lose their health or their 'masters' ('The Twa Dogs', l. 80).[39] Exile is often the shared experience by which Burns's poems and songs draw together otherwise disparate elements in Scottish culture. In 'The Thames flows proudly to the sea', a thirteenth-century Lowland speaker is displaced south to London. Like Burns's exile whose 'heart is not here' but in the Highlands, this speaker, John Comyn (d. 1303), looks to 'the North'. The historical John Comyn ('the Red') was imprisoned in London following his capture at the Battle of Dunbar (1296):

> The Thames flows proudly to the sea,
>   Where royal cities stately stand;
> But sweeter flows the Nith, to me,
>   Where Cummins ance had high command.   (Comyns)
>
> ...
>
> Tho' wandring, now, must be my doom,
>   Far from thy bonie banks and braes,
> May there my latest hours consume,
>   Amang the friends of early days![40]

Other exiled hearts speak not across time but from cultures far removed from Scotland:

> It was in sweet Senegal that my foes did me enthrall
>   For the lands of Virginia-ginia O;

> Torn from that lovely shore, and must never see it more,
>   And alas! I am weary, weary O!
> Torn from &c.
>
> ...
>
> The burden I must bear, while the cruel scourge I fear,
>   In the lands of Virginia-ginia O.
> And I think on friends most dear with the bitter, bitter tear,
>   And Alas! I am weary, weary O!⁴¹

The speaker of 'The Slave's Lament' is another of Burns's despairing exiles 'torn' from his homeland and persecuted by 'foes'. These stanzas come as close as Burns ever did to imagining in a song what really could have been his post-1786 life on a plantation. Here, he sees himself through the eyes of a grieving slave, casting the overly compliant-to-patrons Rob Burness of 1786 as the detested overseer holding the 'cruel scourge'.

We tend to read Burns through the bardolatry of the Victorians, and any attempt to understand pre-Victorian contexts must first strip away Sir Walter Scott's influential reconstruction of Scottish history in the generation following Burns. For Burns cannot be read through the prism of Scott's version of Scotland's eighteenth-century history. In *Waverley*, as mentioned, Scott sees the fall of the Jacobites as fortunate. He begins to make that case as early as his subtitle, '*Tis Sixty Years Since*'. Although the novel goes on to dramatize the attractions of rebellion and insurgency, the subtitle encourages readers from the outset to bear in mind just how long ago the spirit of Highland independence was crushed. In his final chapter, 'A Postscript, which should have been a Preface', Scott's narrator speaks of the 'absurd political prejudice' that vanished with the suppression of the clans.⁴²

Scott's novel frames subversive speech wholly as a language of the dead. The eloquent Highland chief Fergus McIvor ends the tale as a severed head impaled on the north-facing gate of the town of Carlisle. Burns, unlike Scott, introduces Jacobite survivors still voicing defiance after forty years; he brings them into the 'now' of his 1780s and 1790s. In 'Love and Liberty' seditious speech is linked not to self-destruction but to self-respecting survival. Burns's beggars express scorn for 'lawlanders', defined in the closing song as all who place their trust in constituted authority: 'Courts for Cowards were erected / Churches built to please the Priest'.⁴³ Interpreting this concluding song is tricky. Burns has portrayed the beggars as very drunk and more or less antisocial; readers might feel inclined to discount their sentiments accordingly. Most critics and readers have assumed, however, that Burns shares and is promoting the beggars' views, and that reading is possible too, though far from certain. (Burns does not agree, for instance, with the superstitious young speaker of the song 'Tam Glen' or the vindictive speaker of 'Holy Willie's Prayer'.) 'Love and Liberty' transmits the beggars' views on life while remaining bardically ajar, hospitable to multiple interpretations.

Scotland as Burns imagines it is an intricate lacework of past, present and possible futures. Images drawn from Highland landscape and culture are an idealized counterpart to more down-to-earth imagery of the Lowlands, the native region that the poet only once (in 'The Vision') addressed as a visionary space. In his later songs, Highland culture is at the heart (a word used often in these lyrics) of Scottish heritage. Burns's Highland speakers can be read as tragic monologists or as heroic 'inciters': they address a lost world receding into memory but also remind Burns's audience of a spirit of Scottish insurrection that might someday revive. The songs Burns sent to *Scots Musical Museum* could be received by his contemporary audience as museum pieces, touching and aesthetically pleasing memorials; or they might be taken as a lyric history of Scottish resistance, to be held in trust (through continued performance) for a future resurgence. Burns portrays Highland stories as living on in the memories of scattered survivors. All is not quite lost for his rebels, though such free-spoken characters as the Carlin in *Love and Liberty* have fallen on evil days. His exiled Highlanders turn back to Scotland, addressing it across the oceans and the years. His crones and even his Prince look back on the mid-century from the 1780s, if only to record their losses and testify that the high ground they remember has become a nearly empty wasteland.

A Scottish Minstrel

> [T]hese wonderful men, 'Anonymous' and 'Anon' ... have between them caused me more delight than any [other] authors.
>
> Baroness Nairne in her old age[44]

Burns never met Carolina Oliphant (later Baroness Nairne) but she knew of his existence from her early twenties. Her brother, the younger Laurence Oliphant of Gask, subscribed to the Edinburgh edition of *Poems, Chiefly in the Scottish Dialect* and according to Nairne's biographer it was his sister Carolina who 'prevailed upon him' to do so.[45] Her earliest songs circulated wholly by performance. She gave them to friends or performed them herself, never mentioning that she had composed the verses (and in some cases probably the music). Even when many of her songs were printed in the 1820s, they did not appear under her name but were (like many of Burns's) signed by initials (B. B.) or codes (S. M.). Her songs first appeared in an anthology, *The Scotish Minstrel* (1821–4), and at once became widely popular.[46] Nairne signed her first *Minstrel* submissions with an assumed name ('by Mrs. Bogan of Bogan') and sent them in secret. Her stanzas did not pass directly to her publisher Robert Purdie but to an editorial committee of Nairne's friends headed by Elizabeth and Agnes Hume of Edinburgh. She evidently felt that her original pseudonym was too forthcoming even though she had selected it after verifying that 'Bogan of Bogan' was 'to be found in no Directory'.⁴⁷ Even the unmodified 'by' began to trouble her with its claim to authorship and she changed her signature-line to 'Sent by B. B.', implying that her stanzas were collected from folk performance. By the last volumes, Nairne was submitting her songs as of 'Unknown' authorship or printing them under the initials 'S. M.' (Scottish Minstrel).

Jacobite family stories clearly fostered her delight in authorship-by-stealth and conspiracy. When visiting her publisher Purdie, who occasionally met with his best contributor, 'Mrs. Bogan' arrayed herself 'as a gentlewoman of the olden time'.⁴⁸ Swathed in rustic linen and telling no falsehoods, she led Purdie to believe that she had travelled to the capital from the remote countryside.

> To the music dealer it never occurred that his ... contributor was resident in a suburb of the city: and certainly, he still less imagined that her husband held office in connection with Edinburgh Castle, not many hundred yards from his shop.

Purdie knew Nairne for twenty years only under the name 'Mrs. Bogan of Bogan'.⁴⁹ Even though many, perhaps all, of *The Scottish Minstrel* editorial committee were in on the secret, no-one ever told him. Nairne submitted all her work in disguised handwriting. As she wrote to a friend on the committee, 'any queer, backward hand does!'⁵⁰

One motive for cloaking her identity might have been that in Nairne's day, 'Unknown', 'Anon' and 'Anonymous' were presumed, as in her remark quoted in this section's epigraph, to be long-deceased 'wonderful men' rather than living and breathing Edinburgh matrons. Nairne may have feared that her songs' high popularity would suffer if the truth got out. Such a motive would explain why, having begun as 'Mrs. B. of B.', she so quickly shifted to gender-neutral initials or refused to attribute at all: B. B., S. M., 'Unknown'. She wrote to a confidant on the committee:

> If, by any chance ... Purdie were to be asked, 'Who is B. B.?' I think he would do well to make no mention of a lady. As you observed, the more mystery the better: and ... still the balance is in favour of the 'Lords of the Creation'. I cannot help ... undervaluing beforehand what is said to be a feminine production.⁵¹

'Mrs. Bogan's' pose as an elderly female with ties to the peasantry, mere conduit for the high sentiments of unknown male bards of earlier eras, conformed to her era's fantasies about folk songs and their transmission. As more than thirty Burns songs in Purdie's anthology are likewise misidentified as of 'unknown' authorship, at least she was in good company.⁵²

Few women authors have constructed a career so closely supported by women and so closely guarded from men. The all-female editorial committee of *The Scottish Minstrel*; the nieces and grandniece who served as companions after the death of her husband and the premature death of her son: all helped Nairne to keep her secret. Her husband remained in the dark. 'I have not told even Nairne lest he blab', she wrote a friend during the 1820s.[53] In fact, consideration for him might have been her early motive for secrecy. William Murray Nairne bore two famous Jacobite names yet had served from early youth (as had his father) in the British army. From 1806 to 1824, he was Assistant Inspector General of Barracks in Scotland, based in Edinburgh Castle. His own loyalties might have been called into question if it became generally known that Mrs Major Nairne was writing new songs honouring the mid-century rebels. This was especially true before 1824, when he was litigating for the return of the Nairne titles and estates, which were lost after Culloden due to his grandfather's activities in that rising.[54] Even if shielding her husband was an early motive for her secrecy, however, it does not explain why Nairne maintained anonymity for fifteen years after his death. Nairne's style of secrecy had some relation to her negative view of Sir Walter Scott, whom she disliked because she thought that he indulged in unseemly ridicule of Covenanters[55] and had told too many lies to conceal his authorship of *Waverley* (1814). Nairne's own strategy was to say absolutely nothing – but to keep on writing.

A year or two before her death in October 1845, Nairne authorized and began to edit the first songbook to consist solely of her own songs, to be co-edited by her sister, Mrs Keith. This first edition – its title page reads variously *Lays of Strathearn* and *Lays from Strathearn* – appeared in 1845 and prints music as well as her stanzas. Her own plan was for anonymous publication, but after her death the family was more than ready to reveal her authorship, as the preface to *Lays* makes clear.[56] The long-deferred publication of Nairne's writings under her own name has encouraged the misconception that she was a Victorian-era writer; but she wrote most of her songs during the 1790s, the same decade when Burns was sending dozens of lyrics to James Johnson's *Scots Musical Museum* (1787–1803) and George Thomson's *Select Collection of Original Scotish Airs* (1793–1841). According to her biographer, she wrote most of her Jacobite songs to entertain her father, who died in 1792, as well as other Jacobite relatives. Her songs began to circulate locally beginning around 1800 but spread across Britain immediately after they appeared in *The Scottish Minstrel* during the 1820s.

Her long suppression of her authorship has fostered misconceptions about the extent and significance of her song-writing activities. The continuing currency of Nairne's songs in the early twentieth century is clear in Hugh MacDiarmid's frequent echoes of 'Will Ye No Come Back Again' and 'The Regalia' in *A Drunk Man Looks at the Thistle* (1926): MacDiarmid appropriates Nairne almost as often as he does Burns. Her songs live on in performance today as well, although not always linked to her name. Even more than with Burns, whose unsigned Scottish songs often go unrecognized as his work, Nairne's literary reputation remains somewhat obscured by her songs' original circulation as traditional, anonymous, 'Unknown'.

CAROLINE BARONESS NAIRNE
née OLIPHANT OF GASK

Figure 3.1: Carolina Oliphant (later Lady Nairne) at the time she was writing many of her songs. From Margaret S. Simpson, *The Scottish Songstress, Caroline, Baroness Nairne, by her Grandniece* (Edinburgh & London: Oliphant Anderson & Ferrier, 1894), p. 35; author's collection.

Personal History as National Song

> [M]y Fathers had not the illustrious Honours and vast properties to hazard in the contest [in 1715 and 1745] ... yet what they could they did; and what they had they lost.
> Burns, Letter to Lady Winifred Constable, 16 December 1789[57]

Burns and Nairne wrote Jacobite songs in part to honour the mid-century struggle of their own parents and grandparents. Carolina Oliphant was the daughter and granddaughter of exiled Jacobites. Like Baron Bradwardine in Scott's *Waverley*, her grandfather bore arms during the risings of both 1715 and 1745; his son Laurence (father of Nairne) was an aide-de-camp to Charles Edward Stuart. Nairne's maternal grandmother and mother had been fugitives in 1746, taking refuge after Culloden in the Highlands only to be 'driven from a hut in Athole by the threat of military execution'.[58] After six months' wandering through the Buchan district in the north-east, her father and grandfather escaped to Sweden and on to France. In 1763, father and son were allowed to return to Scotland, where a small part of their forfeited estates had been repurchased by kinsmen. Carolina Oliphant's father had married his first cousin at a ceremony at Versailles in 1755. They named their third daughter, born in the Old House at Gask in August 1766, Carolina in honour of Charles Edward Stuart. The names of the Stuarts were 'pasted over the names of the reigning [Hanoverian] family' in the Oliphant children's English Prayer Books: like many in north-east Scotland, the Oliphants worshipped as Episcopalians.[59] Among the relics of the 1745–6 rising displayed in Nairne's house were Charles Edward's 'bonnet, spurs, cockade, crucifix, and [the] lock of his hair' mentioned in 'The Auld House'.[60] Charles Edward had stayed in the house during his flight across Scotland after Culloden.

'The Auld House', the song chosen by Nairne to open *Lays*, links the decline of Nairne's childhood home, abandoned *c.* 1800, with the fallen hopes of the Stuarts:

... Oh the Auld Laird, the Auld Laird,	(Nairne's grandfather)
Sae canty kind and crouse,	'cheerful-kind' 'merry'
How mony did he welcome to	'many'
His ain wee dear Auld House;	
And the Leddy too, sae genty,	'lady' 'dainty'
There shelter'd Scotland's heir,	(Charles Edward Stuart)
And clipt a lock wi' her ain hand,	'own'
Frae his lang yellow hair.	'from'
The Mavis still doth sweetly sing,	'thrush'
The bluebells sweetly blaw,	'blow'
The bonny Earn's clear winding still,	
But the Auld House is awa'.	'away'

> The Auld House, the Auld House,
> Deserted tho' ye be,
> There ne'er can be a new house
> Will seem sae fair to me.[61]

The ruined house calls to mind a superseded dynasty as well as a beloved childhood home. Neither remains intact except in memory but both will always outshine any new replacement.

Like 'the pennyless lass wi' a lang pedigree' of her song 'The Laird o' Cockpen', Carolina Olpihant (known in the family as 'pretty Miss Car')[62] rejected several wealthy suitors, choosing instead her second cousin, a Captain in the British army. They could afford to marry in 1806, when she was forty: he had been promoted to Major and she had received from the head of her mother's family the gift of 'Caroline Cottage', a home in the Edinburgh suburbs. During her protracted engagement, Nairne's family assumed – she remained silent on the topic – that she was writing letters to her fiancé during the long hours that she devoted to her songs. In 1824 during George IV's visit to Edinburgh, William Murray Nairne recovered the peer's title that his family had lost following the rebellion of 1745. Mrs Major Nairne became the Baroness Nairne, but she had passed the first fifty-eight years of her life in genteel poverty.

A sly early song looks at courtship from a perspective that suggests Jacobite disdain for nouveau-riche displays of prosperity; though he does not sport a buff waistcoat, the Laird of Cockpen's blue coat suggests that he is a Whig:

The laird o' Cockpen, he's proud an' he's great,		
His mind is ta'en up wi' things o' the state;	'taken'	
He wanted a wife his braw house to keep,	'fine'	
But favour wi' wooin' was fashous to seek.	'awkward'	
Down by the dyke-side a lady did dwell,	'stone wall'	
At his table head he thought she'd look well,		
McClish's ae daughter o' Claverse-ha' Lee,	'one'	
A pennyless lass wi' a lang pedigree.	'long'	
His wig was weel pouther'd, and as guid as new;	'powdered'	'good'
His waistcoat was white, his coat it was blue;		
He put on a ring, a sword and cock't hat,		
And wha could refuse the laird wi' a' that.		
He took the grey mare, and rade cannily,	'rode cautiously'	
An' rapt at the yett o' Claverse-ha' Lee;	'rapped at the gate'	
'Gae tell Mistress Jean to come speedily ben,	'to the parlor'	
She's wanted to speak to the laird o' Cockpen'.		

Mistress Jean was makin' the elder-flower wine,	'making'
'An' what brings the laird at sic a like time?'	'a time like this'
She put aff her aprin, and on her silk gown,	'off' 'apron'
Her mutch wi' red ribbons, and gaed awa down.	'linen cap' 'goed' (went)
An' when she cam' ben he bowed fu' low,	
An' what was his errand he soon let her know;	
Amazed was the laird when the lady said Na,	'No'
And with a laigh curtsie she turned awa.	'low curtsey'
Dumfounder'd he was, nae sigh did he gie,	'no' 'give'
He mounted his mere – he rade cannily,	'mare' 'rode cautiously'
And aften he thought, as he gaed thro' the glen,	'often'
She's daft to refuse the laird o' Cockpen.⁶³	

Nairne ingeniously reverses a Burns song, itself linked to an older bawdy song. In Burns's unsigned stanzas for 'When She Cam Ben She Bobbed', 'Cockpen' steals a kiss from a 'Collier lassie', preferring her to braw 'Lady Jean'.⁶⁴ In recasting the stanzas, Nairne evidently had something to say about unwanted suitors from Mistress Jean's perspective. Soon after the song began to circulate, someone (not Nairne herself) tried to draw its satiric sting with two final stanzas in which the lady repents and agrees to marry the laird. I have placed these in a note. They appear neither in *The Scottish Minstrel* nor in *Lays of Strathearn*, but Rogers prints them although he knows that they are not by Nairne.⁶⁵ His inclusion of the inferior stanzas is a pity, for they are untrue to the satiric inflections in the original. (Would an editor rewrite Austen's *Pride and Prejudice* by portraying Elizabeth Bennet as happily married to Mr Collins?) Unfortunately, most versions of 'The Laird o' Cockpen' on the internet have been scanned from Rogers's readily available text.

Burns, whose tenant-farming family struggled at the edge of bankruptcy, is well known for songs and poems that satirize displays of arrogant entitlement. It is not so well known that he grew up, like Nairne, with family stories of mid-century displacement although for his family, the exile was economic rather than political. His father settled in Ayrshire in 1750, but William Burnes (as he spelled the family name) was born in Kincardineshire near Inverness. The Burness family (as the north-eastern branch of the family spelled the name) had farmed there as tenants for generations, but the disruption of farming following the battle of Culloden, which occurred nearby in April 1746, was severe enough (along with disastrous weather during the 1740s) to force the poet's grandfather into bankruptcy some two years later. In 1748, Burness's two eldest sons, including the poet's father, left the area in search of work; eleven years later William named his firstborn child after his brother Robert. The tearful parting of the two (mentioned in letters by both Robert and Gilbert as a story often told by their father) is recalled in Burns's stanzas for 'Auld Lang Syne', which dramatize the reunion of long separated 'freres', brothers and playmates. The brothers' families exchanged letters but this joyous reunion never occurred for Burns's own father and uncle.

In his later years, Burns often considered his own life in Jacobite-inflected terms. In stanzas written shortly before his death, he adapts Jacobite toasts to celebrate a forbidden love. These lines are probably his last inspired by 'Clarinda' (Agnes Craig M'Lehose), with whom he had parted on 6 December 1791, a farewell meeting that also inspired 'Ae Fond Kiss', a song better known than 'O May thy morn' but not more beautiful:

> O May, thy morn was ne'er sae sweet,
>   As the mirk night o' December;   'dark'
> For sparkling was the rosy wine,
>   And private was the chamber:
> And dear was she, I dare na name,   'not'
>   But I will ay remember. –   'always'
> And dear was she, I dare na name,
>   But I will ay remember. –
>
> And here's to them, that, like oursel,   'ourselves'
>   Can push about the jorum;   'punchbowl'
> And here's to them that wish us weel,   'well'
>   May a' that's gude watch o'er them: 'good'
> And here's to them, we dare na tell,
>   The dearest o' the quorum. –
> And here's to them, we dare na tell,
>   The dearest o' the quorum.[66]

The air for 'O May thy Morn' was 'The Rashes' and had Jacobite associations, having been set also to stanzas titled 'When the King Came o'er the Water'.[67] The lost lady, like the Jacobites' absent but beloved sovereign, dominates the song all the more for never being named.[68]

'A Waulking Song' by Alexander MacDonald – he was active in the rising of 1745 and an excellent poet in Gaelic – suggests the mixture of political and sexual imagery, the oscillation between different sites of desire, so characteristic of Jacobite lyrics. MacDonald's stanzas praise Charles as 'graceful Morag [Sarah] of the ringlets', concealing his true subject by cross-dressing it. Charles Edward Stuart had himself resorted to this type of disguise, assuming the identity of Flora MacDonald's maid 'Betty Burke' to elude the British before his escape to France:

> Chalk-white, well-set, are the maiden's
> Teeth, carved like the chiselled die.
>
> ... Beautiful budding breasts adorn her,
> And her breath has the musk's fragrance.

> ... Many a sweetheart has my Morag
> Between Morar's hills and Arran.[69]

The Jacobite bard conceals his seditious political message from outsiders by addressing his prince as a seductive young woman; Burns's 'O May Thy Morn' suppresses the identity of his forbidden subject – the lost love he 'dare na tell' – by emulating the indirection of Jacobite toasts.

In a well-known song, Nairne turns to Charles Edward and his lost cause with the same sad love that Burns directs to Agnes M'Lehose. The distinctive tune may be of Nairne's own composition, for no earlier known stanzas are set to it:

> Bonnie Charlie's now awa;
> Safely owre the friendly main;
> Mony a heart will break in twa,   'many' 'two'
> Should he ne'er come back again.
>   Will ye no come back again?   'not'
>   Will ye no come back again?
>   Better lo'd ye canna be,   'loved you cannot'
>   Will ye no come back again?
>
> Ye trusted in your Hieland men,   'Highland'
> They trusted you, dear Charlie!
> They kent your hidin' in the glen,   'knew about'
> Death or exile braving.
>   Will ye no, &c.
>
> English bribes were a' in vain,
> Tho' puir, and puirer, we maun be;   'poor and poorer we must'
> Siller canna buy the heart   'silver [money] cannot'
> That beats aye for thine and thee.   'always'
>   Will ye no &c.
>
> ... We watched thee in the gloaming hour,   'twilight'
> We watched thee in the morning grey;
> *Tho' thirty thousand pound they gie,   (the reward for his capture)
> Oh there is nane that wad betray!   'none that would '
>   Will ye no, &c.

*A fact highly honourable to the Highlanders [original note][70]

Nairne's Jacobite reconstructions focus on grief, that wholly retrospective angle of desire. Although the question asked in the song's chorus was once political, it now is purely rhetorical, for the Prince had died in 1788. Nairne moves Jacobite song in these stanzas (and others like them) from the combination of elegy and submerged social critique in Burns's Jacobite songs to tender eulogy for a long-departed past.

Burns, Nairne and National Song

> [T]he Scotish Muses were all Jacobites. I have paid more attention to every description of Scots songs than perhaps any body living has done, and I do not recollect one single stanza, or even the title of the most trifling Scots air, which has the least panegyrical reference to the families of Nassau or Brunswick; while there are hundreds satirizing them. This may be thought no panegyric on the Scots Poets, but I mean it as such.
> Burns, *Notes on Scottish Song*[71]

Despite Nairne's and Burns's copious references to Scottish history, the distinctive national traits conveyed by their songs have little to do with wearing the tartan or following one king and not another. Both share one injunction learned from the Jacobites: to celebrate resistance as the ground of national consciousness. They express this resistance in very different ways, but both represent 'Scotland' as a *counter*culture. The homeland is for both a site of evocative dissonance, a place where fish vendors inspire art songs ('Caller Herring'), royal princes weep as homeless outcasts ('The small birds rejoice') and every single speaker, as Burns observes in the passage above, has a problem with historical outcome. Both portray rebellion as 'Scottish', although in 1746 many Presbyterian Lowlanders had rejoiced at the defeat of the Highland–Gaelic–Episcopalian–Jacobite coalition. Yet as Nairne and Burns reconstruct this crisis point in Scottish time, speakers from all around Scotland recoil as from a crushing blow. Burns's and Nairne's neo-Jacobite songs emphasize sympathetic interaction between what historically had often been divided or antagonistic Scottish communities. In what they both saw as national song, they brought together art song and folk song, dialect Scots and standard English, Lowland and Highland cultures. Both write mainly to the 'standard' but periodically introduce some non-standard words and variant spellings, so that their stanzas are recognizably 'Scottish' in flavour. These songs are hybrids. While positioning Highlanders as Scotland's heroes, for instance, both Nairne and Burns showcase Scots vernacular (not Gaelic) as the 'national' language. Any contradictions are held together simply by the music, just as in traditional folk songs and ballads. Nairne and Burns chiefly differ from the folk tradition in their preference, not common in folk songs, for dramatic monologue. As has been seen, both often explore a solitary speaker's building mood or wandering thoughts.

Neither Burns nor Nairne saw themselves as recipients of a wise old tradition. Both were active re-constructors. Yet what we think of today as Scottish song is precisely the kind of mixed text that they popularized. In its entry on Burns, the *Grove Dictionary of Music* considers his song project: 'He produced over 350 songs, including more than one-third of those published in the *Musical Museum* and about 114 of those printed in the *Select Collection*: this represents the major part of the published repertory of Scottish song'.[72] Nairne wrote many if not most of her approximately eighty songs during the years before her marriage in 1806. This is not to say, however, that Burns wrote the 'major part' of all songs circulated in Scotland before 1800, with some of the remainder the work of the young Carolina Oliphant. It is only to say that a majority of lyrics that have been *preserved and remembered as Scottish* were their work.

Yet what was this group of regional traditions that they brought together in national song? With Jacobite materials, the question is not easily answered because it is difficult to be sure that any given song said to be old – by tradition, consensus, or even a learned editor – really circulated during the Jacobite wars. The only way to rule out a post-Jacobite genesis for an apparently authentic Jacobite lyric is to find printed texts or manuscripts dating from the years around 1688, 1715 and 1745 – and printed books were rare. Advocating Jacobitism (by spoken word or in print) was seditious, so that these songs were not circulated even in the circuitous and baffling mode of other eighteenth-century songs.

Jacobite Song before Burns and Nairne

> When Political combustion ceases to be the object of Princes & Patriots, it then, you know, becomes the lawful prey of Historians and Poets.
> Burns, enclosing 'There'll Never Be Peace Til Jamie Comes Hame' in a letter to Alexander Cunningham, 11 March 1791[73]

Here several collections are discussed that print older Jacobite writings with which Nairne and Burns were familiar. Both were able, given the four decades since the last rising, to revive the tradition (while carefully remaining anonymous), retelling the stories and redrawing the characters. Both also dramatize the impact of defeat on the ensuing lives of survivors. The immediate impact of war on Scottish ground has been blurred by the passage of time, but Nairne and Burns preserve anecdotes from family members. Whereas earlier Jacobite songs are coded calls to battle, Nairne and Burns often present readers with eulogies and elegies.

In 1933, John Lorne Campbell translated what he calls Highland 'political poetry composed between the years 1640 and 1750'.[74] This material cannot be called folk-derived, for the songs are 'signed, though in some cases little is known about the … authors'.[75] Especially interesting is the work of Alexander MacDonald, Gaelic tutor to Charles Edward. In 'A Waulking Song', briefly cited above, MacDonald speaks as bardic historian of his clan. 'Waulking' is fulling, a process – the work of women, who sang as they worked – that softens and cleans fabric by beating it, as Campbell's note to the song explains. This lyric suggests, even in translation, the grim authority of Macdonald's work:

All the Gaels would gather to thee, (Charles Edward, addressed in dis-
Whoever rose with thee or tarried.   guise as 'Morag' (Sarah))

Ten thousand of them sat a-waulking
In the first King Charles's battles.

Many the cloth they gave a nap to,
Between Sutherland and Annan.

When others had refused to waulk it,
They themselves the band assembled.

God! but they were skilled in battle
When their swords they had unsheathèd.

Every cloth they have waulked for thee,
Firm and goodly did they leave it.

Tight, thick, firm, well waulked and woven,
Scarlet-tinted with blood's colour.[76]

Nairne and Burns knew MacDonald's work, for both adapted some of his lyrics in English.

Another resource for both was James Oswald's *The Caledonian Pocket Companion*, a copy of which Burns owned. First printed in 1751, this seven-volume anthology includes musical texts of many airs whose titles identify them as tributes to an absent king: 'There are few good Fellows when Jamie's awa', 'The King shall enjoy his own again', etc. Yet no stanzas are printed, only the musical settings. For full Jacobite texts, Burns knew MacDonald's work; he knew whatever he was hearing sung in the meetings of the Crochallan Fencibles, or the Freemasons, or in song sessions with his Jacobite friends Allan Masterton and William Nichol. It is also clear from Burns's post-1788 songs that he was well acquainted with the contents of *The True Loyalist* (1779), a collection of English and vernacular Scots Jacobite songs that, like the Gaelic songs translated by Campbell, are evidently not folk derived but simply unattributed. This privately printed and anonymous work may have had some link to Marishal College in Aberdeen, for the only identified contributor is William Meston ('one of the Regents').[77] The publication date of 1779, although long after the catastrophe of 1746, sets *The True Loyalist* well before Burns's and Nairne's careers as adapters of songs. Yet there is no saying whether these songs really circulated during the Jacobite conflicts.

Editorial and antiquarian testimony of the eighteenth and nineteenth centuries is unreliable. Some of the best songs in James Hogg's *Jacobite Relics of Scotland* (1819–21) were almost certainly written by Hogg himself. These include 'Donald Macgillavry' and what are to this day the most often performed versions of 'Cam

Ye by Athol', 'This is no my Ain House', 'Cam Ye o'er frae France', 'Will Ye go to Sheriffmuir' and 'The Piper o' Dundee'.[78] David Johnson has argued that while

> [i]t has been stated that Jacobite songs arose ... out of the Scottish people's deep emotional involvement with the rebellions of 1715 and 1745 ... I can only say that I have seen no evidence supporting this; most of the recorded Jacobite songs were actually written ... by such people as James Hogg and Lady Nairne.[79]

Murray Pittock disagrees, citing numerous Jacobite stanzas that date back to the rebellions. Yet while this material is historically important, he acknowledges that its significance as song is less clear: 'What Johnson ... may really mean is not that the vast majority of all Jacobite song is post Jacobite, but that the vast majority of all *good* Jacobite song is so'.[80]

A case in point are indignant stanzas for 'Over the Water to Ch–rlie' that appeared in *The True Loyalist* in 1779. The song refers to 1746–7, when Jacobite leaders (as in the final chapters of Scott's *Waverley*) were tried and executed in Carlisle:

> No doubt you have heard from C—lisle,   (Carlisle)
> Of such a damnable jury,
> But GOD is just, and will not let pass,
> But will punish them with fury,
> He'll send them headlong down to Hell,
> Which will happen right early,
> Because they hadn't compassion when judg'd
> The friends of the royal P—ce C—lie.[81]   (Prince Charlie)

Burns's version bypasses these stanzas, with which he was familiar, to emulate the simplicity of MacDonald's Gaelic setting. MacDonald's and Burns's lyrics (matched to a boatman's tune) lilt and float. Burns's song appeared unsigned in volume two of *Scots Musical Musum*, published in mid-February 1788, less than a month after Charles Edward Stuart's death:

> Come boat me o'er, come row me o'er;
>   Come boat me o'er to Charlie;
> I'll gie John Ross anither bawbee   (small coin)
>   To boat me o'er to Charlie. –
>   Chorus
> We'll o'er the water, we'll o'er the sea,
>   We'll o'er the water to Charlie;
> Come weal, come woe, we'll gather and go,   'well, wealth'
>   And live or die wi' Charlie. –
>
> ... I swear and vow by moon and stars,
>   And sun that shines so early!
> If I had twenty thousand lives,
>   I'd die as aft for Charlie.[82]   'oft'

Kinsley's note ('A stock Jacobite theme')[83] does not do justice to the seamless fit of words and music in Burns's version, which uses (as the stanzas for *The True Loyalist* do not) the lift in the tune at the end of every second and fourth line: Burns repeatedly names 'Charlie' on a slowly rising note.

The air, titled 'Shawnboy' in Oswald's *Caledonian Pocket Companion*, was also printed in Bremner's *Reels* in 1757. Burns wrote 'fast' stanzas for the tune as well as this famous 'slow' set.[84] MacDonald's lines are slowed by gliding diphthongs and rich vowels: 'O togamaid oirnn thar uisge's thar tuinn, / O falbhmaid thairis gu Tearlach'.[85] Burns's first lines are a free translation of MacDonald's but achieve their flowing liquidity (despite short, mainly monosyllabic words) by assonance – John, Ross, baw – that binds the words closely to the music. Burns's song does not directly seek 'Incitement' (MacDonald's title), but he conveys an implied advocacy. For in the context of 1788's succession crisis (caused by the mental illness of George III and the ensuing controversy over the Regency Bill), this praise of a fallen Stuart and pledge to 'follow' and even 'die' for him has a subversive edge. Still, as in Nairne's 'The Land o' The Leal', those who would literally, in 1788, 'follow' 'Tearlach' (eighteenth-century Gaelic for Charles) would be boating themselves over to the afterlife.

Nairne likewise knew MacDonald's songs, the tunes in *The Caledonian Pocket Companion* and the works printed in *The True Loyalist*. She had learned Scottish music and dancing from Niel Gow, foremost fiddler of the day. Many years after *The True Loyalist* was printed, Nairne took up a central image in one of its songs of an oak tree and the charmed circle of benevolence it casts.[86] Her own version praises the rowan (mountain ash) that grew near her childhood home at Gask. The rowan is recalled as presiding over a family circle now long broken: Nairne's mother, Margaret Robertson, had died in 1774 when Nairne was eight:

> Oh! Rowan Tree, Oh! Rowan Tree! thou'lt aye be dear to me,
> Intwin'd thou art wi' mony ties, o' hame and infancy.   'many' 'home'
> Thy leaves were aye the first o' spring,
> Thy flow'rs the simmer's pride;
> There was nae sic a bonny tree, in a' the countrie side.   'pretty'
>   Oh! Rowan tree.
>
> ... We sat aneath thy spreading shade, the bairnies round thee ran,   'beneath', 'children'
> They pu'd thy bonny berries red, and necklaces they strang.   'pulled', 'strung'
> My Mother! Oh! I see her still, she smil'd oure sports to see,   'our'
> Wi' little Jeanie on her lap, Wi' Jamie at her knee!
>   Oh! Rowan Tree.
>
> Oh! there arose my Father's prayer, in holy evening's calm,
> How sweet was then my Mother's voice, in the Martyr's psalm;
> Now a' are gane! we meet nae mair aneath the Rowan Tree;
> But hallowed thoughts around thee twine o' hame and infancy
>   Oh! Rowan Tree![87]

The final stanza may draw on scenes of family worship in Burns's 'The Cotter's Saturday Night', for Burns's cotter family, led in prayer by the father, also sing the Martyrs' psalm. A possible point of contact with Romantic poetry is Felicia Hemans's 'The Graves of a Household' (1828), which shares some imagery with Lady Nairne's song:

> And parted thus they rest, who played
> Beneath the same green tree;
> Whose voices mingled as they prayed
> Around one parent knee![88]

'The Rowan Tree' did not appear in *The Scottish Minstrel*. If Nairne's song was finished after 1828, the year Hemans's poem appeared in *Records of Woman*, it is likely that she is echoing Hemans; but the contrary might be true, with Hemans adapting imagery from Nairne's song, if the song was circulating in the 1820s without being printed. In Gaelic legend, rowan trees are protective; Highlanders strung necklaces from the berries to ward off evil. The rowan in the song survives but has not been able to shield the family from the passage of time.

'The Auld House', probably completed after the 1820s, may draw one of its images from Wordsworth's 'Immortality' ode:

> The setting sun, the setting sun!
> How glorious it gaed down;   'goed' (went)
> The cloudy splendour raised our hearts
> To cloudless skies aboon!   'above'
> The auld dial, the auld dial!   (old sundial)
> It tauld how time did pass;   'told'
> The wintry winds hae dung it down,   'have beaten it down'
> Now hid 'mang weeds and grass.[89]   'among'

In Nairne, time trumps even war as a blighter of hopes, ruining even its own instruments. She began these stanzas around 1800, evidently both inspired and upset by her brother's decision to abandon the old family home and build a new one. It seems likely however, that she polished the stanzas before their first publication in *Lays*. In the version printed there, a retrospective view of childhood scenes links the song to Wordsworth, who uses the same image of clouds around a setting sun to conclude his 'Immortality' ode, with its own reflections on early childhood. Wordsworth's ode was first published in 1807.

Nairne's 'The Lass of Livingstane', deftly adapted from a bawdy song of the same title, emphasizes the reverberations of political loss in private lives:

> Oh! wha will dry the dreeping tear,   'who'   'dripping'
> She sheds her lane, she sheds her lane?   'alone'
> Or wha the bonie lass will cheer,
> Of Livingstane, Of Livingstane?
> The crown was half on Charlie's head,

Ae gladsome day, ae gladsome day;	'one'
The lads that shouted joy to him,	
Are in the clay[,] are in the clay.	
Her waddin' gown was wyl'd and won,	'wedding' 'artful' 'finished'
It ne'er was on, it ne'er was on;	
Culloden field, his lowly bed,	
She thought upon, she thought upon.	
The bloom has faded frae her cheek	'from'
In youthfu' prime, in youthfu' prime,	
And sorrow's with'ring hand has done	
The deed o' time, the deed o' time.[90]	

The young woman's sexual yearning, mocked in the bawdy text, is re-formulated as grief for a lover killed in battle. In Nairne's distinctively elided Scottish time, even those who survive the conflicts are haunted by memories of a vanished 'then' whose promise will never be fulfilled.

'Scots Wha Hae' versus 'Land o' the Leal'

> I never was for ... retaining silly nonsense, though ever so old.
> Nairne, letter to the Editorial Committee of *The Scottish Minstrel*[91]

If Nairne and Burns both enjoin resistance as a Scottish trait, their stanzas for the old Scottish tune 'Hey tutie tatey' suggest their equally striking differences. Burns probably first encountered the air during his years in Edinburgh, matched to a Jacobite toast.[92] He then made his own drinking stanzas for the tune: 'Hey tutie tatey' appeared unsigned, with the Jacobite source printed below as an alternative text, in *The Scots Musical Museum* volume for 1788. Burns turned again to 'Hey tutie tatey' in 1793, this time writing stanzas with a Jacobin dimension. Robert Bruce, who speaks in this song, is imagined addressing his army before the Battle of Bannockburn (June 1314):

Scots, wha hae wi' WALLACE bled,	'who have'
Scots, wham BRUCE has aften led,	'whom' 'often'
Welcome to your gory bed, –	
Or to victorie. –	
Now's the day, and now's the hour;	
See the front o' battle lour;	'frown'
See approach proud EDWARD's power,	
Chains and Slaverie. –	
... By Oppression's woes and pains!	
By your Sons in servile chains!	
We will drain our dearest veins,	
But they *shall* be free!	

> Lay the proud Usurpers low!
> Tyrants fall in every foe!
> LIBERTY's in every blow!
>   Let us DO – or DIE!!![93]

In his letter transmitting the stanzas, Burns mentions a visit to Bannockburn (late summer 1793) that inspired 'glowing' thoughts of the revolutions in America and France: 'the ... recollection of [Robert Bruce's] glorious struggle for Freedom, associated with the glowing ideas of some other struggles of the same sort, *not quite so ancient*, roused my rhyming Mania –'.[94] William Donaldson points out the Jacobite inflections in one of Burns's phrases: in Scotland at this time 'Usurpers' has 'only one connotation, and ... directly links the Wars of Independence [of the fourteenth century] with the Jacobite Risings as national struggles'.[95]

If Burns's implicit endorsement of struggles 'of the same sort' outside Scotland is missed, 'Scots Wha Hae' will be read as purely nationalistic; in fact, the song is today an anthem of the Scottish National Party. Readings mainly attuned to nationalism, however, will tend to miss the way that these stanzas march ahead in time. Burns speaks from the past but to the future: he even italicizes the future tense ('*shall* be') in imagining the liberation of his sons.

'Hey tutie tatey' is a march (its time signature is 2/4). Burns was sure that the melody had accompanied the soldiers on their historical march to Bannockburn in the fourteenth century; his letter to Thomson titles the stanzas 'Robert Bruce's March to Bannockburn. To its ain tune –'. For other songs set to this popular air in *Scots Musical Museum*, Burns told Johnson to insert that same line about Bruce and Bannockburn. Kinsley rejects Burns's idea as 'improbable', observing that the first known printing of the air was in 1751 in *The Caledonian Pocket Companion*.[96] Early in the twentieth century, however, James C. Dick made a persuasive case supporting Burns's view: 'one of the earliest fragments of Scottish song existing [*c.* 1486] is in the peculiar rhythm of the tune': 'Longe berdes hertles, / Payntyd hodes wytles, / Gay cotes graceles, / Makyth Englond thrifteles'.[97]

In Nairne's stanzas set to 'Hey tutie tatey', the speaker is not a warrior but a dying woman grieving over the loss of her child. She addresses the future, too, but here the better days ahead refer to the afterlife:

I'm wearin awa', John,	'wearing away'
Like snaw wreathes in thaw, John,	'snow drifts'
I'm wearin' awa'	
To the land o' the leal.	'loyal, faithful'
...	
Our bonnie bairn's there, John,	'child's'
She was baith gude and fair, John;	'both good'
And oh! we grudg'd her sair	'sore (sorely)'
To the land o' the leal.	

> ...
> But sorrow's sel wears past, John,   'self'
> And joy's a comin' fast, John,
> The joy that's aye to last   'always'
>   In the land o' the leal.[98]

Like 'Scots Wha Hae' and many of Burns's songs, Nairne's stanzas are emotionally complex in focussing on a single speaker at a moment of crisis. Scottish Jacobitism, at first glance not invoked, in fact frames her song in the frequent repetition of the Jacobite keyword 'leal' (loyal). To a Jacobite exiled in France, the Highlands were the land of the leal, site of a sacred covenant between true believers and the one true king. In Nairne's song, the old hope for a restoration of the Scottish kings is supplanted by a view of that hoped-for other kingdom to which her Jacobite grandparents, parents and brother already had passed. (There is a curious echo of Nairne's conversion of the Highlands into a trope for the afterlife in Dylan's modern song. The Highlands are 'where I'll be', the speaker says, 'when I get called home', l. 17.)

To judge from her biographers, 'The Land o' the Leal' was the Nairne song most admired by the Victorians. Nairne placed the stanzas, written within a year of the death of her brother Charles and soon after an emotional conversion experience, into a letter of condolence written to a childhood friend, Mrs Campbell Colquhoun, who was distraught over the death of her infant daughter.[99] Nairne takes 'Hey tutie tatey' far from Burns's context of battle songs and raucous drinking stanzas; indeed, the song marks a break from her own early work. After her conversion, her songs continue to use Jacobite images but to employ them, often more dogmatically than in these graceful stanzas, to project evangelically tinged scenes of future bliss.

'The Land o' the Leal' circulated briskly. For a long time it was believed that Burns wrote the stanzas (written around 1798) just before his death in July 1796. Bardolaters wishing to document a deathbed repentance for the irreverent and insubordinate national poet were intent on staking Burns's claim to these conspicuously pious stanzas. Decades after the identification of Lady Nairne as the author in 1845, indignant 'proof' of Burns's authorship was still being manufactured, including a note by William Stenhouse during the 1870s that

> sometime in the Sixties ... I remember perfectly reading and discussing ... an account of the production of the song given by Jessie Lewars [Burns's nurse during his final illness]. She said she remembered when it was written, very shortly before Burns's death, that he gave it to her to read, and then placed it under his pillow.[100]

Perhaps Jessie Lewars did tell that story about some other late song, for Burns continued to write almost until the day he died. It could not have been this song, however.

In her old age, Nairne looked back on the composition of the song and the debate about its authorship:

> O yes, I was young then, I wrote it merely because I liked the air so much, and I put these words to it, never fearing questions as to authorship. However a lady ... took it down, and I hadn't Sir Walter's art of denying. I was present when it was asserted that Burns composed it on his deathbed, and that he had Jean instead of John ... I never answered.[101]

The song is among Nairne's contributions to *The Scottish Minstrel*, where it is listed as 'Author Unknown'.

The Prince, the Fishwife and the Honest Man

> The Pith o' Sense and Pride o' Worth,
> Are higher rank than a' that.
>
> Burns, 'Is There for Honest Poverty'[102]

Two songs by Nairne and Burns with strong echoes of Jacobite sources adopt the voices of the labouring poor to engage in social critique. Nairne's 'Caller Herrin'', like 'The Laird o' Cockpen', expresses Jacobite distaste for displays of self-important pomp. The tune follows the cadence of the Newhaven fishwives' street cries, with passages of descending scales intended to sound like the bells of St Giles in the background. It was published (with no words, elaborate musical setting only) by Nathaniel Gow in 1798 or 1799. Nairne's stanzas do not slip right into Gow's music, although the phrasing of about half the setting matches her metre and words. She wrote the stanzas to help Gow through a period of financial trouble, which probably date her lyrics to around 1812–14 after the death of his music-partner. Nairne sent a proxy to Gow bearing the text of the song along with an anonymous note, written like the text in a disguised hand, instructing him to print the stanzas as his own and suggesting to which duchess he should dedicate the song for the best chance of generous assistance. In short, she gave away what may be her best song:

> Wha'll buy caller herrin'?   'fresh, chilled'
> They're bonnie fish and halesome fairin',   'wholesome fare'
> Wha'll buy caller herrin',
> New drawn frae the Forth?   (from the Firth of Forth)
>
> When ye were sleepin' on your pillows,
> Dream'd ye ought o' our puir fellows,   'poor'
> Darkling as they fac'd the billows,
> A' to fill the woven willows,   (the fishwives' baskets)
>   Buy my caller herrin' new drawn frae the Forth.

Wha'll buy my caller herrin'?	
They're no brought here without brave daring;	
Buy my caller herrin'	
Hauld thro' wind and rain.	'hauled'
Wha'll buy my caller herrin'?	
Oh ye may ca them vulgar fairin',	
Wives and mithers maist despairing,	'mothers most'
Ca them lives o' men.	'call'
When the creel o' herrin' passes,	(wicker basket carried on the back)
Ladies, clad in silks and laces,	
Gather in their braw pelisses,	'fine coats; fur coats'
Cast their heads and screw their faces.	'toss'
Wha'll buy caller herrin'? &c.[103]	

Fine ladies may sneer, but this simple food is gathered at the risk of human life.[104] Nairne satirizes the emphasis on material prosperity that for her taints post-Union, post-Stuart Scotland. In this song, descendants of the winners in the eighteenth-century conflicts promenade in their imported silks and laces, turning from Scottish workers and even the Scottish food chain. Nairne's subtext is clear: scorners of herring have gotten above themselves; the fishwives and their families model 'Scottish' values.

'Caller Herrin'' criticizes British gold and the imported luxuries that it pays for. Nairne's song may draw on famous stanzas by Burns:

Is there, for honest Poverty	
That hings his head, and a' that;	'hangs'
The coward-slave we pass him by,	
We dare be poor for a' that!	
For a' that, and a' that,	
Our toils obscure, and a' that,	
The rank is but the guinea's stamp,	
The Man's the gowd for a' that. –	'gold'
What though on hamely fare we dine,	'plain (homely) food'
Wear hoddin grey, and a' that.	'handmade clothes of homespun'
Gie fools their silks, and knaves their wine,	'give'
A Man's a Man for a' that.	
For a' that, and a' that,	
Their tinsel show, and a' that;	
The honest man, though e'er sae poor,	
Is king o' men for a' that. –	
Ye see yon birkie ca'd, a lord,	'spry fellow (suggestion of capering)'
Wha struts, and stares, and a' that,	
Though hundreds worship at his word,	
He's but a coof for a' that	'fool'
For a' that, and a' that,	

> His ribband, star and a' that,   (orders of merit)
> The man of independent mind,
>   He looks and laughs at a' that. –
>   ...
> Then let us pray that come it may,
>   As come it will for a' that,
> That Sense and Worth, o'er a' the earth
>   Shall bear the gree, and a' that.   'be decided victor'
> For a' that, and a' that,
>   It's comin yet for a' that,
> That Man to Man the warld o'er,   'world'
>   Shall brothers be for a' that.[105]

As in 'Caller Herrin'', silken garb has nothing to do with 'Worth', which is linked to honest labour, accurately if grimly rephrased by Burns as 'honest Poverty'. If 'leal' is Nairne's keyword, 'honest' is Burns's: his collected poems use the word (in some form) ninety-four times.

Kinsley's note identifies allusions in Burns's song to Thomas Paine and others but he misses echoes of a song in *The True Loyalist*. I have bolded the phrases that Burns's song revisits:

> Though G—die reign in J—ie's stead   (Geordie; Jamie)
> I'm grieved, yet scorn to shew that;
> I'll ne'er look down, nor **hing my head**
> On Rebel-W-gs for a' that;
> But still I'll trust in Providence,
> And still I'll **laugh at a' that**;
> And sing, He's o'er the hills this night
> That I love weel for a' that.   'well'
>   ...
> The W-gs think a' that Willie's mine,   'Whigs'
> But yet **they mauna fa' that**;
> They think our hearts will be cast down,
> But we'll be blyth for a' that.
> For a' that, and a' that,
> And thrice as meikle's a' that;
> He's bonny that's o'er the hills this night,
> And will be here for a' that.[106]

Two stanzas not quoted above list the Highland accoutrements of Charles ('The target, and the highland plaid, / And shoulder-belt, and a' that'). Burns's song likewise emphasizes dress but contrasts the working poor's homespun and plain diet with the 'silks', 'wine' and marks of royal favour ('ribband, star, and a' that') displayed by the wealthy classes. Burns employs the operatic dyads of Jacobite rhetoric: real work versus place-getting at court; real merit versus 'tinsel show'. Nonetheless, the song also offers a clear instance of Burns's transformation of

Jacobite partisan statement into something else entirely. He loves the energy of resentment that animates the old songs, and he concurs with their rejection of a corrupt political climate and a bad consensus. Yet Burns's lyrics never give a thought to royal prerogatives: this particular song foresees a new world order in which hereditary rank will give way to 'Sense and Worth'.

Nairne never liked Charles Edward Stuart better than when she could imagine him wandering homeless, but her imagination of kingship is not negative. She had no use for regal pomp or stateliness per se; according to a visiting niece, there was much mirth in her household over George IV's delight in ceremony during his visit to Edinburgh in 1824.[107] Nonetheless, for her the Stuart kings have a lustre derived from their long centrality in Scottish history. 'Caller Herrin" celebrates the fishwives of Newhaven; other Nairne songs celebrate the loyalty of the Scots to their Prince: there is no contradiction, for in all cases her speakers follow ancient Scottish ways of life. Nairne is sometimes dismissed as overly sentimental, perhaps because it is so easy to miss how often, as in 'Caller Herrin" or the Laird o' Cockpen', her praise of the Scotland-that-was implies a sharp rebuke of the Scotland-that-is in her own day.

After her fair copy of what was probably her last song ('Would Ye Be Young Again?'), completed when she was seventy-six, Nairne wrote beneath the stanzas a telling sentence: 'The thirst of the dying wretch in the desert is nothing to the pining for voices which have ceased forever!'[108] She adds 'Anon' after the sentence, ensuring that her thoughts, with their tinge of bitterness, will remain decently cloaked. It is possible that Nairne's impulse to write songs originated not in political beliefs but rather this pining for 'lost voices'. Though Nairne's biographers Charles Rogers and George Henderson, who were both ministers, emphasize her steadiness and piety, many of their anecdotes, including the 'dying wretch' sentiment just quoted, suggest not devout resignation but a fierce grief held in check. Her lyrics may look to the past because in her own musings that was where everything valuable was locked away. Her tendency to suppress the political content of a Jacobite song tradition whose reason for existing was political is certainly striking, but her loyalties were divided. Her late parents and brothers had been staunch Jacobites but her husband was an officer in the British army. As in other areas of her creative life, Nairne may have judged it best to leave a great deal unsaid.

A drawing Nairne made of the Old House at Gask suggests some of the ways posterity has misread her. As shown in Figure 3.2, Nairne depicts her childhood home and emphasizes its setting near a public road. She has drawn stairs leading into the road from the kitchen garden, and in full view of sixteen tiny windows, a traveller (or homeless person, or beggar) walks down the highway. He is in the foreground. A large rowan tree is visible behind the house's chimney at the far right. In the revised image that appears in *The Scottish Songstress* (see p. 149), the wanderer and the rowan tree are deleted and the trees are more generic.

THE AULD HOUSE O' GASK, PERTHSHIRE.

Figure 3.2: Carolina Oliphant's sketch of her birthplace, the Old House at Gask, abandoned for a new family house c. 1800. C. Rogers (ed.), *Life and Songs of the Baroness Nairne* (Edinburgh: John Grant, 1905), opposite p. 182; author's collection.

In an even more genteel version in *Lays from Strathearn*, not illustrated here, the highway is replaced by a private driveway to the house and the steps are erased in addition to Figure 3.3's deletion of the traveller and the rowan tree.[109]

Nairne's original drawing links the landed family to the wandering poor: a sturdy representative of the non-owning classes is prominent in the foreground and in full view of the family. In the most radical editing of the image, the Old House becomes a conventional Great House and a broad, blank lawn guards the inhabitants from any sight of the lower orders going about their business: even that shown in Figure 3.3 has redrawn a public highway as a private drive. Those later edits to Nairne's drawing flatter modern ideas of what a Baroness's birthplace should look like, but the original suggests an older Scottish world-view, the view, I think, of Nairne's songs. In her Jacobite-tinged lyric vision, peasants and landed aristocrats coexist in mutual amity and rather close quarters, their solidarity constructed largely out of a shared distaste for imported and newfangled values for 'improvement'. In 'Will Ye No Come Back Again', there is not a single ragged Highlander tempted by the 'thirty thousand pound' offered for information on Charles Edward's whereabouts. There are no silks or laces on the sturdy traveller in Nairne's original sketch and no frills about the house, which looks substantial and old but in no way ornamental. For his part, Burns, though

Drawn by Lady Nairne

Figure 3.3: Victorian revision of Nairne's original sketch of the Auld House, from M. Simpson, *Scottish Songstress*, p. 35; author's collection.

sympathetic to Jacobite dissent, rejects this vision of unity between the king, the landholders and 'the people'. He sees that this coalition is possible only when all parties stay perpetually in their assigned place – their social rank at birth – just as the wanderer in Nairne's drawing looms large but stays on his own side of the road.

I have suggested that wearing the tartan has no essential connection with 'Scottishness' as defined by either Nairne or Burns. There is not a plaidie to be seen in 'Caller Herrin'' or 'Is There for Honest Poverty', songs in which the garb of labouring men and women is proudly adopted by national speakers. Yet the two poets place Scotland in different timeframes. Nairne's song stands up for traditional ways of Scottish life; she puts her faith in religious, not political, dogma. Burns's songs in contrast often appeal to a better future, a world of empowered working people that's coming yet. In July 1999 'Is There for Honest Poverty' was performed when the Scottish Parliament reconvened for the first time in almost 300 years. One cannot imagine Nairne's 'Will Ye No Come Back Again?' being chosen as appropriate for this occasion. Scotland's 'now' was important to Burns as a means to a future for which he had hopes. For Nairne, by contrast, even her closely guarded anonymity suggests a refusal to align herself with her own historical moment. She is the belated survivor of an Old House, a lost world of loyalty and honour. This disparity in Nairne's and Burns's rendering of Scottish time is the main point of difference between Scotland's two greatest writers of national song.

4 THREE DRUNK MEN: VISIONARY MIDNIGHT IN ROBERT FERGUSSON, BURNS AND HUGH MACDIARMID

> The [Scots] poets seem to say ... Be satisfied, if you think it is we who are drunk. As for us, let the contrast be unexplained, and let us make merry in this clash of strange worlds and moods.
> G. Gregory Smith, *Scottish Literature: Character and Influence* (1919)[1]

> These two very different drives exist side by side, mostly in open conflict ... [L]et us think of them ... as the separate art-worlds of *dream* and *intoxication*.
> Friedrich Nietzsche, *The Birth of Tragedy* (1872; trans. 1999)[2]

> If you could imagine dissonance assuming human form – and what else is man? – this dissonance would need, in order to be able to live, a magnificent illusion.
> Friedrich Nietzsche, *The Birth of Tragedy*[3]

Nietzsche's 'separate art-worlds of *dream* and *intoxication*' contend in Hugh MacDiarmid's 'A Drunk Man Looks at the Thistle' (1926) and in many poems by Robert Fergusson and Robert Burns. MacDiarmid's text names Nietzsche, whose trochaic surname summons a Burns-like feminine rhyme: 'Or gin ye s'ud need mair than ane to teach ye, / Then learn frae Dostoevski and frae Nietzsche'.[4] All three Scots, like Nietzsche in his view of human nature as an embodied dissonance, saw poems as sites 'whaur / Extremes meet',[5] including extremes of the heroic and abject. MacDiarmid, Fergusson and Burns all write poems of nocturnal encounter in which a drunken speaker's visions fleetingly illumine a darkened world. Their Drunk Man personae alternate between the roles of bard and poet, at one moment channelling disparate voices of Scotland but at the next offering personal opinions, social commentary and/or poetic critique. Burns uses Drunk Men in bardic – indeed, near-balladic – exposés of local secrets ('Death and Doctor Hornbook') but also in poet-Burnsian performances such as 'Tam o'Shanter', with its celebration of an ale-drunk farmer by a word-drunk narrator.

Nietzsche saw in the birth of Greek tragedy the generative conflict of perfect form – the Apollonian 'magnificent illusion' – and Dionysian energy that is musical, primal, intoxicated.[6] Early in the twentieth century, G. Gregory Smith devised the playful term 'Caledonian antisyzygy' to describe Scottish poetry's analogous spirit of contending contraries. Syzygy describes an alignment of the planets, so Smith's antisyzygy emphasizes Scottish literature's refusal of convergence, its perpetual brawl of opposing statements and entities. W. N. Herbert has argued that Smith's ideas about unresolved tensions in Scottish writing remained useful to MacDiarmid throughout his career. Certainly they were crucial in the early to mid-1920s as he shape-shifted – more dramatically than Burns's 1786 change from 'Burness' to 'Burns' – from Christopher M. Grieve, poet in English, to 'Hugh MacDiarmid', modernist Makar.[7] Taking the idea of antisyzygy from Smith, MacDiarmid made it the cornerstone for a post-Romantic poetics by which he considers literary traditions local and global, long-standing and emerging. Nonetheless, the mood of 'A Drunk Man' is predominantly belated. As Jeffrey Skoblow has observed, 'The Drunk Man's condition is a kind of hangover of great, indeed inescapable, Romantic metaphors'.[8]

Fergusson's best poems likewise portray colliding realms of dream/nightmare and intoxication: Edinburgh roisterers versus the City Guardsmen, who beat them as they stumble homeward; social sing-alongs at the Cape Club versus bizarre encounters with indignant ghosts, talking sidewalks, pregnant cannons, pouting trousers and diabolically clanging church-bells.[9] The door of Fergusson's candle-lit tavern opens on a visionary streetscape. In dialogue poems that he calls 'eclogues', contraries brawl, as in the set-to between Brandy and Whisky in 'A Drink Eclogue', where a shouting match between the French and Scottish bottles is settled only when the Landlady arrives in the cellar to inform Brandy that he is merely Scottish whisky adulterated with saffron. (People of fashion demand imported drink, she says, but who can afford the excise taxes?) Fergusson often offers antisyzygal debates with no moderator, while Burns invents dizzy or corrupt speakers who express views designed to be rejected: among many examples, the best-known is 'Holy Willie's Prayer', whose antihero is a drunk man in the usual sense (l. 51) as well as being drunk with power as an elder of the parish. For all MacDiarmid's sampling of European, American and Scottish novelists and poets, he is more straightforward than either Fergusson or Burns in providing a speaker for 'A Drunk Man Looks at the Thistle' who, however dissonant his wandering thoughts, so clearly looks with a writer's eyes. Burns uses naive speakers designed for alert readers to see through while Fergusson employs conspicuously quotidian surrogates including inanimate objects from whisky bottles to city sidewalks.

In 'Death and Doctor Hornbook', Burns's closest approach to Fergusson's magical night-pieces, a rustic encounters Death while staggering home; fortuitously, he has consumed enough ale to remain undaunted. Burns's title excludes this speaker, however, focussing instead on skeletal, plain-spoken Death, depicted as a disgruntled workman, and overweening 'Hornbook', a schoolmaster in Tarbolton moonlighting as an amateur doctor and drug dispenser. Burns's tall tale – Huck Finn in his American vernacular might call it a 'stretcher' – begins with a suspiciously insistent subtitle ('A True Story'). Its first line informs readers that 'Some books are lies frae end to end' – not including, the narrator hastens to add, the story we are about to hear, every word of which is *completely true*:

> [T]his that I am gaun to tell,
> Which lately on a night befel,
> Is just as true's the Deil's in h-ll,
>   Or Dublin city ...¹⁰

In religious belief of Burns's place and time, the devil lives in hell, but a popular Irish dance tune gives Dublin as his address. The first statement is an article of faith but the second a matter of language, for the Scandinavian name for the city was 'Divelin', in which, in a homophonic sense, the 'divel' does live. Syllepsis (hell ... or Dublin) is a favourite figure for Burns, who often devises compound or serial constructions that are syntactically coordinate but semantically incongruous. Like oxymoron, another favourite figure, syllepsis is a kind of antisyzygy by which language moves through unsettling comparisons to comic dissonance. In 'Love and Liberty', probably written the same year as 'Hornbook', the Carlin swoons for two reasons as the Caird concludes his amorous song: 'partly with LOVE o'ercome sae sair, / An' partly she was drunk'.¹¹

An air of unsteadiness pervades 'Death and Doctor Hornbook', and not only because its ale-fuddled speaker thinks that he has talked all night with Death. Doctor Hornbook's wits are turned by the new words acquired from his home-study of Buchan's *Domestic Medicine*:

Calces o' fossils, earths, and trees;	'fossilized bone, soil, bark'
True Sal-marinum o' the seas;	'salt-water'
The Farina of beans and pease,	'starch'
He has't in plenty;	
Aqua-fontis, what you please,	'fresh water'
He can content ye.¹²	

Fergusson's 'Caller Water', a model for Burns's poem, mocks medical Latin's mystification of these 'simples' or uncompounded substances. Burns probably takes his reference to 'aqua fontis' above from Fergusson's reference in 'Caller Water' to '*aqua font*' (l. 30) as

... the name that doctors use	
Their patients noddles to confuse;	
With *simples* clad in terms abstruse,	
They labour still,	
In kittle words to gar you roose	'tricky, uncertain' 'praise'
Their want o' skill.¹³	

In 'Hornbook', readers are drawn into Burns's vertiginous, barbed exuberance. Resistance is futile in part because, given the title, Death is the alternative to Hornbook's fine words and the speaker's tale-spinning. Even Jock Hornbook and the impaired speaker – studying by candlelight, stumbling in moonlight – are preferable to the silent dark. Yet though most readers have accepted such wild yarns of the Drunk Man as light entertainment, a few (including Hugh MacDiarmid's devoutly Christian father) have always rejected their charm as dangerous: Burns 'was taboo in my father's house', recalled MacDiarmid in *Lucky Poet*, 'and quite unknown to me as a boy'.[14]

In Nietzsche's writings, what people take to be stable truth derives from language and images and therefore stands, despite the seeming objectivity of philosophy and science, on shifting ground:

> What, then, is truth? A mobile army of metaphors, metonymies, anthropomorphisms ... which have been subjected to poetical and rhetorical intensification, translation, and decoration ... and which, after they have been in use a long time, strike a people as firmly established, canonical, and binding; truths are illusions of which we have forgotten they are illusions.[15]

Nietzsche's analysis works for 'Death and Doctor Hornbook', whose mock-hero has mastered not a science but a jargon: he can 'rattle' off the 'Latin names' of drugs as 'fast' as the 'A B C' in which he instructs his youngest scholars.[16] Like a poet and also like the fire-and-brimstone preachers ridiculed in the satirically packed opening stanza, Hornbook's language-use is strictly decorative. He cannot really heal or save, but in this one sense like a poet, he can dazzle and distract.

Burns's rustic speaker tells the reader what Death has told him about Hornbook, who does not speak directly in the poem. This narrator does not knowingly lie, but he is dim-witted and no reliable judge of his own story. 'I was na fou' (not full; i.e., not drunk) (l. 14) that night, he says, though he admits he 'had plenty' (l. 14) and that when he stared at the crescent moon to count her 'horns', he 'cou'd na tell' whether 'she' had 'three or four' (ll. 21–4). This double vision persists in later stanzas that pit Death's authority and prerogatives – 'They're mine', says Fergusson's Death succinctly in 'Auld Reikie', another forerunner of Burns's 'Hornbook' (l. 165) – against the boasts of the '*bauld* Apothecary'(l. 105), whose spiel has half-convinced even Death. The small children of Tarbolton now just mock him and poke at his hips (ll. 83–4), says Death, who is a skeleton, in a grotesque diatribe that includes the rhyming of 'art' with 'fart':

> See, here's a scythe, and there's a dart,
>   (the scythe and dart are his tools)
> They hae pierc'd mony a gallant heart;
> But Doctor *Hornbook*, wi' his art,
>   And cursed skill,
> Has made them baith no worth a f—t,
>   D—n'd haet they'll kill! (ll. 85–90)

A specialist in carnal transactions, Death can see no difference between afflatus (Hornbook's claim to inspired 'art') and merely intestinal flatus; in fact, in this case there is little difference. The poem's mood of wayward joy stems from its speaker's denial of a plain fact: Death rules the body and will one day 'choke the breath', stopping each human story (l. 70). Yet in this telling, Hornbook's magic drugs have thwarted, even routed Death; and the closing lines do the same when the church bell strikes a predawn hour, breaking into the skeleton's tirade and forcing him away. Burns borrows Fergusson's closure in 'The Mutual Complaint of Plainstanes and Causey', in which a quarrelling street and sidewalk must likewise stand mute as early dawn lightens the east. In Burns, Death is silenced at a similar hour and must leave with his tools. This Drunk Man's tale, like Scheherazade's stories in *1001 Nights*, is not closed out so much as broken off, deferring Death to another day.

Among Hornbook's superpowers, reports Death in disgust, is his ability to diagnose and cure patients he has never seen:

> Ev'n them he canna get attended,
> Altho' their face he ne'er had kend it,
> Just sh- in a kail-blade and send it,   'cabbage leaf'
>   As soon's he smells 't,
> Baith their disease, and what will mend it,
>   At once he tells 't. (ll. 109–14)

Death is affronted by Hornbook's rescue of those legitimately scheduled for the scythe and dart but complains too of unauthorized homicides. Heirs are using Hornbook's drugs to bury healthy parents, girls are consulting him about drugs to terminate pregnancies and faithless husbands are murdering inconvenient wives. Buried secrets are a fact of life and death in every community, but this poem's deep investment is in looking away from facts, just as Doctor Hornbook feels no pressing need to examine his patients before prescribing for them. For all its grim topic, the work is aglow with Hornbook's insane overconfidence. Having vanquished illiteracy through technologies of early reading, as suggested by his metonymic name Hornbook, the portly dominie has gone on to challenge Death, or at any rate to drive him out of Tarbolton. And for all the speaker, who is not bright, can tell, Hornbook will win this fight. Death has a plan to defeat his rival but readers never learn the details; and as matters stand in the last lines, Hornbook remains in sole charge of all the bodies in the village, including those in the spare field currently being used as a graveyard (ll. 130–50). No matter that his claims to medical expertise and clinical prowess stand on ground as shaky as the speaker's gait:

> I was come round about the hill,
> And todlin down on *Willie's mill*,   'walking unsteadily'
> Setting my staff wi' a' my skill,   'walking stick, cudgel'
>   To keep me sicker,   'secure (steady)'

> Tho' leeward whyles, against my will,   'to the side sometimes'
> I took a bicker.   'staggered'
>   (ll. 25–30)

MacDiarmid's 'A Drunk Man Looks at the Thistle' opens with an echo of the early stanzas in 'Death and Doctor Hornbook' ('I wasna fou', l. 14) though his speaker is jaded rather than dizzily naive:

> I amna fou' sae muckle as tired – deid dune,
> It's gey and hard wark coupin' gless for gless
> Wi' Cruivie and Gilsanquhar and the like,
> And I'm no' juist as bauld as aince I wes.[17]

His Drunk Man cannot keep 'free [of] the ditches' like Burns's speaker (l. 16) but begins with a fall; and if Burns's rustic sits down with Death for a long conversation, MacDiarmid's, immobilized and alone, talks to himself. His thoughts range far, sometimes touching on contraries reminiscent of those in 'Hornbook':

> Guid sakes, ye dinna need to pass   'do not'
> Ony exam, to dee   'die'
> – Daith canna tell a common flech   'flea'
> Frae a performing flea! ... (ll. 799–802)

Doctor Hornbook is, at least in his own mind, splendidly empowered, while MacDiarmid's Drunk Man sees himself more as a performing insect. Yet MacDiarmid is like Burns in his focus on fluency, the acrobatic interplay of dialect Scots with standard English and literary allusions from all over. His speaker muses on Melville and Hawthorne, translates Russian and Belgian poetry into Scots, transcribes passages of French and Italian, and alludes to poems from Coleridge's 'The Rime of the Ancient Mariner' to Eliot's 'The Wasteland' – all while moving between topics public (the failure of the General Strike) and private (meditations on marriage).

As in Burns's 'Hornbook', drunken fancy looks at Death, though MacDiarmid's Drunk Man takes a longer, closer look:

> It is Mortality itsel' – the mortal coil,
> Mockin' Perfection, Man afore the Throne o' God
> He has yet bigged himsel', Man torn in twa   'built' 'two'
> And glorious in the lift and grisly on the sod! ...   'sky'
>
> There's nought sae sober as a man blin' drunk.   'so'
> I maun ha'e got an unco bellyfu'   'must have' 'uncommon'
> To jaw like this – and yet what I am sayin'
> Is a' the apter, aiblins, to be true.   'perhaps'
>   (ll. 273–80)

MacDiarmid embraces Smith's antisyzyzy, Nietzsche's idea of human nature as an embodied dissonance, and Burns's juxtaposition of truth and lying as filtered through a tipsy speaker. MacDiarmid's Drunk Man, however, is not so much shaky as frozen in place. He lies still, seeing only the thistle round the ditch above him and higher still a moonlit sky. The phantasmagoric shiftings of thistle and moon, refusing syzygy, produce images by turns beautiful and bizarre:

> Is it the munelicht or a leprosy
> That spreids aboot me; and a thistle
> Or my ain skeleton ... (ll. 369–72)

In his dismissive comments about Cruivie and Gilsanquhar, the drinking cronies he has just left, MacDiarmid echoes the ancient Scottish tradition of what might be called male *anti-bonding* poems:

> What are prophets and priests and kings,
> What's ocht to the people o' Scotland?
> Speak – and Cruivie'll goam at you,   'stare blankly'
> Gilshanquhar jalouse you're dottlin!   'suspect'   'crazy'
>
> ... And whiles I wish I'd nae mair sense   'sometimes'   'no more'
> Than Cruivie and Gilsanquhar,
> And envy their rude health and curse
> My gnawin' canker. (ll. 783–86; ll. 795–99)

Quarrels and contests mark Scottish insult-matches, from 'Peblis to the Play' (1430–50) and 'Chrystis Kirk on the Green' to 'The Flyting of Dunbar and Kennedie' (*c*. 1503): the first two mentioned begin at a convivial gathering but culminate in a riot.[18] If the Greeks wrote Anacreontics lightly praising wine and love, the Scots for centuries have been depicting large- and small-scale scenes of boozing, boasting and brawling.

In the 1770s, Fergusson brought back this Scottish free-for-all in such raucous performances as 'The King's Birth-day in Edinburgh'. His epigraph for that poem was taken from William Drummond of Hawthornden's 'Polemo-Middinia' ('Battle of the Midden', pub. 1684), described by George Gilfallan as 'a grotesque mixture of bad Latin and semi-Latinised Scotch'.[19] In these fight-poems, even the diction is a 'gallimaufry', to use a term of MacDiarmid's – a word-hash in which languages as well as men contend.[20] Another of Fergusson's holiday poems, 'Leith Races', inspired the opening stanzas of Burns's 'The Holy Fair': both poets use the rhyme-rich, rollicking 'Chrystis-Kirk' stanza of earlier Scottish fight-poems, drawing anarchic energy from the depiction of colliding realms: celebration and incarceration, sermonizing and houghmagandie. The old Scots texts emphasize direct assaults, physical or verbal; but Fergusson, Burns and MacDiarmid adapt the tradition for purposes ranging from allegory to satire to self-mocking language play. Though all take up a drunk-and-disorderly setting and/or speaker, MacDiarmid and Fergusson lean to haunted midnight social commentary while Burns specializes in sly mock epic. In all three, however, drunken speakers cross a threshold to see incredible things. Their Drunk Men, like Burns's rustic in 'Death and Doctor Hornbook', pass their story along to readers presumably sober, if not presumed to be wholly innocent themselves. As MacDiarmid said in 1926, 'Drunkenness has a logic of its own, with which, even in these decadent days, I believe a sufficient minority of my countrymen remain *au fait*'.[21]

Critics have had no difficulty in perceiving the visionary element in MacDiarmid but have often misread Fergusson's and Burns's 'Drunk Man' poems as literal self-portraits. During the 1820s, Henry Mackenzie assumed that Burns's love of Fergusson derived solely from his attraction to scenes of drunkenness:

> Fergusson, dissipated and drunken, died in early life after having produced poems faithfully and humorously describing scenes of Edinburgh festivity and somewhat of blackguardism ... Burns, originally virtuous, was seduced by dissipated companions, and after he got into the Excise addicted himself to drunkenness, tho' the rays of his genius sometimes broke through the mist of his dissipation ... His great admiration of Fergusson shewed his propensity to coarse dissipation.[22]

This is not only circular in logic but chronologically inaccurate: such works as 'Death and Doctor Hornbook' and 'Love and Liberty' were written years before Burns's appointment to the Excise in 1788. Mackenzie's statement fails to acknowledge Burns's legitimate gratitude for Fergusson's technical legacy: his rich vernacular vocabulary, development of standard Habbie and other Scots stanza-forms, and virtuoso rhyming. Family testimony likewise contradicts Mackenzie. The poet's brother Gilbert recalled of their years together on Lochlie and Mossgiel farms that 'I do not recollect, during ... seven years [*c.* 1779–86] ... to have ever seen him intoxicated, nor was he ... at all given to drinking'. Gilbert notes that Burns received the same income as all his siblings – £7 per year – and says that when Burns was writing such poems as 'Doctor Hornbook', his brother's

> expenses never ... exceeded his slender income. As I was intrusted with the keeping of the family accounts, it is not possible that there can be any fallacy in this statement, in my brother's favor. His temperance and frugality were everything that could be wished.[23]

Evidence about Burns and drink during his later years is mixed, as is the biographers' consensus.[24] Yet his use of a drunken speaker cannot at any rate be read as exclusively confessional. For the Drunk Man is a recurring trope in literary Scots from Dunbar and Kennedie to Fergusson and Burns to MacDiarmid – generally, as in 'Death and Doctor Hornbook', unmasking not the poet but the culture he looks at and speaks to. The Scottish vernacular poets' reliance on this Drunk

Man persona, especially for satire, raises doubt about critics who take as directly autobiographical Tam o'Shanter's weekly binge on market day (or who read the witches' dance later in the poem as proof that Burns was prone to superstitious terror).[25] Supported by centuries of Scottish brawl poems, 'Tam o'Shanter' in fact stoutly repels all efforts, such as Wordsworth's in the passage below, to see an improving message in the tale:

> The poet fears not to tell the reader in the outset that his hero was a desperate and sottish drunkard, whose excesses were as frequent as his opportunities ... I pity him who cannot perceive that, in all this, though there was no moral purpose, there is a moral effect: [']Kings may be blest, but Tam was glorious, / O'er a' the ills of life victorious.['] What a lesson do these words convey of charitable indulgence for the vicious habits of the principal actor of this scene, and of those who resemble him! ('Letter to a Friend of Robert Burns')[26]

In his irritated response to Wordsworth's comments, William Hazlitt remarks that

> 'till some puritanical genius should arise to do these things equally well without any knowledge of them, the world might forgive Burns the injuries he had done his health and fortune in his poetical apprenticeship to experience, for the pleasure he had afforded them.[27]

Yet Hazlitt too, reading 'Tam o'Shanter' as a disclosure of personal 'experience', overlooks the poem's roots in one of oldest, and for modern readers most alien, traditions in Scottish poetry.

Burns's letters correct any impulse to read these poems as not-so-veiled accounts of personal conduct. In 1791, he describes the drunken scene at Ellisland farm that followed the sale of his harvest:

> I sold my crop on this day se'ennight past, & sold it very well: a guinea an acre, on an average, above value. – But such a scene of drunkenness was hardly ever seen in this country. – After the roup [auction] was over, about thirty people engaged in a battle, every ma [3 or 4 letters illegible] his own hand, & fought it out for three hours. Nor was the scene much better in the house. – No fighting, indeed, but folks lieing drunk on the floor, & decanting, untill both my dogs got so drunk by attending them, that they could not stand. – You will easily guess how I enjoyed the scene as I was no farther over than you used to see me.[28]

The phrase 'farther over' sees drunkenness as a spectrum, its extreme degree here viewed with distaste. A similar disdain marks lines on being appointed to the Excise in 1788, a position in which measuring ale barrels would be among Burns's duties: '[t]hat clarty barm [dirty yeast] should stain my laurels'.[29]

Robert Fergusson, only twenty-four when he died, left few written records except for his poems; and most of his biographers, notably David Irving, read poems of drunken encounter directly back into his life.³⁰ Fergusson's surviving friends were horrified at the censorious early biographies, and Thomas Sommers tried to set the record straight in 1803, though to little effect. Late in the nineteenth century, Robert Louis Stevenson could still deplore the fate of the 'poor, white-faced, drunken, vicious boy that raved himself to death in the Edinburgh madhouse', though he admits that this is not all there is to say: 'Surely there is more to be gleaned about Fergusson'.³¹ One point is clear despite scanty records of the poet's personal life: Fergusson, loosely linking the Scottish midnight brawl poem to scenes of ghostly encounter in 'Mutual Complaint of Plainstanes and Causey' and other poems, inspired Burns, who himself inspired (or annoyed) MacDiarmid sufficiently to be addressed in 'A Drunk Man Looks at the Thistle'. One of Fergusson's richest gifts to Burns was this poetic plot so memorably adapted and updated by MacDiarmid in 1926: the homeward journey of a Drunk Man – alone, outside and open to marvellous encounter.

Before turning to 'Tam o' Shanter' and its relation to the Drunk Man trope in general as well as MacDiarmid's poem in particular, I turn to a teasing auxiliary image: the whistle, a child's trifle and a shepherd's tool. Fergusson and MacDiarmid use it as a symbol for poetry, while Burns makes the whistle the centrepiece in a surreal ballad about a drinking match. The whistle calls readers to equivocal poetic as opposed to literal readings, for as a signifier it points back to numerous contradictory signifieds, among them poetry, poverty, pastoral simplicity and piratical drunken combat.

Whistle Hall

> Gin ever ye come here awa',
> I hope ye'll be sae gude as ca',
> For Andrew Gray, at Whistle-ha,
>   The riddle-macker ...   (maker of sieves, riddles, or puns)
>   A. Gray, 'To R. Fergusson'³²

The poet who addressed Fergusson from Whistle Hall was Andrew Gray, a minister at Abernethy. His verse-letter was published in a Perth newspaper in June 1773, with Fergusson's reply printed a few weeks later. In choosing Whistle Hall as his poetic home, Gray summons a wealth of possible meanings. A whistle suggests a whimsical reference to drink – as in 'wetting your whistle', a phrase that both Fergusson and Burns adapt in Scots.³³ It can be a noun or a verb and can identify the song of a bird or song of a poet, or a shepherd's way of calling his flock. Vaguely onomatopoeic, 'whistle' is not high-literary or learned; it suggests the natural. A whistle is a trifle, too: a toy, an empty thing. Tam o' Shanter, elevated by ale, enters a fierce midnight storm blithely, not minding it 'a whistle' (l. 52). In Burns's 'Author's Earnest Cry and Prayer', which protests a rise in the price of whisky, old

Mother Scotland, thirsting for drink, is described as angrily brandishing a half-pint tankard that is 'as toom's [empty as] a whissle' (l. 38). 'Kist o' whistles', a scornful reference to a cathedral organ as a 'chest of whistles', remembers the violence of the Reformation in Scotland; *A Kist of Whistles* is also the title of MacDiarmid's 1947 collection of poems in English. In 'A Drunk Man', 'whistle' is paired in rhyme with 'thistle' (l. 372) as a subsidiary 'Scottish' image.

On the exact location of Whistle Hall, Gray's poem offers a trail of false clues: 'About a rig length frae Coolsa, / Just o'er the water' (l. 30). As Matthew MacDiarmid writes in his note to Gray's epistle, 'the topography, the dialect and the occupation are assumed in order to mystify ... [T]he most careful research ... [has] failed to identify the place-name Coolsa'.[34] Fergusson's reply to Gray comments on this indeterminate return address:

'Frae *Whistleha*' your muse doth cry;   'call' (summon me)
Whare're ye win I carena by;   'wherever you live, I don't care'
Ye're no the laird of *Whistledry*,
    As lang's ye can
Wi routh o' reikin *kail* supply   'plenty of hot kale' (cabbage)
    The inward man. (ll. 7–12)

Subsequent stanzas consider other means of feeding the inner man: the study of nature, which 'can gie scouth [room] to *muses nine* / At *Whistle-ha*'; steady application to the crafting of poems, lest Whistle-hall become '*idleseat*' (l. 47). The final stanza imagines a future sociable after-dinner meeting over a whisky.

Fergusson's mild and pleasant rejoinder to Gray offers a good introduction to his sensitive gentleness, always a counterpoint to his emphatic word-choices and the revolting details his poems supply about life in the reeking capital, including such perils as being knocked down by the cats tossed during celebrations ('The King's Birth-day in Edinburgh', ll. 75–7). Fergusson's verse-epistle is self-deprecating: he praises nature, sets application over genius as a means to poetic success, and – this is like Burns, who often proceeds to a similar conclusion – finally imagines a meeting in which the brother-poets will sing, laugh and talk '*cheek* for *chow*' (close together; l. 59). When the topic is not an urban riot, Fergusson's catalogue of pleasures always begins with simple foods and beverages (kail, fresh oysters, chilled water) and continues on to poetry; drink in these quieter poems is imagined in conjunction with friendly conversation.

Even Fergusson's more over-the-top celebrations of feasting and revelry ('Good Eating'; 'Leith Races') should be interpreted in the light of his extreme poverty: he wrote of food and drink with the avidity of a hungry man. He worked as a 'Writer' or clerk for law and court proceedings and was remembered by his friends as being extremely frail in appearance. 'Rising of the Session' describes the chronic hunger of the clerks during the Scottish court's long recesses (13

August to 11 November and 13 March to 11 June); in that poem, a starving Writer 'racks his wits, / How he may get his buick [body] weel clad, / And fill his guts'.³⁵ Fergusson's slovenly attire is also mentioned by surviving friends; a passage in 'Auld Reikie' describes the old-clothes merchants in St Mary's Wynd, a probable source for the poet's wardrobe:

... mony a hungry Writer, there	
Dives down at Night, wi' cleading bare,	'clothing'
And quickly rises to the View	
A Gentleman, perfyte and new.	
Ye rich Fock, look no wi' Disdain	
Upo' this ancient Brokage Lane!	'brokerage'
For naked Poets are supplied ...	(ll. 305–11)

A section in 'Auld Reikie' gives thanks for Edinburgh's havens for debtors around Holyrood Abbey and the King's Park: 'May I, whenever DUNS come nigh, / And shake my Garret wi' their Cry, / Scour here wi' Haste, Protection get, / To screen myself frae them and Debt' (ll. 295–8). For an indignant Burns, who studied these poems closely, the two extremes that met in the figure of his most admired predecessor were poetry and destitution: 'My curse upon your whunstane [whinstone] hearts, / Ye Enbrugh Gentry! / The tythe o' what ye waste at *cartes* [cards] / Wad stow'd his pantry!' (ll. 21–4).³⁶ A poet can address the world from Whistle Hall but cannot make a living there, Fergusson's poem to Gray warns between the lines. Fergusson, whose singing voice was so fine that his club-name was Sir Precentor, once won a bet that he could pose successfully as a street-singer; he sold out his stock of ballads in less than in two hours and regaled his friends with the profits. In any steady material sense, however, the poet's whistle was for Fergusson linked to a 'toom' or empty stomach.³⁷

The setting of Burns's 'The Whistle. A Ballad' is not Whistle Hall but Friar's Carse, home of Captain Robert Riddell, a patron and friend. The song describes a drinking contest in which Riddell and two cousins competed for an heirloom ebony whistle on 16 October 1789: in closing, Burns compares the trifle for which the gentry are competing with the valuable stanzas that their contest has inspired. In celebrating the family's unusual trophy, Burns revives this teasing image so often associated with song and drink. Here the whistle is used to contrast the heavy consumption of the gentry with a poet's joyous and more sociable creation.

Alexander Fergusson of Craigdarroch won the match that night in 1789 and 'blew on the Whistle' the 'requiem shrill' of his fallen cousins (l. 12). Most other details are fabricated or exaggerated. The ballad was a favourite either of the poet himself or of the publisher William Creech, who then held copyright and made the decisions for the 1793 edition. For 'The Whistle' appears as the last poem printed in this last edition of Burns's *Poems* to be published during his lifetime.

The song's metre is 'a derivative of the old alliterative line ... common in ballads and popular drinking songs';[38] but Burns's words are set to a new tune that may have been composed by Robert Riddell, the evening's host.[39] The plot is ballad-like in its narrative of a 'battle' in which a knight falls – one unlucky contender was in fact a Baronet – while another retires and a third emerges triumphant. Yet the song is not balladic but mock-epic in its elaborate back-story, which Burns constructs by allusion to Ossianic and Greek mythology. Burns's stylized diction recalls ancient epic as translated by Dryden and Pope: one such epic trait is the interest in the contention of mortal heroes shown by the god Phoebus and goddess Cynthia.[40] As in both epic and 'Ballad' (as the subtitle defines this song), Burns narrates as facts improbable and/or impossible heroic feats; seen in this light, the song also partakes, like 'Death and Doctor Hornbook', of the folk genre of the tall-tale.

Although featuring a character called 'the Bard', this is not anonymous/bardic but Poet Burnsian in its explicit final insistence on poetic song as the supreme self-indulgent pleasure. The claims to heroism of the carousing Drunk Men are repeatedly undercut by various poetic devices, including rhetorical question and syllepsis in the second line below:

> The gallant Sir Robert fought hard to the end;
> But who can with Fate and Quart Bumpers contend?
> Though Fate said, a hero should perish in light;
> So uprose bright Phoebus – and down fell the knight. (ll. 61–4)

Bacchus (Dionysus) appears in the song but only as a subordinate under Loda's command. It is Apollo, god of music, poetry and form, who triumphs in the end as his avatar, the sun, rises. Like Belinda in Pope's 'The Rape of the Lock', one of Burns's favourite poems, the contending men of property in 'The Whistle' are at once stars of the ballad and the targets of intermittent satire.

A few hours before the contest, Burns wrote to Riddell in terms that anticipate the song's hyperbole, wondering why 'the elements ... seem to take the matter very quietly: they did not even usher in this morning with triple suns and a shower of blood, symbolical of the three potent heroes and the mighty claret-shed of the day'.[41] The ballad opens on a parodic echo of Virgil's *Aeneid* – 'I sing of a Whistle'. Yet as if realizing that the 'whistle' is incongruous as an epic topic, the line goes on to insist that this is 'a Whistle of worth', the poem's first oxymoron. Alternating inflation and deflation also mark the Bard's introduction of the three combatants:

> Three joyous good fellows with hearts clear of flaw;
> Craigdarroch so famous for wit, worth, and law;
> And trusty Glenriddel, so skilled in old coins;
> And gallant Sir Robert, deep-read in old wines. (ll. 21–4)

Burns devises two epic genealogies for the whistle. The 'authentic Prose history' inserted in a note above the text is bogus, greatly exaggerating its age,[42] while in the ballad itself the whistle's origins are traced even farther back to the Ossianic sagas, in Burns's view equally spurious.[43] According to the early stanzas, it was bestowed in ancient times by Loda (spirit of Odin) on Bacchus, 'god of the bottle', who was commanded to carry the whistle to Scotland and avenge the wrongs of Loda by inciting Fingal's descendants - the Scots nation - to ruinous feats of competitive drinking:

> This Whistle's your challenge, to Scotland get o'er,
> And drink them to hell, Sir! or ne'er see me more!   (ll. 7–8)

The ballad then describes the triumph of the ancestral Sir Robert who brought the whistle into the family after winning a competition with Bacchus:

> He drank his poor god-ship as deep as the sea,   (the poor god-ship is Bacchus)
> No tide of the Baltic e'er drunker than he.   (ll. 15–16)

This noble heritage of drunken contention lives on in 1789, the speaker solemnly asserts, in the present generation of cousins.[44]

According to a surviving memorandum of the real-life wager and its outcome, Craigdarroch 'drank upds. of 5 Bottles of Claret' that night.[45] This is increased to eight quarts in the ballad, with 'cautious and sage' Riddell giving up and leaving the room after the sixth quart (l. 57) and Sir Robert Lawrie falling down after swallowing a seventh quart in a single bumper. In Burns's telling, Craigdarroch declares victory exactly as the doomed Scottish pirate-hero Sir Andrew Barton fights on in the old ballad, blowing on his whistle in defiance of his enemies.[46] All the while that he is lauding the cousins' epic exploits, the unnamed Bard sits somehow apart, like the omniscient voice-over narrator of 'Tam o'Shanter' or the herald in Homer who lives on to tell a true account of the slaughter of Penelope's suitors. The Bard bears witness as the early bumpers draw the kinsmen together:

> The dinner being over, the claret they ply,
> And every new cork is a new spring of joy;
> In the bands of old friendship and kindred so set,
> And the bands grew the tighter the more they were wet. (ll. 45–8)

Yet the cousins are truly communal in spirit only in this first phase of the match; they become antagonistic and separate as the night wears on and camaraderie disintegrates into drunken combat. The speaker, in contrast, remains socially connected, indulgently observant.

Undoubtedly the cousins are supreme as claret-consumers, but it is the Bard, Apollo's votary, who shapes the night's events into a song. He serves as Apollo's surrogate in another sense as well, staying during the long hours that the sun, introduced in early stanzas as another interested spectator, has been tactfully nudged offstage by his prudent twin-sister, the moon:

> Bright Phoebus ne'er witnessed so joyous a corps,
> And vow'd that to leave them he was quite forlorn,
> Till Cynthia hinted he'd see them next morn. (ll. 50–2)

The judge of the contest, John M'Murdo, must have attended but is not mentioned, nor is Patrick Miller, the poet's landlord, who had signed a memorandum agreeing to witness 'if possible'.[47] Contender in a different field, the Bard addresses Craigdarroch in the final stanza as a co-winner - 'thine be the laurel, and mine be the bay' (l. 71). As 'bay' and 'laurel' refer to the same plant, he asserts a parallel victory, although disappointed that Craigdarroch has ignored his earlier request for further feats of wine-consumption to lift his ballad to even higher, 'immortal' levels:

> Next uprose our Bard, like a prophet in drink: –
> 'Craigdarroch, thou'lt soar when creation shall sink!
> But if thou would flourish immortal in rhyme,
> Come – one bottle more – and have at the sublime!' (ll. 65–8)

Like Loda, prophetic Burns has his revenge on the hard-drinking Scottish gentry, treating their contest in his final lines as a command performance staged for his amusement and inspiration.

According to a servant of the Riddells interviewed years later, the poet was seated during the contest at a distance, not at table, taking notes and refreshing himself occasionally with rum and brandy. Burns himself 'drank none of the claret' and 'left a good deal' of the liquor he had been given; he 'walked home without assistance, not being the worse for drink' '[w]hen the gentlemen were put to bed'.[48] The other surviving account of the evening likewise affirms that Burns himself was not intoxicated: his wife recalled that 'he came home' from Friar's Carse that night 'in his ordinary trim'.[49] During the contest, Burns sketched a few lines, but the ballad took over a year to complete. It was popular, printed in Scottish and London newspapers during 1791 and fair-copied for friends several times in Burns's hand. (A prominent drawing of the family whistle adorns the frontispiece of both volumes of the Glenriddell Manuscript, as yet unpublished writings that Burns collected and partly transcribed as a gift for Riddell.) In 1789, Captain Riddell ceded possession of the family whistle to his cousin but also to a poet who made it his own by transforming it, as Pope transformed Belinda's ravished lock, into a memorable if incongruous poetic prop.

For Andrew Gray, Whistle Hall is the ancestral seat of a distinctively Scottish type of comical/pastoral/fraternal vernacular poetry. For Fergusson, the whistle signifies the nature-inspired song of the poet but also the empty coggie and threadbare clothing of chronic poverty.[50] In Burns's ballad the whistle is at the heart of a song that, like the sun, outshines the dubious pleasure-seeking of the landed gentry, their cult of excessive consumption. Captain Riddell had sold Glenriddell, his family's large holding; Friar's Carse was a smaller inherited property. The Bard's realm is smaller still, only a ballad, a piece of unreal estate that nonetheless demonstrates a mode of companionable sharing more 'joyous' – to use a word frequent in the song – than wine. 'The Whistle', a mock-epic, conveys a mixed message on drinking matches but wholeheartedly promotes the alternative pleasures of ballad-making. Burns's oxymoronic song is an Anacreontic with reservations. As for the whistle, Gray, Fergusson and Burns invoke it as a by turns riddling, empty, melodious, shrill, natural, whimsical, trifling and, in the case of Burns's ballad, silly-decadent accessory and accompaniment to poetic song.

A Drunk Man Looks

> Gin I was sober I micht think
> It was like something drunk men see!
> 'A Drunk Man Looks at the Thistle' (ll. 1351–2)

These poets thwart readers hoping for a didactic 'lesson', to quote again Wordsworth on 'Tam o' Shanter', let alone the culminating moral in boldface type sought by so many nineteenth-century critics. What could be the moral of 'The Whistle', with its giddy account of excess, its distance – fully appropriate in a ballad – from normal daily life? In Burns's mock-epic practice, poetry is more or less the antithesis of common sense: for him, as for Hugh MacDiarmid, poets are, or should be, 'mair than dominies yet' ('A Drunk Man', l. 1323). Doctor Hornbook, pedagogue and quack, inhabits a realm of self-deluding language that readers at once recognize as double-talk; and if 'The Whistle' recommends any behaviour to readers, it is not that they carry out a similar bacchanalia at home but that they learn the words and sing along. The plots of most ballads discourage literal emulation: in 'Lamkin' (Child #93), a mason who receives no payment for his work on Lord Wearie's castle is hanged for his revenge-murder of Lord Wearie's infant son and wife. Ballads, like mock-epics (and 'The Whistle' is both), tell their stories parabolically. Direct advice within them is often weirdly evil, as when the nurse in 'Lamkin', asked whether the pleading mother should be spared, counsels Lamkin to 'kill her, kill her ... / for she neer was good to me'.[51]

Gilbert Burns, who like his brother knew John Wilson from the Freemasons, asked the model for 'Hornbook' his reaction to the poem. Wilson replied sadly that Burns had been 'pretty severe'.[52] Yet Burns is more severe on preachers in the opening stanza, who are said to invent a 'rousing whid' (thumping lie) and then 'nail' it 'wi' Scripture' (ll. 5–6). Themselves drunk with 'holy rapture', ministers use sermons to dictate to everyone in the parish, taking charge of every soul just as Doctor Hornbook assumes custody of every body. From the dissonant rhyming of stanza one ('rapture'/'Scripture') down to the poem's arbitrary closure because Death hears a bell ring, 'Death and Doctor Hornbook' resists one-size-fits-all *prescriptions*, whether for living, dying, or even telling a story.

Burns's Drunk-Men poems look at cultural institutions (drinking customs, articles of faith, medical practice) to raise questions, not to answer them, at least not in any simple way. During the evening reconstructed in 'The Whistle', Burns was a formal witness to the cousins' bet, an observer whose role was fully compatible with his other task as a poet meditating a ballad. In an early letter (1782) to his Kirkoswald schoolmate Thomas Orr, Burns mentions the pleasure he takes in observing, 'going on in my old way ... studying men, their manners, & their ways, as well as I can. Believe me Tom, it is the only study in this world will yield solid satisfaction'.[53] A year later, he wrote to his former schoolmaster in London that he was no 'pushing, active fellow' but the 'reverse':

> I seem to be one sent into the world, to see, and observe; and I very easily compound with the knave who tricks me of my money, if there be anything original about him which shews me human nature in a different light.[54]

Asked in 1810 for his memories of the poet, the physician who had treated Burns's ailing father during the early 1780s spoke of the poet's watchful demeanour:

> [he was] distant, suspicious, and without any wish to interest or please. He kept himself very silent in a dark corner of the room; and before he took part in the conversation, I frequently detected him scrutinising me during my conversation with his father and brother. But ... when the conversation ... had taken the turn he wished, he began to engage in it.[55]

Mock-epic may have appealed to Burns because it encouraged the reformulation of his observing eye not as hostile but as amused.

'Tam o'Shanter', much concerned with 'men, their manners and their ways'[56] as well as with the poet's gaze, is a companion piece to 'The Whistle' in its enigmatic presentation of high-risk behaviours; but in its dark subject-matter lightly reported, it is 'Death and Doctor Hornbook's' soul-twin. According to its subtitle, 'Hornbook' is a 'True Story', and 'Tam o'Shanter', according to line 219, a 'tale o' truth'. Yet in both poems, teasingly unreliable narrators keep all meanings unsettled and in play. In the earlier poem, a Drunk Man converses with Death; in the second, a conspicuously literary narrator sings a Drunk Man's midnight ride. The epigraph of 'Tam o'Shanter' - '*Of Brownyis and of Bogillis full is this buke*'- reveals mock-epic intentions, as it is taken from Gavin Douglas's *Eneados* (1513), a translation of Virgil's epic into middle-Scots. Burns's title, like Virgil's, is eponymous with his hero, although 'Tom of Shanter' lacks the gravitas of

'Aeneas of Troy'. Mock-epic parody and hyperbole allow Burns to present Tam as an embodied oxymoron, a *local hero* whose once and future domain is a rented farm, not two fabled cities. In Virgil's Book 6, Aeneas descends to the underworld to consult the shade of his father Anchises; Burns's poem likewise revisits the spirit of William Burnes (d. 1784), who was buried in Alloway churchyard, backdrop for this poem's culminating vision, a dance of witches. Tam's descent into Hell is technically heroic: he returns victorious from his brush with witches and Satan, avoiding the violent death suffered not only by Virgil's hero but by various entities and characters in Burns's own poem, where Care commits suicide in line 53 and where landmarks along Tam's first homeward miles commemorate places where the chapman suffocated in a snowbank (l. 90), drunken Charlie broke his neck (l. 92), the murdered infant was found by hunters (l. 94) and Mungo's mother hanged herself (l. 96).

Burns takes the epigraph of 'Tam o' Shanter' from the preface Douglas added to Book 6: Douglas's wording familiarly refers to Aeneas's guide, the sibyl at Cumae, as a 'brownie' - in Scottish lore, often a tricky but helpful spirit - while the ghostly dead become 'bogles' or spooks. In his own tale, Burns miniaturizes and localizes further. Tam's adventures do not require twelve books (Douglas in fact added a thirteenth, translating a medieval Latin continuation of Virgil's story) but can be fully told in 224 octosyllabic lines. Just as Death is partly domesticated in Burns's 'Death and Doctor Hornbook', seen in a village setting and cast as a speaker of broad rural Scots, the devil is reduced in 'Tam o' Shanter' to a supporting role as piper for the dancing warlocks and witches.

The stylistic devices and plot-twists of epic - digression, allusion, amplification, simile, travel by water, descent into madness, connection of the hero to death and the preternatural, etc. - infuse Burns's mock-epic with an eerie energy that has very little to do with folklore or the poet's own level of superstition. In its very familiarity as Burns's best-known extended poem, 'Tam o' Shanter' disinclines readers to the closer look that reveals it as his strangest, most intense work - more bizarre even than 'Death and Doctor Hornbook', possibly because of its echoes of disguised or displaced childhood and adolescent memories. The poet looks from age thirty-one ('Tam' was written late in 1790) back to Alloway, scene of his early childhood; he also revisits events of his middle teens circa 1775.

The newly enlisted witch Nannie, whose country dancing is the object of lecherous and middle-aged Tam's voyeuristic 'glow'r' or fascinated stare, displays unspecified parts of her nubile body. Yet Nannie is at the same time a flash-back to Rob Burness himself at sixteen. She dances; she is a spiritual renegade: and from the first of these began a lasting estrangement between the poet and his father.

Burns reports in his autobiographical letter to John Moore that in his 'seventeenth year', he deeply offended William Burnes when he defied his father's command to stay away from a country dancing school:

> from that instance of rebellion he took a kind of dislike to me, which, I believe was one cause of that dissipation which marked my future years. – I only say, Dissipation, comparative with the strictness and sobriety of Presbyterean country life.

Burns wanted to give his 'manners a brush' and in his letter to Dr. Moore says that he saw his father's 'antipathy' to dancing lessons as 'unaccountable'.[57]

A family story suggests that this paternal dislike developed into a fear for Robert's soul. Years after the original quarrel, as William Burnes lay near death in 1784, he told his assembled family that 'there was one member ... for whose future conduct he feared. He repeated the expression, and then Robert came up to the bed and asked: "oh, father, is it me you mean?" The old man said it was.'[58] Robert Chambers probably softened the wording in retelling this anecdote from the poet's youngest sister, although even his own wording suggests that William Burnes had expressed a dying fear that one among them would not join the others in heaven. The 'priestlike' father in 'The Cotter's Saturday Night' uses a similar phrase in the prayer he speaks in stanza 16, which asks God 'That *thus* they all shall meet in future days' (l. 139). The poet's sister reports something different: a dying patriarch denying this comfort and singling out his grown son for severe reproof. 'The Cotter's Saturday Night' honours the memory of William Burnes by reconstructing his multiple roles as 'The *Saint*, the *Father*, and the *Husband*' (l. 137), celebrating his patriarchal authority. Under cover of various mock-epic distortions and transpositions, 'Tam o'Shanter' revisits that same upright, judgmental viewpoint chiefly to let it go.

During William Burnes's later years, first-born Robert clearly became the designated family rebel. In 'Tam o'Shanter' that spirit of insubordination crosses genders to inhabit Carrick's youngest witch, whose more extreme degree of shameless audacity justifies every reproof an alarmed adult may ever have administered. Nannie is a teenage outlaw, and as we learn from a flash-forward digression by the omniscient narrator (ll. 166–70), her future conduct will continue to range from mischievous to reprehensible. Youthful Rob Burness broke the fourth commandment, precipitating a family rupture that rankled for years. Positively forbidden to go, he went out one night to dance in 'absolute defiance of his [father's] commands'.[59] Nannie goes further, renouncing all ten commandments for all eternity. Not a rebel but an apostate, Nannie dances nearly naked, for her ragged and outgrown shift from childhood, a gift from her grandmother, no longer covers her, while Tam and the devil view her with desire (ll. 185–6). She will pay the piper, Satan, for these pleasures stolen at midnight. Rob Burness's dancing lesson, like Tam o'Shanter's irresponsible drinking, begins to look almost innocent by comparison – but only almost innocent, and only by comparison, for here Burns has no interest in portraying unmixed characters. As a boy, he had heard sermons coloured by a belief that 90 per cent of souls were predestined to Hell; God's grace had justified the remaining 10 per cent, who already were living saints.[60] 'Tam o'Shanter' identifies zero percent of human beings as living saints. The poem considers a spectrum of misbehaviours and the scene involving the witches' dance actually moves venal Tam nearer to the median. Even a Drunk Man will trend closer to average when contrasted with a capering mob of murderous Satanists.

Alloway kirk, scene of the witches' dance, stands a few hundred yards from the cottage where Burns was born and where he lived until age seven. The kirk had been abandoned in 1690 when Alloway parish was absorbed by Ayr some three miles away; reroofed in 1740, it was again in ruins during Burns's childhood.[61] William Burnes repaired the churchyard's outer wall to prevent cattle from grazing among the graves and in time came to think of having his own grave there. The Burnes children 'learned the reverence for it', said Gilbert, that 'people generally have for the burial-place of their ancestors'[62] and Burnes was duly interred there in 1784. Oblique, displaced life-echoes contribute to the psychodramatic complexity of 'Tam o'Shanter', wherein sketchily attired witches perform a lewd country dance more or less on William Burnes's grave: he might even be imagined as among the dead whose coffins have been opened so that lights in their hands can illuminate the church interior for the dancers (ll. 125–9).[63] So much for respecting the burial place of one's ancestors or accepting the guidance of caution, virtue and patriarchal authority. Yet to word the matter in that way makes the poem sound retributive or angry, and the tone is far otherwise. Its mood combines glinting satiric commentary with a kind of radiant indulgence: virtuoso style and the mock-epic format call readers to marvel at word-play, not to shake their heads at enormities. Caution is never scorned outright but it is put aside for a time, first depicted as drowned in ale and then upstaged by a spectacular witches' dance with its display of exposed bodies both dead and alive, almost all of them hideous – all but one.

'Tam o'Shanter', in short, takes to a mock-epic extreme William Burnes's viewpoint that dancing is a gateway sin. The Alloway witches and warlocks, mostly elderly – some are dancing with the assistance of their canes (l. 161) – link arms, leap about in abandon, become heated and remove most of their clothing, all while worshipping Satan. Aside from using the denizens of the graveyard to light the dance, the unrepentant dancers have displayed on the abandoned altar their grisly gifts for the devil: among them are a variety of bloodied murder weapons and the body of a newly hanged thief. In the narrator's epic list, the last item mentioned is a knife encrusted with a murdered father's blood:

> A garter, which a babe had strangled;
> A knife, a father's throat had mangled,
> Whom his ain son o' life bereft,
> The grey hairs yet stack to the heft;
> Wi' mair o' horrible and awefu',
> Which e'en to name wad be unlawfu'.[64]

Burns inverts word-order, a form of stylization that can introduce local ambiguities, even possible confusion. One of the inverted lines if read without the preceding line as context makes the son the victim ('Whom his ain son o' life bereft'). The murdered father is also described just after a reference to a strangled babe. Burns's darkly fantastic imagery conveys deathly harm, parent to child and child to parent. The three lines devoted to the parricide's grisly knife perhaps acknowledge the psychic wound Burns himself had inflicted the night he insisted on leaving the house for dancing school, defying his father, whom he did revere and honour yet whose demand for strictest obedience he was no longer willing to meet.

Burns's antiquary acquaintance Francis Grose had requested a supernatural story about Alloway kirk, inspiring 'Tam o'Shanter'.[65] Its chief ghost, laid with gentle authority in this caustic yet deeply tolerant poem, is not William Burnes himself so much as the spectre of those hard words between father and son: in the lines just quoted, both fatal attacks are to the throat. Such quarrels, poisoning memory, have residual power repeatedly to wound again. 'Tam o'Shanter' has a therapeutic rather than (in Wordsworth's phrase quoted earlier) 'moral effect', for it is (like the early poem 'Address to the Unco Guid, or the Rigidly Righteous') an anti-sermon for flawed adults. It repudiates repudiation, the Auld Licht Calvinist emphasis on predestination, from which, as will soon be discussed, a catechism written during the 1760s by William Burnes for his young children likewise had strongly dissented. The witches and warlocks in 'Tam o'Shanter' are not condemned to the dark side; they choose it.

A dead father and a church in ruins, linked by association, geography and the poem's atmospheric lighting arrangements, suggest (in a more figurative and symbolic way than 'Death and Doctor Hornbook') the strange egotism of any institution or individual who seeks to direct and control human bodies and souls. In early lines, Tam's wife Kate delivers a blistering scold, an epic recapitulation of his drunken misdeeds:

> She tauld thee weel thou was a skellum,
> A blethering, blustering, drunken blellum;
> That frae November till October,
> Ae market-day thou was nae sober ...
>   (ll. 19–22; six lines of further execration follow)

Kate's intervention perfectly summarizes Tam's failings but has no effect on his behaviour. In a letter of 1788, Burns ruefully compares reason, which always arrives too late, to the reprimands of 'an unlucky wife':

> Men of grave, geometrical minds ... may cry up reason as much as they please; but I have always found an honest passion, or native instinct, the trustiest auxiliary in the warfare of this world. - Reason almost always comes to me, like an unlucky wife to a poor devil of a husband - just in time enough to add her reproaches to his other grievances.[66]

In 'Tam o' Shanter', reason, 'the unlucky wife', shapeshifts into Kate.

According to Burns's Kirkoswald classmate and early correspondent William Niven, the character of Tam was based on Douglas Graham, tenant of Shanter farm near Kirkoswald, a village some thirteen miles from Ayr.[67] Tam's presence in the background - he happens on the midnight dance three miles into his homeward journey from Ayr and observes it at first in concealment - is inadvertent but hardly blameless. Kate has warned him to avoid Alloway's abandoned church when coming home in the dark:

> She prophesied that late or soon,
> Thou would be found deep drown'd in Doon;
> Or catch'd wi' warlocks in the mirk,
> By *Alloway's* auld haunted kirk. (ll. 29–32)

Tam would never have seen forbidden sights if he had only followed Kate's advice, however intemperately worded (for Kate is not perfect, either). Like the Bard in 'The Whistle', Tam is in the poem mainly to witness, though not in this case on behalf of poetry and song, a task left to the narrator managing the mock-epic special effects.[68] Tam, the Drunk Man, is there to look at sin, misdeeds encouraged by compulsive pleasure-seeking. Yet flawed and pleasure-driven Tam remains, at least until the next market-day, unharmed and unpunished. He does not drown, nor is he carried off to Hell to be roasted like a herring (l. 202). Instead, he sees something beautiful, a glimpse of Nannie's flesh, and approves – 'Weel done!' (l. 189).

Tam is a man in the middle, and not only in terms of his age. He does not embrace sobriety as a God-fearing farmer should, yet he is not actively anti-social as the witches are. He is not horrified by the Satanic orgy he sees but he does not join it. When he sees young Nannie dancing among the witches and warlocks, he shouts approval but from a prudent distance; and when the witches fly out to seize him, he turns his horse and gallops home to Kate. Curious but unseduced, Tam is just looking.

His destination, Kirkoswald, is like Alloway linked to Burns's early years: the poet's letter to Moore describes an extended stay there at age sixteen. He had been sent to Hugh Rodger's school to study surveying and mathematics, but his letter admits that he made 'greater progress in the knowledge of mankind'.[69] He failed to 'do any more good at school' after meeting Margaret Thomson, heroine and muse of 'Song, Composed in August', a lyric that remembers that late summer. Kirkoswald, he tells Moore, was also the scene of his first exposure to tavern bills and to 'scenes of swaggering riot and roaring dissipation': due to the smuggling trade on that part of the Scottish coast, brandy was plentiful and cheap.[70] Characteristically, Burns flavours his account with the mathematical words he was also learning that summer:

> I went on with a high hand in my Geometry; till the sun entered Virgo, a month which is always a carnival in my bosom, a charming Fillette who lived next door to the school overset my Trigonomertry [sic], and sent me off in a tangent from the sphere of my studies. - I struggled on with my Sines and Co-sines for a few days more; but stepping out to the garden one charming noon, to take the sun's altitude, I met with my Angel,
>
>   - 'Like Proserpine gathering flowers,
>   Herself a fairer flower' -
>
> It was vain to think of doing any more good at school. - The remaining week I staid, I did nothing but craze the faculties of my soul about her, or steal out to meet with her; and the two last nights of my stay in the country, had sleep been a mortal sin, I was innocent.[71]

Margaret Thomson, 'my Angel', inspires an allusion, the line invoking Proserpine, to Book IV of *Paradise Lost*, the scene introducing Adam and Eve in their bower. Peggy Thomson may have been the poet's Eve in the sense of being object of his first reciprocated passion. In summer of 1775, she was like Burns himself in that year and in one sense like Nannie in 'Tam o' Shanter': an adolescent recruit to adult pleasures forbidden under the strict codes of what Burns calls Presbyterian country life in his letter to Moore.[72] The couple continued to meet after he left Kirkoswald, although the details are not clear. There is no doubt that Burns remembered her with deep affection, visiting her home - she had married by that time - when he was taking leave of friends during those weeks in late summer 1786 when he was sure he would soon be sailing to Jamaica. She was one of just three people, and the only woman, who received a presentation copy of the Kilmarnock *Poems*.[73]

Tam's tale, told by a narrator who is watching Tam watching, is always travelling, always shifting ground. Its last lines offer scolding advice with a Kate-like flavour, as if she has pushed aside the narrator and re-entered to shake her finger one more time:

> Now, wha this tale o' truth shall read,
> Ilk man and mother's son, take heed:
> Whene'er to drink you are inclin'd,

> Or cutty-sarks run in your mind,
> Think, ye may buy the joys o'er dear,
> Remember Tam o'Shanter's mare. (ll. 219–24)

These final lines speak in imperatives, verbs that command. Yet readers are like Tam, and refuse to turn their so-called thoughts to Meg/Maggie (both names appear as required by the metre), the horse who has lost her tail. After all, she is now safe at home. Just as Nannie's short sark exposes her body, Meg's missing tail no longer can cover her genitals; yet this is a reversible harm: the tail will grow back. Any readers who do take closer heed of Maggie will inevitably conclude that having saved Tam with her bold leap across the keystone of the brig of Doon (a note informs us that witches can cross running water only half way), the little mare is far more the hero of the tale than its incorrigible protagonist. Nannie has in her enraged pursuit clutched at and removed Meg's tail, but otherwise rider and horse are spared. Maggie, Meg and Peggy are frequent forms of Margaret in Scotland: Burns's name for Tam's mare may be another dreamlike transposition and echo of Peggy Thomson of Kirkoswald, that 'charming Fillette' - does he mean 'filly'? - as he refers to her in his 1787 letter to John Moore.

'Tam o'Shanter's' cautionary closing lines address the workings of adult human impulse about as adequately as Doctor Hornbook's ABCs explain the rich multiplicity of poetic language. These Kate-like 'sage advices' could only be accepted as imperative in some radically diminished world-view in which desire is placed wholly under interdiction. In his letter to Moore, Burns writes of his teens as a time of contrary impulses fuelled by contending forces: 'though will-o'-wisp meteors of thoughtless Whim were almost the sole lights of my path, yet early engrained Piety and Virtue never failed to point me out the line of Innocence'.[74] The wording acknowledges that to have a line of conduct pointed out is not always to follow it. 'Tam o'Shanter' was written 130 years before Sigmund Freud published *Beyond the Pleasure Principle* (1920), but the two works' appraisal of the compulsion to seek pleasure is curiously analogous, especially in a shared refusal to propose any remedy. (The narrator's warnings throughout are, like Kate's, plainly dysfunctional, serving, like the protests of the chorus in ancient tragedy, mostly to alert the audience as to which norms are about to be transgressed.) Burns also adds some intimation of Freud's death-drive, the pleasure principle's destructive/aggressive counterpart, in the poem's extended pan across the murder weapons and other ghastly trophies displayed on the church's desecrated altar (ll. 131–42; also some additional lines that he later cancelled).

Burns's greatest mock-epic (though all are eye-openers) looks back in disguised and distorted dreamlike fashion at emotion-laden scenes from his own early life. He transforms many early memories: his father's tending of a neglected graveyard at Alloway, an early courtship, geometry school, dancing school, his first sight of tavern fighting and tavern camaraderie, a bitter quarrel with and subsequent estrangement from his father and perhaps even his mother's connection with Kirkoswald, for Agnes Burnes had lived nearby on her father's farm until age 12.[75] As the poet's letter to Moore tells his life's story, all but the first and last of these events happened in the same year, 1775. 'It is during this climacterick that my little story is most eventful', he says, introducing these formative episodes of his mid-adolescence.[76] Witch Nannie in 'Tam o' Shanter' is among other things a surrogate, a caricature of how his own family viewed Rob Burness in his 'seventeenth year'; and the forbidden sight revealed by Nannie's cutty sark may serve not only as a fleeting delight for Tam, clearly in the throes of some eighteenth-century version of mid-life crisis, but also as a visual flashback of what a young poet first saw during all-night trysts with Margaret Thomson in Kirkoswald, nights laughingly associated in his letter to Moore with 'mortal sin'. Kate is usually taken as a stand-in for Burns's wife, who once on record did chide the poet for arriving home in a drunken state, although in fact Jean Armour was quite unlike Kate: her temperament was generally forbearing and mild.[77] Kate's intolerance of any infraction, her execrations and prophecies of doom, are more reminiscent of the 'headlong, ungovernable Irrascibillity' of his father, William Burnes.[78] Mock-epic format allows Burns to recast a life-altering battle of wills with his father as merely a lively spousal squabble, like the domestic disputes in *opere buffe*.

On its shadow-side, the poem descends to the underworld of Satan and witchcraft to revisit Burns's Anchises, the father whose disapproval he had long carried not on his back but in painful memory. The admonitions of the patriarch, tenderly recalled in 'The Cotter's Saturday Night', are here laid aside as insufficient guide for the 'benighted' human 'traveller' (l. 206n). Poet Burns, as a poet, is called to look at the whole world, not just the sunlit realm of well-conducted people. In the poem's series of impracticable final cautions, the voice of authority would repress and crush impulse - if it had any power. But it has none in the 'mirk' of Tammie's midnight, where discretion is drowned out by the crazy dance of impulse, what Burns, recalling in his letter to Moore his courtship of Margaret Thomson, calls the 'carnival' in his 'bosom'.[79] It behoves a grown man like Tam to behave more like an adult and less like a heedless adolescent, to be sure; and 'Tam o'Shanter' emphasizes the often catastrophic cost of pleasure (l. 223): drunken Charlie breaks his neck and dancing Nannie has pledged her soul. Yet notwithstanding the casualty rate, the people depicted in this poem follow primal impulses, not prudent left-brain 'advices' (l. 35), no matter how 'sage' or 'lengthen'd'. Burns's autobiographical letter traces his failure to learn trigonometry to his first sight of Peggy Thomson: 'It was *vain to think* of doing any more good at school' (emphasis added).[80] 'Tam o'Shanter' likewise depicts thinking and desiring as mutually exclusive.

The poem's final lines are spoken from a grave, geometrical viewpoint, a domain of dire consequences if impulse is preferred to prudent conformity with moral algorithms like those that conclude 'A Bard's Epitaph'. Yet the only left-brained creature in this poem is Tam's Sibylline guide, his mare Maggie, and she does not need the advice, being already responsive to command, sagacious, orderly. It is her human rider who is out of control. In this poem, guiding words of wisdom are like Nannie's sark, a lovely gift for a child that is now too skimpy to cover adult yearnings for power and pleasure as unquenchable as Souter Johnny's thirst.

Divine Inebriety

Whan Sibyl led the Trojan down	the Trojan: Aeneas
To haggard PLUTO's dreary Town,	'the underworld'
Shapes waur nor thee, I freely ween,	'thee: a dead-deal, board to carry a corpse'
Could never meet the Soldier's Ein.	the Soldier: Aeneas
	Fergussson, 'Auld Reikie', ll. 191–4

For all these poets, to be under the influence is among other things to play, to suspend work. (Burns's 'Scotch Drink', for instance, dwells on whisky's use in easing labour, both that of childbirth and the heaviest work of farming.[81]) As the market closes for another week, these poets' speakers linger in darkness, freed from daylight responsibilities and identities: '[F]ain I wad be free / O' my eternal me' ('A Drunk Man Looks at the Thistle', ll. 1898–99):

> These are the moments when a' sense
> Like mist is vanished and intense
> Magic emerges frae the dense
> Body o' bein' ...   ('A Drunk Man', ll. 1913–16)

These observant speakers record the *passing* moment, joy but also its quick eclipse, another reason drink is a useful topic: 'Ilka pleasure I can ha'e / Ends like a dram ta'en yesterday' (ll. 841–2). MacDiarmid's octosyllabic couplet darkens Burns's parallel lament in 'Tam o' Shanter': 'pleasures are like poppies spread, / You seize the flower, its bloom is shed' (ll. 59–60). Burns's narrator is addressing Tam's victory over 'a' the ills o' life' at a tavern in Ayr but also foreshadowing his stormy homeward ride (l. 58). As always when in mock-heroic mode, Burns's style is expansive: the broad metonym 'pleasures' in Burns becomes the specific, non-figurative 'dram' in MacDiarmid.

These Drunk Man poets, their attention withdrawn from daily cares, all consider the soul and especially the body, whether rapidly approached on horseback in 'Tam o' Shanter', carried away for burial in Fergusson or ambiguously transfixed in 'A Drunk Man Looks at the Thistle', whose speaker cannot remember how he came to 'sprawl here 'neath the mune' (l. 96). For MacDiarmid and Fergusson, drink and the body are shifting signifiers, as is midnight. The hours of darkness for Fergusson are sometimes 'chief for fun' ('Auld Reikie' l. 67) but sometimes a cavernous blank dark that leaves his speaker 'dead with fear!' ('Ode to Hope', l.

28). MacDiarmid is similarly haunted by images of death: 'Thou Daith in which my life / Sae vain a thing can seem / Frae whatna source d'ye borrow / Your devastatin' gleam?' (ll. 691–4). When considering his own body, MacDiarmid's speaker often laments its incongruity: 'I canna feel it has to dae wi' me' (l. 329).

Among the three, Burns is most inclined to view the body with approval; he is also unlike Fergusson and MacDiarmid in so often staging his speaker as an onlooker, as in 'The Whistle' and 'Tam o'Shanter', rather than directly as a pleasure-seeker. Even in the early song inspired by his youthful passion for Margaret Thomson, the young couple 'stray' but also 'view':

> Come let us stray our gladsome way,
>   And view the charms o' Nature;
> The rustling corn, the fruited thorn,
>   And ilka happy creature.   (ll. 29–32)

In 'A Drunk Man', MacDiarmid occasionally falls into Tam o'Shanter's octosyllabic couplets: lines 825–44 refer directly to Burns's poem, naming Nannie, as Tam does, by her metonym, 'Cutty Sark' (l. 831). Yet the twentieth-century Drunk Man is entirely frozen in place:

> I canna ride awa' like Tam,
> But e'en maun bide juist whaur I am.   'must stay just where I am'
>   (ll. 833–4)

In other parts of his poem, MacDiarmid employs unrhymed eight-syllable lines, including a series of lyric questions he addresses to the shade of Dostoevski:

> Is Scotland big enough to be
> A symbol o' that force in me,
> In wha's divine inebriety
> A sicht abune contempt I'll see?   (ll. 2010–13)

Here the rhyme - be / me / inebriety / see – doubles the couplet, repeating the rhyme four times. MacDiarmid reshapes the Fergusson/Burns octosyllabic line even as he loosely readopts it.[82]

MacDiarmid also reintroduces the figure of the Kate-like cautionary spouse. Early in the poem, his speaker, like Tam, worries about the trouble he will face when he arrives home so late: 'For even Jean maun natter, natter, natter' (l. 163). When the speaker lapses into 'Silence' two lines before the end, Jean returns like scolding Kate in the concluding lines of 'Tam o'Shanter', as the speaker ventriloquizes her reaction to his fantastic visions. Jean's lines close and also close off the poem, marking a return to the daily world of sober, practical, non-poetic speaking:

> O I ha'e Silence left
>
>> 'And weel ye micht',
>> Sae Jean'll say, 'efter sic a nicht!' (ll. 2683–5)

Though a space is inserted to mark a break, there is no period after the Drunk Man's final line, no closure but simply, as in 'Death and Doctor Hornbook', a breaking off. Practical Jean takes over for two final lines as the speaker's voice fades; in effect she reprises Kate's role in 'Tam o'Shanter' as the absent wife whose common sense is administered at poem's end as a kind of antidote to poetic flight.[83]

In their night-pieces, the Scots poets, their senses deranged, see things in which, as in many an old ballad, life and death are enmeshed:

> Dae what ye wull ye canna parry
> This skeleton-at-the-feast that through the starry
> Maze o' the warld's intoxicatin' soiree
>> Claughts ye ...   'clutches'
>>   (ll. 652–5)

Fergusson often dives into horror in closing: 'We reap the fruit of our unkindly lusts, / And feebly totter to the silent grave'.[84] In a paraphrase of the book of Job, remembered and quoted by Burns before his own premature death in 1796,[85] Fergusson's final lines convey bewildered agony as death moves in on his weakened body and spirit:

> Wild visag'd fear, with sorrow-mingled eye,
> And wan destruction piteous stared me nigh;
> For tho' no rest nor safety blest my soul,
> New trouble came, new darkness, new controul. (ll. 51–4)

The speaker of 'On Seeing a Butterfly in the Street' rejoices in the fluttering creature ranging above a city street; but then Fergusson imagines the capricious girl who will strip off its wings and leave it to die:

> Kind NATURE lent but for a day
> Her wings to make ye sprush and gay;   'spruce'
> In her habuliments a while   'habilaments' (dress)
> Ye may your former sel' beguile,   'forget you ever were a caterpillar'
> And ding awa' the vexing thought   'drive away'
> Of hourly dwyning into nought   'dwindling, wasting away'
>   (ll. 19–24)

A *carpe diem* poem reminds readers of mortality to turn them to pleasure now, but Fergusson's show a contrary movement from delight to despair. He looks about, observant and watchful, but as he looks, as he writes, joy and beauty diminish and go dark.

For Fergusson, embodiment is a fading delight that cannot conceal imminent doom. He gave Burns 'Auld Reikie' as a pattern for sardonic celebration and satire; in 'To My Auld Breeks', another octosyllabic poem, Fergusson's speaker offers his worn-out blue breeches to any takers, giving Burns the idea for his narrator's similar offer in ll. 155–8 of 'Tam o'Shanter'. Yet Burns is so different in both tone and mood, not in awe of the dark and caring little about the dead-deal, the board that will carry him to his grave ('Auld Reikie', l. 193), but thinking much about the world that his children will inherit. Especially in the last decade of his life, having survived the crisis of 1786, Burns typically looked into the future with hope, not horror. In a letter to a dying friend and patron, Burns offered a rare comment about the afterlife:

> an honest man has nothing to fear. – If we lie down in the grave, the whole man a piece of broke machinery, to molder with the clods of the valley, - be it so; at least there is an end of pain, care, woes and wants: if that part of us called Mind, does survive the apparent destruction of the man - away with old-wife prejudices and fears! Every age and every nation has had a different set of stories; and as the many are always weak ... they have often, perhaps always been deceived.[86]

Here the beliefs of different cultures and nations are equally unverifiable in that they each tell 'a different set of stories'. If a 'great unknown Being' does summon the soul after death, the letter continues, it will not be for a scene of denunciation, the fear that tormented Robert Fergusson. In wording reminiscent of the family catechism memorized in his early boyhood, Burns consoles Robert Muir, to whom this letter is addressed, with the thought that this 'unknown Being' is not cruel and 'could have no other end in giving [a man] ... existence but to make him happy; who gave him ... passions and instincts, and well knows their force.'[87]

This optimism and distrust of religious dogmatism may well have descended to the poet from his late father, that irascible and unbending man whom John Murdoch nonetheless praised as 'by far the best of the human race that ever I had the pleasure of being acquainted with.'[88] A close look at William Burnes's catechism, structured as a series of questions from a son to a father, suggests that the poet only travelled further down a road laid out by early teaching. Ashamed of his faulty handwriting, Burnes had asked the schoolmaster John Murdoch, who sometimes boarded with the family, to transcribe this work; but Murdoch assured James Currie that the wording is wholly that of William Burnes. This 'little manual of religious belief', as James Currie calls it, has a theological tendency that Currie sees as 'approaching to Arminianism'.[89] Writing in the *Burns Chronicle* in 1933, James Muir, a Presbyterian minister, can find in it 'no Calvinism':

> it is oddly devoid of Scripture reference, especially the words of Jesus. Nothing is said of regeneration, or foreordination; or the Divinity of Jesus Christ, or of the oneness of the Son of God with the Divine Father. Jesus is referred to simply as 'the seed of

the woman', 'the Messiah', 'the Saviour'. In the views expressed [by the poet's father], law and prophecy weigh more than grace or faith, salvation is largely by 'works', and not simply a free gift of God for Jesus' sake. The origin and spread of sin in the world is represented as due to our first parents and to the devil. Yet every man is held by the author to have his 'eternal destiny in his own hands' ... [T]here is here no Calvinism ... [and] Jesus is not conceived to be central.[90]

Burnes's catechism answers the son's first question – 'How shall I evidence to myself that there is a God?' – with an eerie premonition of Burns's songs, for it wholly rejects the idea that Nature fell with the first sin of Adam and Eve. The chief proof of God is to be found 'By the works of creation ... this fabrick of Nature demonstrates its Creator to be possessed of all possible perfection'.[91] William Burnes did not see permeating evil in postlapsarian nature like the rustic speaker in 'Address to the Deil', whose superstitious grandmother has taught him to see and hear the devil everywhere: down by the wall, over by the bull-rushes, howling in the winter winds. Burnes taught his children differently: in his view, the matchless beauty of the natural world reveals its faultless creator. The answer to the catechism's second question (' ... how shall we account for so much wickedness in the world?') emphasizes that evil has 'made great progress' since the fall of Adam and Eve but does not mention Hell or punishment. To the third question, 'But has God left His own rational offspring thus, to the tyranny of His and their enemy', the extended answer begins with a single consoling word:

> No. For God hath addressed His rational creatures, by telling them in his revealed word ... [that] ... everyone oppressed with the tyranny of the Devil, should, through the promised seed, by faith in Him, and humble supplication, and *a strenuous use of their own faculties*, receive such measures of Grace ... as should make them able to Overcome.[92] [emphasis added]

The catechism later advises restraint in sensual indulgence on the grounds that more pleasure is derived when restraint is exercised:

> setting the rational part above the animal ... tends to compose the mind more and more, not to the utter destruction of the animal part, but to the real and true enjoyment of them ... and not only so, but gives animal life pleasure and joy, that we could not have had without [the struggle].[93]

A man disappointed, William Burnes evidently became difficult in his declining years; but the catechism written during the happiest time in his life, the years at Alloway, attempts to teach his children a spirit of self-reliant, self-respecting optimism. Burns, in a letter of 1795 to Anna Wallace Dunlop, speaks, although equivocally in context, of religious faith as 'a never-failing anchor of hope'.[94] Yet the poet departs from his father's beliefs in basing his ideas not on Scripture (many Biblical verses are cited in the catechism) or logical inference from established dogma but on instinct:

> I have no objection to what the Christian system tells us of Another world; yet I own I am partial to those proofs & ideas of it which we have wrought out of our own heads & hearts. - The first has the demonstration of an authenticated story, the last has the conviction of an intuitive truth.[95]

As an adult Burns was less preoccupied with thoughts of an afterlife than with the other world that might come into being (with a 'strenuous use' of personal 'faculties') despite the political struggles and injustices of his own day:

> In politics if thou would'st mix,
>   And mean thy fortunes be;
> Bear this in mind, be deaf and blind,
>   Let great folks hear and see.[96]

This sardonic versicle was inscribed on a Dumfries tavern window (Burns's diamond-tipped pen was a gift from a patron) during the counterrevolutionary 1790s. That Burns chose a tavern window suggests his association between the camaraderie of tavern life and the more open political atmosphere that might ensue in times to come. '[C]ome it will for a' that': one day people will interact more like brothers and social equals, sharing thoughts freely, as in meetings of the Freemasons or pleasant socializing at the Globe Inn.[97]

Tam o'Shanter is happy as he rides through the midnight storm because he has warmed himself at a 'bleezing' ingleside not only with 'reaming swats' (foaming new beer) but with Souter Johnnie's 'queerest stories' (l. 49) and the landlady's kisses (ll. 47–8). MacDiarmid's Drunk Man, who has not enjoyed his tavern visit, is alone when he has his visions of the thistle and the moon but for Burns, the tavern is in itself a vision, a space where working people gather to play.[98] While the poet-narrator watching Tam clearly sees his 'hero' for what he is, a locally notorious toper, he is also happy for him. For he is watching the escape of a fellow mortal not so much from angry witches as from the drudging life of a tenant farmer *c*. 1790: the daily labour for meagre results, the weekly pressure each Sabbath from Auld Light Calvinism. Tam's social evening at the tavern each market-day is his alternative weekly observance, his personal ritual. The Drunk Man's most unusual dimension in Burns's usage is this association of the trope not with antisyzygal brawling but with community, shared pleasure, social interaction. In 'Tam o'Shanter' tavern life is syzygal. Moreover, while Burns gives drink its due in his 'Drunk Man' poems, consumption per se is always upstaged in the end by some energetic act of creation, whether a dance of leaping witches, an epidemic of houghmagandie ('The Holy Fair') or the construction of a hyper-allusive ballad ('The Whistle').

In social and political terms, his own day was for Burns the dark corner in which he sat, waiting for the conversation to take a more congenial turn. His assumption that better times were possible may well have been rooted in teachings of his father that cleared space for a largely affirmative reading of human nature ('every man, even the worst, have something good about them', he says in *The First Commonplace Book*)[99] despite the folly, false dogma and crime that his satires plentifully document. MacDiarmid's call for revolution is more systematic and fully theorized than Burns's, for MacDiarmid was schooled in Marx's program for global change. Burns put little faith in grave, geometrical systems, embracing with politics (as with theological issues) an intuition rather than a dogma. In the Dumfries years, one anchor of hope was his implicit belief in the future, when those of 'mean' fortunes would see improved opportunities for power and pleasure. The tavern may have been as good as social interaction got in 1790 for people like Burns but the future promised better. In this light, it can be said that such mock-epics as 'Tam o' Shanter' and 'Death and Doctor Hornbook' share a utopian element, for Burns portrays in them behaviour *not yet* heroic in Scotland in his day, including Tam's unrepentant pursuit of small social pleasures and the wholly unterrified conversation with Death enjoyed by the unnamed speaker of 'Hornbook'.

Four short poems are inscribed on windows of Burns's favourite tavern in Dumfries. That on the danger of political activity for those of 'mean' fortune has just been quoted; its warning to leave politics to 'great folk' shares all these poets' customary association between drink and social-political commentary. The three further short poems respectively address rapture, desire and the body. The first printed in Kinsley's edition saucily reverses Milton's message in 'Il Penseroso', urging the pursuit of folly:

> The greybeard, old wisdom, may boast of his treasures,
>   Give me with gay folly to live;
> I grant him his calm-blooded, time-settled pleasures,
>   But folly has raptures to give.[100]

The second and best-known ('I murder hate') is longer, sixteen extraordinary and in his day quite unpublishable lines praising the joys of begetting over the mass murder of war: 'I'm better pleased to *make one more* / Than be the death of twenty'.[101] The last of the short poems, a quatrain that echoes ancient pagan beliefs, emphasizes drink's healing properties:

> My bottle is a holy pool,
>   The heals the wounds o' care an' dool,
> And pleasure is a wanton trout,
>   An ye drink it, ye'll find him out.[102]

Belief in the healing power of holy pools probably dates back to the Bronze Age but survived in Burns's day in many parts of Britain and Northern Europe. In folklore, sacred fish were said to guard many, including St Beans's Well in Argyll, Scotland; further away in Cardigan (Wales) and Herefordshire (England), two such pools were thought to be protected by a magic trout wearing a golden chain.[103] When the poet calls his bottle a holy pool, he conveys the idea of sharing drink as a social sacrament. (His bawdy songs and poems suggest the same about consensual adult sexuality). Burns is rarely spatial in imagery, looking down into the abyss like Fergusson or up to the stars like MacDiarmid.[104] He is temporal, looking *across* time; and beyond his headlong gallop through the darkening moor of his own life, he saw an unborn world ablaze with possibility, just as in 'Tam o'Shanter' light pours out from the ruins of Alloway church.

EPILOGUE: BURNS AND APHORISM; OR POETRY INTO PROVERB

> Aphorism lives on, it lives much longer than its present and it lives longer than life.
> Jacques Derrida, 'Aphorism Countertime'[1]

Derrida's deconstruction of Juliet's 'What's in a name?' speech in *Romeo and Juliet* considers the 'contretemps' that ensue in Shakespeare's play from the dissonance between the characters' names (Montague, Capulet) and their desires and identities. Derrida also observes that 'every name can take on the figure of an aphorism,'[2] perhaps because names and wise sayings both come down to posterity as gifts, or at any rate givens, from earlier generations. As seen in Chapter 1, Burns in his early years as a poet adjusted his father's spelling of the family name, changing 'Burnes' to 'Burness' and then back to 'Burns'. He neither accepted nor wholly rejected his given name: he worked on it; and throughout his life his relation to literary traditions and languages (both Scottish and English) was analogous. These closing pages briefly consider Burns's literary afterlife, the channels through which his words and thoughts live on in literary and popular contexts.

He survives first of all as a signature, a famous name toasted during birthnight celebrations around the world. Yet he also persists as 'X' and 'Z', those tricky codes he used in *The Scots Musical Museum*. This ghostly yet formidable presence likewise continues to influence writers, readers and daily speech. The passing of Burns's writings into semi-anonymous cultural memory is hardly unique: memorable writing always becomes common (if fragmented) cultural property. Yet it is remarkable that Burns himself began this breakdown of his own voice into general literary culture through frequent suppression of his signature. There is some explanation for his covert literary activities in the eighteenth-century history of Scotland, the impact of the Jacobite wars, which had ended only a generation before Burns's birth in 1759. Lady Nairne and Sir Walter Scott likewise published writings powerfully addressing Scottish identity while refusing (in part because of the continuing controversy about Jacobitism's role in Scottish history) to disclose their authorship. Like Burns, they shielded themselves from political reprisal while offering one voice, their own, as that of Scottish history and culture. Burns's lifelong alternation between conspicuous claims to public attention in his signed work (as in the preface of the 1786 Kilmarnock *Poems*) and provocative evasion in his unsigned poems and songs explains his dual persistence in both literary and popular imagination. For Poet Burns and Rob Burness live on in contrary ways. The signature persona, Poet Burns, retains a strong cult value. Some of the manuscripts are now almost beyond price; and a plaster casting of his skull (made in the nineteenth century after an intrusion into the mausoleum by crazed phrenology-devotees[3]) is still a sought-after souvenir among the poet's more fanatical admirers. Yet both Burns and anonymous or semi-anonymous Burness are also notable for their use-value in the form of a trove of aphoristic sayings still freely circulating. Burns himself not only reworked Scots adages but 'aphorized' – isolated and sententiously condensed – memorable moments in English poetry and Scripture.

The Scots are drawn to aphorism. During the 1730s, vernacular poet Allan Ramsay compiled forty-four chapters of alphabetically listed Scots proverbs. Although published twenty-three years before Burns was born, many express sentiments that will sound familiar to Burns's readers:

> He has mickle Prayer but little devotion.
> Love's as warm among Cotters as Courtiers.
> The simple Man's the Beggars [*sic*] Brother.[4]

Burns uses such sayings to illustrate a speaker's passing mood; a measure of character for him is the type of aphorism – whether kindly or caustic, literary/biblical or folk/proverbial – on which a speaker relies. In Burns's adaptation, however, truisms are offered to readers not as 'truths' but as representative utterances. Moreover, no matter how homely their speech, his proverb users are engaging in a proto-literary activity, for aphorisms, although they come to hand readymade, nonetheless must be selected and approved, as a poet chooses words and rhymes, from a near infinite menu of conflicting possibilities. One of the proverbs from Ramsay quoted above, 'The simple Man's the Beggars Brother', is preceded by the very different proposition that 'The lazy Man's the Beggar's Brother'.[5]

In a Burns song published in 1792, the betrayed speaker consoles himself with stereotypes and proverbs:

> Whae'er ye be that woman love,
>   To this be never blind;
> Nae ferlie 'tis tho' fickle she prove,   'no wonder'
> A woman has't by kind.[6]   'nature'

That last line recalls a proverb in Ramsay: 'He has't of kind, he coft [purchased] it not'.[7] The sententious narrator of 'Tam o' Shanter' (1790), too, aside from lifting phrases from the English poets, adapts one of Ramsay's proverbs ('Time and Tide will tarry for nae Man'), which resurfaces in Burns's 'Nae man can tether time or tide'.[8] The adage in Ramsay itself can be traced to 'the tide tarieth no man', first collected and printed by John Heywood in 1546.[9]

For Burns's speakers, to talk in proverbs is often to establish credentials as a rustic. Happily enmeshed in the realm of the proverbial, for instance, is the pert country girl who speaks in broad Scots in Burns's late song 'Scottish Ballad'. She rapidly narrates the tale of her courtship, darkly revisiting her indignation, several weeks after spurning his first marriage proposal, when she learned that her 'braw wooer' had been seen with her cousin:

> But what wad ye think? in a fortnight or less,
>   The deil tak his taste to gae near her!
> He up the lang loan to my black cousin, Bess,
>   Guess he how, the jad! I could bear her, could bear her,
>   Guess ye how the jad! I could bear her.
>
> ... I spier'd for my cousin fu' couthy and sweet,
>   Gin she had recover'd her hearin,
> And how her new shoon fit her auld shachl't feet;
>   But, heavens! how he fell a swearin, a swearin,
>   But, heavens! how he fell a swearin.[10]

This unnamed speaker energetically applies to Bess an insulting adage in Ramsay – 'Ye shape shoon by your ain shachled feet' – unconsciously revealing her possessive love for the wooer she has been resisting.[11]

Burns uses homely Scots proverbs just as he uses echoes from prior poets or Scripture: to bring his speakers to life. When portraying exalted heroes, he is likely to turn to the English poets, as a stanza in 'Scots Wha Hae' suggests:

> Wha will be a traitor-knave?
> Wha can fill a coward's grave?
> Wha sae base as be a Slave? -
> – Let him turn and flie – ... [12]

The song, especially when performed to its old Scottish air, sounds quintessentially 'Scots', but Burns is drawing on a famous scene in Shakespeare. In Act 3 of *Julius Caesar*, Brutus, Caesar's adopted son and assassin, poses a parallel series of rhetorical questions: 'Who is here so base that would be a bondman? If any, speak, for him have I offended. Who is here so rude that would not be a Roman? ... Who is here so vile that will not love his country?'[13] In Burns's revision, a Roman forum becomes the field at Bannockburn, republican Brutus becomes Robert Bruce, a Roman mob becomes a fiercely loyal army, and the diction shifts from formal English to idiomatic Scots. Shakespeare's revolutionary context is retained, but Burns moves the point of national crisis from the last days of the Roman republic to June 1314, eve of the Battle of Bannockburn, the military victory that restored Scottish independence. A large part of Burns's art or craft lies in such submerged yet seismic shifts in the register and context in which he re-purposes old songs, the poems of predecessors and also proverbial phrases and sayings.[14]

Sometimes he introduces contradictory aphorisms, as in a coat of arms he designed in 1794 to replace his lost seal. He wanted the design inscribed on a 'Highland pebble':

> 'On a field, azure, a holly bush, seeded, proper, in base; a Shepherd's pipe & crook, Saltier-wise, also proper, in chief. – On a wreath of the colours, a woodlark perching on a sprig of bay-tree, proper, for Crest. – Two Mottoes: Round the top of the Crest – "Wood-notes wild" - At the bottom of the Shield, in the usual place – "Better a wee bush than nae bield"'.[15]

'Wood-notes wild' echoes line 134 of Milton's 'L'Allegro'; Milton is praising Shakespeare. In the upper image, a native wood-lark alights on a sprig of bay, but 'in base' stands a tree of northern growth. Any coat of arms brings together the disparate history of male and female ancestors: Burns selects a visual image well designed to represent his own poetic identity as a crisscrossing (a display 'Saltier-wise') of divergent elements. This is especially true of the mottos: Burns's quotation of Milton is countered by a proverb collected in Ramsay: 'A wee Bush is better than nae Bield'.[16]

If aphorism 'separates', as Derrida argues – 'it marks dissociation (apo), it terminates, delimits, arrests (horizō)'[17] – Burns, in reusing familiar phrases (whether from literary classics or anonymous folk sources), often brings them back in this way as elements in a pair or series. Rather than settling things as aphorisms do, such serial quotations raise questions. Do the two 'mottos' (high-literary and folk-derived) compete on his coat of arms or is Burns promoting the cosy cohabitation of contraries? Milton's phrase is higher than the proverb, as high as can be on the top. Yet the literal grounding of the folk saying at the base of the image could be read as marking Ramsay's aphorism not as lesser but as foundational.

The Burns-derived aphorisms still in circulation have in Derrida's terms been cut away from their original context of juxtaposed counter-proverbs, so that wise sayings taken from Burns as aphorisms today preserve only a partial view even of Burns's characters. They do not define the poet himself, who is often widely removed from his speakers, whether historically (King Robert Bruce), in gender and age (the adolescent girl in 'Scottish Ballad'), or in temper, as in 'Holy Willie's Prayer'. The last-named poem is a dramatic monologue whose speaker, almost in the same breath, confesses to habitual drunken adultery and boasts of his affinities with the apostle Paul:

> Maybe thou lets this fleshly thorn
> Buffet thy servant e'en and morn,
> Let he o'er proud and high should turn,
>   That he's sae gifted;
> If sae, thy hand maun e'en be borne
>   Untill thou lift it. –[18]

William Fisher deftly perverts the spirit of Paul's second letter to the Corinthians: 'of myself I will not glory, but in mine infirmities ... And lest I should be exalted above measure ... there was given to me a thorn in the flesh, the messenger of Satan to buffet me, lest I should be exalted above measure'.[19] Such shifts in meaning and adapted micro-allusions are precisely what is lost in posterity's aphoristic reduction of Burns to a handful of memorable phrases.

Nonetheless, the stripped-of-context or proverbial Burns soon became, especially in North America, an important element in posterity's memory of him. Wise sayings drawn from Burns were, like his songs, convenient links to the home-culture for the numerous Scots emigrants of the nineteenth century. The Scottish-born naturalist John Muir had memorized Burns, reciting whole poems to himself as he strode alone through the North American wilderness.[20] Other nineteenth-century emigrant Scots remembered Burns as a coiner of phrases, often encountered in casual speech or even in secondary sources. The original edition of Bartlett's *Familiar Quotations*, for instance, self-published in 1855 by Cambridge, Massachusetts bookseller John Bartlett, included a section on Burns. The ninth edition (1891), the last edited by Bartlett before his death in 1905, incorporates seventy Burns passages, citing forty poems and songs.[21] Bartlett selects across a broader range than one might expect, broader than the Burns selections of most anthologists today. The poet's aphoristic tour de force 'Tam o' Shanter' generates eleven entries, while the sententious 'The Cotter's Saturday Night' is cited five times; yet less famous works are included, too: 'A Winter Night', 'The Twa Dogs', 'Ode, Sacred to the Memory of Mrs Oswald' and 'Epistle from Esopus to Maria', along with songs that are today all but forgotten. If phrases from Burns were still current only by means of such genteel compendia as *Familiar Quotations*, we would have to think of Burns's words as surviving today, at least outside Scotland, on artificial life-support. However, aphorisms drawn from Burns were culled by numerous writers during the twentieth century.[22] As this work has shown, even as Burns re-shaped Brutus's speech from Shakespeare to bring Robert the Bruce to life, nineteenth- and twentieth-century writers from Wordsworth and Nairne to MacDiarmid adapted 'familiar quotations' and phrases from Burns to delineate their own vision, their own characters and settings.

Burns is still honoured by name each late January. Both his name and his words were celebrated by Frederick Douglass, said to have made Burns's complete works his first book purchase after escaping from slavery in Maryland. He offered the formal toast to Burns's 'Immortal Memory' on 25 January 1849 in a speech that ended with one of Burns's most often quoted aphorisms:

> though I am not a Scotchman ... I am proud to be among you this evening. And if any think me out of my place on this occasion ... I beg that the blame may be laid at the door of him who taught me that 'a man's a man for a' that'.[23]

Over a century later, *The Autobiography of Martin Luther King, Jr.* (compiled by Clayborne Carson in 1998 from Dr King's papers) used the phrase 'Man's inhumanity to Man'[24] from Burns's song 'Man was Made to Mourn' (discussed in Chapter 2) no fewer than six times. 'Man's inhumanity to man', he writes, speaking of the murder of four schoolgirls in the Birmingham, Alabama church-bombing of 1963, 'is not only perpetrated by the vitriolic actions of those who are bad. It is also perpetrated by the vitiating inaction of those who are good'.[25]

Whether the 'yes' of aphoristic echo – in Derrida's terms, the countersigning that affirms the anterior 'event', Burns's poetic career itself – is linked, as in Douglass, to Burns's name or remains, as in King, unattributed, is not as important today as it must have been for Burns himself in the years of struggle before he published *Poems, Chiefly in the Scottish Dialect* (1786). For like the lovers he depicts in 'Corn Rigs', who lie 'among' the rigs, his poems and songs are at this point fully embedded in literary and colloquial speech. This was already the case when Emerson offered the principle toast at a centennial Burns celebration in January 1859:

> [E]very boy's and girl's head carries snatches of his songs, and they say them by heart, and, what is strangest of all, never learned them from a book, but from mouth to mouth. The wind whispers them, the birds whistle them, the corn, barley, and bulrushes hoarsely rustle them, nay, the music-boxes at Geneva are framed and toothed to play them; the hand-organs of the Savoyard in all cities repeat them, and the chimes of bells ring them in the spires. They are the property and the solace of mankind.[26]

A culminating toast to the 'Immortal Memory' of Burns is repeated in celebrations each 25 January that honour a particular person and a particular nation. Yet Emerson, himself speaking as part of a splendid Burns celebration at Boston's Parker House hotel, is closer to the mark in celebrating not a personality or national culture but an extraordinary gift of language and song. The philosopher emphasizes the poet's appeal not only to those like himself but to those who never pick up a book, who encounter Burns's writings in 'snatches' through poetic phrases and song-lyrics that pass 'from mouth to mouth'. Burns's words and images are not exclusively Scottish but global, 'the property and the solace of mankind'. Emerson situates Burns's 'immortal memory', then, precisely in the *memory of mortals*, the interactive matrix of living cultural exchange.

Emerson's comments reflect how dramatically Burns's fame increased throughout the nineteenth century; with each decade, he conveyed more joy to more people. Like his early hero John Barleycorn, he has renewed delight with each encounter for several centuries now. The bardolaters of the nineteenth century who invaded Burns's mausoleum in order to handle and measure Burns's skull,[27] misunderstood the nature of poetic authority, for a poem is not an object to be grasped but a voice waiting to be heard. As long as Burns's writings are spoken and sung, or transplanted into new contexts, his 'poetry' will continue to outlive his 'poverty', as he phrased the matter in that letter quoted in the epigraph of this volume's Introduction. Poets survive as long as their words are remembered, and to this day Burns's writings invite – and reward – renewed performance and interpretation.

NOTES

Introduction, with a Brief History of Burns's Relation to Literary Canons

1. G. R. Roy and J. D. Ferguson (eds), *The Letters of Robert Burns*, 2nd edn, 2 vols (Oxford: Clarendon Press, 1985), vol. 2, p. 32.
2. An exception is Thomas Crawford, who uses a shifting rubric ('Poet of the Parish', 'Poet of Scotland', 'World Poet'), adding eighty pages on Burns as a 'Maker of Songs' in *Burns: A Study of the Poems and Songs* (Stanford, CA: Stanford University Press, 1960).
3. Susan Manning sees this preference for 'purer' Scots as 'linguistic nationalism' (pp. 90–1) and the ranging of Scots against English as a 'crude binary'. See *'Heaven-Taught' Fergusson, Robert Burns's Favourite Scottish Poet*, ed. R. Crawford (East Linton: Tuckwell Press, 2003), pp. 87–112, on p. 90.
4. J. Berryman, from *'Pereant qui ante nos nostra dixerunt'* ('May they perish who have expressed our bright ideas before us'; the phrase is from Marcus Aurelius), in *The Dream Songs* (1969; New York: Farrar, Straus, and Giroux, 2007), p. 244.
5. D. Paterson, *Robert Burns: Poems Selected by Don Paterson* (London: Faber & Faber, 2001), p. vii.
6. W. Whitman, 'Robert Burns as Poet and Person', in *November Boughs* (1882), in *The Complete Poetry and Prose of Walt Whitman*, 2 vols (New York: Pellegrini and Cudahy, 1948), vol. 2, p. 409.
7. Recent monographs, critical biographies and essay collections from 2013 back to 2009 include A. Broadhead, *The Language of Robert Burns: Style, Ideology and Identity* (Lewisburg, PA: Bucknell University Press, 2013), S. Alker, L. Davis and H. F. Nelson (eds), *Robert Burns and Transatlantic Culture* (Farnham, Surrey: Ashgate, 2012), P. Scott and K. Simpson (eds), *Robert Burns and Friends: Essays by W. Ormiston Roy Fellows Presented to G. Ross Roy* (Columbia, SC: University of South Carolina Libraries, 2012), D. Sergeant and F. Stafford (eds), *Burns and Other Poets* (Edinburgh: Edinburgh University Press, 2012), M. G. H. Pittock (ed.), *Robert Burns and Global Culture* (Lewisburg, PA: Bucknell University Press, 2011), N. Leask, *Robert Burns and Pastoral: Poetry and Improvement in Late Eighteenth-Century Scotland* (Oxford: Oxford University Press, 2010), F. Stafford, *Local Attachments: The Province of Poetry* (Oxford: Oxford University Press, 2010), G. Carruthers (ed.), *Edinburgh Companion to Robert Burns* (Edinburgh: Edinburgh University Press, 2009), R. Crawford, *The Bard: Robert Burns, A Biography* (Princeton, NJ: Princeton University Press, 2009) and I. McIntyre, *Robert Burns: A Life* (Edinburgh: Constable and Robinson, 2009).

8. See D. Cook (ed.), *Annotations of Scottish Songs by Burns*, in *Songs of Robert Burns* and *Notes on Scottish Songs by Robert Burns*, by James C. Dick, together with *Annotation of Scottish Songs* (Hatboro, PA: Folklore Associates, 1962). It begins 'By the bye, it is singular enough that the Scotish [*sic*] Muses were all Jacobites' and ends with a clue to his own interest in these songs insofar as they attack the current royal family: 'surely the gallant though unfortunate, house of Stewart, the kings of our fathers for so many heroic ages, is a theme much more interesting than an obscure beef-witted insolent race of foreigners whom a conjuncture of circumstances kickt up into power and consequence' (pp. 4–5).
9. W. Benjamin, 'The Storyteller', in *Walter Benjamin: Selected Writings, vol. 3, 1935–8* trans. H. Eiland and M. W. Jennings (Cambridge, MA: Harvard University Press, 2002), p. 162.
10. F. Kermode, *The Art of Telling: Essays on Fiction* (Cambridge, MA: Harvard University Press, 1983), p. 171.
11. T. S. Eliot, *The Use of Poetry and the Use of Criticism: Studies in the Relation of Criticism and Poetry* (London: Faber & Faber, 1933), p. 106. While rebuking Matthew Arnold's condescension to Burns, Eliot himself opens by declaring his 'partiality for small, oppressive nationalities like the Scots' (ibid.).
12. From 'Was there a Scottish Literature?', a review of Smith's *Scottish Literature*, an inspiration to Hugh MacDiarmid (in *Atheneaum*, 1 August 1919, pp. 680–1, on p. 681).
13. Ibid.
14. H. K. Bhabha, *The Location of Culture* (1994; London: Routledge, 2004), p. 2.
15. Quoted in Leask, *Robert Burns and Pastoral*, p. 9.
16. J. Speirs, *The Scots Literary Tradition: An Essay in Criticism*, 2nd edn (London: Faber & Faber, 1962), p. 9.
17. Ibid., p. 117.
18. G. Tillotson et al. (eds), *Eighteenth Century English Literature* (Fort Worth: Harcourt, 1969), p. 1458.
19. B. H. Smith, *Contingencies of Value: Alternative Perspectives for Critical Theory* (Cambridge, MA: Harvard University Press, 1988), pp. 46–47.
20. J. Kinsley (ed.), *The Poems and Songs of Robert Burns*, 3 vols (Oxford: Clarendon Press, 1968), vol. 3, p. 971.
21. Thomas Gray's 'Elegy in a Country Churchyard', l. 81, in Tillotson et al. (eds), *Eighteenth Century English Literature*, p. 944.
22. For more on Ramsay's *Gentle Shepherd*, see T. Crawford, *Society and the Lyric: A Study of the Song Culture of Eighteenth-Century Scotland* (Edinburgh: Scottish Academic Press, 1979), pp. 70–96, and S. Newman, *Ballad Collection, Lyric, and the Canon: The Call of the Popular from the Restoration to the New Criticism* (Philadelphia, PA: University of Pennsylvania Press, 2007), pp. 48–60.
23. The italicized phrase '*I, Rob, am here*' occurs in line 60 of Burns's second verse-letter to John Lapraik; see Kinsley (ed.), *The Poems and Songs of Burns*, vol. 1, p. 91. Even Burns's title, *Poems, Chiefly in the Scottish Dialect*, is new and provocative. Eighteenth-century precursors had not advertised dialect in their titles. Fergusson's 1773 title, like Ramsay's in 1721, had been simply *Poems*, although this was changed in 1779 to *Poems in Two* [i.e., English and Scottish] *Parts*. Fergusson had hoped to publish 'Auld Reikie', his celebration of Edinburgh, in book form but had taken ill after publication of the first canto and had died in 1774. If 'Auld Reikie' had been completed and published under that title, it might have been the first book of Scottish poetry bearing a title in Scots since the Union of Parliaments in 1707. It is typical of Burns that he finesses – negotiates – his

dialect-use. By titling his book 'Poems, Chiefly in the Scottish Dialect', he announces dialect without actually using it, preparing readers for what is to come. All the prefatory matter is in standard English. Dialect-use is reserved for the poems themselves but is emphasized in those, especially in the poems that open the volume. From the first title of the first poem ('The Twa Dogs', not 'The Two Dogs'), these are poems 'chiefly' in 'Scottish'; indeed, 'The Twa Dogs', at 238 lines, is the second longest poem Burns ever wrote: a sustained dialect performance opens Burns's debut volume.

24. R. Williams, 'Dialect', in *Keywords: A Vocabulary of Culture and Society*, rev. ed. (New York: Oxford University Press, 1983), p. 106.
25. P. Bourdieu, *Distinction: A Social Critique of the Judgment of Taste*, trans. R. Nice (Cambridge, MA: Harvard University Press, 1984), p. 7.
26. A. K. Mellor and R. E. Matlak (eds), *British Literature, 1780–1830* (Fort Worth, TX: Harcourt, 1996), p. 354.
27. R. L. Stevenson, 'Some Aspects of Robert Burns', in *Familiar Studies of Books and Men* (London: Chatto & Windus, 1889), in pp. 30–90, on p. 80.
28. A. Noble, 'Introduction', in A. Noble and P. S. Hogg (eds), *Canongate Burns: Complete Poems and Songs of Robert Burns* (Edinburgh: Canongate, 2001), p. lxxi. See also C. McGuirk's 'The Politics of the Collected Burns', *Gairfish 2: Discovery* (1991), pp. 37–50; M. Butler, 'Burns and Politics', in *Robert Burns and Cultural Authority*, ed. R. Crawford (Edinburgh: Edinburgh University Press, 1997), pp. 86–112; L. McIlvanney, *Burns the Radical: Poetry and Politics in Late-Eighteenth Century Scotland* (East Linton: Tuckwell Press, 2002), pp. 189–240; Noble and Hogg (eds), *The Canongate Burns*, pp. xxi–xlvi and *passim*; and C. Kidd, 'Burns and Politics', in *The Edinburgh Companion to Robert Burns*, ed. G. Carruthers (Edinburgh: Edinburgh University Press, 2009), pp. 61–73.
29. Kinsley (ed.), *The Poems and Songs of Robert Burns*, vol. 3, p. 1534.
30. Ibid., vol. 1, p. 322.
31. D. A. Low, (ed.), *Robert Burns: The Critical Heritage* (London: Routledge, 1974), p. 70.
32. Williams, *Keywords*, p. 219.
33. Kinsley considers conflicting anecdotes about performances of 'To a Haggis' in 1786: 'Chambers had a story that the final stanza, in the form printed in the Edinburgh periodicals ... was produced extempore during a dinner in the house of John Morrison, a Mauchline cabinet-maker ... and it will stand alone as a short grace ... Hogg's statement, that Burns wrote the poem to celebrate a haggis dinner at the house of Andrew Bruce ... is – if it implies extempore composition – too simple. But the publication of 'To a Haggis' in two Edinburgh periodicals, within a few weeks of Burns's arrival in the city, suggests that it took final shape for – or after – some 'occasion' there in early December, and was applauded into print', Kinsley (ed.), *The Poems and Songs of Robert Burns*, vol. 3, p. 1221. James Mackay describes a third version of the story, John Richmond's. Burns's wild-child friend remembered an earlier 'extempore' performance in autumn 1785: 'Burns sat down in the company of five lawyers at what was then constituted the Haggis Club. Matthew Dickie of Edinburgh ... asked Burns to say a grace, but instead he addressed the haggis which was the main dish of the evening', *RB: A Biography of Robert Burns* (Edinburgh: Mainstream, 1992), p. 281.
34. Kinsley (ed.), *The Poems and Songs of Robert Burns*, vol. 1, p. 311.
35. C. McGuirk (ed.), *Robert Burns: Selected Poems* (London: Penguin Books, 1993), p. xxvi.
36. V. Woolf, *To the Lighthouse* (1927; London: CRW Publishing, Ltd, 2004), p. 102.
37. G. C. Spivak, 'A Literary Representation of the Subaltern', in *In Other Worlds: Essays in Cultural Politics* (New York: Routledge Classics, 2006) pp. 332–70, on p. 365.

38. J. Kinsley (ed.), *The Poems and Songs of Robert Burns*, 3 vols (Oxford: Clarendon Press, 1968), vol. 1, p. 194. The printing of 'To a Louse' in the Kilmarnock *Poems* shows that Burns (who evidently worked closely with the printer, as he stayed in Kilmarnock while the book was being printed) suggested emphasis in several ways:

TO A
LOUSE,
On Seeing one on a Lady's Bonnet at Church.

The effect of the interplay between font-sizes and between roman and italic type is that of hearing a voice in two distinct registers: loud for the main title, especially 'LOUSE', which parades itself in capital letters in what looks like 16-point type on a separate line; then, in smaller italics, a conspiratorial stage-whisper of a subtitle: 'On seeing one ... '

39. Low (ed.), *Robert Burns: The Critical Heritage*, p. 435.
40. H. K. Bhabha, 'Signs Taken for Wonders', in *The Location of Culture*, pp. 145–74, on p. 154.
41. L. Colley, *Britons: Forging the Nation, 1707–1832* (New Haven, CT: Yale, 1992), p. 117.
42. R. Crawford (ed.), *Devolving English Literature* (Oxford: Clarendon, 1992), p. 62.
43. Postcolonial approaches are discussed in the introduction of Crawford's *Devolving English Literature*, pp. 1–15; in T. Preston's 'Contrary Scriptings: Implied National Narratives in Burns and Smollett', *Love and Liberty: Robert Burns*, ed. K. Simpson (East Linton: Tuckwell, 1997), pp. 198–216; in J. Skoblow's 'Resisting the Powers of Calculation: A Bard's Politics', in C. McGuirk (ed.), *Critical Essays on Robert Burns* (New York, G. K. Hall, 1998), pp. 17–31; and in M. Butler's 'Burns and Politics', in *Burns and Cultural Authority*, ed. Crawford, pp. 86–112.
44. G. C. Spivak, *The Spivak Reader: Selected Writings*, ed. D. Landry and G.Maclean (eds) (London: Routledge, 1995), pp. 224, 238–9.
45. C. Jones, *A Language Suppressed: The Pronunciation of the Scots Language in Eighteenth-Century Scotland* (Edinburgh: J. Donald, 1995), p. 81.
46. Kinsley (ed.), *The Poems and Songs of Robert Burns*, vol. 2, p. 762.
47. Anderson notes that the goal of the American colonies 'was not to have New London succeed, overthrow, or destroy Old London, but rather to safeguard their continuing parallels'. B. Anderson, *Imagined Communities: Reflections on the Origin and Spread of Nationalism*, rev. edn (1983; London: Verso, 1991), p. 191.
48. Kinsley (ed.), *The Poems and Songs of Robert Burns*, vol. 1, p. 501.
49. Burns's reference to ribbon remembers the English 'Greensleeves', which lists clothing items purchased for an unfaithful mistress, who has cast off the speaker like one of those old garments. Tartan is not merely a decorative fabric: as the dress of Highland Jacobites, it was an emblem of Scottish resistance. From 1747 to 1782, the wearing of tartan was proscribed under penalty of transportation. The ban had been lifted only seven years before Burns added tartan ties to English green sleeves.
50. Anderson, *Imagined Communities*, p. 90; original italics.
51. Ibid.
52. D. Fuss, *Essentially Speaking: Feminism, Nature, Difference* (London: Routledge, 1989), p. 28.
53. As McIlvanney describes them, 'The Crochallan Fencibles was a mock-regiment, named in derision of the volunteer defence forces raised during the war with the Americans. William Dunbar, for instance, was Colonel, and William Smellie ... was described by Burns as a 'Veteran' in bawdry (McIlvanney, *Burns the Radical*, p. 181). The introduction to *Canongate Burns* sees the Fencibles as one of two opposing factions: '[Burns]

was ... a member of the boozy, boisterous, in many instances brilliant, radical, reformist club, The Crochallan Fencibles. He was also taken up, [and] mildly patronized, by the aesthetically, politically, and religiously conformist pro-Hanoverian group led by Henry Mackenzie and Hugh Blair. What has never been understood is not only how partisan to their own causes both groups were but ... the degree to which, as the political scene darkened in the 1790s, they were sucked into active participation either towards not simply reform but insurrection on the radical side and covert anti-revolutionary activity on the government side'. Noble, 'Introduction', p. xlii.

54. As G. R. Roy writes in introducing his facsimile printing of *Merry Muses*, Burns's name does not appear on the title page (xvii). The texts of twelve (out of some eighty-five songs) exist in Burns's holograph and are thought to be his work, while a further nine songs also in his own handwriting are thought by many to have been copied and transmitted but not composed by the poet. Most scholars see the balance of the texts in *Merry Muses* as folk erotica added by various members of the Fencibles. My own sense is that all but five or six of these songs are by Burns – or pastiches drawn from traditional songs but revised rather than merely copied. My reason is the volume's emphasis on mutual consent: Burns is notable for this emphasis, whereas the folk tradition is rife with cautionary tales of rape and incest. There are only a few such songs in this collection. The facts are too scanty for certainty except in the case of the twenty-one songs that exist in Burns's handwriting. This volume is extremely rare (two known copies survive).

55. McGuirk (ed.), *Robert Burns: Selected Poems*, p. 176 and the note on p. 279. I have not used Kinsley's edition for the text of 'Logan Water' because I disagree with his printing of 'How can your flinty hearts enjoy' for the original line 'Ye mind na, mid your cruel joys'. Burns changed the line under duress.

56. Kinsley (ed.), *The Poems and Songs of Robert Burns*, vol. 2, p. 822.

57. Ibid., vol. 1, p. 346.

58. Ibid, vol. 2, p. 914. Although Kinsley places this song-text under 'Dubia and Undated', a copy exists in Burns's hand. The chorus of 'Buy broom besoms' is traditional. Ewan McColl and Dr Fred Freeman each include the song among their excellent Burns recordings. A 'besom' is a broom, sometimes a witch's broom and, by hostile extension, a pejorative term for a woman.

59. M. M. Bakhtin, *The Dialogic Imagination: Four Essays*, ed. M. Holquist, trans. C. Emerson and M. Holquist (Austin, TX: University of Texas Press, 1981), p. 287.

60. In Scotland alone, 'Is there for honest Poverty' ('A Man's a Man') appeared in the *Glasgow Magazine* (1795), *The Oracle* (June 1796, a Paisley chapbook (Paisley was a centre for radical weavers) and the *Scots Magazine* (1797).

61. Kinsley (ed.), *The Poems and Songs of Robert Burns*, vol. 1, p. 454.

62. Roy and Ferguson (eds), *Letters of Burns*, vol. 2, p. 169.

63. M. Shiach, *Discourse on Popular Culture: Class, Gender and History in Cultural Analysis, 1730 to the Present* (Stanford, CA: Stanford University Press, 1989), p. 43.

64. Ibid.

65. M. B. Ross, 'The Birth of a Tradition: Making Cultural Space for Feminine Poetry', in M. B. Ross, *Contours of Masculine Desire: Romanticism and the Rise of Women's Poetry* (New York: Oxford University Press, 1989), pp. 187–231, on p. 218.

66. Ibid.

67. Roy and Ferguson (eds), *Letters of Burns*, vol. 2, p. 173.

68. C. Carswell, *Life of Robert Burns* (London: Chatto & Windus, 1930), pp. 398–9.

69. Mackay, *RB*, p. 519.

70. Kinsley (ed.), *The Poems and Songs of Robert Burns*, vol. 2, p. 661.
71. Ibid., vol. 2, p. 662
72. A 1789 letter of Burns to Helen Maria Williams – she wrote him several times, having seen and admired the Kilmarnock 1786 *Poems*– enclosed an analysis of Williams's *A Poem on the Bill Lately Passed for Regulating the Slave Trade* (1788). Burns praises some passages as 'uncommonly beautiful' while critiquing others, telling Williams that in offering detailed advice he is 'doing as I would be done by'. Roy and Ferguson (eds), *Letters of Burns*, vol. 1, p. 431. Miss Williams was a friend of Burns's correspondent Dr John Moore. Liam McIlvanney mentions that Burns may have corresponded with Mary Wollstonecraft in *Burns the Radical*, p. 197.
73. The image of Burns walking a tightrope is from David Daiches's 'Robert Burns: The Tightrope Walker', in K. Simpson (ed.), *Love and Liberty: Robert Burns, A Bicentenary Celebration* (East Linton: Tuckwell Press, 1997), pp. 18–31.
74. Roy and Ferguson (eds), *Letters of Burns*, vol. 2, p. 301.
75. C. Kaplan, 'Pandora's Box: Subjectivity, Class and Sexuality in Socialist-Feminist Criticism', in T. Lovell (ed.), *British Feminist Thought: A Reader* (Oxford: Blackwell, 1990), pp. 956–75, on p. 957.
76. E. Stetson and L. David, *Glorying in Tribulation: The Life Work of Sojourner Truth* (East Lansing, MI: Michgan State University Press, 1994), p. 118. That the wording of Truth's speech as printed reflected her actual speech has sometimes been challenged, but Stetson and David disagree with the sceptics: 'It has been argued that Truth never said 'Ain't I a woman'. This is surprising since [the newspaper accounts that] ... report "she said she was a woman" can be reasonably understood as ... re-statements ... Truth's entire speech was a transformation worked on the ... abolitionist slogan "Am I not a Man and a Brother"'. Sojourner Truth and Josiah Wedgewood (who used the caption 'Am I not a Man and a Brother?' for an anti-slavery medallion in the 1780s) used gender-specific imagery as Burns did, invoking gender to raise consciousness about injustice and to call for social change.
77. The stocky silhouette by John Myers (or Miers) in 1787 bears out this point, as does Sir Walter Scott's memory of his one encounter with Burns: 'His person was strong and robust ... His features are represented in Mr. Nasmyth's picture, but ... they are diminished ... I think his countenance was more massive than it looks in any of the portraits'. Low (ed.), *Robert Burns: The Critical Heritage*, p. 262.
78. M. Lindsay (ed.), *The Burns Encyclopedia*, 3rd edn (New York: St Martin's, 1980), p. 32.
79. Kinsley (ed.), *The Poems and Songs of Robert Burns*, vol. 2, p. 624.
80. On Wordsworth's ambivalence, see chapter 2 and also A. Noble, 'Wordsworth and Burns: The Anxiety of Being Under the Influence', in McGuirk (ed.), *Critical Essays on Robert Burns*, pp. 49–62. Austen's reservations are conveyed by a conversation in *Sanditon* between the heroine and a tiresome admirer of Burns: Low (ed.), *Robert Burns: The Critical Heritage*, pp. 293–5); this Austen passage is discussed in F. Stafford, 'Burns and Romantic Writing', in G. Carruthers (ed.), *The Edinburgh Companion to Robert Burns* (Edinburgh: Edinburgh University Press, 2009), pp. 97–109, on p. 97. A. Noble's article on Wordsworth (see the first citation in this note) also discusses Hazlitt's enthusiasm for Burns (pp. 59–60); I discuss Carlyle's in my Introduction to *Critical Essays*, p. 2. S. Sweeney-Turner considers Carlyle and Burns in 'Pagan Airts: Reading Critical Perspectives on the Songs of Burns and Tannahill', in McGuirk (ed.), *Critical Essays*, pp. 182–207.

81. See text and note for 'From Esopus to Maria: or, Fragment – Part Description of a Correction House', in Noble and Hogg (eds), *Canongate Burns*, pp. 853–8.
82. Kinsley (ed.), *The Poems and Songs of Robert Burns*, vol. 1, p. 182.
83. Ibid , vol. 3, p. 972.
84. Roy and Ferguson (eds), *Letters of Burns*, vol. 2, p. 3.
85. Kinsley (ed.), *The Poems and Songs of Robert Burns*, vol. 3, p. 971.
86. G. Deleuze and F. Guattari, *A Thousand Plateaus: Capitalism and Schizophrenia*, trans. B. Massumi (Minneapolis, MN: University of Minnesota Press, 1987), p. 7.
87. R. W. Emerson, 'Ralph Waldo Emerson: An American Tribute', in Low (ed.), *Robert Burns: The Critical Heritage*, pp. 434–6.

1 Rob^r. Burness to Poet Burns: Bard, Interrupted

1. A. Cunningham (ed.), *Works of Robert Burns, with Life and Notes by Allan Cunningham. Illustrated Edition with Music*, 2nd edn, 4 vols (Edinburgh: Thomas C. Jack, 1835), vol. 1, p. 17.
2. Roy and Ferguson (eds), *Letters of Burns*, vol. 1, p. 41.
3. Seven early letters use the signature 'Robert Burns'. Six are addressed to former school friends at Kirkoswald, with the seventh and last (dated January 1783) to Burns's schoolmaster John Murdoch in London. Then for several years the signature reverts to Burness. 'Burns' is used always from April 1786 on, with the exception of letters to the branch of the family who spelled the name 'Burness'. The two major early gatherings of manuscript poems are signed 'Burness'.
4. See C. Ricks on Burns's allusions to Shakespeare and the Bible in 'Burns', in *Allusion to the Poets* (Oxford: Oxford University Press, 2002), pp. 43–82, on pp. 45–7, 61–5).
5. 5. On the contradictory stories about when and where Jean Armour met the poet, see Crawford, *The Bard*, p. 183. The parish records in Mauchline note Jean Armour's baptism on 25 February 1765. The later birth-date sometimes given, 27 Feb. 1767, is in the Burns family Bible, an entry in Burns's hand.
6. Roy and Ferguson (eds), *Letters of Burns*, vol. 1, p. 30.
7. Jean Armour was the mother of nine, all with Burns and all legitimate under the 'marriage lines' co-signed early in 1786. 'Irregular marriage' was not unusual. James Currie begins his edition and biography of Burns with an extended essay on 'the Character and Condition of the Scottish Peasantry'. This emphasizes that 'the law respecting marriage ... requires neither the ceremonies of the church, nor any other ceremonies, but simply the deliberate acknowledgment [*sic*] of each other as husband and wife, made by the parties before witnesses, or in any other way that gives legal evidence of such an acknowledgment having taken place'. J. Currie (ed.), *The Works of Robert Burns; with an Account of his Life, and a Criticism on his Writings. To which are Prefixed, Some Observations on the Character and Condition of the Scottish Peasantry*, 2nd edn, 4 vols (London: T. Cadell and W Davies, 1801), vol. 1, pp. 1–31, on p. 20. Even children born before any such agreement were, according to Currie, retroactively legitimated whenever parents made mutual acknowledgement of their partnership: 'the law of Scotland legitimating all children born before wedlock, on the subsequent marriage of their parents, renders the actual date of the marriage itself, of little consequence' (p. 21). The 1896 edition of Robert Chambers and William Wallace – influential on subsequent critical biographies – questions whether the paper co-signed by the poet and Jean Armour constituted a marriage. Yet the only dated legal judgement cited that supports their view is not from

1786 but from 1796, when Lord Braxfield declared from the Bench that consent *de presenti* does not constitute marriage 'without the priest's blessing or something equivalent'. No date is given in Chambers and Wallace's edition for the similar quoted opinion of Sir Ilay Campbell (who retired in 1808 but had had a long career in Scottish law): he likewise denied that 'consent makes marriage'. No date is given for an opposing judgement from 'Erskine' (probably Henry Erskine (1746–1818), Burns's correspondent). Erskine's opinion as cited in Chambers and Wallace is favourable to the view of marriage as mutual contract: 'Marriage may be without doubt perfected by the consent of parties declared by writing ... The proof of marriage is not confined to the testimonies of the clergyman and witnesses present at the ceremony'. See R. Chambers (ed.) and W. Wallace (rev.), *Life and Works of Robert Burns*, 4 vols (Edinburgh and London: W & R Chambers, 1896), vol. 1, p. 313n (for all citations above). Marriage customs in Scotland were clearly in transition at the end of the eighteenth century, but it is also clear from the letters of spring 1786 that Burns considered his agreement with Jean Armour to constitute a marriage. Burns, so far as we know the father of twelve who survived birth, had children (again so far as we know) by four women. Four of his children died during his lifetime and two died soon after the poet's death, including the son born to Jean Armour on the day of Burns's funeral. Two of three known illegitimate children were raised in the family. Bess, his firstborn, was reared by the poet's mother until 1796 (R. Fitzhugh, *Robert Burns, the Man and the Poet: A Round, Unvarnished Account* (Boston, MA: Houghton Mifflin, 1970), p. 68). The second illegitimate child, a son born in Edinburgh, was raised by his mother, who refused Burns's offer to adopt: 'I would have taken my boy from her long ago, but she would never consent' (Roy and Ferguson (eds), *Letters of Burns*, vol. 2, p. 122). This child's mother, Jenny Clow, died of tuberculosis two months after the poet last saw her in December 1791, but according to nineteenth-century anecdote, their son Robert survived and prospered in London (Mackay, *RB*, p. 425). Burns's third known illegitimate child was born in Dumfries in 1791 and raised by Jean Armour, who nursed her along with her own newborn son, William Nichol Burns. His three out-of-wedlock children and three of Jean Armour's nine children survived into adulthood.
8. Roy and Ferguson (eds), *Letters of Burns*, vol. 1, p. 44.
9. R. Sher, *The Enlightenment and the Book: Scottish Authors and their Publishers in Eighteenth-Century Britain, Ireland, and America* (Chicago, IL: University of Chicago Press, 2007), p. 230.
10. In 1796, Wilson's visits to Jean Armour in Paisley are revisited in 'The Gallant Weaver', a Burns song set in Paisley and told from the viewpoint of the young woman the weaver courts.
11. Mackay, *RB.*, p. 187.
12. Roy and Ferguson (eds), *Letters of Burns*, vol. 1, p. 30; original emphasis.
13. 'Marriages contracted in Scotland without the ceremonies of the church, are considered as *irregular*, and the parties usually submit to a *rebuke* for their conduct in the face of their respective congregations, which is not however necessary to render the marriage valid' (Currie (ed.), *The Works of Robert Burns*, vol. 1, p. 21). When the poet and Jean Armour reaffirmed their marriage in 1788 shortly after the death of their newborn twin girls, the ceremony (according to testimony in the Train MS – no formal record survives) did not take place in church but in the law office of Gavin Hamilton.
14. The dating of a letter by Burns to John Arnot that mentions Jamaica is open to question. The original is lost but Burns preserved a copy in vol. 2 of the Glenriddell Manuscript

(begun in 1793; vol. 1 was begun in 1789 and finished in 1791). For some letters in vol. 2, Burns used an amanuensis, but the two that open the volume – copies of part of a 1787 letter to William Nicol in broad Scots dialect and then the only text we have of Burns's letter to Arnot – are in the poet's hand. In the Glenriddell MS, Burns says that he sent the letter to Arnot 'about the latter end of 1785' (vol. 2, p. 9) but this cannot be, as it predates Jean Armour's pregnancy, topic of the letter, which describes the poet's battle with the Armours in a style of giddy *double entendre* reminiscent of Sterne's *Tristram Shandy*. *Letters* conjectures a date of April 1786 because the heading in Glenriddell mentions 'enclosing in it a subscription-bill for my first edition'. Yet Burns's letters enclose subscription blanks for the 1786 *Poems* as late as 10 August 1786, when Burns returned some forms to John Logan until 'the quantum of Copies' had been 'called for' (vol. 1, p. 46). Burns could even be remembering subscriptions for the Edinburgh edition (1787), for which a John Arnot, Esq., Dalwhatswood did subscribe. See R. Burns, *Poems, Chiefly in the Scottish Dialect* 3rd edn (London: T. Cadell, 1787), p. xi: my copy is the 'London' edition, which J. W. Egerer says was based on the 1787 Edinburgh ('stinking' variant). See J. W. Egerer, *A Bibliography of Robert Burns* (Edinburgh and London: Oliver & Boyd, 1964), pp. 13–15. Arnot's listing among the 'Subscriber's Names' in the 1787 Edinburgh and London editions is his only clear connection with Burns other than vol. 2 of the Glenriddell MS. According to the accounts of John Wilson, he was not among the Kilmarnock edition subscribers, although it is possible that he and Burns met in late March 1786 when Burns attended a Masonic meeting at Newmilns. Arnot, who lived near Newmilns and was a Freemason, might have taken one of the forty copies that Gavin Hamilton distributed in August 1786. The Arnot letter, like 'Holy Willie's Prayer' (which exists in two versions, John Richmond's copy of the mid-1780s and the much embellished Glenriddell MS text of 1791) was probably altered when transcribed. (The poet's dialect letter to William Nicol, a partial transcript of which opens the Glenriddell volume – the original is held by Mitchell Library, Glasgow – copies only the first two paragraphs (of six), and there are many variants from the original. See Roy and Ferguson (eds), *Letters of Burns*, vol. 1, pp. 120–1.) Burns's reference to 'the mountains of Jamaica' in the letter he copied years later into the Glenriddell MS might have originated anytime between April 1786 and 1793. As mentioned above, among surviving letters, Burns's first reference to Jamaica is in June 1786 in his letter to David Brice.

15. Roy and Ferguson (eds), *Letters of Burns*, vol. 1, p. 36.
16. Ibid., vol. 1, p. 144.
17. *Robert Burns: Poems 1786 and 1787* [facsimile of the Kilmarnock edition, with facsimiles of poems added in 1787] (Menston: Scolar Press, 1971), p. 152.
18. Roy and Ferguson (eds), *Letters of Burns*, vol. 1, p. 39.
19. Ibid., vol. 1, p. 138.
20. Ibid., vol. 1, p. 43. Infant Bess, born 22 May 1785, had just been weaned and was joining the Mossgiel household, where she stayed until 1796. The elder Elizabeth, whom the poet had met during his father's final illness when she worked at Lochlie farm, initialled a settlement agreement on 1 December 1786 (witnessed by Gavin Hamilton and James Smith; the poet was then in Edinburgh) by which she is thought to have received £20, or about 40 per cent of the profits from the Kilmarnock 1786 *Poems* (Lindsay (ed.), *The Burns Encyclopedia*, p. 280). (In the settlement document in the National Library of Scotland, the elder Bess's mark is a tall, very shaky 'E P'; it is likely she could write no more than her initials.) The December agreement suggests that Burns no longer was intent on emigrating: it makes no mention of the copyright and stipulates for the

child's maintenance ('Board wages, cloathing, and Education') through age ten, not fourteen (see National Library of Scotland, Dep. 308). This may explain Elizabeth Paton's reclaiming of Bess in 1796 when she turned eleven, although Burns's death in July of that year might also have had some bearing. By 1796, the elder Elizabeth was married to a farm worker and settled in life.
21. See H. Barclay, *Notes on the Law and Practice, Relative to Applications Against Debtors as in Meditatione Fugae* (Edinburgh: Thomas Clark, 1832).
22. Roy and Ferguson (eds), *Letters of Burns* , vol. 1, p. 145.
23. Mackay sees Burns's fear of legal pursuit in mid-1786 as 'exaggerated' (*RB*, p. 240). Currie, however, had a different reaction in 1800. He was shocked by the Armours' legal pursuit for a money settlement. 'The poet mentions his "skulking from covert to covert, under the terror of a jail" – The "pack of the law" were "uncoupled at his heels", to oblige him to find security for the maintenance of his twin-children, whom he was not permitted to legitimate by a marriage with their mother!' Currie (ed.), *The Works of Robert Burns*, vol. 1, p. 78. Mackay, despite questioning the validity of Burns's terror of being jailed (*RB*, p. 240), emphasizes in an earlier chapter that the poet 'was being hounded' so vengefully by the Armours that he vanished from public sight, taking shelter in the home of Jean Allan, a half-sister of his mother, in Gateshead near Kilmarnock (*RB*, p. 192). Burns chose a hiding place convenient to his printer's office.
24. Currie (ed.), *The Works of Robert Burns*, vol.1, pp. 74–6; original emphasis. The Armour's rejection of Burns most likely stemmed from his satires and (as Burns believed and Gilbert Burns's letter hints) his family's precarious situation following seizure of their stock and goods in 1784. Then there was the poet's daughter Bess, about whom Gilbert's 1797 letter to Mrs Dunlop is utterly silent but whose existence was no secret in Mauchline.
25. Robert Crawford mentions correspondence in December 1785 that discusses '"the planting line" – that is, sugar plantations' (Crawford, *The Bard*, p. 205). The reference is to an abstract made by Burns's biographer Currie, however, which is itself damaged. The letter it abstracts has not survived. Currie's précis of John Hutchison's letter to Burns is (in its entirety) as follows: 'Has recd. one from Burns dated D ... Will be glad to return the kindness ... B. in the planting line, tho' he must ... good advice. – Thanks for account of h ... ' (Roy and Ferguson (eds), *Letters of Burns*, vol. 2, p. 396). The fragmentary 'dated D' does suggest a December 1785 date for Burns's lost letter; although the Roy and Fergusson edition records no letters sent by Burns in that month. (Hutchinson's reply that Currie abstracted was mailed on 10 July, received on 23 September). Yet 'B. in the planting line, tho' he must' need not refer to the poet's emigration. No reference to Jamaica appears in what little survives, and Hutchinson might have been thanking the poet for 'good advice' as well as offering it. The letter could even be referring to Burns's farming activities in Scotland. David Daiches was puzzled by Gilbert Burns's assertion that the Armours' pursuit of Burns and the Jamaica voyage were the reasons for Burns's decision to publish: 'if we look at the date of publication of the proposals and realize that the decision to publish must have been arrived at a considerable time before the proposals were drawn up, it seems clear that Burns had determined to bring out a volume of his poems some time before he thought of emigrating to Jamaica'. See *Robert Burns* (London: G. Bell & Sons, 1952), p. 95.
26. Roy and Ferguson (eds), *Letters of Burns*, vol. 1, p. 30.
27. Sher, *The Enlightenment and the Book*, p. 230.
28. Roy and Ferguson (eds), *Letters of Burns*, vol. 1, p. 144.

29. Ibid., vol. 1, p. 144. See also C. Andrews, 'Lament for Slavery? The Case for Robert Burns', in F. R. Shaw (ed.) *Robert Burns Lives!* http://www.electricscotland.com/familytree/frank/Burns_lives93.htm [accessed 20 November 2013]; G. Carruthers, 'Burns and Slavery', in Shaw (ed.), *Burns Lives!*; and N. Leask, 'Burns and the Poetics of Abolition', in G. Carruthers (ed.), *The Edinburgh Companion to Robert Burns* (Edinburgh: Edinburgh University Press, 2009), pp. 47–60. Moore's *Zeluco* opens the chapters describing his dissolute protagonist's murder of slaves with this comment: 'If the reign of many European proprietors of estates in the West Indies were faithfully recorded, it is much to be feared, that the capricious cruelties which disgrace ... Caligula and Nero would not seem so incredible as they now do'. J. Moore, *Zeluco. Various Views of Human Nature, Taken from the Life and Manners, Foreign and Domestic* (1786), 2nd edn, 2 vols (London: Strahan, 1789), vol. 1, p. 121.

30. Robert Aiken's son left for Liverpool to learn a trade in May 1786, prompting Burns to rework 'Epistle to a Young Friend' as a parting gift. Andrew Aiken eventually became wealthy as a merchant in an unspecified trade (Lindsay (ed.), *The Burns Encyclopedia*, p. 3). His work might have been linked to the slave trade. By 1740, Liverpool was the most active slave-port in Europe, with 10 per cent of its traffic stemming from slavery. The port was responsible for 69.4 per cent of the English slave trade in 1786 and by 1804 that percentage had increased to 89.8 per cent. See E. Halcrow, *Canes and Chains: A Study of Sugar and Slavery* (Oxford: Heinemann Educational Publishers, 1982), p. 14. In 1792, 131 ships sailed to Africa from Liverpool laden with 'cottons and woollens, guns, iron, alcohol and tobacco' to be exchanged for African captives (ibid.). There were, in contrast, forty-two such ships sailing from Bristol and twenty-two from London. I should add, however, that Liverpool was a centre for abolition as well, electing William Roscoe as the first abolitionist Member of Parliament in 1806. Nonetheless, it is possible that Robert Aiken was not deterred by links to the slave trade when settling his own son in life.

31. Roy and Ferguson (eds), *Letters of Burns*, vol. 1, pp. 58–9.

32. The letter, dated 19 June 1786, from Charles Douglas in Jamaica to his brother Patrick, owner of the properties, is held by the Burns Birthplace Museum (NBC247) and is also available online at http:www.burnsmuseum.org.uk/collections/transcript/1574.

33. 'S. R. G.', 'If Burns Had Gone to Jamaica', *Burns Chronicle and Club Directory*, 20 (1911), pp. 79–82, on pp. 80–1. An earlier unsigned account of 'Burns's Jamaica Connections', mentioning the same estates, had appeared in the 1903 *Burns Chronicle*, pp. 79–83.

34. *Jamaican Family Genealogy Research Library*, 'Slaves and Slavery', '1788 Slave Count' at http://jamaicanfamilysearch.com/Samples2/1788tab.htm [accessed 20 November 2013].

35. T. Burnard, '"Not a Place for Whites?" Demographic Failure and Settlement, 1655–1780', K. E. A. Montieth and G. Richards (eds), *Jamaica in Slavery and Freedom: History, Heritage and Culture* (Kingston: University of the West Indies Press, 2002), pp. 73–88.

36. T. Burnard, '"Grand Mart of the Island": The Economic Functions of Kingston, Jamaica in the Mid-Eighteenth Century', K. E. A. Montieth and G. Richards (eds), *Jamaica in Slavery and Freedom*, p. 228.

37. As in S. R. G.'s account (see above, note 33), alcohol abuse (rather than mosquito-borne fever) was thought to be the chief cause of premature death in the tropics. Writing about the construction of the Panama Canal, David McCullough quotes one French engineer: 'only drunkards and the intemperate take the yellow fever and die there'. D. McCullough, *Path between the Seas: The Creation of the Panama Canal, 1870–1910* (New York: Simon & Shuster, 1978), p. 154.

38. Roy and Ferguson (eds), *Letters of Burns*, vol. 1, p. 56.
39. D. Harrison, "'A Most Miserable Trade": David Harrison Reveals the Involvement of Freemasons in the Slave Trade', *Freemasonry Today*, 39 (Winter 2006/7), online at http://webarchive.org/web/20070621004422/http:freemasonrytoday.com/39/p12.php [accessed 20 November 2013].
40. J. Boswell, *Life of Samuel Johnson*, unabridged, ed. R. W. Chapman (Oxford: Oxford University Press, 1980), p. 878.
41. Roy and Ferguson (eds), *Letters of Burns*, vol. 1, p. 44.
42. Mackay, *RB*, p. 200.
43. Roy and Ferguson (eds), *Letters of Burns*, vol. 1, p. 47.
44. Mackay, *RB*, p. 249. Coincidentally, the 'Roselle' was the same ship on which Burns's 'Clarinda' (Agnes M'Lehose) sailed from Leith several years later (February 1792) in an unsuccessful attempt to reconcile with her husband in Jamaica.
45. Burns sent mixed signals on emigration even before 1 December. His accounts with the printer were settled on 28 August; so no later than (probably before) 28 August, he had paid for his passage. The name of the agent (James Allen of Irvine) is known, but not the date of purchase (Mackay, *RB*, p. 237). In a letter of 26 September Burns calls his departure 'uncertain ... I do not think it will be till after harvest', Roy and Ferguson (eds), *Letters of Burns*, vol. 1, p. 54. To John Richmond he writes a day later that 'I am going perhaps to try a second edition ... If I do, it will detain me a little longer in the country; if not, I shall be gone as soon as harvest is over' (ibid., vol. 1, pp. 54–5). In his incoherent October letter to Robert Aiken cited above, Burns makes his first mention of an alternative to emigration: pursuing a position in Scotland as an Exciseman. Excise officers received a salary higher than that offered by the Douglases, with extra income possible in the form of a share in any goods seized. Moreover, unpopular as tax-collectors were, this was nothing to profiting from slavery. Even in the letter in which the Excise is introduced as an alternative, however, Burns admits in deference to his patrons that 'the consequences of my follies ... may perhaps make it impracticable to stay at home' (ibid., vol. 1, p. 58). Talk of emigration ceased only when Burns became a part-time Excise officer in summer 1788. As late as June 1787, the poet wrote to James Smith of still unsettled plans: 'Farming ... I cannot, dare not risk on farms as they are. If I do not fix, I will go for Jamaica' (ibid., vol. 1, p. 121). Smith himself, following the failure of a venture in calico printing in 1788, took ship for St Louis, Jamaica, or perhaps St Lucia in the Windward Islands: R. H. Cromek's *Reliques of Robert Burns* (1808) reports him as having died soon after arrival (Lindsay (ed.), *The Burns Encyclopedia*, p. 338).
46. Low (ed.), *Robert Burns: The Critical Heritage*, p. 70.
47. Roy and Ferguson (eds), *Letters of Burns*, vol. 1, p. 72.
48. Ibid., vol. 1, p. 73.
49. For detailed discussions of Highland Mary, see the Burns biographies by C. Carswell and J. Mackay. Mackay examined parish birth records to establish that her forename was not Mary but Margaret. The poet, referring to this courtship, says only that their acquaintance was 'pretty long', wording that to me suggests it was brief (R. H. Cromek (ed.), *Reliques of Robert Burns* (London: Cadell and Davies, 1808), p. 237). On 14 May 1786, they parted. The poet gave her his two-volume Bible inscribed with such oaths as 'and ye shall not swear by name falsely', but her own name is not written in the volumes. The Bible itself still exists but only the biblical quotations remain intact; other inscriptions (shades of Jean Armour's story) were mutilated. Her gravesite was opened in 1920, when it was found that the grave also contained the remains of at least three adults as well as

an infant in a wooden coffin. Whether this infant was a child of 'Highland Mary' by the poet is addressed in numerous biographies. (It could be a child whose burial occurred around 1827.) So the matter of a possible third child of Burns being born in 1786 is not settled. It is known that Margaret Campbell died in Greenock in autumn 1786 of typhus; she had brought her brother safely through the same illness. It might seem that her travel to Greenock was related to the poet's rendezvous with the ship *The Bell*, which embarked for Jamaica from Greenock in late September, but there is contrary evidence that she was in Greenock waiting for transport to Glasgow, having accepted a job offer there. Burns could not have arranged with her in May that they would sail from that port, for he did not himself know until August, although there could have been later letters between them that were destroyed or lost. One song inscribed to her, 'Will ye go to the Indies, my Mary', links her name with emigration; but like the other 'Highland Mary' songs, this was composed long after 1786: Burns sent it to *The Scots Musical Museum* in 1792.

50. This quatrain by Shenstone is the second epigraph. J. C. Ewing and D. Cook (eds), *Robert Burns's Commonplace Book. 1783–85. Reproduced in Facsimile from the Poet's Manuscript and the Original Introduction and Notes of James Cameron Ewing and Davidson Cook. This Edition Introduced by David Daiches* (Carbondale, IL: Southern Illinois University Press, 1965), p. 1. Page numbers in my citations are to the printed transcript in the facsimile volume, checked against the manuscript facsimile.
51. Ewing and Cook (eds), *Robert Burns's Commonplace Book*, p. vii.
52. Ibid., p. 4.
53. Ibid., p. 1.
54. Roy and Ferguson (eds), *Letters of Burns*, vol. 2, p. 153.
55. Kinsley (ed.), *The Poems and Songs of Robert Burns*, vol. 3, p. 968.
56. Ewing and Cook (eds), *Robert Burns's Commonplace Book*, p. 32.
57. Kinsley (ed.), *The Poems and Songs of Robert Burns*, vol. 3, p. 971.
58. Ewing and Cook (eds), *Robert Burns's Commonplace Book*, p. 40. The refrain is repeated in brackets because repetition is required by the tune. Ian F. Benzie has recorded a lively version (*Robert Burns: Complete Songs*, Vol. 1. Linn CKD047 [1995]).
59. Ibid., pp. 37–9. In calling tunes 'Scots', I suggest only that these were songs circulating in Scotland in Burns's day. In many cases, including the ballad 'John Barleycorn', Burns's airs might in origin be English or Irish. 'The Weaver and His Shuttle', musical setting for 'My Father Was a Farmer', is said in one of Burns's own later song-notes to be popular in both Ireland and Scotland, where it was called 'Jockie's Grey Breeks', Kinsley (ed.), *The Poems and Songs of Robert Burns*, vol. 3, p. 1015. 'Cold and Raw', another air used both for English and Scottish stanzas, is discussed by in Newman, *Ballad Collection, Lyric, and the Canon*, pp. 19, 24–6. Printed in Thomas D'Urfey's seventeenth-century song-collections, 'Cold and Raw' was adopted by John Gay in *The Beggar's Opera* and by Burns, early and late in his career.
60. See Liam McIlvanney's indispensable account of Burns's schooling. The book shared by the Burnes children during the mid-1760s has not itself survived. This was a popular textbook for decades: in a later edition, Burns's own poems appeared soon after his emergence into fame. McIlvanney suggests that the Burnes children studied the edition of 1764 (*Burns the Radical*, p. 47, n. 39).
61. I quote the opening four lines as printed in D. J. Maclagan, *Scottish Paraphrases, being the Translations and Paraphrases in Verse of several Passages of Sacred Scripture, Collected and Prepared by a Committee of the General Assembly of the Church of Scotland, In Order*

to be Sung in Church (Edinburgh: Andrew Elliot, 1889), p. 162. This was added to the approved paraphrases in 1781, so was not used in worship when Burns studied it in his schoolbook.

62. *Presbyterian Social Psalmodist: Being an Abridgment of the Presbyterian Psalmodist with a Selection of Hymns from the Assembly's Collection Adapted to the Respective Tunes* (Philadelphia, PA: Presbyterian Board of Publication, 1857), p. 4.
63. Ewing and Cook (eds), *Robert Burns's Commonplace Book*, p. 18.
64. Ibid., p. 34.
65. Kinsley (ed.), *The Poems and Songs of Robert Burns*, vol. 2, p. 573.
66. Ibid., vol. 2, p. 840. This stanza from 'Tam Lin' evidently remembers midsummer 1786, to which there are numerous references, by turns comic and elegiac, in later Burns songs. The elder Armours had done all in their power to shake their daughter's bond with him and to demonize their prospective son-in-law.
67. Ibid., vol. 1, p. 149.
68. Ewing and Cook (eds), *Robert Burns's Commonplace Book*, pp. 9–10. The annotation on Young does not appear in *1CPB* but was added by Burns to the Kilmarnock edition. Kinsley (ed.), *The Poems and Songs of Robert Burns*, vol. 1, p. 16 (note to line 9).
69. Paterson (ed.), *Robert Burns: Poems*, p. viii.
70. Ewing and Cook (eds), *Robert Burns's Commonplace Book*, p. 21. The pun in l. 10 is clearer in the revised later text printed in Kinsley's edition: 'For her a, b, e, d and her c, u, n, t', Kinsley (ed.), *The Poems and Songs of Robert Burns*, vol. 1, p. 61.
71. Ewing and Cook (eds), *Robert Burns's Commonplace Book*, p. 43.
72. Roy and Ferguson (eds), *Letters of Burns*, vol. 1, p. 28; spelling of Fergusson's name as in the original.
73. D. Sneddon (ed.), *Burns Holograph Manuscripts in the Kilmarnock Manuscript Museum, With Notes* (Kilmarnock: D Brown & Co, 1889), p. iii. Both quoted phrases are in the first paragraph of Sneddon's 'Introductory Remarks'.
74. As Tom Scott well observed, Fergusson found standard Habbie 'used only for comic elegy and left it fit for many purposes'; 'A Review of Robert Fergusson's Poems', *Akros*, 2:6 (December 1967), pp. 15–26, on p. 24.
75. E. Morgan, 'A Poet's Response to Burns', in K. G. Simpson (ed.), *Burns Now* (Edinburgh: Canongate Academic, 1994), pp. 1–12, on p. 10.
76. According to Gilbert Burns's account, quoted in Currie, 'Hugh Williams, a curious looking awkward boy ... came to us with much anxiety ... with the information that the ewe had entangled herself in the tether, and was lying in the ditch. Robert was much tickled with *Huoc*'s appearance and postures on the occasion. Poor Maillie [*sic*] was set to rights, and when we returned from the plough in the evening, he repeated to me her *Death and dying Words* pretty much in the way they now stand'. Currie (ed.), *The Works of Robert Burns*, vol. 3, p. 330.
77. Sneddon (ed.), *Burns Holograph Manuscripts*, p. 82.
78. Ibid., p. 81.
79. Ibid., p. 83.
80. The poet did not copy 'To a Mouse' or 'To a Louse' into Kilmarnock Manuscript. They may not have been finished early in 1786. A manuscript of 'To a Mouse' owned by one Alfred Morrison is cited by Henley and Henderson in their 1896 Centenary edition (W. E. Henley and T. F. Henderson (eds), *The Poetry of Robert Burns*, 4 vols (Edinburgh: T. C. and E. C. Jack, 1901), vol. 1, on p. 365). Yet Kinsley was unable to trace its whereabouts six decades later and Henley and Henderson do not say whether it bore any date.

(The seven variants they list are not major and also not improvements.) The sole manuscript of 'To a Louse' is at Oxford (Bodleian MS. Add. A. 111) and is not dated; it was acquired at the same time as a letter of the 1790s, but the letter itself does not refer to any enclosed poem.

81. Kinsley numbers 'Poor Mailie's Elegy' as #25, not due to its date of composition but because it must appear as the poet intended just after the early poem presenting Mailie's 'Dying Words', Kinsley (ed.), *The Poems and Songs of Robert Burns*, vol. 3, p. 1018.
82. For more on Fergusson's influence, see C. McGuirk, 'The "Rhyming Trade": Fergusson, Burns, and the Marketplace', in R. Crawford (ed.), *'Heaven-Taught Fergusson': Robert Burns's Favourite Scottish Poet* (East Linton: Tuckwell, 2003), pp. 135–59. On his mettle in contending with one of Fergusson's best poems, Burness strictly replicates Spenser's rhyme-scheme; Fergusson had recast the rhyme to return less often (see p. 158 in 'The "Rhyming Trade"').
83. Cunningham (ed.), *Works of Robert Burns*, vol. 1, p. 36.
84. Late in December of 1787, Burns wrote to Brown thanking him for early encouragement: 'Do you recollect a sunday we spent in Eglinton woods? you told me, on my repeating some verses to you that you wondered I could resist the temptation of sending verses of such merit to a magazine: 'twas actually this that gave me an idea of my own pieces which encouraged me to endeavour at the character of a Poet'. In Roy and Ferguson (eds), *Letters of Burns*, vol. 1, p. 192.
85. Roy and Ferguson (eds), *Letters of Burns*, vol. 1, p. 145.
86. 'The [£6 discrepancy in Burns's account of his Kilmarnock profits] might represent … a 50% down payment to "Robert Burn, Architect" for Fergusson's headstone', in C. McGuirk, 'Burns's Two Memorials to Fergusson', in Scott and Simpson (eds), *Robert Burns and Friends*, pp. 5–23, on p. 6n. The final payment was not made until February of 1792. Roy and Ferguson (eds), *Letters of Burns*, vol. 2, p. 133.
87. Kinsley (ed.), *The Poems and Songs of Robert Burns*, vol. 3, p. 971.
88. Ibid., vol. 3, p. 972.
89. Ibid., vol. 3, p. 971.
90. Ibid.
91. Ibid.
92. Roy and Ferguson (eds), *Letters of Burns*, vol. 1, p. 137.
93. More will be said on Wordsworth's reaction to the 1786 *Poems* in Chapter 2.
94. Low (ed.), *Robert Burns: The Critical Heritage*, p. 122.
95. Leask, *Robert Burns and Pastoral*, pp. 118–22.
96. 'The Twa Dogs' also refers to Ossian in the name given to the Scottish dog ('Cesar' has been imported from Newfoundland). Luath, the name of Cuchullin's dog in *Fingal*, was also the name of Burns's dog: '*Luath* was a great favourite. The dog had been killed by the wanton cruelty of some person the night before my father's death. Robert said to me, that he should like to confer such immortality as he could upon his old friend *Luath*' (Currie (ed.), *The Works of Robert Burns*, vol. 3, p. 383). As this part of my chapter focusses on Burns's choices in editing and arranging his first published book, I have taken line numbers from the Scolar Press facsimile of the Kilmarnock 1786 *Poems*. Kinsley's edition relies on the second edition (1787 *Poems*), in which some of Burns's choices were constrained by genteel advice. Having sold copyright, Burns had little say in the edition of 1793.

97. 'Caller Water', in M. McDiarmid (ed.), *The Poems of Fergusson*, 2 vols (Edinburgh: Blackwood for the Scottish Text Society, 1954–6), vol. 2, p. 106. All citations to Fergusson's texts are from this exemplary edition.
98. *Poems, Chiefly in the Scottish Dialect* (1786), pp. 22.
99. The final image of Mother Scotland's involuntary urination was too graphic even for Burns on reflection, for he made a holograph change in a copy of the 1793 edition of *Poems*. Kinsley (ed.), *The Poems and Songs of Robert Burns*, vol. 3, p. 1145.
100. Kinsley (ed.), *The Poems and Songs of Robert Burns*, vol. 1, p. 128.
101. Prior vernacular poets' tend to minimize the subversive element in their blend of Scots and English (McGuirk, 'Burns's Two Memorials to Fergusson', p. 13). Allan Ramsay defended vernacular as a 'Doric' variant on the standard language, fully compatible with classical literary standards. Fergusson never defended his use of dialect: there is no preface in the volume of poems that appeared during his lifetime, in 1773. It could be said, however, that he hedged his bet, for in *Poems by Robert Fergusson*, the only book published in his lifetime, only a few of his dialect poems are included and they are placed in the back of the volume.
102. Low (ed.), *Robert Burns: The Critical Heritage*, p. 82. Blair also recommends cutting part of Burns's 'Dedication to Gavin Hamilton' on the grounds that 'it will give offence' (p. 81). In Blair's short notes – 400 words or so – the terms 'indecent' and 'inadmissible' are used freely. He condemns imagery for giving 'Offence', being 'coarse', and being 'very exceptionable' to religious propriety.
103. C. McGuirk, 'Loose Canons: Milton and Burns, Artsong and Folksong', in K. Simpson (ed.), *Love and Liberty: Robert Burns. A Bicentenary Celebration* (East Linton: Tuckwell, 1997), pp. 315–25, on pp. 317–20.
104. Kinsley (ed.), *The Poems and Songs of Robert Burns*, vol. 1, p. 152.
105. *Robert Burns: Poems 1786 and 1787*, p. 101.
106. See the comments on Burns's notes to 'Halloween' in L. Davis, 'Re-Presenting Scotia: Robert Burns and the Imagined Community of Scotland', in McGuirk (ed.), *Critical Essays on Robert Burns*, pp. 63–78, on pp. 71–2.
107. Hallowmas Fair, described by Fergusson, was a major festival held the first week of November. Burns in contrast describes a group of friends gathered on a farm for an evening of fun. A line in Fergusson's 'Hallow-Fair' – 'Here chapman billies tak their stand' (l. 28) – is echoed in the opening line of Burns's 'Tam o'Shanter': 'When chapman billies leave the street'.
108. 'Halloween' portrays young people using spells to predict the names of their future partners and the nature, stormy or tranquil, of their future courtships. Though tone is very different, this emphasis on love-spells may have turned John Keats in the direction of love-charms in 'Eve of St Agnes' (1819), although he displaces his lovers to a much earlier era of superstition. Madeleine and Porphyro escape in the final lines from her family's benumbed winter castle, while Burns's seekers-after-signs, venturing outdoors, manage only to startle the farm animals.
109. Kinsley (ed.), *The Poems and Songs of Robert Burns*, vol. 3, p. 971.
110. Describing the hardships of life on his father's farm ('we lived very poorly'), Burns notes that 'A Novel-Writer might perhaps have viewed these scenes with some satisfaction; but so did not I'. He never romanticized the difficulties of farming without capital. Roy and Ferguson (eds), *Letters of Burns*, vol. 1, p. 137.
111. Ibid., vol. 1, p. 139; original emphasis.

112. 'Despondency, an Ode' is among the texts praised in Henry Mackenzie's review of December 1786, named first among the Burns poems offering 'strains ... solemn and sublime' (Low (ed.), *Robert Burns: The Critical Heritage*, p. 69). The poem echoes Gray's 'Ode on a Distant Prospect of Eton College'; two other lines in Gray about the schoolboys ('No sense have they of ills to come, / Nor care beyond today' (ll. 53–4) may also resonate in 'To a Mouse' ('The *present* only toucheth thee', l. 44).
113. Low (ed.), *Robert Burns: The Critical Heritage*, p. 131.
114. Roy and Ferguson (eds), *Letters of Burns*, vol. 1, p. 30.
115. C. McGuirk, *Robert Burns and the Sentimental Era* (Athens, GA: University of Georgia Press, 1985), p. 13.
116. Roy and Ferguson (eds), *Letters of Burns*, vol. 1, p. 142.
117. McDiarmid (ed.), *Poems of Fergusson*, vol. 2, p. 148.
118. 'Corn Rigs' is not transcribed in *The First Commonplace Book* but Burns says in his autobiographical letter of 1787 that is it among his earliest songs. Anne Rankine was delighted to have her name associated with a song felt in the nineteenth century to border on racy indecency; perhaps she shared her father's cheerfully carnal disposition. 'Anne Rankine ... not only "owned the soft impeachment" but to her dying day boasted that she was the Annie of "Rigs o' Barley"'. G. Gebbie (ed.), *Complete Works of Robert Burns (Self-Interpreting)*, 6 vols (New York: Dumont, *c.* 1880), vol. 1, p. 49.
119. Mackay, *RB*, pp. 88–9.
120. Three satiric epitaphs were the only texts cut from the 1786 edition when the 1787 edition was prepared. These epitaphs were used mainly to fill up, or as David Daiches says 'pad out', the final signature. D. Daiches, *Robert Burns* (London: Bell, 1952), p. 194.
121. While only a few marked printers' copies for texts in the 1786 *Poems* survive, Burns himself (not the printer) most likely chose that final flourish of FINIS. In *The First Commonplace Book* Burns ends his first song, 'Handsome Nell', the same way: 'Finis' (2). A similar 'Le fin' appears after eight of fifteen texts in Kilmarnock Manuscript. This announcement of The End carries some editorial significance, possibly as a seal of approval ('There, I've finished this one'). One of the seven texts in 'Scotch Poems' that does not receive the 'Le fin', 'John Barleycorn', may have been seen as unfinished early in 1786: 'Barleycorn' was also the only text copied for the Kilmarnock MS that then was then held back from 1786 *Poems*. Burns may have hoped to add new stanzas but in the event the song appeared in the 1787 edition of *Poems* as transcribed in the Kilmarnock MS. The 1786 volume of his poems was in every sense under Burns's control: he determined sequence, contents, and spelling and produced the glossary and the remarkable preface. The two later editions (1787 and 1793) added to the contents of the 1786 volume.
122. Kinsley (ed.), *The Poems and Songs of Robert Burns*, vol. 1, p. 292.
123. Roy and Ferguson (eds), *Letters of Burns*, vol. 1, p. 145.
124. Kinsley (ed.), *The Poems and Songs of Robert Burns*, vol. 1, p. 292.
125. Corinna Hewat has recorded an excellent performance of 'The Gloomy Night' in *Robert Burns: Complete Songs*, volume 5 (Linn, 1998: CKD086).
126. L. Braudy, *The Frenzy of Renown: Fame and Its History* (New York: Vintage, 1997), p. 404.

2 'If Thou Indeed Derive Thy Light from Heaven': Wordsworth Responds to Burns

1. R. L. Brett and A. R. Jones (eds), *Lyrical Ballads; Text of the 1798 Edition with the Additional 1800 Poems and the Preface* (London and New York: Routledge, 1988), pp. 255–6.
2. Ibid., p. 7. In Burns's case, those Scottish middle and lower classes seasoned their speech with a strong spice of vernacular.
3. Wordsworth wrote that 'With the poems of Burns I became acquainted almost immediately upon their first appearance in the volume printed at Kilmarnock'. Low (ed.), *Robert Burns: The Critical Heritage*, p. 162. His headmaster at Hawkshead School, Thomas Bowman, loaned Wordsworth the volume. See D. Wu, *Wordsworth's Reading, 1770–1799* (Cambridge: Cambridge University Press, 1993), p. 24.
4. Russell Noyes discusses many parallels in 'Wordsworth and Burns'. He suggests that the Lucy poems were inspired by Burns's songs to Highland Mary, citing parallel phrases, and sees the link between Wordsworth's 'Lines Written in Early Spring' and 'Man Was Made to Mourn'. Noyes traced the link between 'great Nature's plan' in Burns's 'Second Epistle to John Lapraik' and Wordsworth's phrase 'Nature's holy plan'. (Both probably go back to Alexander Pope's *An Essay on Man* of 1733–4.) Noyes sees similar links between Burns's 'Epistle to Davie' and Wordsworth's 'To my Sister' and Burns's 'To a Mountain Daisy' and Wordsworth's 'To a Daisy'. Some of the expressions are images frequently used in that era; those interested should consult his article itself and see whether they agree with all Noyes's parallels. He notes the importance of Burns's 'The Vision' to Wordsworth, but does not mention 'If thou indeed derive thy light from Heaven'. He observes the correspondences between Burns's 'A Bard's Epitaph' and Wordsworth's 'A Poet's Epitaph' but does not discuss Burns's cameo appearance in 'Resolution and Independence'. I would never have seen the echoes and revisions of elements from Burns in 'Benjamin the Waggoner' without this pioneering article. R. Noyes, 'Wordsworth and Burns', *PMLA* [*Publications of the Modern Language Association*], 59 (1944), pp. 813–32.
5. In most of the *Lyrical Ballads* (1798), Wordsworth used plain diction, whereas Burns loved the dramatic juxtaposition of multiple levels of language, from bawdy language to the high-flown 'poetic diction' that Wordsworth deplores in the 1800 Preface to *Lyrical Ballads*, calling it 'falsehood of description'. Brett and Jones (eds), *Lyrical Ballads*, p. 251.
6. See Wordsworth's letter of 23 November 1825 to Allan Cunningham, quoted by S. Gill in 'Wordsworth and Burns', in D. Sergeant and F. J. Stafford (eds) *Burns and Other Poets* (Edinburgh: Edinburgh University Press, 2012), pp. 156–67, on p. 159. Wordsworth also copied this into a note he added in 1842 to 'At the Grave of Burns', cited above in note 3. In Low (ed.), *Robert Burns: The Critical Heritage*, p. 162.
7. For Wordsworth's quoting 'most of' the second epistle to John Lapraik, see Kinsley (ed.), *The Poems and Songs of Robert Burns*, vol. 3, p. 1060. For Wordsworth's recitation 'with much emotion' of the 'eighth and ninth stanzas' of 'On a Scotch Bard Gone to the West Indies', see Kinsley (ed.), *Poems and Songs of Burns*, vol. 3, p. 1176.
8. 'On Fergusson', in Kinsley (ed.), *The Poems and Songs of Robert Burns*, vol. 1, p. 323.
9. See Kinsley (ed.), *The Poems and Songs of Robert Burns*, vol. 3, p. 971. For further discussion of Burns's emulation of Fergusson, see McGuirk, 'Burns's Two Memorials to Fergusson', pp. 5–23.
10. 'A Day with Wordsworth', recording the poet's conversation with James Patrick Muirhead in 1841, was not published until 1927 in *Blackwood's Magazine*; it was rediscovered

by A. Noble in 'Wordsworth and Burns; The Anxiety of Being Under the Influence', in McGuirk (ed.), *Critical Essays*, pp. 49–62.
11. T. Crawford, *Burns: A Study of the Poems and Songs* (Stanford, CA: Stanford University Press, 1960), pp. 182–92; Ricks, *Allusion to the Poets*, pp. 46–7, 54–5; Leask, *Robert Burns and Pastoral*, pp. 98–103; and F. Stafford, 'Robert Burns's Addresses', in *Local Attachments*, pp. 176–223.
12. Gill, 'Wordsworth and Burns', p. 158.
13. Burness and Poet Burns alternate in both poems 'The Cotter's Saturday Night' pays sentimental tribute to Burns's father but Burns's speaker also fiercely defends the peasant classes and refers to himself as a 'Patriot Bard' in the closing lines. Diction varies in both poems – grand in some stanzas, homely and quaint in others, as in the portrait of the mother in 'The Cotter's Saturday Night', with her pride in her homemade cheese and relief to find that her daughter's suitor is respectful and mannerly. 'The Vision' exhibits similarly contrasting moods and diction.
14. 'When I composed my Vision long ago, I had attempted a description of Koyle, of which the additional stanzas are a part, as it originally stood', 'Letter to Mrs. Dunlop', 15 January 1787, in Roy and Ferguson (eds), *Letters of Burns*, vol. 1, p. 85.
15. Ibid.
16. Robert Dewar, who from 1930 to 1955 planned the Burns edition subsequently carried out by James Kinsley, tracked the many changes in the three printed versions of the poem, for which there are no manuscripts. Kinsley (ed.), *The Poems and Songs of Robert Burns*, vol. 3, pp. 1069–71.
17. 'A Dream' was inspired, says its headnote in the Kilmarnock edition, by 'reading, in the public papers, the Laureate's Ode, with the other parade of June 4th, 1786'. The 1786 birthday ode for King George III was the second of six by Warton; Burns's 'A Dream' therefore was composed in less than a week if he first saw Warton's poem on 4 June and sent 'A Dream' off to the printer with the rest of the Kilmarnock manuscripts on 13 June. 'A Dream' does seem loosely (if delightfully) improvised, but perhaps the newspapers printed the ode in advance of the birth-date. In the poem a 'humble Bardie' (l. 4), lulled to sleep by perusal of the Warton ode, dreams he is at court. Promising that unlike a pensioned laureate he will not flatter (l. 20), he offers birthday greetings before turning to George and Charlotte's many grown children. Ten final stanzas offer advice on their various marriage options, which adds self-mockery to satire given Burns's own courtship disasters in 1786. Citations from 'A Dream' and all other Kilmarnock poems quoted in this chapter are from the facsimile *Robert Burns, Poems 1786–1787*, p. 79. Kinsley's edition of Burns's complete poems and songs is cited for texts not printed in Kilmarnock or for references to Kinsley's notes.
18. The Warton ode of 1786 is a bit of a 'parade', as Burns describes it in his note to his rejoinder-poem (see note 17 above). Warton suggests that only the greatest poets of Greece could do King George sufficient 'honour'. G. Gilfillan (ed.), *Poetical Works of Goldsmith, Collins and Thomas Warton, with Lives, Critical Dissertations, and Explanatory Notes* (New York: D. Appleton & Co., 1860), pp. 250–1.
19. *Robert Burns, Poems 1786–1787*, p. 97. The Kilmarnock text of 'The Vision' is the version Wordsworth read in 1786.
20. I use the term 'sonnet' despite the poem's sixteen-line length and absence of rhyme. George Meredith's *Modern Love* (1862) consists of fifty sixteen-line sonnets tracing stages in a failed marriage, although Meredith uses rhyme.

21. T. Hutchinson (ed.) and E. De Selincourt (rev.), *Wordsworth: Complete Poetical Works, With Introduction and Notes* (Oxford: Oxford University Press, 1936), p. v.
22. M. Y. Hughes (ed.), *Complete Poems and Major Prose of John Milton* (New York: Odyssey Press, 1957), p. 77.
23. Hutchinson (ed.) and De Selincourt (rev.), *Wordsworth*, p. 226. Burns rises like a star – but (paradoxically) a star that touches earth. The imagery is similar to that of his later sonnet 'If thou indeed derive thy light from heaven'.
24. Because the Oxford Standard Authors volume (on which I am chiefly relying for poems later than the early editions of *Lyrical Ballads*) does not reprint this note, I have taken it from *Complete Poetical Works of William Wordsworth, Part 1* (Boston, MA: Houghton Mifflin, 1904), p. 700.
25. Low (ed.), *Robert Burns: The Critical Heritage*, p. 258.
26. Both at Hawkshead School and St Johns College, Cambridge, Wordsworth's studies emphasized mathematics and science. He especially loved geometry.
27. In 1718 Edmund Halley discovered that the stars were not fixed but in 'proper motion'. While Aristotle and many (not all) ancients thought that the speed of light was infinite, in 1676 the Danish astronomer Ole Roemer had proved that light takes time to transmit and had estimated its speed.
28. Hughes (ed.), *Complete Poems and Major Prose of John Milton*, p. 168.
29. In later printings of 'Resolution and Independence', each stanza is headed with a number, decisively separating the stanza describing Wordsworth's speaker from the next stanza describing Chatterton and Burns. In the 1807 edition of *Poems in Two Volumes*, where this poem of 1802 first was printed, there is no numbering, so I have used that first version. Wordsworth, *Poems. In Two Volumes* (London: Longman, Hurst, Rees and Orme, 1807).
30. *Robert Burns Poems 1786 and 1787*, p. 165.
31. Hutchinson (ed.) and De Selincourt (rev.), *Wordsworth*, p. 460.
32. Brett and Jones (eds), *Lyrical Ballads*, p. 69, and Hutchinson (ed.) and De Selincourt (rev.), *Wordsworth*, p. 378.
33. *Robert Burns: Poems 1786 and 1787*, p. 98.
34. In 'Tam o'Shanter' Burns's pace is furious: 'The piper loud and louder blew; / The dancers quick and quicker flew; / They reel'd, they set, they cross'd, they cleekit, / Till ilka carlin swat and reekit, / And coost her duddies to the wark, / And linket at it in her sark!' Kinsley (ed.), *The Poems and Songs of Robert Burns*, vol. 2, p. 562. In 'Benjamin the Waggoner' the strenuous dancing is only overheard: the dancers on an upper floor soon descend to watch the sailor's exhibition of his model ship. Wordsworth offers steady slow lines as Benjamin's horses pull the heavily laden wagon up a hill: 'Up against the hill they strain, / Tugging at the iron chain, / Tugging all with might and main, / Last and foremost, every Horse / To the utmost of his force. / And the smoke and respiration / Rises like an exhalation / Which the merry, merry sun / Takes delight to play upon' (ll. 648–56). P. F. Betz (ed.), *Benjamin the Waggoner, by William Wordsworth* (Ithaca, NY: Cornell University Press, 1981), p. 100.
35. Of Coila's three zenith-poets, Wordsworth was most sympathetic to Thomson. In 1829 he recalled that 'I had once a hope to have learned some unknown particulars of Thomson, around Jedburgh, but I was disappointed ... These three writers, Thomson, Collins, and Dyer, had more poetic imagination than any of their contemporaries, unless we reckon Chatterton as of that age'. 'William Wordsworth to Alexander Dyce', 12 January

1829, in W. Knight (ed.), *Letters of the Wordsworth Family, Vol. 2* (Boston, MA: Ginn and Company, 1907), p. 359.
36. Brett and Jones (eds), *Lyrical Ballads*, pp. 245–6.
37. Ibid., p. 251.
38. Thomson, 'Summer', *The Seasons*, Project Gutenberg Australia (August 2008) at gutenbergbook.net.au/ebooks08 [accessed 3 September 2013]. This passage may be remembered in Burns's description of the fleeting nature of pleasure in 'Tam o'Shanter': 'Or like the rainbow's lovely form, / Evanishing amid the storm' (ll. 65–6).
39. T. Gray, 'Elegy in a Country Churchyard', in L. I. Bredvold, A. D. McKillop and L. Whitney (eds), *Eighteenth Century Poetry and Prose*, 2nd edn (New York: Ronald Press, 1956), pp. 392–5.
40. W. Shenstone, 'The School-mistress', in Bredvold et al. (eds), *Eighteenth Century Poetry and Prose*, pp. 550–6.
41. Burns's epitaph for his father quotes from l. 164 of Goldsmith's 'The Deserted Village' ('even his failings leaned to virtue's side') and many of Burns's poems echo Goldsmith's lament for the dispossession of tenants (Bredvold et al. (eds), *Eighteenth Century Poetry and Prose*, p. 811).
42. As J. C. Weston writes, 'For twelve crucial years [*c.* ages seven to eighteen, when the family endured its worst struggle at Mount Oliphant], Burns helped his ageing father farm seventy-five acres of mossy, rocky uplands ... The land was unimproved, that is undrained ... The steading was isolated, not even on the main pony path from Ayr to Dalrymple. They lived in a stone, thatched house, along with their stock, no bigger than the mud cottage with a turf roof Burns was born in. It was heated by peat, dug by themselves from the muirs. They were forced by lack of cash, not ignorance, to use the old-style farming methods ... Oats were cut with a sickle, thrashed with a flail, winnowed by wind, and ground by hand daily on a knocking-stone. They tethered (not having fences) a sufficient number of sheep and grew enough flax to make their own clothes. They ate nothing but skim milk, oats, cabbage, and maybe potatoes and when there was none of that they starved. The little lime they used to make the soil less sour, they bought because they had no kiln to burn it themselves. They hauled it in on sledges or creels on horseback, for they had no cart with wheels'. J. C. Weston, 'Robert Burns's Satire', in McGuirk (ed.), *Critical Essays on Robert Burns*, pp. 117–33, on p. 121.
43. The 'Air Library Society' was founded in 1762 and William Burnes was highly esteemed by several of its founding members. Robert Crawford thinks it probable that he had access to its books. Burnes had other 'friends with good libraries' as well. In Crawford, *The Bard*, p. 52.
44. Quoted in Currie (ed.), *The Works of Robert Burns*, vol. 1, p. 79. Gilbert Burns's account is taken from notes he made responding to his brother's autobiographical letter to Moore.
45. Ibid., p. 66. Currie reprints here a letter of Gilbert Burns written several years after his brother's death at the request of Mrs Dunlop.
46. Preface, *Poems, Chiefly in the Scottish Dialect*, in *Robert Burns: Poems 1786 and 1787*, p. 2.
47. Skoblow, *Dooble Tongue*, p. 117.
48. See L. McIlvanney, 'A Real Whig Reading-Book? Masson's Collection and the Politics of Burns', in *Burns the Radical*, pp. 46–63.
49. James Currie's biography assumes that Burns was schooled through the extensive Scottish parish system, but Alloway had been absorbed by the parish of Ayr in 1690. There was no school at Alloway. Ayr's school, several miles away, was not in walking distance for young

children. With several neighbours Burnes interviewed five candidates and they selected John Murdoch to teach their children, paying privately. Burnes hired the candidate with the best handwriting and clearest competency in English grammar. The families took turns boarding Murdoch, who soon became a fast friend of the poet's father.

50. Currie (ed.), *The Works of Robert Burns*, vol. 1, pp. 88–9, from a letter John Murdoch sent to Currie from London, where by the late 1790s he was established as a French teacher.
51. W. Shenstone, 'The School-mistress', ll. 245–8, in Bredvold et al. (eds), *Eighteenth Century Poetry and Prose*, pp. 550–6.
52. Crawford (ed.), *Devolving English Literature*, p. 90.
53. 'Thoughts, Suggested the Day Following, on the Banks of the Nith, near the Poet's Residence', in Hutchinson (ed.) and De Selincourt (rev.), *Wordsworth*, p. 226.
54. Ricks, 'Burns', in *Allusion to the Poets*, p. 67.
55. '[He drew on] the vast store of Scots songs he already knew and … [collected] others, using fragments of existing lyrics as a basis for his own poems and selecting suitable airs on which to compose new lyrics. He produced over 350 songs, including more than one third of those published in the *Musical Museum* and about 114 of those printed in the *Select Collection*: this represents the major part of the published repertory of Scottish national song'. *Grove Music Online* at http://www.oxfordmusiconline.com/article/q=Robert+Burns [accessed 22 October 2013].
56. After 1787, perhaps regretting sale of the copyright of *Poems* to William Creech, Burns generally refused payment for songs and poems. In 1789 and 1790 he declined offers from Peter Stuart of the *Star*, a Whig evening newspaper in London, that would have doubled his income by matching his Excise salary. Stuart required only that Burns send material to him regularly, but Burns would not agree, even though he was then writing numerous songs, sent gratis to song-editors James Johnson and George Thomson. Although freely giving permission to publish, Burns retained copyright (the right to reprint in any way he wished), a matter that Thomson later tried to obfuscate.
57. 'Letter from John Mitchell to Robert Graham of Fintry, 24 July 1796', National Records of Scotland, at http://www.nas.gov.uk/about/090717.asp [accessed 22 October 2013].
58. By Jessie Lewars's account, Burns 'bought for … [his wife] the best clothes he could afford. She was … one of the first persons in Dumfries who appeared in a dress of gingham … at its first introduction, rather costly, and almost exclusively used by persons of superior conditions'. Lindsay (ed.), *The Burns Encyclopedia*, p. 214.
59. McGuirk (ed.), *Robert Burns: Selected Poems*, p. xxvii.
60. Mackay, *RB*, p. 523.
61. Hutchinson (ed.) and De Selincourt (rev.), *Wordsworth*, p. 704.
62. Roy and Ferguson (eds), *Letters of Burns*, vol. 2, p. 152.
63. R. Chambers, J. Currie, R. H. Cromek (eds), *Prose Works of Robert Burns: With the Notes of Currie and Cromek, and Many by the Present Editor* (Edinburgh: W & R Chambers, 1839), p. 120; the note is marked §.
64. [J. C. Ewing (ed.)], 'Maria Riddell's Letters to Dr Currie, (1796–1805)', *Burns Chronicle*, first series, 32 (1921), pp. 59–133, on p. 105.
65. Low (ed.), *Robert Burns: The Critical Heritage*, p. 183.
66. Currie, who lived in Liverpool, solicited accounts of Burns from a wide circle of informants but many of those he trusted were unreliable or malicious. George Thomson never met Burns (they had exchanged letters) but wrote to Currie in September 1799 speculating about whether 'Clarinda' was currently having an affair with Burns's old friend Robert Ainslie. He hints too that old gossip about Burns and 'the Lady' was true: 'The

poet it is said knew all her charms: the secret however must have been well kept, for understand the Lady visits where no woman of frail character would be admitted'. For more on Currie and his informants, see C. McGuirk, 'The Politics of the Collected Burns', *Gairfish 2: Discovery* (1991), pp. 40–1.
67. Currie (ed.), *The Works of Robert Burns*, vol. 1, pp. 214–15.
68. *Robert Burns: Poems 1786 and 1787*, pp. 172–3.
69. Hutchinson (ed.) and De Selincourt (rev.), *Wordsworth*, p. 373.
70. Roy and Ferguson (eds), *Letters of Burns*, vol. 1, p. 142.
71. Kinsley cites 'Temora', 'Cath-Loda' and 'Carthon' among the Macpherson texts echoed by Burns, who had admired Sir James Hunter-Blair and was disappointed in this elegy: 'The performance is but mediocre but the grief was sincere'. Kinsley (ed.), *The Poems and Songs of Robert Burns*, vol. 3, p. 1239.
72. Allan Cunningham's anecdote is quoted in Noble and Hogg (eds), *Canongate Burns*, p. 198.
73. 'In the fleeting expression of a human face, the aura beckons from early photographs ... This is what gives them their incomparable beauty', in 'The Work of Art in the Age of its Technological Reproducibility', in *Walter Benjamin, Selected Writings 1935–38, vol. 3*, trans. Eiland and Jennings, pp. 101–33, on p. 108.
74. Brett and. Jones (eds), *Lyrical Ballads*, p. 284.
75. Hutchinson (ed.) and De Selincourt (rev.), *Wordsworth*, p. 371.
76. Hughes (ed.), *Complete Poems and Major Prose of John Milton*, p. 399.
77. Burns, *Poems 1786–1787*, p. 155; original emphasis.
78. Ibid., p. 157; original emphasis.
79. Kinsley (ed.), *The Poems and Songs of Robert Burns*, vol. 3, pp. 1174–7.
80. 'Ode on a Distant Prospect of Eton College', in Bredvold et al. (eds), *Eighteenth Century Poetry and Prose*, pp. 591–2.
81. Low (ed.), *Robert Burns: The Critical Heritage*, p. 131.
82. I quote from the 1817 version of Coleridge's 'Dejection'; in D. Wu (ed.), *Romanticism: An Anthology* (Oxford: Blackwell, 1998), pp. 544–8.
83. The ballad was printed in Percy's *Reliques* (1775). Sir Patrick Spens, commanded to sail by the king despite bad weather, fears the worst but is forced to set out. (Here the ballad diverges from history, for the urgent voyage in a season of storms was undertaken because Scotland had no king. He had died and the heir was a small girl living in Norway who had to be brought home without delay.) The storm sinks the ship and all on board are drowned. See F. J. Child (ed.), *English and Scottish Popular Ballads*, 5 vols (Mineola, NY: Dover Publications, Inc., 2003), vol. 2, p. 22.
84. D. Dunn, '"A Very Scottish Kind of Dash": Burns's Native Metric', in Crawford (ed.), *Robert Burns and Cultural Authority*, pp. 58–85, on p. 67.
85. Kinsley (ed.), *The Poems and Songs of Robert Burns*, vol. 1, pp. 234–5.
86. Ibid., vol. 3, p. 1180.
87. *Robert Burns: Poems 1786 and 1787*, p. 235; original emphasis.
88. 'Letter to a Friend of Robert Burns' (1816), in Low (ed.), *Robert Burns: The Critical Heritage*, p. 288.
89. Brett and Jones (eds), *Lyrical Ballads*, pp. 213–14.
90. Hutchinson (ed.) and De Selincourt (rev.), *Wordsworth*, p. 226.
91. Ibid., p. 586.
92. Ibid., p. 501.
93. Ibid, p. 513.

94. Kinsley (ed.), *The Poems and Songs of Robert Burns*, vol. 1, p. 322.
95. 'Letter from Keats to Richard Woodhouse, 27 October 1818', in Wu (ed.), *Romanticism*, p. 1042.
96. In a letter dated 13 November 1788 to Mrs Dunlop, Burns describes the coding system for his contributions to *The Scots Musical Museum*. Stanzas entirely by him would be coded R, B or X while songs marked Z would identify traditional songs lightly retouched. He goes on, however, to say that 'Those [songs] marked Z, I have given to the world as old verses to their respective tunes; but in fact, of a good many of them, little more than the Chorus is ancient; tho' there is no reason for telling every body this piece of intelligence'. Three weeks later, on 7 December, he wrote again enclosing the Z-coded 'Auld Lang Syne' and unsigned 'Silver Tassie'; he slyly informed Mrs Dunlop that both were, in his opinion, the work of a 'heaven-inspired Poet'. Roy and Ferguson (eds), *Letters of Burns*, vol. 1, p. 337 and vol. 1, p. 345.
97. Burns himself uses this image of his body 'stretched at … full length' in a letter to Agnes M'Lehose: 'I am as proud as ever; & when I am laid in my grave, I wish to be stretched at my full length, that I may occupy every inch of ground which I have a right to'. Wordsworth could not have been aware of this letter in 1799, however, when he wrote 'A Poet's Epitaph', published in 1800. Two years after 'A Poet's Epitaph' appeared in *Lyrical Ballads* Burns's letter appeared in *Letters Addressed to Clarinda, &c.* (Glasgow: Niven, Napier and Khull, for T. Stewart, 1802).
98. 'Letter from Keats to Richard Woodhouse', in Wu (ed.), *Romanticism*, p. 1042.

3 Highlands: Burns, Lady Nairne and National Song

1. B. Dylan, 'Highlands', *Time Out of Mind* (1997), BobDylan.com at http://www.bobdylan.com./us/songs/highlands [accessed 14 December 2013], ll. 34–5. Dylan has named Burns as a strong influence: see S. Michaels, 'Bob Dylan: Burns is my Biggest Inspiration', *Guardian*, 5 October 2008.
2. Roy and Ferguson (eds), *Letters of Burns*, vol. 1, p. 124.
3. Kinsley (ed.), *The Poems and Songs of Robert Burns*, vol. 2, p. 528. I have not followed Kinsley's printing of the song in quatrains. The text appears in 1790 in *The Scots Musical Museum* as two octaves; and also in a reprint re-edited by William Stenhouse. See J. Johnson and R. Burns (eds), W. Stenhouse (rev.), *The Scots Musical Museum; Consisting of Upwards of Six Hundred Songs, with Proper Basses for the Pianoforte. Originally Published by James Johnson, and Now Accompanied by Copious Notes and Illustrations of the Lyric Poetry of Scotland, by the late William Stenhouse, with Additional Notes and Illustrations. New Edition*, 4 vols (Edinburgh: William Blackwood & Sons, 1853), vol. 2, p. 268. Octaves correspond with a note in Burns's interleaved copy of *The Scots Musical Museum*: 'the first half-stanza of this song is old', quoted in Kinsley (ed.), *The Poems and Songs of Robert Burns*, vol. 3, p. 1344. The 'old lines' number four, which would make the first stanza eight lines in Burns's reckoning. Ashmead and Davison concur: 'Tune and text both have an unhurried octave structure, with the two verbal octaves using the whole melody'. J. Ashmead and J. Davidson (eds), *The Songs of Robert Burns* (New York: Garland, 1988), p. 242.
4. J. C. Dick describes Sir Walter's performance of the song, although he may be referring to 'Strong Walls of Derry' (Burns's source). 'The ballad was a favourite of Sir Walter Scott, who sometimes sang it at convivial meetings'. J. C. Dick and D. Cook (eds), *Songs of*

Robert Burns and *Notes on Scottish Songs by James C. Dick, Together with Annotation of Scottish Songs by Burns by D. Cook* (Hatboro, PA: Folklore Associates, 1962), p. 453.
5. Dylan, 'Highlands', ll. 9–10.
6. Thirteenth-century Thomas the Rhymer had foreseen depopulation of the Highlands: 'The teeth of the sheep will lay the plough on the shelf', *Read and Run Library* in *Tait's Edinburgh Magazine*, 26 (January–December 1859), p. 544.
7. When jotting down notes as he travelled, Burns more often focussed on turnip cultivation than on picturesque landscape.
8. Kinsley (ed.), *The Poems and Songs of Robert Burns*, vol. 1, p. 350. Kinsley identifies the speaker as eldest son of the fourth Viscount, who died in the battle (vol. 3, p. 1243). Murray Pittock notes that after Culloden the speaker's dying father, a legendary Jacobite martyr, took emergency Communion in the form of sanctified oatmeal and whisky (M. G. H. Pittock, 'Burns and the Jacobite Song', in K. Simpson (ed.), *Love and Liberty: Robert Burns – A Bicentenary Celebration* (East Linton: Tuckwell, 1996), pp. 308–14, on p. 311).
9. The final lines of Milton's epic: 'The world was all before them, where to choose / Thir place of rest, and Providence thir guide: / They hand in hand with wandering steps and slow, / Through Eden took their solitary way' (ll. 646–9). 'Paradise Lost', in Hughes (ed.), *Complete Poems and Major Prose of John Milton*, p. 469.
10. In 'Here's a health to ane I lo'e dear', Jessie Lewars's name is repeated at the close of each stanza: 'Thou are sweet as the smile when fond lovers meet, / And soft as their parting tear – Jessy'. Kinsley (ed.), *The Poems and Songs of Robert Burns*, vol. 2, p. 810. Galloway Tam was the sexual miscreant in many songs: 'Tradition has neglected to tell us who this Gallovidian hero was, of whose prowess so many bards have sung'. A. Cunningham (ed.), *Songs of Scotland, Ancient and Modern, with an Introduction and Notes, Historical and Critical, and Characters of the Lyric Poets*, 4 vols (London: John Taylor, 1825), vol. 2, p. 206.
11. Kinsley (ed.), *The Poems and Songs of Robert Burns*, vol. 3, p. 1334.
12. Ibid.
13. Burns used his Z code for 'Auld Lang Syne' but takes his title-phrase and opening line ('Should old acquaintance be forgot') from 'The Kind Reception', a standard-English song by Allan Ramsay. See C. McGuirk, 'Augustan Influences on Allan Ramsay', *Studies in Scottish Literature*, 16:1 (1981), pp. 97–109. Burns's version reprises sentiments expressed in earlier Scottish songs, but with the exception of his echo of Ramsay in his first line, he does not repeat exact phrases.
14. Johnson (ed.), *The Scots Musical Museum*, vol. 3, pp. 314–15. Another stanza in 'Strong Walls of Derry' has become famous through its association with the film, television and graphic novel franchise *Highlander*: 'Oh, bonie Portmore, thou shines where thou stands, / The more I look on thee, the more my heart warms, / But when I look from thee, my heart is full sore, / Then I think of the lilly I lost at Portmore' (p. 314). Loreena McKennit has recorded a version for the series.
15. Johnson (ed.), *The Scots Musical Museum*, vol. 3, p. 314.
16. Ibid., vol. 3, p. 315.
17. 'Derry' seems set before the battle. A sternly beautiful Burns song conveying the devastating outcome is 'It Was a' For Our Rightfu' King', unsigned, like most of Burns's Jacobite lyrics. Kinsley quotes a chapbook ballad that supplied Burns with four lines: 'The trooper turn'd himself about all on the Irish shore, / He has given the bridal [*sic*]-reins a shake, saying / 'Adieu for ever more, / My dear, / Adieu for ever more', Kinsley

(ed.), *The Poems and Songs of Robert Burns*, vol. 3, p. 1515. Burns's close adaptation is as follows: 'He turned him right and round about, / Upon the Irish shore, / And gie his bridle-reins a shake, / Wi' adieu forevermore, my dear, / Wi' adieu forevermore', Kinsley (ed.), *Poems and Songs of Burns*, vol. 2, p. 876. As in 'Farewell to the Highlands', framing stanzas intensify the context of the four traditional lines, which become #3 of five stanzas in Burns. The mood in Burns's version conveys exile and mourning: 'When day is gane, and night is come, / And a' folk bound to sleep, / I think on him that's far awa, / The lee-lang night and weep, my dear, / The lee-lang night and weep'.

18. 'To compose *Don Quixote* at the beginning of the seventeenth century was a reasonable ... perhaps inevitable undertaking; at the beginning of the twentieth century it is almost impossible', p. 51; in J. L. Borges, 'Pierre Menard, Author of the Quixote', *Ficciones*, trans. A. Bonner (New York: Grove Press, 1962), pp. 45–55.
19. Ashmead and Davison note that the tune 'climbs, descends, leaps up again, back and forth through its length and through its large octave-and-a-sixth range ... It has a pentatonic substructure but has been ... filled out into a major-mode tune which is not a cheerful major but a nostalgic, even melancholy outpouring'. Ashmead and Davison (eds), *The Songs of Robert Burns*, p. 242.
20. Johnson (ed.), *The Scots Musical Museum*, vol. 3, p. 314.
21. The speaker's repetition of 'Highlands' conveys his homesickness: 'In addition to the repeated ... "Farewell" (five in all), and the nine "My Heart's", there are eleven "Highlands" which occur not at the ends of line, but at strong caesural pauses'. Ashmead and Davison (eds), *The Songs of Robert Burns*, p. 242.
22. 'Museumification' is Jean Baudrillard's pejorative term for the out-of-context ways in which we display older objects, stripping them of their original significance. Burns was not thinking of *The Scots Musical Museum* project in such terms, however: *The Scots Musical Museum* title was selected by James Johnson before he met Burns; and Johnson had in mind only an inexpensive alternative to available song-collections: he cut costs by engraving on inexpensive pewter plates. J. Baudrillard, 'The Precession of Simulacra', in *The Norton Anthology of Theory and Criticism*, ed. V. Leitch (New York: Norton, 2010), pp. 1553–65, on pp. 1562–4.
23. 'Bob Dylan's Dream', *Freewheelin' Bob Dylan* (1963), ll. 25–8, at http://www.bobdylan.com./us/songs/highlands [accessed 16 December 2013].
24. Kinsley (ed.), *Poems and Songs of Burns*, vol. 1, p. 200.
25. Ibid., p. 201.
26. The tavern run by 'Poosie Nansie' was 'much frequented by beggars'; it is still operating (now respectably) across from the Mauchline churchyard. Lindsay (ed.), *The Burns Encyclopedia*, p. 290.
27. Kinsley (ed.), *The Poems and Songs of Robert Burns*, vol. 2, p. 865.
28. W. Scott, *Waverley; or, 'Tis Sixty Years Since*, ed. C. Lamont (New York: Oxford World Classics, 2008), p. 340.
29. T. Crawford, 'Burns, Love and Liberty', in *Critical Essays on Robert Burns*, ed. McGuirk, pp. 95–116, on p. 97.
30. Kinsley (ed.), *The Poems and Songs of Robert Burns*, vol. 2, p. 835. A song-chorus that parallels Burns's 'O an ye were dead Guidman' is transcribed in Herd's collection; its diction is predominantly English: 'I wish that you were dead, goodman, / And a green sod for your head, goodman, / That I might ware my widowhead / Upon a ranting highlandman', quoted in Kinsley (ed.), *The Poems and Songs of Robert Burns*, vol. 3, p. 1498.

The use of a denser vernacular in Burns's version suggests that the speaker herself is a Lowlander, a renegade 'Lawlander'.
31. Songs about the Highland rover's sexual prowess predate the mid-century Jacobite rising and were adapted to political purposes by the Loyalists, as W. Donaldson discusses in *The Jacobite Song: Political Myth and National Identity* (Aberdeen, Aberdeen University Press, 1988), p. 55. Such songs often dramatize the seduction of a Lowland girl by a Highland thief.
32. Kinsley (ed.), *Poems and Songs of Burns*, vol. 1, p. 188.
33. Donaldson, *The Jacobite Song*, p. 4.
34. In 1819–21, James Hogg collected Jacobite songs in *Jacobite Reliques of Scotland, Being the Songs, Airs and Legends of the Adherents of the House of Stuart*, ed. M. G. H. Pittock (Edinburgh: Edinburgh University Press, 2002 [1st series] and 2003 [2nd series]. 'Donald Macgillavry' is in vol. 1, pp. 101–2.
35. Kinsley (ed.), *The Poems and Songs of Robert Burns*, vol. 1, pp. 374–5.
36. Ibid., vol. 1, pp. 411–12.
37. For the ballad, see O. Ritter (ed.), *Neue Quellenfunde zu Robert Burns* (Halle: Ehrhardt Karras, 1903), pp. 8–12. Burns introduced innuendo more subtly than this particular source: 'Yet we will go a milking, / let them say what they will, / And if we dare not milk the cow, / our maids will milk the bull' (pp. 10–11).
38. Kinsley (ed.), *The Poems and Songs of Robert Burns*, vol. 2, pp. 846–7. Burns did not sign the song.
39. Ibid., vol. 1, p. 140.
40. Ibid., vol. 1, p. 424.
41. Ibid., vol. 2, pp. 647–8.
42. Scott, *Waverley*, p. 340.
43. Kinsley (ed.), *The Poems and Songs of Robert Burns*, vol. 1, p. 209.
44. C. Rogers, *Memoir of Baroness Nairne*, in C. Rogers (ed.), *Life and Songs of the Baroness Nairne With a Memoir and Poems of Caroline Oliphant the Younger* (Edinburgh: John Grant, 1905), pp. 13–156, on p. 82.
45. Ibid., p. 32. 'Laurence Oliphant, jun. of Gask' is listed on p. xxxviii of the Subscribers' List of *Poems, Chiefly in the Scottish Dialect* (Edinburgh, 1787). The spelling of Nairne's forename varies between 'Carolina' (before her marriage) and 'Caroline' (later in life). *Lays of Strathearn* has 'Caroline, Baroness Nairne'. Charles Rogers's *Memoir of Baroness Nairne* uses 'Carolina', as does Henderson's memoir of Nairne. I have used Carolina here.
46. The title will hereafter be spelled as '*Scottish*' (not '*Scotish*') *Minstrel* to avoid confusion: 'Scottish Minstrel' is the spelling used in *Lays from Strathearn* when referring to Purdie's edition.
47. Rogers, *Memoir of Baroness Nairne*, p. 43.
48. Ibid., p. 45.
49. Ibid., p. 46.
50. Ibid., p. 45.
51. Ibid., p. 44.
52. Purdie wrote that his series would de emphasize Burns: 'we have made it our invariable rule to prefer dulnes to wit, if it bordered on profanity'. *Scottish Minstrel* nonetheless printed numerous Burns songs as being of 'Unknown' authorship, slipping the national poet in through a side door. R. Purdie (ed.), *Scotish Minstrel: A Selection from the Vocal Melodies of Scotland, Ancient and Modern. Arranged for the Piano Forte by R. A. Smith*, 4 vols (Edinburgh: Purdie, 1821–4), p. v.

53. Rogers (ed.), *Memoir of Baroness Nairne*, p. 41.
54. A family quarrel and disinheritance evidently laid the groundwork for Major Nairne's legal difficulties. One petition survives, part of a lawsuit to regain his title and property; it is a three-page document bound in MS 3142 of the National Library of Scotland (the binding is stamped 'Jacobite Miscellaneous'). A date of 1807 has been pencilled in; the document is headed 'The Case of Major William Nairne, Grandson and Heir to the late John Lord Nairne'. The petition argues that while the Major's grandfather, John Lord Nairne, had been a Jacobite leader, the Major's father (also named John Nairne) had differed politically with Lord Nairne and had served in the British Army, including one campaign in Flanders in which he had served under William, Duke of Cumberland. The younger John Nairne was disinherited by his Jacobite father. In the next generation, William Murray Nairne served as a Lieutenant in the American War from 1776, when he was around nineteen ('Case' 1). As the petition observes, 'the heirs of all those whose Estates were forfeited in the year 1746, got Possession of them again, either by the grant of the crown, or by purchase at a low price, excepting Major Nairne alone, whose father was actually serving in the War against the Enemies of his Majesty's Royal Grandfather' (2).
55. Nairne avoided Scott. 'Poor Sir Walter! ... we did not put ourselves in his way, or we might have seen much of him. One so attractive as he was, and who had yet been bold enough to single out God's servants for derision, as he did the Covenanters, placing them in a light so false, would have been a dangerous friend' (Rogers (ed.), *Memoir of Baroness Nairne*, p. 72).
56. 'LADY NAIRNE ... [had] no intention of revealing her name. But, now that she is departed hence, her nearest ... relatives have ... [agreed to identify her], as the legacy of a true-hearted Scotswoman for her "ain countrie"', Caroline [sic] Baroness Nairne, *Lays of Strathearn by Caroline Baroness Nairne, Symphonies and Accompaniments by the Late Finlay Dun* (Edinburgh: Patterson & Sons, n.d.), p. vi. Both copies of Nairne's songbook in the National Library of Scotland are undated. The title page of one reads *Lays from Strathearn* (the titled used by Nairne's biographer Charles Rogers); another reads *Lays of Strathearn*. I cite the latter. The song texts in this elusive family-authorized (probably, in its planning stages, author-supervised) edition are superior to those in Purdie or Rogers, so songs quoted here are texts from *Lays*.
57. Roy and Ferguson (eds), *Letters of Burns*, vol. 1, p. 461.
58. Rogers (ed.), *Memoir of Baroness Nairne*, p. 17.
59. Ibid., p. 16.
60. Ibid., p. 24. Her father received some of these relics later in life as gifts or by purchase: they were not all acquired during Charles Edward's visit as a fugitive.
61. Nairne, *Lays of Strathearn*, 'The Auld House', pp. 2–5.
62. Rogers, *Memoir of Baroness Nairne*, p. 31. Considered strikingly beautiful in her youth, Nairne was known as the 'Flower of Strathearn'.
63. Nairne, *Lays of Strathearn*, pp. 55–6.
64. Here is Burns's polite version: 'O when she cam ben she bobbit fu' law [curtsied full low], / O when she cam ben she bobbed fu' law; / And when she cam ben she kiss'd Cockpen, / And syne denied she did it at a''. Kinsley (ed.), *The Poems and Songs of Robert Burns*, vol. 2, p. 625. Mistress Jean's low curtsey in Nairne's text does not precede a kiss but follows a scornful 'Na'. For notes on earlier versions, see Kinsley (ed.), *The Poems and Songs of Robert Burns*, vol. 3, p. 1396.

65. Rogers's note attributes the added stanzas to Miss Ferrier (Rogers (ed.), *Memoir of Nairne*, p. 284.) Susan Ferrier, a novelist, had denied authorship, however, saying that the stanzas were by Sir Alexander Boswell, James Boswell's son, a song-writing Baronet. If Boswell was author, the stanzas were completed before 1822, when he died in a duel. This suggests lively circulation of 'The Laird o' Cockpen' in the Edinburgh area before its first printing in vol. 3 of *Scottish Minstrel* (1821–4). Here is one (of the two) non-Nairne additional stanzas. Both are online at bartleby.com as the authentic conclusion: 'And now that the Laird his exit had made, / Mistress Jean she reflected on what she had said; / "Oh, for ane I'll get better its waur I'll get ten, / I was daft to refuse the Laird o' Cockpen"', Rogers (ed.), *Memoir of Baroness Nairne*, p. 284.
66. Kinsley (ed.), *The Poems and Songs of Robert Burns*, vol. 2, pp. 861–2.
67. Ibid., vol. 3, p. 1500. 'Lewis Gordon' is another song in *The True Loyalist* echoed in Burns's song for 'Clarinda': 'O! send my Lewis Gordon home, / And the Lad I darena name'. *The True Loyalist; or, Chevalier's Favourite: Being a Collection of Elegant Songs, Never Before Printed, Also Several Other Loyal Compositions, Wrote by Eminent Hands* (np, 1779), p. 32.
68. Pittock captures the paradox: 'Jacobite "language" ... conceals as it reveals itself, [and] in its own speechlessness makes its most profound articulations', in M. G. H. Pittock, *Material Culture and Sedition, 1688–1760: Treacherous Objects, Secret Places* (Houndmills: Palgrave Macmillan, 2013), p. 16.
69. J. L. Campbell (ed.), *Highland Songs of the Forty-Five, Edited and Translated with Glossary and Notes* (Edinburgh: John Grant, 1933), pp. 147–9.
70. Nairne, *Lays of Strathearn*, p. 7.
71. Dick and Cook (eds), *The Songs of Robert Burns* and *Notes on Scottish Songs*. This is a portmanteau volume printing a selection of Burns's songs with excellent notes by Dick and Burns's commentary on songs, culled mainly from his correspondence with the song-editor James Johnson. The different components all keep their original pagination. The passage quoted is in D. Cook (ed.), [Burns's] *Notes on Scottish Song*, pp. 4–5.
72. *Grove Music* online at http://www.oxfordmusiconline.com/article/q=Robert+Burns [accessed 22 October 2013].
73. Roy and Ferguson (eds), *Letters of Burns*, vol. 1, p. 82.
74. Campbell (ed.), *Highland Songs*, p. xiii.
75. Ibid.
76. Ibid., pp. 151–3. This edition includes facing pages of the original Gaelic and the English translation.
77. Anon., *The True Loyalist*, p. 11. A note refers to Meston's wanderings in 1716. Hogg attempted to trace *The True Loyalist* but could conclude only that it was 'printed privately in A.D. 1779, nobody knows where'. Hogg (ed.), *Jacobite Reliques of Scotland*, ed. Pittock, vol. 1, p. 172.
78. Campbell writes sceptically of 'thirteen poems in the second volume of Hogg's *Jacobite Relics* "translated from the Gaelic" of which I have not discovered one original version. Hogg says that they were sent to him by different people, translated into English prose, which he versified. The result is something very unlike Gaelic poetry', Campbell, *Highland Songs*, p. xxi, 1n. Donaldson concludes that Hogg wrote many of the songs in *Jacobite Relics*, citing 'a number of pieces with a very strong family likeness to one another which suddenly appear for the first time in the *Relics*. There is not a trace of them in the earlier tradition and it is highly improbable that earlier collectors would have missed them had they been genuinely old. They are artistically of high quality, outstanding in

their command of the vernacular, and fitted to their beautiful airs with the utmost guile by somebody who knew in the highest degree what he was about'. Donaldson, *The Jacobite Song*, p. 108.

79. D. Johnson, quoted in M. G. H. Pittock, *Poetry and Jacobite Politics in Eighteenth-Century Britain and Ireland* (Cambridge: Cambridge University Press, 1994), p. 4.
80. Ibid., p. 4; original emphasis.
81. *The True Loyalist*, p. 81.
82. Kinsley (ed.), *The Poems and Songs of Robert Burns*, vol. 1, p. 400.
83. Ibid., vol. 3, p. 1270 .
84. An example of 'fast' words to the tune 'Shawnboy' was performed by Burns at a gathering of Freemasons. In 'Sons of old Killie', multi-syllabic words and feminine rhyme encourage rapid recitation: 'Within this dear mansion may wayward contention / Or wither'd envy never enter; / May secrecy round be the mystical bound, / And brotherly love be the centre'. Kinsley (ed.), *The Poems and Songs of Robert Burns*, vol. 1, p. 300.
85. Kinsley (ed.), *The Poems and Songs of Robert Burns*, vol. 3, p. 1270.
86. 'Then shaded beneath this great Royal Tree, / Let us from all strife, from all discord be free; / Tho' hardships surround us let us make amends, / A friend in our need is the surest of friends. / Firm as the Oak let us stand, friends sincere let us be ... ', 'Tree of Friendship' as printed in *The True Loyalist*, pp. 14–16.
87. Nairne, *Lays of Strathearn*, pp. 102–4. Jean Redpath's memorable performance of 'The Rowan Tree' (in a fine album consisting entirely of Nairne's songs) is now available at iTunes.
88. F. Hemans, 'Graves of a Household', in Wu (ed.), *Romanticism*, p. 1365.
89. Nairne, *Lays of Strathearn*, p. 5.
90. Ibid., pp. 33–4. The third song printed in *Merry Muses of Caledonia* offers bawdy stanzas: 'She has a black and a rolling eye / And a dimplit chin, a dimplit chin, / And no to prie her rosy lips / Wad be a sin, wad be a sin', G. R. Roy (ed.), *Merry Muses of Caledonia; A Collection of Favourite Scots Songs, Ancient and Modern; Selected for the Use of the Crochallan Fencibles. Printed in the Year 1799* (Columbia, SC: University of South Carolina Press, 1999), p. 7. In its sombre mood, Nairne's song may also emulate another Burns song, 'The Bonie Lass of Inverness'.
91. Rogers, *Memoir of Baroness Nairne*, p. 62.
92. Burns's first stanza in 'Hey tuti tatey': 'Landlady count the lawin, / The day is near the dawin, / Ye're a' blind drunk, boys, / And I'm but jolly fou'; Kinsley (ed.), *The Poems and Songs of Robert Burns*, vol. 1, p. 395. Kinsley quotes Jacobite toasts also set to this air (vol. 3, p. 1268). Nairne was intent on replacing drinking songs and bawdry with less uproarious stanzas, a chief motive also of Purdie's *The Scottish Minstrel*. See Nairne, *Lays of Strathearn*, p. iii.
93. Kinsley (ed.), *The Poems and Songs of Robert Burns*, vol. 2, p. 707.
94. Roy and Ferguson (eds), *Letters of Burns*, vol. 2, p. 236; original emphasis.
95. Donaldson, *The Jacobite Song*, p. 87.
96. Kinsley (ed.), *The Poems and Songs of Robert Burns*, vol. 3, p. 1268.
97. Dick and Cook (eds), *The Songs of Robert Burns*, p. 449.
98. Nairne, *Lays of Strathearn*, pp. 10–12.
99. Rogers, *Memoir of Baroness Nairne*, p. 35.
100. W. Stenhouse, 'Introduction', in *'Land o' the Leal' Irrefutably Proved from a Searching Investigation to be the Deathbed Valediction of Robert Burns*, by A[lexander] Crichton, 3rd edn (Peterhead: Scrogie, 1919), pp. 3–10. The thesis of this slender volume is that

'The claim of Lady Nairne is ... the invention of Dr. Rogers'. Yet 'Land o' the Leal' had been printed under Nairne's signature (in *Lays from Strathearn*) over twenty years before Rogers wrote his biography. (This gives some indication of how rare a book *Lays from Strathearn* is: Crichton is unaware of its existence.) I thank Thomas Keith for bringing this work to my attention. In the Roy Collection at the Thomas Cooper Library (University of South Carolina) is also a copy of Burns's 1793 Edinburgh *Poems* augmented (*c.* 1811) with a tipped-in version of Nairne's song, which has been retitled 'Burns's Deathbed Song'; 'John' has been changed to 'Jean'. This 'Burns's deathbed' text appears also in vol. 2 of the *Caledonian Musical Museum* (Edinburgh 1810), whose editor was Robert Burns the Younger, the poet's eldest son. Finally, one chapbook (*c.* 1800–10) held by the Roy Collection in South Carolina reprints Nairne's stanzas accurately (with 'John', not 'Jean') yet is illustrated with a portrait of Burns.
101. Rogers (ed.), *Memoir of Baroness Nairne*, p. 48.
102. Kinsley, The Poems and Songs of Robert Burns, vol. 2, p. 763.
103. Nairne, 'Caller Herring', in *Lays of Strathearn*, pp. 28–30.
104. An undated song-collection interprets 'Caller Herrin' as a satire *against* the herring-vendors: 'These women are notorious for their exorbitant demands ... which generally [end ...] with the irresistible appeal alluded to in the song, –'Lord bless ye, mem! It's no fish ye're buying, it's the lives o' honest men!' It is likelier that the herring-vendors began to echo Nairne's song than that she had intended to mock them. *Lyric Gems of Scotland: A Collection of Scottish Songs, Original and Selected, with Music* (Glasgow: n. p., n. d.), p. 16.
105. Kinsley (ed.), *The Poems and Songs of Robert Burns*, vol. 2, pp. 762–3.
106. *The True Loyalist*, pp. 21–3.
107. King George's visit to Edinburgh led to the Nairnes' ejection from their grace-and-favour rooms in Holyrood Palace. A niece staying with them at the time was still chuckling, late in her life, at the gilded throne set up in the very spot where their cook's bed once had been. See G. Henderson, *Lady Nairne and Her Songs*, 3rd edn (Paisley: Gardner, 1905), pp. 99–100 and [M. S. Simpson], *Caroline, Baroness Nairne: Scottish Songstress. By Her Great-Grand-Niece* (Edinburgh: Oliphant, 1894), p. 33.
108. Henderson, *Lady Nairne and Her Songs*, unpaginated Appendix of facsimiles at the end of his volume.
109. Figure 3.2, which includes the wandering traveller and rowan tree, is an illustration in Rogers's *Memoir of Baroness Nairne*. Figure 3.3 deletes the traveller and the rowan tree. The version that looks most like a stately home (not reprinted in this volume) is in *Lays of Strathearn*. There, in addition to the deletions in Figure 3.2, the steps from the house into the road disappear; indeed a much broader lawn and drive replace the road.

4 Three Drunk Men: Visionary Midnight in Robert Fergusson, Burns and Hugh MacDiarmid

1. G. G. Smith, *Scottish Literature: Character and Influence* (London: Macmillan, 1919), p. 23.
2. F. Nietzsche, *'The Birth of Tragedy' and Other Writings*, ed. R. Geuss and R. Speirs, trans. R. Speirs (Cambridge: Cambridge University Press, 1999), pp. 14–15; original emphasis.
3. Ibid., p. 115.

4. M. Grieve and W. R. Aitken (eds), *Hugh MacDiarmid: Complete Poems*, 2 vols (Ashington, Northumberland: Carcanet Press, 1993), vol. 1, p. 106. Unless otherwise noted, subsequent references to MacDiarmid's poems are from this edition.
5. Ibid., p. 87.
6. Nietzsche sees in Greek tragedy 'an ... opposition ... between the Apolline art of the image-maker [*Bildner*] and the imageless art of music, which is that of Dionysos. These two very different drives [*Triebe*] exist side by side, mostly in open conflict, stimulating and provoking one another ... until eventually, by a metaphysical miracle ... they ... engender a work of art which is Dionysiac and Apolline in equal measure: Attic tragedy'. In *'The Birth of Tragedy' and Other Writings*, p. 14.
7. MacDiarmid takes up Smith's term 'Caledonian antisyzygy' and a related idea, 'the Scottish antithesis of the real and the fantastic' (W. N. Herbert, 'The Significance of Gregory Smith', *Gairfish 2: Discovery* (1991), pp. 16–27, on p. 19). Herbert notes, however, that MacDiarmid rejected Smith's idea that 'the various [Scots] dialects had become incompatible' (p. 18) by the twentieth century. Smith condemns as 'a jumble' any modern attempts, such as MacDiarmid's would become in the 1920s, to revive Scottish poetry by synthesizing dialects from different regions and eras (p. 18).
8. Skoblow, *Dooble Tongue*, p. 64.
9. For these images in the order mentioned, see Fergusson's poems 'The Daft Days', 'The Ghaists: A Kirk-yard Eclogue', 'The Mutual Complaint of Plainstanes and Causey, in their Mother-tongue' 'The King's Birth-Day in Edinburgh', 'To my Auld Breeks' and 'To the Tron Kirk Bell'.
10. Kinsley (ed.), *The Poems and Songs of Robert Burns*, vol. 1, p. 79.
11. Ibid., vol. 1, p. 205.
12. Ibid., vol. 1, p. 82.
13. M. McDiarmid (ed.), *The Poems of Robert Fergusson*, vol. 2, p. 106. Subsequent citations are to this edition.
14. H. MacDiarmid, *Lucky Poet: A Self-Study in Literature and Political Ideas* (London: Methuen, 1943), p. 191.
15. Nietzsche, *'The Birth of Tragedy' and Other Writings*, p. 146.
16. Kinsley (ed.), *Poems and Songs of Burns*, vol. 1, p. 82.
17. Grieve and Aitken (eds), *Hugh MacDiarmid: Complete Poems*, vol. 1, p. 83.
18. 'Peblis to the Play' (1430–50) is set in the border town Peebles. 'Chrystis Kirk of the Green', which mentions the brawl in 'Peblis', features a wild archery match during a festival; a fight begins when drunken Robin Ray begins to revel and his friend Jock takes issue. Kennedy's flyting of Dunbar is a war of words in which he assaults the great Makar, in my loose translation, as an 'ape, disorderly owl, scabby shit-bird and vulgar parasite, bastard foundling that nature made a dwarf'.
19. '"Polemo-Middinia", a grotesque mixture ... has created, among many generations, inextinguishable laughter', G. Gilfillan (ed.), *Specimens with Memoirs of the Less-Known British Poets, Vol. 1* (1860), Project Gutenberg (25 November 2011), at Gutenberg.org/cache/epub/9667/pg9667.txt [accessed 8 July 2013].
20. K. Buthlay (ed.), *A Drunk Man Looks at the Thistle. An Annotated Edition* (Edinburgh: Scottish Academic Press, 1987), p. 196. Fergusson taught Burns the gallimaufry-pairing of incongruous words: for example, 'fash us' with 'Parnassus' in 'The King's Birth-day in Edinburgh'. In 'Hallow-Fair' Fergusson echoes the dialect of Sawny from Aberdeen (l. 37ff) and later quotes a City Guardsman from the Highlands: 'Pring in da drunken sot' (l. 96). The clashing dialect in Edinburgh sound to Fergusson's speaker similar to the

cacophany around the Tower of Babel: 'sic yellochin and din, / Wi' wives and wee-anes gabblin, / That ane might trou they were a-kin / To a' the tongues at Babylon, / Confus'd that day' (ll. 68–72), *Poems of Fergusson*, vol. 2, pp. 90–2.
21. Preface to 1926 edition of 'A Drunk Man', in Buthlay (ed.), *A Drunk Man*, p. 196.
22. H. Mackenzie, *Anecdotes and Egotisms of Henry Mackenzie, 1745–1831, Now First Published*, ed. H. W. Thompson (Oxford: Oxford University Press, 1927), p. 150.
23. Currie (ed.), *The Works of Robert Burns*, vol. 1, p. 73.
24. The topic of Burns and drinking has strongly affected his critical reputation. It is difficult to separate probable fact from innuendo or political enmity. In *RB*, J. Mackay refutes 'obituary notices in the newspapers, both local and national, [which] hinted that he had spent his last years in abject poverty and a close approximation to disgrace' (*RB*, p. 482). That many of these reports were fabrications is well argued by McIlvanney in *Burns the Radical* and Noble and Hogg in *Canongate Burns*. Malicious stories influenced (and were reported in) important early biographies by James Currie (1800), John Gibson Lockhart (1828) and Alexander Cunningham (1834). Early biographers imply an improbable degree of debauchery and reckless improvidence. I have argued elsewhere that the idea of a self-destructive poet was selected by Currie as the best focal point for his edition, whose profits were assigned to the poet's widow and children. He solicited the sympathy of readers of their behalf. To highlight Burns's increasingly intense political opinions, some radical and all unpalatable in the repressive climate of the late 1790s, would drive too many potential subscribers away. Currie actually shared some of Burns's political sentiments but suppressed any account of them, frankly stating in his Dedication to Captain Graham Moore that 'Generous minds will receive the posthumous works of Burns with candour ... as the remains of an unfortunate man of genius, published for the benefit of his family – as the stay of the widow and the hope of the fatherless. To secure the suffrages of such minds, all topics are omitted in the writings, and avoided in life of Burns, that have a tendency to awake the animosity of party' (Currie (ed.), *The Works of Robert Burns*, vol. 1, p iv). For more, see McGuirk, 'The Politics of the Collected Burns', pp. 36–51. Among twentieth-century biographers who refute Currie in some detail were Franklyn Bliss Snyder (1932), J. DeLancey Ferguson (1939), David Daiches (1952), Maurice Lindsay (1954) and Robert Fitzhugh (1970); but during the later twentieth century the pendulum began to swing back with Robert D. Thornton's energetic and admiring biography of Currie (1963). Thornton takes as simple fact Currie's charge that Burns was '[p]erpetually stimulated by alcohol in one or other of its various forms' (*Works of Burns*, vol. 1, p. 220). Gilbert Burns testified to the contrary, cautiously restricting his comments from Burns's 20th to 27th years, after which point the brothers lived far apart (see note 23 above). In a recent biography, Robert Crawford's nuanced conclusion is that 'The bard's conduct was orderly, not disorderly, his drinking usually contained ... [but] protesting his own drinking grew significant to him' (*The Bard*, p. 351). Such concerns do surface in Burns's letters. One sent to Mrs Dunlop on 2 January 1793 suggests that he has made a resolution for the New Year: 'You must not think, as you seem to insinuate, that in my way of life I want exercise. – Of that I have enough; but occasional hard drinking is the devil to me. – Against this I have again & again bent my resolution & have greatly succeeded'; Roy and Ferguson (eds), *Letters of Burns*, vol. 2, p. 170. An otherwise undated letter of 1794 by Burns, sent to Samuel Clarke, asks Clarke's help in combating rumours in Edinburgh: 'Some of our folks about the Excise office, Edinr, had and perhaps still have conceived a prejudice against me as being a drunken, dissipated character. – I might be all this, you know, & yet be an hon-

est fellow, but you know that I am an honest fellow and am nothing of this' (Roy and Ferguson (eds), *Letters*, vol. 2, pp. 281–2).

25. Currie was too literal-minded to be a good commentator on poetry. He takes Burns's poems and songs as factual: 'If fiction be, as some suppose, the soul of poetry, no one ever had less pretension to the name of poet than Burns' (*The Works of Robert Burns*, vol. 1, p. 259). Such poems as 'Tam o'Shanter' supplied Currie, a physician, with evidence for his diagnosis of drunkenness and vice as the cause of Burns's death at thirty-seven. For, factoring in the portrayal of the witch Nannie in 'Tam o'Shanter' and Burns's hundreds of love songs, he adds to charges of dipsomania a strong hint of sexually transmitted disease: 'He who cannot escape the pollution of inebriation, how shall he escape other pollution?' (vol. 1, p. 214). The same charges of personal misconduct and artistic failure that marked Robert Fergusson's critical heritage for almost two centuries (ended only by Matthew McDiarmid's exemplary scholarly edition) were repeated when Burns died in 1796 (see also note 30 below). It has long been agreed that the poet died of heart disease, perhaps infective endocarditis. His brother Gilbert remembered Burns as suffering from young manhood with such symptoms as 'palpitation of the heart, and a threatening of fainting and suffocation in his bed, in the nighttime' (Currie (ed.), *The Works of Robert Burns*, vol. 1, p. 70). Burns himself mentions fainting fits in a heading for *The First Commonplace Book* above 'Prayer in the Prospect of Death', a poem that Kinsley assigns to 'the Irvine period' (1781), when the poet was twenty-one (*The Poems and Songs of Robert Burns*, vol. 3, p. 1012). R. H. Fowler's biography of Burns suggests another possibility: brucellosis, caused by contact with animal carcasses or unpasteurized dairy products. Easily treated with tetracycline today, brucellosis can progress to infective endocarditis; R. H. Fowler, *Robert Burns* (London: Routledge, 1988), pp. 235–6.
26. W. Wordsworth, in Low (ed.), *Robert Burns: The Critical Heritage*, p. 206.
27. W. Hazlitt in ibid., p. 299.
28. Roy and Ferguson (eds), *Letters of Burns*, vol. 2, p. 104.
29. Kinsley (ed.), *The Poems and Songs of Robert Burns*, vol. 1, p. 382.
30. David Irving wrote the first biography of Fergusson in 1800. Like the first Burns *Works* with biography by Currie (see notes 24 and 25 above), Irving set a most unfortunate tone while becoming (and remaining) influential. A rival memoir, published in 1803 by Thomas Sommers – for early 'Extempore' lines from Fergusson to Sommers, see McDiarmid, *Poems of Fergusson* (vol. 2, p. 51) – indignantly rejected the 'foul calumnies' of Irving's account. Sommers hoped that his first-hand account (he was a school-mate of Fergusson's) would finally ensure that 'justice shall be done to the deeply injured Fergusson' [A. B. Grosart (ed.),] *Works of Robert Fergusson Edited with a Life of the Author and an Essay on his Genius and Writings* (London: Fullarton, 1857), p. xviii). Yet a century later Robert Ford acknowledged the continuing hold of 'Dr Irving's ... slanderously extravagant' portrayal of the poet (p. xiv). See R. Ford (ed.), *Poetical Works of Robert Fergusson with Biography, Introduction, Notes, and Glossary, Etc.* (Paisley: A Gardner, 1905), p. xiv.
31. A contemporary described Fergusson's tavern behaviour: 'The entertainment almost invariably consisted of a few boards of raw oysters, porter, gin, and occasionally a rizzared (dried) haddock ... The best gin was then sold at about five shillings a gallon, and accordingly the gill at Lucky Middlemass's cost only threepence. The whole debauch of the young men seldom came to more than sixpence or sevenpence. Mr S— [Sommers] distinctly recollects that Fergusson always seemed unwilling to spend any more. They generally met at eight o'clock, and rose to depart at ten'. In T. L. Reed, *The Transform-*

ing Draught: Robert Louis Stevenson and the Alcohol Debate (Jefferson, NC: McFarland, 2006), p. 57. A physician has sifted through written records of the events leading to Fergusson's decline and death. Chalmers Davidson rejects the charge of Irving and other early biographers that syphilis and alcohol abuse figured in Fergusson's premature death: 'From 1769 he attended very regularly at the office of the Commissary Clerk, where he was employed as a writer, but in February 1774, the *Caledonian Mercury* reported that "Mr Robert Fergusson has had a very dangerous sickness". Previously Fergusson's temperament had been gay and sociable, but a significant change was now apparent ... all social invitations were refused, no poetry was written and his reading was confined to the Bible. In August he fell downstairs, striking his head on the stone steps; he was severely concussed and did not regain consciousness until next morning, following which he was maniacal for several days. He was then admitted into the Edinburgh Bedlam, and though very confused he quickly recognized his new surroundings, whereupon his suffering became extreme ... Apart from a few rational periods his condition quickly deteriorated, and he died on 16 October 1774'. See McDiarmid (ed.), *The Poems of Robert Fergusson*, vol. 1, pp. 199–200. Davidson diagnoses a manic depressive psychosis 'precipitated by the effects of a severe physical illness on a susceptible temperament' (p. 200); he adds that the prospect for recovery, even in the eighteenth century, would have been good with rest and proper care. Like Fergusson's friends, he concludes that the poet's death was brought on by his extreme distress over being hospitalized.

32. A. Gray, 'To R. Fergusson', in McDiarmid (ed.), *The Poems of Robert Fergusson*, vol. 2, p. 151.
33. Kinsley (ed.), *The Poems and Songs of Robert Burns*, vol. 1, p. 413.
34. McDiarmid, 'To R. Fergusson', in McDiarmid (ed.), *The Poems of Robert Fergusson*, vol. 2, p. 151.
35. Robert Ford quotes an 'evening-associate' on the wasted appearance of Fergusson. The poet was 'about five feet nine, slender and handsome. His face never exhibited the least trace of red, but was perfectly and uniformly pale, or rather yellow. He had all the appearance of a person in delicate health; and Mr S— [Sommers?] remembers that, at last, he could not eat raw oysters, but was compelled ... to ask for them pickled. His forehead was elevated, and his whole countenance open and pleasing. He wore his own fair brown hair, with a long massive curl along each side of the head, and terminating in a queue, dressed with a black silk riband. His dress was never very good, but often much faded, and the white thread stockings, which he generally wore ... he often permitted to become considerably soiled before changing'. See Ford (ed.), *The Poetical Works of Robert Fergusson*, p. xxxvii.
36. Kinsley (ed.), *The Poems and Songs of Robert Burns*, vol. 1, p. 94.
37. C. McGuirk, '"Rhyming Trade": Fergusson, Burns, and the Marketplace', in *'Heaven-Taught Fergusson'*, ed. Crawford, pp. 135–60, on p. 150.
38. Kinsley (ed.), *The Poems and Songs of Robert Burns*, vol. 3, p. 1021.
39. Ibid., vol. 3, p. 1317. Kirsten Easdale offers a contagiously joyous performance of 'I Sing of a Whistle', in F. Freeman (comp.), *The Complete Songs of Robert Burns*, various artists, 12 vols (Linn Music, 1997–2003), vol. 10, Linn CDK199 (2002).
40. In calling the sun 'Phoebus', Burns echoes Fergusson. Both poets found 'Phoebus' useful as the second word in iambic lines: 'Whan *Phoebus* ligs in *Thetis* lap, / Auld Reikie gies them shelter', in McDiarmid (ed.), *The Poems of Robert Fergusson*, vol. 2, p. 91.
41. Roy and Ferguson (eds), *Letters of Burns*, vol. 1, p. 443.

42. James Kinsley, perhaps missing the burlesque dimension of 'The Whistle', reports with irritation that 'Burns's account of the legend is inaccurate' (*The Poems and Songs of Robert Burns*, vol. 3, p. 1316). It is useful to have correct details supplied by Kinsley, for they clarify the extent of Burns's epic amplification.
43. For Burns's scepticism about Ossian's authenticity, see a sly reference in 'The Twa Dogs' (ll. 27–9).
44. The duration of the cousins' 'battle' is most likely exaggerated like other details. According to the ballad, the dinner party begins while the sun is still bright and ends at sunrise the next morning. Sunset occurs at around 6:09p.m. in October in Scotland; the sunrise would be around 6:47a.m., so those limits would mean a contest lasting at least twelve hours, depending on the customary dinner hour of the Riddells.
45. Kinsley (ed.), *The Poems and Songs of Robert Burns*, vol. 3, p. 1316.
46. The pirate-hero of 'Sir Andrew Barton', a ballad included in Percy's *Reliques*, was described by Francis Child as 'ever ... [blowing] on his whistle'. Child (ed.), *The English and Scottish Popular Ballads*, vol. 3, p. 335.
47. Kinsley (ed.), *The Poems and Songs of Robert Burns*, vol. 3, p. 1316.
48. Quoted in Mackay, *RB*, p. 466.
49. Kinsley (ed.), *The Poems and Songs of Robert Burns*, vol. 3, p. 1316.
50. In the splendid 'To my Auld Breeks', Fergusson's speaker commands the ghost of his ragged trousers to find 'some bard, in lucky times' and haunt him: 'Glowr in his face, like spectre gaunt, / Remind him o' his former want'. McDiarmid (ed.), *The Poems of Robert Fergusson*, vol. 2, p. 217.
51. 'Lamkin' (version A), in Child (ed.), *The English and Scottish Popular Ballads*, vol. 2, p. 322.
52. Chambers (ed.) and Wallace (rev.), *The Life and Works of Robert Burns*, vol. 1, p. 157n.
53. Roy and Ferguson (eds), *Letters of Burns*, vol. 1, p. 14.
54. Ibid., vol. 1, p. 17.
55. Mackay, *RB*, p. 124.
56. The phrase 'men, their manners and their ways' occurs in Alexander Pope's early poem 'January and May': 'Sir, I have liv'd a Courtier all my days, / And studied men, their manners, and their ways; / And have observ'd this useful maxim still, / To let my betters always have their will. / Nay, if my Lord affirm'd that black was white, / My word was this, "Your honour's in the right"'. *The Works of Alexander Pope*, 9 vols (London: J. F. Dove, 1822), vol. 2, p. 116.
57. Roy and Ferguson (eds), *Letters of Burns*, vol. 1, p. 139.
58. Chambers (ed.) and Wallace (rev.), *The Life and Works of Robert Burns*, vol. 1, pp. 109–11.
59. Roy and Ferguson (eds), *Letters of Burns*, vol. 1, p. 139. Gilbert Burns questioned his brother's account: 'I wonder how Robert could attribute to our father that lasting resentment of his going to a dancing-school ... I believe the truth was, that he about this time began to see the dangerous impetuosity of my brother's passions, as well as his not being amenable to counsel, which often irritated my father; and which he would naturally think a dancing-school was not likely to correct. But he was proud of Robert's genius, which he bestowed more expense in cultivating, than on the rest of the family ... and he was greatly delighted with his warmth of heart, and his conversational powers. He had indeed that dislike of dancing-schools which Robert mentions; but so far overcame it during Robert's first month of attendance, that he allowed all the rest of the family that were fit for it, to accompany him during the second month. Robert excelled in dancing,

and was for some time distractedly fond of it'. Currie (ed.), *The Works of Robert Burns*, vol. 1, pp. 78–9.
60. That 90 per cent of human souls are bound for hell and 10 per cent for heaven is the estimate offered William Fisher in 'Holy Willie's Prayer' (l. 3).
61. Mackay, *RB*, p. 30.
62. Henley and Henderson (eds), *The Poetry of Robert Burns*, vol. 1, p. 438.
63. The dancers are not in the graveyard but within the church walls: the altar holds the witches' gifts to Satan. The devil sits piping the in 'winnock-bunker' (window) on the east side. Kinsley points out that an illuminated dance was 'part of the ritual. Dr Murray expresses the importance, in the witch cult, of the spring festival of Candlemas ... Burns cancelled a significant detail: witch-candles are made of pitch, and burn with a blue flame'. Kinsley (ed.), *The Poems and Songs of Robert Burns*, vol. 3, p. 1360, paraphrasing M. Murray, *The Witch Cult in Western Europe* (1921).
64. The passage quotes ll. 137–42. Four lines describing the relics on the altar were removed at the suggestion of early readers of the manuscript. In the first drafts these lines followed the description of the parricide's knife: 'Three Lawyers' tongues, turn'd inside out, / Wi' lies seam'd like a beggar's clout; / Three [or And] Priests' hearts, rotten, black as muck, / Lay stinking, vile, in ev'ry neuk' (Kinsley (ed.), *The Poems and Songs of Robert Burns*, vol. 2, p. 561n). In '"Tongues Turn'd Inside Out": The Reception of "Tam o' Shanter"', G. Carruthers has argued that the cancelled lines should be restored (in P. Scott and K. Simpson (eds), *Robert Burns & Friends: Essays by W. Ormiston Roy Fellows: Presented to G. Ross Roy* (Columbia, SC: University of South Carolina Libraries, 2012), pp. 47–57, on pp. 56–7.
65. According to David Daiches, Burns considered the small churchyard at Alloway his own likely place of burial (*Robert Burns*, p. 280): that, as well as his father's maintenance of the wall and grounds, may be why he suggested that Grose include Alloway in his book on antiquities of Scotland. Grose replied that Burns first should send him a story about the kirk.
66. Roy and Ferguson (eds), *Letters of Burns*, vol. 1, p. 257.
67. Douglas Graham was a neighbour and crony of John Davidson (called 'Souter *Johnny*' in Burns's poem), a cobbler whose wife Anne Gillespie had worked for Gilbert Broun, Burns's maternal grandfather (Lindsay (ed.), *The Burns Encyclopedia*, p. 100). While Davidson is a surname occurring frequently among Burns's associates, perhaps Souter Johnny, known for convivial humour and storytelling, was some relative of Betty Davidson, the widow who sometimes helped Agnes Burnes at Alloway and had told the children such memorable stories.
68. One trait of epic in 'Tam o'Shanter' is prophecy. Kate's predicts Tam's drowning and the omniscient narrator knows Nannie's future misdeeds: 'For mony a beast to dead she shot [note: not a literal gun-shot; a witch's evil glance] / And perish'd mony a bonie boat, / And shook baith mickle corn and bear, / And kept the countryside in fear', ll. 166–70.
69. Roy and Ferguson (eds), *Letters of Burns*, vol. 1, p. 140.
70. Douglas Graham's boat was named the 'Tam o'Shanter'. It may have been used for smuggling (Lindsay (ed.), *The Burns Encyclopedia*, p. 149).
71. Roy and Ferguson (eds), *Letters of Burns*, vol. 1, pp. 140–1.
72. Ibid., vol. 1, p. 139.
73. Burns bought three copies of *Poems Chiefly in the Scottish Dialect* (1786), giving them to his cousin James Burness in Montrose, to Richard Brown, who as early as 1781 had encouraged him to publish his poems, and to Margaret Thomson. He wrote a short

poem in her copy, with the last four lines alluding to his projected emigration to Jamaica but the first four to their courtship. 'Once fondly lov'd, and still remember'd dear, / Sweet early Object of my youthful vows, / Accept this mark of friendship, warm, sincere, / Friendship – "Tis all cold Duty now allows"' (Kinsley (ed.), *The Poems and Songs of Robert Burns*, vol. 1, p. 290).

74. Roy and Ferguson (eds), *Letters of Burns*, vol. 1, p. 139.
75. The poet's mother, Agnes Broun Burns, was raised near Kirksowald on her father's farm but after her mother's death and father's remarriage, she stayed with her grandmother in Maybole, about five miles from Kirkoswald. Some of her relatives still lived nearby or in the town in 1775, including her brother Samuel. As formidable a character as Burns's father but of a generous and fiery rather than stubborn and inflexible temperament, Agnes Burnes long outlived her firstborn son, dying in 1820 at the age of eighty-eight. Betty Davidson, with ties also to Kirkoswald, was a widowed cousin of Burns's mother who sometimes stayed with the Burnes family at Alloway, delighting the children with her stories.
76. Roy and Ferguson (eds), *Letters of Burns*, vol. 1, p. 138.
77. 'My wife scolds me!', ibid., vol. 2, p. 121.
78. Ibid., vol. 1, pp. 134–5.
79. Ibid., vol. 1, p. 140.
80. Ibid., vol. 1, p. 141.
81. In 'Scotch Drink', Burns praises barley as a food but says that it 'shines chief' as whisky, the 'life o' public haunts' and holidays. Whiskey eases childbirth for the mother and her 'gossips' gathered to help; it calms the fears of the anxious father. It fizzes and froths in the wooden cup provided for blacksmith and workers as they repair the farm gear (Kinsley (ed.), *The Poems and Songs of Robert Burns*, vol. 1, pp. 173–6).
82. It is not only octosyllabics that MacDiarmid borrows from the earlier Scots poets; parts of 'A Drunk Man Looks at the Thistle' use ballad meter: 'The orderin' o' the thistle means / Nae richtin' o't to them. / Its loss they call a law, its thorns / A fule's fit diadem' (ll. 1199–202).
83. The name Jean, not that of MacDiarmid's own wife in 1926 (Peggy Skinner), might be intended to recall the name of Burns's wife. Although F. G. Scott, who helped MacDiarmid decide the final shape of the poem, claimed that he had himself written the last two lines of *A Drunk Man*, MacDiarmid, 'while not saying that this was untrue, did state repeatedly that he did not recollect it as having happened' (Buthlay (ed.), *A Drunk Man*, p. 193). That Scott's story has seemed plausible has to do with how the lines, switching from the perspective of the Drunk Man to Jean, so decisively break with the speaker's extended poetic reverie.
84. McDiarmid (ed.), *The Poems of Robert Fergusson*, vol. 2, p. 47.
85. 'I look on vernal day, & say with poor Ferguson – "Say wherefore has an all indulgent Heaven / Light to the comfortless and wretched given?"' Roy and Ferguson (eds), *Letters of Burns*, vol. 2, p. 378.
86. Ibid., vol. 1, p. 258.
87. Ibid.
88. Currie (ed.), *The Works of Robert Burns*, vol. 1, p. 92.
89. Ibid., vol. 1, p. 82.
90. J. Muir, 'William Burnes's Manual of Religious Belief', *Burns Chronicle* (1933), pp. 78–80, on p. 80.

91. W. Burnes, *A Manual of Religious Belief. Composed by William Burnes, (the Poet's Father) for the Instruction of his Children*; with Biographical Preface (Kilmarnock: McKie & Drennan, 1875), p. xl.
92. Ibid., p. xli.
93. Ibid., p. xlvii.
94. Roy and Ferguson (eds), *Letters of Burns*, vol. 2, p. 333.
95. Ibid., vol. 2, p. 34.
96. Kinsley (ed.), *The Poems and Songs of Robert Burns*, vol. 2, p. 822.
97. Ibid., vol. 2, p. 763.
98. Burns once observed that it was not taverns but 'the private parties among the hard-drinking gentlemen of this country' that encouraged him to overindulge. Roy and Ferguson (eds), *Letters of Burns*, vol. 2, p. 170 (see also note 24 above). The poet frequented taverns to work on his songs as well as to socialize. At the time he wrote this letter (January 1793) his family were still living in a three-room, second floor flat in Dumfries. They leased a house later that year, but in early 1793 Burns and his wife were rearing five young children in this flat: Robert (aged seven), Frank (four), William (two), Betty (two) and Elizabeth (two months). His widow and his eldest son Robert both left accounts of Burns during the Dumfries years that recall his working at home with the children playing around him ('their prattle never disturbed him', said Jean) but he also sought his special chair and corner at the Globe Inn. For Jean's and the younger Robert's Dumfries memories, see *Robert Burns: Selected Poems*, ed. McGuirk, pp. xxvi and xxvii.
99. Ewing and Cook (eds), *Robert Burns's Commonplace Book*, p. 7.
100. Kinsley (ed.), *The Poems and Songs of Robert Burns*, vol. 2, p. 821.
101. Ibid., vol. 2, p. 822.
102. Ibid.
103. The sick visited these wells and pools to bathe, tying messages on nearby bushes or fastening on nearby branches the rags in which they had wrapped their wounds. See P. Jones and N. Pennick, *A History of Pagan Europe* (London: Routledge, 1995), pp. 38, 81.
104. Late in life, Wordsworth told a Scottish newspaper reporter of his deep regret that Burns refused to look far in a spatial sense: 'he nowhere in all his poems mentions the mountains of Arran which constantly before him, had he raised his eye or his mind so much'. Noble, 'Wordsworth and Burns', p. 52.

Epilogue: Burns and Aphorism; or Poetry into Proverb

1. J. Derrida, 'Aphorism Countertime', in *Acts of Literature*, ed. D. Attridge, trans. N. Royle (New York: Routledge, 1992), pp. 414–34, on p. 421.
2. Ibid., p. 416.
3. For more on Burns's visitors in the mausoleum, see C. McGuirk, 'Burns and Nostalgia', in K. Simpson (ed.), *Burns Now* (Edinburgh: Canongate Academic, 1994), pp. 31–69. Nathaniel Hawthorne learned of the 1857 exhumation (there were at least three) during his tour of Burns country (1857), which he mentions in 1860 in *Atlantic Monthly*. Writing anonymously, Hawthorne describes his visit to the Burns mausoleum: 'the bones of the poet, and of Jean Armour, and of some of their children, lie in the vault over which we stood. Our guide ... said that the vault was opened about three weeks ago, on occasion of the burial of the eldest son of Burns. The poet's bones were disturbed, and the dry skull, once so brimming over with powerful thought and bright and tender fantasies, was taken away, and kept for several days by a Dumfries doctor. It has since been deposited in

a new leaden coffin, and restored to the vault'. [N. Hawthorne], 'Some of the Haunts of Burns, by a Tourist Without Imagination or Enthusiasm', *Atlantic Monthly, a Magazine of Literature, Art, and Politics*, 6:36 (October 1860), pp. 385–95.
4. A. Ramsay (ed.), *A Collection of Scots Proverbs* (1737), in *The Works of Allan Ramsay*, A. M. Kinghorn and A. Law (eds), 6 vols (Edinburgh: Scottish Text Society, 1944–74), vol. 5, pp. 59–133. Subsequent quotations from *Scots Proverbs* are from this volume.
5. Ibid., p. 111.
6. Kinsley (ed.), *The Poems and Songs of Robert Burns*, vol. 2, p. 655.
7. Ramsay (ed.), *Scots Proverbs*, p. 81.
8. For the line in Burns, see Kinsley (ed.), *The Poems and Songs of Robert Burns*, vol. 2, p. 559.
9. J. Sharman (ed.), *The Proverbs of John Heywood* (London: Bell, 1874), p. 11. Sharman describes Heywood's collection as 'the most popular of all popular books ... [P]oets, playwriters, and statesmen made capital of its mine of proverbs. The Elizabethan dramatists are brimming with them' (p. xv). These adages were old when Heywood printed them. Here are a few, given in modern form: 'the more the merrier'; 'better late than never'; 'the fat's in the fire'; 'one good turn deserves another'; 'beggars can't be choosers'; 'a penny for your thoughts'; 'haste makes waste'; 'out of sight, out of mind'; 'make hay when the sun shines'; 'strike while the iron is hot'; 'look before you leap'; 'can't see the forest for the trees'; 'two heads are better than one'; 'love me, love my dog'; 'many hands make light work'; and 'all's well that ends well'.
10. Kinsley (ed.), *The Poems and Songs of Robert Burns*, vol. 2, p. 796.
11. Ramsay (ed.), *Scots Proverbs*, p. 128.
12. Kinsley (ed.), *The Poems and Songs of Robert Burns*, vol. 2, p. 708.
13. G. B. Evans and J. J. M. Tobin (eds), 'Julius Caesar', in G. B. Evans and J. J. M. Tobin (eds), *Riverside Shakespeare*, 2nd edn (Boston, MA: Houghton Mifflin, 1997), p. 1166.
14. In *Allusion to the Poets*, Christopher Ricks considers echoes of *King Lear* in 'A Poet's Welcome to His Love-Begotten Daughter', whose 'allusions range wildly ... Burns embraces *King Lear*. His pair of lines, "tho' ye come here a wee unsought for" and "Tho' ye come to the world asklent", is itself paired with the opening scene of *King Lear*: "though this Knave came somthing [*sic*] sawcily to the world before he was sent for ..."' (p. 64). Gloucester also reminisces in this scene that 'there was good sport at his making' (ibid., p. 65), a matter Burns's lines may reflect when he addresses newborn Elizabeth as the 'sweet fruit of monie a merry dint'.
15. Roy and Ferguson (eds), *Letters of Burns*, vol. 2, p. 285.
16. Ramsay (ed.), *Scots Proverbs*, p. 70.
17. Derrida, 'Aphorism Countertime', p. 416.
18. Kinsley (ed.), *The Poems and Songs of Robert Burns*, vol. 1, p. 76.
19. Holy Willie is echoing 2 Cor. 12:5, 7.
20. In a diary entry for 25 January 1906 (Burns's birthday) John Muir wrote that 'On my lonely walks ... [Burns] was always with me, for I had him by heart'. L. M. Wolfe (ed.), *John of the Mountains: The Unpublished Journals of John Muir* (Boston: MA: Houghton Mifflin, 1938), pp. 434–5.
21. J. Bartlett (ed.), *Familiar Quotations: A Collection of Passages, Phrases, and Proverbs. Traced to their Sources in Ancient and Modern Literature*, 9th edn (Boston, MA: Little, Brown, 1891).
22. For discussion of nineteenth and twentieth century US and British writers who reworked Burns's language into their own projects, see C. McGuirk, 'Burns and Aphorism: or,

Poetry into Proverb: His Persistence in Cultural Memory Beyond Scotland', in S. Alker, L. Davis and H. Faith Nelson (eds), *Robert Burns and Transatlantic Culture* (Burlingon, VT: Ashgate, 2012), pp. 169–86.
23. F. Douglass, 'Speech at a Burns Supper, January 1849', online at http://www.bulldozia.com/ projects/ index.php?section_id=25 [accessed 30 March 2014].
24. Kinsley (ed.), *The Poems and Songs of Robert Burns*, vol. 1, p. 118.
25. C. Carson (ed.), *Autobiography of Martin Luther King, Jr.* (New York: Warner Books, 1998), p. 220.
26. R. W. Emerson, 'Speech at Burns Centenary Dinner in Boston, January 1859', in Low (ed.), *Robert Burns: The Critical Heritage*, p. 436.
27. McGuirk, 'Burns and Nostalgia', pp. 48–51.

WORKS CITED

Alker, S. L., L. Davis and H. F. Nelson (eds), *Robert Burns and Transatlantic Culture* (Farnham, Surrey: Ashgate Press, 2012).

Anderson, B., *Imagined Communities: Reflections on the Origin and Spread of Nationalism*, rev. edn (1983; London: Verso, 1991).

Andrews, C., 'Lament for Slavery? The Case for Robert Burns', in F. R. Shaw (ed.) *Robert Burns Lives!* http://www.electricscotland.com/familytree/frank/Burns_lives93.htm [accessed 20 November 2013].

Ashmead, J., and J. Davison (eds), *The Songs of Robert Burns* (New York: Garland, 1988).

Bakhtin, M. M., *The Dialogic Imagination: Four Essays*, ed. M. Holquist, trans. C. Emerson and M. Holquist (Austin, TX: University of Texas Press, 1981).

Barclay, H., *Notes on the Law and Practice, Relative to Applications Against Debtors as in Meditatione Fugae* (Edinburgh: Thomas Clark, 1832).

Bartlett, J. (ed.), *Familiar Quotations: A Collection of Passages, Phrases, and Proverbs. Traced to their Sources in Ancient and Modern Literature*, 9th edn (Boston, MA: Little Brown, 1891).

Baudrillard, J., 'The Precession of Simulacra', in *The Norton Anthology of Theory and Criticism*, 2nd edn (New York: Norton, 2010), pp. 1553–65.

Benjamin, W., 'The Storyteller', in *Walter Benjamin: Selected Writings*, vol. 3, trans. H. Eiland and M. W. Jennings (Cambridge: MA, Harvard University Press, 2002), pp. 143–66.

—, 'The Work of Art in the Age of its Technological Reproducibility', in *Walter Benjamin, Selected Writings 1935–38, vol. 3*, trans. Eiland and Jennings, pp. 101–33.

Benzie, I. F. (singer), 'Montgomerie's Peggy', *The Complete Songs of Robert Burns*, vol. 1, Fred Freeman (comp.), Linn CKD047 (1995).

Berryman, J., *The Dream Songs* (1969; New York, NY: Farrar, Straus, and Giroux, 2007).

Betz, P. F. (ed.), *Benjamin the Waggoner, by William Wordsworth* (Ithaca, NY: Cornell University Press, 1981).

Bhabha, H. K., *The Location of Culture* (1994; London: Routledge, 2004).

Borges, J. L., 'Pierre Menard, Author of the Quixote', *Ficciones*, trans. A. Bonner (New York: Grove Press, 1962), pp. 45–55.

Boswell, J., *Life of Samuel Johnson*, unabridged, ed. R. W. Chapman (Oxford: Oxford University Press, 1980).

Bourdieu, P., *Distinction: A Social Critique of the Judgment of Taste*, trans. R. Nice (Cambridge, MA: Harvard University Press, 1984).

Braudy, L., *The Frenzy of Renown: Fame and Its History* (New York: Vintage, 1997).

Bredvold, L. I., A. D. McKillop and L. Whitney (eds), *Eighteenth Century Poetry and Prose*, 2nd edn (New York: Ronald Press Company, 1956).

Brett, R. L., and A. R. Jones (eds), *Wordsworth and Coleridge: Lyrical Ballads: The Text of the 1798 Edition, with the Additional 1800 Poems and the Prefaces* (London: Routledge, 1988).

Broadhead, A., *The Language of Robert Burns: Style, Ideology and Identity* (Lewisburg, PA: Bucknell University Press, 2013).

Broadside ballad entitled 'Christs Kirk on the Green', National Library of Scotland, at http://www.scran.ac.uk/database/record.php?usi=000-000-528-056-C [accessed 8 July 2013].

Burnard, T., '"The Grand Mart of the Island": The Economic Functions of Kingston, Jamaica in the Mid-Eighteenth Century', K. E. A. Montieth and G. Richards (eds), *Jamaica in Slavery and Freedom: History, Heritage and Culture* (Kingston: University of the West Indies Press, 2002), pp. 225–41.

—, '"Not a Place for Whites?" Demographic Failure and Settlement, 1655–1780', in K. E. A. Montieth and G. Richards (eds), *Jamaica in Slavery and Freedom: History, Heritage and Culture* (Kingston: University of the West Indies Press, 2002), pp. 73–88.

Burnes, W., *A Manual of Religious Belief. Composed by William Burnes, (the Poet's Father) for the Instruction of his Children; with Biographical Preface* (Kilmarnock: McKie & Drennan, 1875).

Burns, R., The Glenriddell Manuscripts, 2 vols, National Library of Scotland, MSS 86 and 87.

—, *Poems, Chiefly in the Scottish Dialect* (Kilmarnock, 1786).

—, *Poems, Chiefly in the Scottish Dialect* (London: A. Strahan, 1787).

—, *Letters Addressed to Clarinda, &c.* (Glasgow: Niven, Napier and Khull, for T. Stewart, 1802).

—, *Robert Burns's Commonplace Book. 1783–85. Reproduced in Facsimile from the Poet's Manuscript and the Original Introduction and Notes of James Cameron Ewing and Davidson Cook. This Edition Introduced by David Daiches* (Carbondale, IL: Southern Illinois University Press, 1965).

—, *Poems, 1786–1787* [facsimile printing of *Poems, Chiefly in the Scottish Dialect*, 1786 with additional facsimiles of the poems added in 1787] (Menston: Scolar Press, 1971).

—, *The Glenriddell Manuscripts of Robert Burns* [facsimile of Burns's transcriptions only, omitting other copyists]. *With an Introduction and Notes by D. Donaldson* (Wakefield: Archon, 1973).

[Burns, R. et al.], *The Merry Muses of Caledonia; A Collection of Favourite Scots Songs, Ancient and Modern; Selected for the Use of the Crochallan Fencibles*, facsimile with notes by G. Ross Roy (1799; Columbia, SC: University of South Carolina Press, 1999).

Buthlay, K., (ed.), *A Drunk Man Looks at the Thistle. An Annotated Edition* (Edinburgh: Scottish Academic, 1987).

Butler, M., 'Burns and Politics', in *Robert Burns and Cultural Authority*, ed. R. Crawford (Edinburgh: Edinburgh University Press, 1997), pp. 86–112.

Campbell, J. L. (ed.), *Highland Songs of the Forty-Five, Edited and Translated with Glossary and Notes* (Edinburgh: John Grant, 1933).

Carruthers, G. (ed.), *The Edinburgh Companion to Robert Burns* (Edinburgh: Edinburgh University Press, 2009).

—, '"Tongues Turn'd Inside Out": The Reception of "Tam o' Shanter"', in P. Scott and K. Simpson (eds), *Robert Burns & Friends: Essays by W. Ormiston Roy Fellows: Presented to G. Ross Roy* (Columbia, SC: University of South Carolina Libraries, 2012), pp. 47–57.

—, 'Burns and Slavery', in F. R. Shaw (ed.), *Burns Lives!* http://www.electricscotland.com/familytree/frank/Burns_lives55.htm [accessed 20 November 2013].

Carson, C. (ed.), *The Autobiography of Martin Luther King, Jr* (New York: Warner, 1998).

Carswell, C., *The Life of Robert Burns* (London: Chatto & Windus, 1930).

'The Case of Major William Nairne, Grandson and Heir to the late John Lord Nairne', MS 3142 [Jacobite Miscellaneous]. National Library of Scotland, Edinburgh [1807?].

Chambers, R. (ed.), and W. Wallace (rev.), *The Life and Work of Robert Burns*, 4 vols (Edinburgh and London: W & R Chambers, 1896).

Chambers, R., J. Currie, R. H. Cromek (eds), *Prose Works of Robert Burns: With the Notes of Currie and Cromek, and Many by the Present Editor* (Edinburgh: W & R Cambers, 1839).

Child, F. J. (ed.), *The English and Scottish Popular Ballads*, 5 vols (Mineola, NY: Dover Publications, 2003).

Colley, L., *Britons: Forging the Nation, 1707–1832* (New Haven, CT: Yale, 1992).

Complete Poetical Works of William Wordsworth, Part 1 (Boston, MA: Houghton Mifflin, 1904).

Cook, D. (ed.), *Annotations of Scottish Songs by Burns*, in *The Songs of Robert Burns* and *Notes on Scottish Songs by Robert Burns*, by J. C. Dick, together with *Annotation of Scottish Songs* (Hatboro, PA: Folklore Associates, 1962).

Crawford, R. (ed.), *Devolving English Literature* (Oxford: Clarendon, 1992).

—, 'Robert Fergusson's Robert Burns', in *Robert Burns and Cultural Authority*, ed. R. Crawford (Edinburgh: Edinburgh University Press, 1997), pp. 1–22.

—, *The Bard: Robert Burns, A Biography* (Princeton, NJ: Princeton University Press, 2009).

Crawford, T., *Burns: A Study of the Poems and Songs* (Stanford, CA: Stanford University Press, 1960).

—, *Society and the Lyric: A Study of the Song Culture of Eighteenth-Century Scotland* (Edinburgh: Scottish Academic Press, 1979).

—, 'Burns, Love, and Liberty', in McGuirk (ed.), *Critical Essays*, pp. 95–116.

Cromek, R. H. (ed.), *Reliques of Robert Burns* (London: Cadell and Davies, 1808).

Cunningham, A., *Songs of Scotland, Ancient and Modern, with an Introduction and Notes, Historical and Critical, and Characters of the Lyric Poets*, 4 vols (London: John Taylor, 1825).

— (ed.), *Complete Works of Robert Burns, with Life and Notes by Allan Cunningham*, 2nd edn, 4 vols (Edinburgh: Thomas C. Jack, 1835).

— (ed.), *Works of Robert Burns. With Life and Notes by Allan Cunningham. Illustrated Edition with Music*, 4 vols (Edinburgh: Thomas Jack, 1835).

Currie, J. (ed.), *The Works of Robert Burns; with an Account of his Life, and A Criticism on His Writings. To which are Prefixed, Some Observations on the Character and Condition of the Scottish Peasantry*, 2nd edn, 4 vols (London: Cadell and Davies, 1801).

Daiches, D., *Robert Burns* (London: Bell, 1952).

—, 'Robert Burns: The Tightrope Walker', in K. Simpson (ed.), *Love and Liberty: Robert Burns, A Bicentenary Celebration* (East Linton: Tuckwell Press, 1997), pp. 18–31.

Davis, L., 'Re-Presenting Scotia: Robert Burns and the Imagined Community of Scotland', in McGuirk (ed.), *Critical Essays*, pp. 63–78.

Deleuze, G., and F. Guattari, *A Thousand Plateaus: Capitalism and Schizophrenia*, trans. B. Massumi (Minneapolis, MN: University of Minnesota Press, 1987).

Derrida, J., 'Aphorism Countertime', in *Acts of Literature*, ed. D. Attridge, trans. N. Royle (London: Routledge, 1992), pp. 414–34.

Dick, J. C., and D. Cook (eds), *The Songs of Robert Burns* and *Notes on Scottish Songs by James C. Dick, Together with Annotation of Scottish Songs by Burns by Davidson Cook* (Hatboro, PA: Folklore Associates, 1962).

Donaldson, W., *The Jacobite Song: Political Myth and National Identity* (Aberdeen: Aberdeen University Press, 1988).

Douglas, C., 'Letter to Patrick Douglas Port Antonio 19 June 1786'. Burns Birthplace Museum (NBC247) and online at http:www.burnsmuseum.org.uk/collections/transcript/1574 [accessed 20 November 2013].

Douglass, F., '"Speech at a Burns Supper, January 1849", Bulldozia: Douglas, Burns and Scott', http://www.bulldozia.com/projects/index.php?section_id=25 [accessed 30 March 2014].

Dunn, D., '"A Very Scottish Kind of Dash": Burns's Native Metric', in R. Crawford (ed.), *Robert Burns and Cultural Authority* (Edinburgh: University of Edinburgh Press, 1997), pp. 58–85.

Dylan, B., 'Highlands', *Time Out of Mind* (1997), BobDylan.com at http://www.bobdylan.com./us/songs/highlands [accessed 14 December 2013].

—, 'Bob Dylan's Dream', *Freewheelin' Bob Dylan* (1963) at http://www.bobdylan.com./us/songs/highlands [accessed 16 December 2013].

Easdale, K. (singer), 'I Sing of a Whistle', *Robert Burns: The Complete Songs*, vol. 10, comp. F. Freeman, Linn CDK199 (2002).

Egerer, J. W. (ed.), *A Bibliography of Robert Burns* (Edinburgh and London: Oliver & Boyd, 1964).

Eliot, T. S., 'Was there a Scottish Literature?', *Atheneaum*, 1 August 1919, pp. 680–1.

—, *The Use of Poetry and the Use of Criticism: Studies in the Relation of Criticism and Poetry* (London: Faber & Faber, 1933).

Emerson, R. W., 'Ralph Waldo Emerson: An American Tribute', in Low (ed.), *Robert Burns: The Critical Heritage*, pp. 434–6.

—, 'Speech at Burns Centenary Dinner in Boston, January 1859', in Low (ed.), *Robert Burns: The Critical Heritage*, p. 436.

Evans, G. B., and J. J. M. Tobin (eds), *The Riverside Shakespeare*, 2nd edn (Boston, MA: Houghton Mifflin, 1997).

[Ewing, J. C. (ed.)], 'Maria Riddell's Letters to Dr Currie (1796–1805)', *Burns Chronicle*, first series, 32, part 2 (1921), pp. 96–108.

Ewing, J. C., and D. Cook (eds), *Robert Burns's Commonplace Book. 1783–85. Reproduced in Facsimile from the Poet's Manuscript and the Original Introduction and Notes of James Cameron Ewing and Davidson Cook. This Edition Introduced by David Daiches* (Carbondale, IL: Southern Illinois University Press, 1965).

Fergusson, R., *Poems of Robert Fergusson*, ed. M. McDiarmid, 2 vols (Edinburgh: Blackwood for the Scottish Text Society, 1956), vol. 2.

Fitzhugh, R., *Robert Burns, the Man and the Poet: A Round, Unvarnished Account* (Boston, MA: Houghton Mifflin, 1970).

Ford, R. (ed.), *The Poetical Works of Robert Fergusson with Biography, Introduction, Notes, and Glossary, Etc.* (Paisley: A Gardner, 1905).

Fowler, R. H., *Robert Burns* (London: Routledge, 1988).

Freeman, F. (comp.), *The Complete Songs of Robert Burns*, various artists, 12 vols (Linn Music, 1997–2003).

Fuss, D., *Essentially Speaking: Feminism, Nature, Difference* (London: Routledge, 1989).

Gebbie, G. (ed.), *Complete Works of Robert Burns (Self-Interpreting)*, 6 vols (New York: Dumont, c. 1880).

Gilfillan, G. (ed.), *Poetical Works of Goldsmith, Collins and Thomas Warton, with Lives, Critical Dissertations, and Explanatory Notes* (New York: D. Appleton & Co., 1860).

—, *Specimens with Memoirs of the Less-known British Poets, Vol. 1* (1860), Project Gutenberg (25 November 2011), at gutenberg.org/cache/epub/9667/pg9667.txt [accessed 8 July 2013].

Gill, S., 'Wordsworth and Burns', in D. Sergeant and F. J. Stafford (eds) *Burns and Other Poets* (Edinburgh: Edinburgh University Press, 2012), pp. 156–67.

Gray, T., 'Elegy in a Country Church-yard', in L. I. Bredvold, A. D. McKillop, L. B. Whitney (eds), *Eighteenth Century Poetry and Prose*, 2nd edn (New York: Ronald Press, 1956), pp. 392–5.

—, 'Ode on a Distant Prospect of Eton College', in L. I. Bredvold, A. D. McKillop, L. B. Whitney (eds), *Eighteenth Century Poetry and Prose*, (New York: Ronald Press, 1956), pp. 591–2.

Grieve, M., and W. R. Aitken (eds), *Hugh MacDiarmid: Complete Poems*, 2 vols (Ashington, Northumberland: Carcanet Press, 1993).

[Grosart, A. B. (ed.)], *Works of Robert Fergusson Edited with a Life of the Author and an Essay on his Genius and Writings* (London: Fullarton, 1857).

Grove Music Online at http://www.oxfordmusiconline.com/article/q=Robert+Burns [accessed 22 October 2013].

Halcrow, E., *Canes and Chains: A Study of Sugar and Slavery* (Oxford: Heinemann Educational Publishers, 1982).

Harrison, D., '"A Most Miserable Trade": David Harrison Reveals the Involvement of Freemasons in the Slave Trade', *Freemasonry Today* 39 (Winter 2006/7), http://webarchive.org/web/20070621004422/http:freemasonrytoday.com/39/p12.php [accessed 20 November 2013].

[Hawthorne, N.], 'Some of the Haunts of Burns, by a Tourist Without Imagination or Enthusiasm', *Atlantic Monthly, A Magazine of Literature, Art, and Politics*, 6:36 (October 1860), pp. 385–95.

Hemans, F., 'Graves of a Household', in D. Wu (ed.), *Romanticism: An Anthology*, 4th edn, (Malden, MA: Wiley-Blackwell, 2012), p. 1365.

Henderson, G., *Lady Nairne and Her Songs*, 3rd edn (Paisley: Gardner, 1905).

Henley, W. E., and T. F. Henderson (eds), *The Poetry of Robert Burns*, 4 vols (Edinburgh: T. C. and E. C. Jack, 1901).

Herbert, W. N., 'The Significance of Gregory Smith', *Gairfish 2: Discovery* (1991), pp. 16–27.

Hewat, C. (singer), 'The Gloomy Night is Gath'ring Fast', in *The Complete Songs of Robert Burns*, vol. 5, F. Freeman (comp.), Linn CKD086 (1998).

Hogg, J. (ed.), *Jacobite Reliques of Scotland, Being the Songs, Airs and Legends of the Adherents of the House of Stuart*, ed. M. G. H. Pittock (Edinburgh: Edinburgh University Press, 2002 [1st series] and 2003 [2nd series]).

Hughes, M. Y. (ed.), *Complete Poems and Major Prose of John Milton* (New York: Odyssey Press, 1957).

Hutchinson, T. (ed.), and E. D. Selincourt (rev.), *Wordsworth: Complete Poetical Works, With Introduction and Notes* (Oxford: Oxford University Press, 1936).

Jamaican Family Genealogy Research Library, 'Slaves and Slavery', '1788 Slave Count', http://jamaicanfamilysearch.com/Samples2/1788tab.htm [accessed 20 November 2013].

Johnson, J., and R. Burns (eds), W. Stenhouse (rev.), *The Scots Musical Museum; Consisting of Upwards of Six Hundred Songs, with Proper Basses for the Pianoforte. Originally Published by James Johnson, and now Accompanied by Copious Notes and Illustrations of the Lyric Poetry of Scotland, by the late William Stenhouse, with Additional Notes and Illustrations. New Edition*, 4 vols (Edinburgh: William Blackwood & Sons, 1853).

Jones, C., *A Language Suppressed: The Pronunciation of the Scots Language in the 18th Century* (Edinburgh: John Donald, 1995).

Jones, P., and N. Pennick, *A History of Pagan Europe* (London: Routledge, 1995).

Kaplan, C., 'Pandora's Box: Subjectivity, Class and Sexuality in Socialist-Feminist Criticism', in T. Lovell (ed.), *British Feminist Thought: A Reader* (Oxford: Blackwell, 1990), pp. 956–75.

Kermode, F., *The Art of Telling: Essays on Fiction* (Cambridge, MA: Harvard University Press, 1983).

Kidd, C., 'Burns and Politics', *The Edinburgh Companion to Robert Burns*, ed. G.Carruthers (Edinburgh: Edinburgh University Press, 2009), pp. 61–73.

Kinsley, J. (ed.), *The Poems and Songs of Robert Burns*, 3 vols (Oxford: Clarendon Press, 1968).

Knight, W. (ed.), *Letters of the Wordsworth Family, Vol. 2* (Boston, MA: Ginn and Company, 1907).

Leask, N., 'Burns and the Poetics of Abolition', in G. Carruthers (ed.), *The Edinburgh Companion to Robert Burns* (Edinburgh: Edinburgh University Press, 2009), pp. 47–60.

—, *Robert Burns and Pastoral: Poetry and Improvement in Late-Eighteenth Century Scotland* (London: Oxford University Press, 2010).

'Letter from John Mitchell to Robert Graham of Fintry, 24 July 1796', Graham of Fintry Papers, GD151/11/26/46, National Records of Scotland: http://www.nas.gov.uk/about/090717.asp. [accessed 22 October 2013].

Lindsay, M., *Robert Burns: The Man, His Work, His Legend* (London: MacGibbon & Kee, 1954).

Lindsay, M. (ed.), *The Burns Encyclopedia*, 3rd edn (New York: St Martin's, 1980).

Lockhart, J. G., *Life of Robert Burns* (Edinburgh: Constable and Co., 1828).

Low, D. A. (ed.), *Robert Burns: The Critical Heritage* (London: Routledge, 1974).

Lyric Gems of Scotland: A Collection of Scottish Songs, Original and Selected, With Music. (Glasgow: n. p., n. d.).

MacDiarmid, H., *Lucky Poet: A Self-Study in Literature and Political Ideas* (London: Methuen, 1943).

Mackay, J., *RB: A Biography of Robert Burns* (Edinburgh: Mainstream Press, 1992).

Mackenzie, H., *The Anecdotes and Egotisms of Henry Mackenzie, 1745–1831, Now First Published*, ed. H. W. Thomson (Oxford: Oxford University Press, 1927).

Maclagan, D. J. (ed.), *The Scottish Paraphrases, being the Translations and Paraphrases in Verse of several Passages of Sacred Scripture, Collected and Prepared by a Committee of the General Assembly of the Church of Scotland, In Order to be Sung in Church* (Edinburgh: Andrew Elliot, 1889).

Manning, S., 'Robert Fergusson and Eighteenth-Century Poetry', on *'Heaven-Taught' Fergusson, Robert Burns's Favourite Scottish Poet*, ed. R. Crawford (East Linton: Tuckwell Press, 2003), pp. 87–112.

McColl, E., *Songs of Robert Burns* (Library of Congress recording, 1959).

McCullough, D., *The Path between the Seas: The Creation of the Panama Canal, 1870–1910* (New York: Simon & Schuster, 1978).

McDiarmid, M., (ed.), *The Poems of Robert Fergusson*, 2 vols (Edinburgh: Blackwood for the Scottish Text Society, 1954–6).

McGuirk, C., 'Augustan Influences on Allan Ramsay', *Studies in Scottish Literature*, 16:1 (1981), pp. 97–109.

—, *Robert Burns and the Sentimental Era* (Athens, GA: University of Georgia Press, 1985).

—, 'The Politics of the Collected Burns', *Gairfish 2: Discovery* (1991), pp. 36–50.

— (ed.), *Robert Burns: Selected Poems* (London: Penguin Books, 1993).

—, 'Burns and Nostalgia', in *Burns Now*, ed. K. Simpson (Edinburgh: Canongate Academic Press, 1994), pp. 31–69.

—, 'Loose Canons: Milton and Burns, Artsong and Folksong', in K. Simpson (ed.), *Love and Liberty: Robert Burns. A Bicentenary Celebration* (East Linton: Tuckwell, 1997), pp. 315–25.

— (ed.), *Critical Essays on Robert Burns* (New York, G. K. Hall, 1998).

—, The '"Rhyming Trade": Fergusson, Burns, and the Marketplace', in *'Heaven-Taught Fergusson': Robert Burns's Favourite Scottish Poet*, ed. R. Crawford (East Linton: Tuckwell, 2003), pp. 135–59.

—, 'Burns and Aphorism: or, Poetry into Proverb: His Persistence in Cultural Memory Beyond Scotland', in *Robert Burns and Transatlantic Culture*, ed. S. Alker, L. Davis and H. Faith Nelson (Burlington, VT: Ashgate, 2012), pp. 169–86.

—, 'Burns's Two Memorials to Fergusson', in *Robert Burns & Friends: Essays by W. Ormiston Roy Fellows Presented to G. Ross Roy*, ed. P. Scott and K. Simpson (Columbia, SC: University of South Carolina Libraries, 2012), pp. 5–23.

McIlvanney, L., *Burns the Radical: Poetry and Politics in Late-Eighteenth Century Scotland* (East Linton: Tuckwell Press, 2002).

McIntyre, I., *Robert Burns: A Life* (Edinburgh: Constable and Robinson, 2009).

Mellor, A. K., and R. E. Matlak (eds), *British Literature, 1780–1830* (Fort Worth, TX: Harcourt, 1996).

Michaels, S., 'Bob Dylan: Burns is my Biggest Inspiration', *Guardian*, 5 October 2008.

Moore, J., *Zeluco. Various Views of Human Nature, Taken from the Life and Manners, Foreign and Domestic* (1786), 2nd edn, 2 vols (London: Strahan, 1789).

Morgan, E., 'A Poet's Response to Burns', in K. G. Simpson (ed.), *Burns Now* (Edinburgh: Canongate Academic, 1994), pp. 1–12.

Muir, J., 'William Burnes's Manual of Religious Belief', *Burns Chronicle* (1933), pp. 78–80.

Nairne, C., *Lays of Strathearn by Caroline Baroness Nairne, Symphonies and Accompaniments by the Late Finlay Dun* (Edinburgh: Patterson & Sons, n.d.).

Newman, S., *Ballad Collection, Lyric, and the Canon: The Call of the Popular from the Restoration to the New Criticism* (Philadelphia, PA: University of Pennsylvania Press, 2007).

Nietzsche, F., *'The Birth of Tragedy' and Other Writings*, ed. R. Geuss, and R. Speirs, trans. R. Speirs (Cambridge: Cambridge University Press, 1999).

Noble, A., 'Wordsworth and Burns: The Anxiety of Being Under the Influence', in C. McGuirk (ed.), *Critical Essays*, pp. 49–62.

—, 'Introduction', in A. Noble and P. S. Hogg (eds), *The Canongate Burns: The Complete Poems and Songs of Robert Burns*, Canongate Classics 104 (Edinburgh: Canongate, 2001), pp. ix–xcii.

Noble, A., and P. S. Hogg (eds), *The Canongate Burns: The Complete Poems and Songs of Robert Burns*, Canongate Classics 104 (Edinburgh: Canongate, 2001).

Noyes, R., 'Wordsworth and Burns', *PMLA [Publications of the Modern Language Association]*, 59 (1944), pp. 813–32.

Paterson, D., *Robert Burns: Poems Selected by Don Paterson* (London: Faber & Faber, 2001).

Pittock, M. G. H., *Poetry and Jacobite Politics in Eighteenth-Century Britain and Ireland* (Cambridge: Cambridge University Press, 1994).

—, 'Burns and the Jacobite Song', in K. Simpson (ed.), *Love and Liberty: Robert Burns – A Bicentenary Celebration* (East Linton: Tuckwell, 1996), pp. 308–14.

— (ed.), *Robert Burns and Global Culture* (Lewisburg, PA: Bucknell University Press, 2011).

—, *Material Culture and Sedition, 1688–1760: Treacherous Objects, Secret Places* (Houndmills: Palgrave Macmillan, 2013).

Presbyterian Social Psalmodist: Being an Abridgment of the Presbyterian Psalmodist with a Selection of Hymns from the Assembly's Collection Adapted to the Respective Tunes (Philadelphia, PA: Presbyterian Board of Publication, 1857).

Preston, T., 'Contrary Scriptings: Implied National Narratives in Burns and Smollett', in K. Simpson (ed.), *Love and Liberty: Robert Burns* (East Linton: Tuckwell, 1997), pp. 198–216.

Purdie, R. (ed.), *The Scotish Minstrel: A Selection from the Vocal Melodies of Scotland, Ancient and Modern. Arranged for the Piano Forte by R. A. Smith*, 4 vols (Edinburgh: Purdie, 1821–4).

Ramsay, A., *Journal of the Easy Club*; *A Collection of Scots Proverbs*; *The Early Drafts of 'The Gentle Shepherd'*, in *The Works of Allan Ramsay*, ed. A. M. Kinghorn and A. Law (Edinburgh: Scottish Text Society, 1944–74).

— (ed.), *A Collection of Scots Proverbs* (1737), in *The Works of Allan Ramsay*, ed. Kinghorn and Law, vol. 5, pp. 59–133.

Read and Run Library: Scotland, Review in *Tait's Edinburgh Magazine*, 26 (January–December 1859), p. 544.

Reed, T. L., *The Transforming Draught: Robert Louis Stevenson and the Alcohol Debate* (Jefferson, NC: McFarland, 2006).

Ricks, C., *Allusion to the Poets* (Oxford: Oxford University Press, 2002).

Ritter, O. (ed.), *Neue Quellenfunde zu Robert Burns* (Halle: Ehrhardt Karras, 1903).

Rogers, C., *Memoir of Baroness Nairne*, in C. Rogers (ed.), *The Life and Songs of the Baroness Nairne, With a Memoir and Poems of Caroline Oliphant the Younger* (Edinburgh: Grant, 1905), pp. 13–156.

Ross, M. B., 'The Birth of a Tradition: Making Cultural Space for Feminine Poetry', in M. B. Ross, *The Contours of Masculine Desire: Romanticism and the Rise of Women's Poetry* (New York: Oxford University Press, 1989), pp. 187–231.

Roy, G. R. (ed.), *The Merry Muses of Caledonia; A Collection of Favourite Scots Songs, Ancient and Modern; Selected for the Use of the Crochallan Fencibles. Printed in the Year 1799* (Columbia, SC: University of South Carolina Press, 1999).

Roy, G. R., and J. D. Ferguson (eds), *The Letters of Robert Burns*, 2nd edn, 2 vols (Oxford: Clarendon Press, 1985).

Scott, P., and K. Simpson (eds), *Robert Burns and Friends: Essays by W. Ormiston Roy Fellows Presented to G. Ross Roy* (Columbia, SC: University of South Carolina Libraries, 2012).

Scott, T., 'A Review of Robert Fergusson's Poems', *Akros*, 2:6 (December 1967), pp. 15–26.

Scott, W., *Waverley: or, 'Tis Sixty Years Since*, ed. C. Lamont (New York: Oxford, 1986).

Sergeant, D., and F. Stafford (eds), *Burns and Other Poets* (Edinburgh: Edinburgh University Press, 2012).

Sharman, J. (ed.), *The Proverbs of John Heywood* (London: Bell, 1874).

Shenstone, W., 'The School-mistress', in L. I. Bredvold, A. D. McKillop, and L. Whitney (eds), *Eighteenth Century Poetry & Prose*, 2nd edn (New York: Ronald Press Company, 1956), pp. 550–6.

Sher, R., *The Enlightenment and the Book: Scottish Authors and Their Publishers in Eighteenth-Century Britain, Ireland, and America* (Chicago, IL: Chicago University Press, 2007).

Shiach, M., *Discourse on Popular Culture: Class, Gender and History in Cultural Analysis, 1730 to the Present* (Stanford, CA: Stanford University Press, 1989).

[Simpson, M. S.], *Caroline, Baroness Nairne: The Scottish Songstress. By Her Great-Grand-Niece* (Edinburgh: Oliphant, 1894).

Skoblow, J., *Doouble Tongue: Scots, Burns, Contradiction* (Newark, DE: University of Delaware Press, 2001).

—, 'Resisting the Powers of Calculation: A Bard's Politics', in McGuirk (ed.), *Critical Essays*, pp. 17–31.

Smith, B. H., *Contingencies of Value: Alternative Perspectives for Critical Theory* (Cambridge, MA: Harvard University Press, 1988).

Smith, G. G., *Scottish Literature: Character and Influence* (London: Macmillan, 1919).

Sneddon, D. (ed.), *Burns Holograph Manuscripts in the Kilmarnock Manuscript Museum, With Notes* (Kilmarnock: D. Brown & Co., 1889).

Snyder, F. B., *The Life of Robert Burns* (New York: Macmillan, 1932).

Speirs, J., *The Scots Literary Tradition: An Essay in Criticism*, 2nd edn (London: Faber & Faber, 1962).

Spivak, G. C., 'A Literary Representation of the Subaltern', in *In Other Worlds: Essays in Cultural Politics* (New York: Routledge, 1988), pp. 241–68.

—, *The Spivak Reader: Selected Writings*, ed. D. Landry and G. Maclean (London: Routledge, 1995).

'S. R. G', 'If Burns Had Gone to Jamaica', *Burns Chronicle and Club Directory*, 20 (1911), pp. 79–82.

Stafford, F., 'Burns and Romantic Writing', in G. Carruthers (ed.), *The Edinburgh Companion to Robert Burns* (Edinburgh: Edinburgh University Press, 2009), pp. 97–109.

—, 'Robert Burns's Addresses', in F. Stafford, *Local Attachments: The Province of Poetry* (Oxford: Oxford University Press, 2010), pp. 176–223.

Stenhouse, W., 'Introduction', in *'The Land o' the Leal' Irrefutably Proved from a Searching Investigation to be the Deathbed Valediction of Robert Burns, by A[lexander] Crichton*, 3rd edn (Peterhead: Scrogie, 1919), pp. 3–10.

Stetson, E., and L. David, *Glorying in Tribulation: The Life Work of Sojourner Truth*. (East Lansing, MI: Michigan State University Press, 1994).

Stevenson, R. L., 'Some Aspects of Robert Burns', in *Familiar Studies of Books and Men* (London: Chatto & Windus, 1889), pp. 30–90.

Sweeney-Turner, S., 'Pagan Airts: Reading Critical Perspectives on the Songs of Burns and Tannahill', in McGuirk (ed.), *Critical Essays*, pp. 182–207.

Thomson, J., 'Summer', *The Seasons*, Project Gutenberg Australia (August 2008) at gutenbergbook.net.au/ebooks08 [accessed 3 September 2013].

Thornton, R. D., *James Currie the Entire Stranger and Robert Burns* (Edinburgh: Oliver & Boyd, 1963).

Tillotson, G. et al. (eds), *Eighteenth Century English Literature* (Fort Worth, TX: Harcourt, 1969).

The True Loyalist; or, Chevalier's Favourite: Being a Collection of Elegant Songs, Never Before Printed, Also Several Other Loyal Compositions, Wrote by Eminent Hands (np, 1779).

Weston, J. C., 'Robert Burns's Satire', in McGuirk (ed.), *Critical Essays*, pp. 117–33.

Whitman, W., 'Robert Burns as Poet and Person', in *November Boughs* (1882), in *The Complete Poetry and Prose of Walt Whitman*, 2 vols (New York: Pellegrini and Cudahy, 1948).

Williams, R., 'Dialect', in *Keywords: A Vocabulary of Culture and Society*, rev. ed. (New York: Oxford University Press, 1983), p. 106.

Wolfe, L. M. (ed.), *John of the Mountains: The Unpublished Journals of John Muir* (Boston, MA: Houghton Mifflin, 1938).

Woolf, V., *To the Lighthouse* (1927; London: CRW Publishing, Ltd, 2004).

Wordsworth, W., *Poems. In Two Volumes* (London: Longman, Hurst, Rees and Orme, 1807).

The Works of Alexander Pope, 9 vols (London: J. F. Dove, 1822).

Wu, D., *Wordsworth's Reading, 1770–1799* (Cambridge: Cambridge University Press, 1993).

— (ed.), *Romanticism: An Anthology* (Oxford: Blackwell, 1998).

INDEX

Addison, Joseph, 46, 91–2
Aiken, Andrew, 69
Aiken, Robert, 5, 30–1, 36–9
Ainslie, Robert, 109
'Alexander's Feast', *see* Dryden, John
Alloway, 91–2, 168, 170–2, 174, 180, 183
Alloway kirk, 168, 170–2, 174, 183
    see also 'Tam o'Shanter', *under* Burns, Robert, poems and songs
An Evening Walk, 75, 89
    see also Wordsworth, William
Anacreontics, 157
Anchises, 168, 175
    see also Virgil, *Aeneid*
Anderson, Benedict, 18–20
Apollo, 151, 163–5
    see also Cynthia
Apollonian and Dionysian, 151
    see also Nietzsche, Friedrich
aporia, 79
    see also Derrida, Jacques
Armour, James and Mary, 30–1, 35, 68, 94, 103
Armour, Jean, 26, 37, 59, 78, 99
    1786 agreement with Burns, 5, 30–5, 40, 68–9, 99, 103
    Dumfries and later life in, 15, 94, 96, 175
Augustan poets, 89, 92
Austen, Jane, 26, 132

Bacchus, 61, 163–4
Bachelor's Club (Tarbolton), 20
Baillie, Joanna, 9
Bakhtin, M. M., 22
ballads, 4, 75, 101, 135, 178
    Burns and, 118, 122–3, 151, 166, 187–8

'The Whistle', 7, 160, 162–7, 181
    see also 'Whistle. A Ballad, The', *under* Burns, Robert, poems and songs
Coleridge and, 101
Fergusson and, 162
metre, 46, 52
music in, 135, 162
Ballantine, John, 38–9
Balliol, John, 124
Bannockburn, Battle of, 141–2, 187
    see also 'Scots Wha Hae', *under* Burns, Robert, poems and songs,
Barbauld, Anna Aiken, 23, 26
bawdry, 18, 20
Beattie, James, 12, 42
Bécourt, 24
    see also 'Ça ira'
Benjamin, Walter, 7, 98
Berryman, John, 1
Bhabha, Homi K., 9, 17
Blair, Hugh, 16, 26, 63, 72
Blake, William, 21, 27
Bonnie Prince Charlie, *see* Charles Edward Stuart
Borges, Jorge Luis, 114
Boswell, James, 9, 38
Bourdieu, Pierre, 12
Boyne, Battle of the, 113–14
    see also 'Strong Walls of Derry' and *Scots Musical Museum, The*
Bradwardine, Baron, 119, 130
    see also Sir Walter Scott and *Waverley*
Braudy, Leo, 73
brawl poems, Scottish, 7, 53, 152, 157, 159–60, 181
Bremner's *A Collection of Scots Reels*, 139
Brice, David, 32

Brown, Richard, 56
Bruce, Robert, 141–2, 187–8
  see also Bannockburn, Battle of
Buchan, William, *Domestic Medicine*, 153
Burnes, Agnes (poet's mother), 31, 175
Burnes, William (poet's father), 4, 7, 29, 42, 65, 132
  A Manual of Religious Belief, 179–80
  schooling of Burns, 90–1
  and 'Tam o'Shanter', 168–71
Burns, Elizabeth (Bess), 33, 36–7, 39, 42, 122
Burns, Francis Wallace, 96
Burns, Gilbert, 31, 33, 39, 132, 166
  narratives about Robert Burns, 34–8, 91, 158, 170
Burns, Isabella (Isobel), 169
Burns, Robert, poems and songs:
  'Address of Beelzebub', 26
  'Address to the Deil', 30, 53, 62, 66, 180
  'Ae Fond Kiss', 83, 133
  'Auld Lang Syne', 133
  'Author's Earnest Cry and Prayer, The', 30, 53, 55, 61, 120–1, 160
  'Bard's Epitaph, A', 5, 76, 98, 104–6
    symbolic burial in, 30, 70, 72
  'Broom Besoms' [B], 22
  'Charlie is My Darling',123
  'Corn Rigs', 70, 190
  'Cotter's Saturday Night, The', 5, 7, 11, 30, 54, 189
    influence on Nairne, 140
    mixed diction of, 56, 71, 77, 90
    Robert Aiken addressed in, 37–8
    virtuous peasantry and national character in, 22, 47, 53, 79
    William Burnes remembered in, 54, 65, 169, 175
  'Death and Dr Hornbook', 2, 41, 151–6
    aligned with 'Tam o'Shanter', 167, 171, 174, 178, 182
    as tall tale, 153, 158, 163, 166–7
    domestication of death in, 168
    exposé of local secrets, 151, 155
    Fergusson's influence on, 152
    MacDiarmid's 'A Drunk Man' and, 7, 156
    medical overconfidence in, 152, 154–5

    misread as autobiographical, 158
    resists prescription, 167
  'Death and Dying Words of Poor Mailie, The', 3, 11, 44, 52, 62–4
    as comic elegy, 54
  'Despondency, an Ode', 5, 32, 98–102
    influence on Coleridge's 'Dejection, an Ode', 5, 68, 76
  'Dream, A', 56, 64, 78–9
  'Epistle from Esopus to Maria', 26, 189
  'Epistle to Davie', 41, 67, 72–3, 102
    homelessness in, 53, 68
    stanza form of, 102
    see also 'Cherry and the Slae'
  'Epistle to James Smith', 13, 53, 64, 66–7, 76, 104
  'Epistle to John Lapraik', 13, 44, 70, 96
    JL's imprisonment for debt, 67
  'Epitaph on a Henpeck'd Country Squire', 70
  'Farewell to the Highlands', 109–10, 112, 114–16
    see also *Scots Musical Museum*
  'Flow Gently, Sweet Afton', 112
  'From thee, Eliza, I must go', 70
  'Gloomy Night is Gathering Fast, The', 71–2, 112
  'Green Grow the Rashes', 46
  'Greensleeves', 19
  'greybeard, old wisdom, may boast of his treasures, The', 182
  'Halloween', 53, 55–6, 64–5
  'Handsome Nell' ('O once I lov'd'), 44, 46
  'Hey tutie tatey', 141–2
  'Highland balou, The', 118–19
  'Holy Fair, The', 30, 50, 53, 55, 62–4, 181
    Chrystis Kirk stanza in, 157
  'Holy Willie's Prayer', 31, 38, 41, 62, 125, 188
    as 'drunk man' poem, 152
    see also Fisher, William
  'I murder hate', 21, 182
  'In politics if thou would'st mix', 181
  'Is there, for honest Poverty' ('A Man's a Man'), 18, 22–3, 145–6, 149, 189
  'Jeremiah 15.th Ch. 10 V', 102–3
  'John Barleycorn', 44, 52–3, 190

'Lament, The', 32, 68, 99, 103
'Logan Water', 20, 22–3
'Love and Liberty: A Cantata', 116–17, 125–6, 158
  recitativo sections, 102
  speakers in, 3, 16, 22, 119–21, 126, 153
  suppression of, 63, 72, 103, 116
'Man Was Made to Mourn', 46, 68, 76, 190
  death in, 27, 69
  metre and stanza, 46–7
  social criticism in, 85–6, 88
'Montgomerie's Peggy', 45
'My bottle is a holy pool', 182–3
'My girl she's airy', 49
'O an ye were dead, guidman', 120
'O May thy morn', 133
'O'er the Water to Charlie', 114, 122
'On a Scotch Bard Gone to the West Indies', 67, 69, 77
'On the Death of Sir J. Hunter Blair', 96–7
'Poor Mailie's Elegy', 52, 55, 79
'Prayer in the Prospect of Death, A', 68
'Rights of Woman, The', 23–5
'Scotch Drink', 30, 53, 61, 176
'Scots Ballad' ('Bonie Lass of Albanie'), 122
'Scots Wha Hae', 73, 83, 141–3, 187
'Scottish Ballad' ('Last May a braw wooer'), 187–8
'Slave's Lament, The', 73, 125
'small birds rejoice, The', 110, 122–3, 135
'Song, Composed in August', 68, 70, 173
'Strathallan's Lament', 110–12, 114
'Tam Glen', 125
'Tam Lin', 47
'Tam o'Shanter', 2–3, 83, 151, 158–60, 166–79, 181–9
  Hugh MacDiarmid's adaptation of, 7, 160, 176–7
  see also MacDiarmid, Hugh
  mock epic, as, 73
  see also mock-epic
  narrator as witness in, 164, 172, 176
  utopian element in, 182
  Wordsworth and, 76, 88–9, 166
  see also 'Benjamin the Waggoner', under Wordsworth, William, shorter poems
'Tam Samson's Elegy', 76, 96–8
'Thames flows proudly to the sea, The', 124
'Thou lingering star', 112
'To a Haggis', 14–15, 21
'To a Louse', 15–17, 55, 70, 73, 78
'To a Mountain Daisy', 5, 32, 55, 68–9, 88, 95–6
  Wordsworth and, 76, 95–6
'To a Mouse', 55, 65–8, 73, 78, 96
  emergence of the Poet Burns persona, 5, 71
  homelessness in, 66–7
'To Ruin', 69, 101
'To the Same' (Second Epistle to Lapraik), 44, 67, 70, 96
  Wordsworth's recitation of, 77
'To William S*****n' (William Simson), 162
'Vision, The', 2, 56, 79–80, 92–3, 96–100, 126
  addressed in Wordsworth's 'Resolution and Independence', 84–5
  Burns as laureate of Kyle in, 56, 69, 77–8, 84, 110
  complaints about poverty in, 64, 79, 81
  descriptive stanzas cut for the 1786 *Poems*, 78
  Jean Armour's name removed from, 32, 68
  mixed personae (Burness and Burns) in, 65–6, 77, 79
  poetry and transgression in, 83
  poets and landscapes in, 81, 83
  Wordsworth's interpretation of, 5, 76–7, 80, 93–5, 96, 98–9
  Wordsworth's recitation of, 77
  'zenith' poets, and, 82
  see also Coila
'When she cam ben she bobbed', 132
'Whistle. A Ballad, The', 160–7, 172, 177, 181
  as mock epic, 2–3, 7, 164, 166
  see also mock-epic

use of Greek and Ossianic mythologies in, 163
'Winter Night, A', 189
'Winter, a Dirge', 52–3, 68
'Ye flowery banks o' bonie Doon', 47
'Yon wild mossy mountains', 21
Burns, Robert,
  as editor of songs, 27, 41, 113, 115
  coded authorship, 1, 27, 106, 112, 114, 185
  copyright, 1, 33, 39, 162
  death, 63, 89, 96, 98, 178
  diction
    English, 45, 50, 92, 117, 156
    hybrid, 1, 4, 9, 16, 56, 90, 135
    in songs, 41
    'natural', 8, 23
    neoclassical, 7, 82
    stylised, 11, 163, 171
    vernacular, 3, 49, 61, 90
    working people, of, 12, 18, 149,
  Highland landscape in, 111, 114–15, 119, 121, 123, 126
  Lowland landscape in, 48, 71, 78–9, 81
  masculinism and, 20–3, 25
  mock-elegy, 55, 70, 96–7
  mock-epic, 21, 96–7, 154, 158, 163, 166–72
  mixed diction in, 7, 92, 174–6
  and 'Poet Burns' persona, 3, 73
    see also Poet Burns persona
  national song and, 6, 93, 135–6, 150
  observing eye, his, 166–7, 172
  oxymoron, 62, 153, 163, 166, 168
  'Patriot-bard', as, 11, 65, 103
    see also 'The Cotter's Saturday Night', under Burns, Robert, poems and songs
  speech acts in, 66
  syllepsis in, 62, 153, 163
  tavern cameraderie in, 7, 20, 56–7, 173–4, 176, 181–2
Burns, Robert, the Younger, 94
Byron, George Gordon Noël, Baron, 81

'Ça ira', 23–26
  see also Bécourt
Calvinism, 31, 33, 53–4, 78, 171, 179–81
Cameron, May, 124
Campbell, John Lorne, 136–7
Campbell, Margaret, see Highland Mary
Campbell of Colquhoun, Mrs, 143
Carlisle, 125, 138
Carlyle, Alexander, 17
Carlyle, Thomas, 26
Carswell, Catherine, 24
Cervantes, Miguel de, 114
Chalmers, Margaret, 124
Chambers, Robert, 14–15, 169
Charles Edward Stuart, 134, 138, 147
  as portrayed in Burns, 110, 118, 119, 121–2, 123–4, 126
  death of, 122, 138
  disguise as Betty Burke, 133
  Nairne and, 6, 130, 134–5, 136, 147–8
  see also Stuart, Charlotte, Duchess of Albany
Chatterton, Thomas, 84–5
'Cherry and the Slae' metre, 52, 54, 59, 101–2
  see also Montgomerie, Alexander
Chevalier, The, see Charles Edward Stuart
'Chrystis Kirk of the Green', 157
  stanza-form and rhyme, 52–4, 59
Clanranald, Clan Macdonald of, 117–18
Clarinda, see Agnes M'Lehose
Clow, Jenny, 124
Coila (Muse of Kyle), 56, 59, 64, 66, 71–2
  in 'The Vision' 77–84, 87, 89, 93, 110
Coleridge, Samuel Taylor, 97, 99, 107, 156
  Burns texts admired by, 5, 68
  'Dejection', 5–6, 101
  friendship with Wordsworth, 76, 88, 93, 97, 105, 107
  'Rime of the Ancient Mariner, The', 156
Comyn, John (Red Comyn), 124
Count of Albany, The, see Charles Edward Stuart
Covenanters' tunes ('Dundee', 'Elgin', 'Martyrs'), 47–8
Craigdarroch, Alexander Fergusson of, 162–5
Crawford, Robert, 92
Crawford, Thomas, 12, 77, 119
Creech, William, 20, 39, 162
Crochallan Fencibles, 20, 124, 137

Cromek, R. H., *Reliques of Robert Burns*, 44, 49, 94
crones, 117, 120–1, 124, 126
Culloden, 17, 112, 123, 141
   Burns's family and, 132
   Nairne's family and, 6, 128, 130
Cunningham, Alexander, 94, 136
Cunningham, Allan, 29, 56, 58, 76–7
Currie, James, 94–5, 179
   Works of Burns, With an Account of His Life, 21, 34, 49, 123
Cynthia (goddess), 163–5

Daiches, David, 9
death-drive (Freud), 174
Deleuze, Gilles and Félix Guattari, 27
Derrida, Jacques, 79, 185, 188–90
'Deserted Village, The', *see* Goldsmith, Oliver
Dick, James C., 142
Dods, Captain, 25
Domestic Medicine, *see* Buchan, William
Donaldson, William, 121, 142
Douglas, Charles, 35, 37, 39
Douglas, Gavin, *Eneados*, 167–8
Douglas, Patrick, 35, 37–9
Douglass, Frederick, 4, 189–90
Dress Act, The (1746), 111
Drummond of Hawthornden, William, 197
Dryden, John, 91, 163
Duck, Stephen, 12
Dumfries, 93–4, 112, 181–2
Dunbar, William, 9, 157–8
Dunlop, Anna Wallace, 34, 36, 78, 180
Dunn, Douglas, 101
Dylan, Bob, 109–10, 113, 116, 143

Edinburgh, Burns and, 27, 39, 57, 111, 123–4, 141
Edinburgh Castle, 6, 127–8
Edinburgh Review, 13
Eliot, T. S., 1, 8–9, 156
Ellisland farm, 27, 159
Emerson, Ralph Waldo, 2, 16, 27, 190
emigration, 31–5, 37–40, 70, 73, 110, 189
epic, 163–4, 167–8, 170–1
erotic songs, *see* bawdry

exile, 5, 18, 24–5, 88
   in Burns's family, 26, 71–4, 96, 124–6, 132
   in Burns's Highland songs, 109–16, 143
   in Dante, 88
   in Nairne, 130
Excise, The, 23, 27, 74, 91, 93–4, 158–9
Fencibles, Crochallan, 20, 124, 137
Fénelon, François, *Les Adventures de Télémache*, 91
Fergusson, Robert, 18, 29, 57, 102–3, 153–5, 183
   biography, 7, 57, 77, 103, 159–60, 183
   bodies and embodiment, 176–7, 179
   'brawl' poem reinvented by, 157–8
   death in, 154, 160, 176, 178–9
   drink and, 6–7, 62, 64, 151–2, 177
   Edinburgh and, 11, 62–5, 152, 160–1, 162
   emulation by Burns, 4, 51, 53, 54, 60–5, 77
   midnight in, 158, 160
   poems:
      'Auld Reikie', 154, 161–2, 176
      'BUGS, The', 70
      'Caller Water', 61–2, 153
      'Canongate Playhouse in Ruins, The', 63, 102
      'Drink Eclogue, A', 152
      'Good Eating', 161
      'Farmer's Ingle, The', 4, 53, 56
      'Hallow-Fair', 62
      'Hame Content', 60
      'Job. Chap III. Paraphrased', 178
      'King's Birth-day in Edinburgh, The', 157, 161
      'Leith Races', 62, 157
      'Mutual Complaint of Plainstanes and Causey, The', 155, 160
      'On Seeing a Butterfly in the Street', 178
      'Ode to Hope', 176–7
      'Rising of the Session, The', 161
      'To Andrew Gray', 160–1
      'To My Old Breeks', 179
   Poems (1773), 63
   poverty of, 161–62
   slovenly attire, 162

vernacular forms and dialect, 18, 53–4, 63
  standard Habbie, 29, 53–4, 62
  whistle as trope in, 160–2, 165–6
Findlater, Alexander, 93–4
First Commonplace Book, The, 40–50, 68–9, 73, 182
  experiments with text placement and commentary, 36, 55
  metres used in, 3, 29, 71, 102, 106
  songs and poems in, 2–4
  speakers as observers in, 32
  title page of, 40–1, 49, 57–8
Fisher, William, 11, 189
  see also 'Holy Willie's Prayer', *under* Burns, Robert, poems and songs
Fletcher, Elizabeth, 77, 84
Fontenelle, Louisa, 23–4
  see also 'The Rights of Woman', *under* Burns, Robert, poems and songs
Franklin, Benjamin, 24, 38
Freud, Sigmund, *Beyond the Pleasure Principle*, 174
Freemasons, 20, 38, 137, 166, 181
Fuss, Diana, 20

gaberlunzie (beggar), 119
Gaelic, 9, 17, 19, 112, 133, 135–40
  Burns's Gaelic-derived words, 116–17
  Fergusson's Gaelic speakers, 63
Galloway Tam (song-protagonist), 112
Gebbie, Eliza, 69–70
The Gentle Shepherd, *see* Ramsay, Allan
George IV, 131, 147
  as Prince of Wales, 22, 122
Gilfallan, George, 157
Gill, Stephen, 77
Glenriddell Manuscript, 49, 103, 165
'God Save the King', 24–6
Goldsmith, Oliver, 42, 62, 90
  'The Deserted Village', 4, 11
Gow, Nathaniel, 144
Gow, Niel, 139
Graham, Douglas, 7, 172
Graham of Fintry, Robert, 23
Gray, Andrew, 160–2, 165–6
Gray, Thomas, 6–7, 55, 62, 82–3, 89–90
  'Elegy in a Country Churchyard', 10–11, 19, 49, 51, 90, 92

illiteracy in, 19, 70, 90, 105
'Ode on a Distant Prospect of Eton College', 68, 92, 100–1
Grieve, Christopher M., *see* Hugh MacDiarmid
Grove Dictionary of Music, 93, 135

Habeas Corpus Suspension Act (1794), 118
Hamilton, Gavin, 31, 35–6, 69–70
Hazlitt, William, 26, 159
hell, 62, 138, 153, 168, 172, 180
Hemans, Felicia, 26, 140
Henryson, Robert, 9
Herbert, W. N., 152
Heron, Robert, 58
'Hey tutie tatey' (old Scottish air), 141–3
Highlands, 109–16, 118–21, 124, 126, 135
  John Highlandman ('Love and Liberty'), 116–17, 119–20
  in Nairne, 6, 130, 140, 148
'Highlands' (song), *see* Bob Dylan
'Highland Mary' (Margaret Campbell), 40, 112
Hogg, James, 14, 122, 137–8
holy pools, 182–3
homelessness, 18, 35, 117, 119, 135
Homer, 164
Hume, David, 9, 19
Hume, Elizabeth and Agnes, 126

Imagined Communities, *see* Anderson, Benedict
'Inferno' (Dante Alighieri), 87–8
Irving, David, 159–60

Jacobinism, 88, 111, 141
Jacobitism, Burns and, 130, 110–16, 121–2, 125, 133–7, 149
  Burns's Jacobite speakers, 114, 121
Jacobite history, 17–18, 111–13, 118–19, 121–5, 135–8, 185
  see also Nairne, Carolina (Baroness), née Carolina Oliphant, songs
  see also Scottl, Sir Walter
  see also MacDonald, Alexander
  see also Burns, Robert, poems and songs
Jacobite Relics of Scotland, *see* Hogg, James
Jacobite songs, 1, 6, 88, 112–13, 118, 141–7

Jamaica, 5, 69, 96, 111, 173
   Burns's projected emigration to, 31–3, 35–8, 56–7, 96, 111, 173
      see also 'On a Scotch Bard Gone to the West Indies', under Burns, Robert, poems and songs
   plantations, slavery
Johnson, David, 138
Johnson, James, see Scots Musical Museum, The
Johnson, Samuel, see The Rambler

Kaplan, Cora, 25
Keats, John, 106
Kermode, Frank, 8, 10
King Charles III, 121, see Charles Edward Stuart
Kilmarnock MS, 2, 29, 32, 50, 52–6, 73
   relation to Poems (1786), 36, 54
Kinsley, James, 59, 99–100, 139, 142, 146, 182
   conjectural dating of Burns texts, 41–4, 48, 55, 104
Kirkoswald, 5, 7, 56, 90, 167, 172–5
Kyle, 5, 82, 92, 103, 112
   district boundaries, 56, 79, 90, 106, 110, 112
   poems and songs mentioning, 43, 69
   Burns as laureate of, 64–6, 69, 77–8, 84
   see also Coila

'Lamkin' (ballad), 166
Lapraik, John, 13
   see also 'Epistle to John Lapraik', under Burns, Robert, poems and songs
   see also 'To the Same', under Burns, Robert, poems and songs
Leask, Nigel, 77
Leavis, F. R. and Queenie D., 9
Lewars, Jessie, 93, 112, 143
literati of Edinburgh, 8, 18, 63
Lochlie farm, 54, 158
Loda, 163–5
Lowlands, 17, 19, 120, 124, 126, 135
   as 'Lawlanders', 117–18, 125
Lawrie, Sir Robert, 164
Lunardi, Vincenzo, 16
Lyrical Ballads, 75–6, 89, 97, 106
   see also Wordsworth, William

MacDiarmid, Hugh, 13, 158, 182, 183
   Burns and, 73, 156, 160, 177, 181
   adapts 'Tam o'Shanter', 7, 160, 176–7
   Drunk Man Looks at the Thistle, A, 151–7, 166, 176–7, 181–3
   Kist of Whistles, A, 161
   Lucky Poet, 154
   Nairne and, 128
McDiarmid, Matthew, 161
MacDonald, Alexander, 133–4, 136–9
MacDonald, Flora, 118, 133
McIvor, Fergus, 125
   see also Waverley
Mackay, James, 56
Mackenzie, Henry, 13, 26, 39, 158
M'Lehose, Agnes, 124, 133–4
M'Murdo, John, 165
Marx, Groucho, 72
Marx, Karl, 27, 182
Arthur Masson's Collection of Prose and Verse, from the Best English Authors, 46, 91–2
Masterton, Allan, 111, 137
Mauchline, 5, 14, 31, 62, 117, 119
Meston, William, 137
Miller, Patrick, 165
Milton, John, 7, 21, 62, 76, 88, 98–9
   Adam and Eve in PL, 61–2, 92, 112, 173
   'How soon hath time', 80
   'Il Penseroso', 182
   'L'Allegro', 188
   'Lycidas', 14, 64
   Paradise Lost, 13, 53, 91, 111–12
   'When I consider', 83
Mitchell, John, 93
mock elegy, 55, 96–7
Moore, Dr. John, Burns's autobiographical letter to, 34, 56–7, 66, 69, 169, 173–5
   Zeluco, 36
Montgomerie, Alexander, see 'Cherry and the Slae' metre
Morgan, Edwin, 53–4, 72
Mossgiel farm, 34–6, 65, 158
Mount Oliphant farm, 85, 90
Muir, Edwin, 9
Muir, Robert, 31, 179
Muirhead, James Patrick, 77
Murdoch, John, 90–2, 179

Nairne, Carolina (Baroness), née Carolina Oliphant, 4, 9, 126–32
  belated perspective, 6, 134, 136, 150
  Burns's influence on, 2, 4, 73, 116, 122, 189
  coded or anonymous authorship, 6, 126–8, 143–4, 147, 150, 185
    'Mrs Bogan of Bogan' (B. B.), 126–7
  homeless people in, 6, 135, 147
  Jacobitism, and, 122, 127–8, 130–1, 134, 143–4, 147–9
    Jacobite sources, 136–9
  Lays of Strathearn [*Lays from Strathearn*], 128, 130, 132
  misconceptions about, 128, 147–9
  national song and, 6, 135–6, 150
  Scottish Minstrel, 126–8, 132, 140–1, 144
  songs:
    'Auld House, The', 130, 140
    'Caller Herring', 6, 135, 144–5
    'Laird o' Cockpen, The', 131–2
    'Land o' the Leal, The', 142–4
    'Lass of Livinstane, The', 140–1
    'Regalia, The', 128
    'Rowan Tree, The', 139–40
    'Will Ye No Come Back Again?', 6, 128, 134, 148, 150
    'Would Ye Be Young Again?', 147
  'The Auld House' (drawing), 147–9
Nairne, Lady, *see* Nairne, Baroness
Nairne, William Murray, 6, 128, 131
New Licht, 54
Newman, Steve, 12
Nichol, William, 137
Nietzsche, Friedrich, 151, 154, 157
Noble, Andrew, 13

odes, 78, 86, 92, 176, 189
  Burns's 'Despondency', 5–6, 32, 68, 99–102
    see also Burns, Robert, poems and songs
  Coleridge's' 'Dejection', 5, 101
    see also Coleridge, Samuel Taylor
  Gray's 'Eton College ode', 68, 92, 100
    see also Gray, Thomas
  Warton's laureate odes, 56, 78
    see also Warton, Thomas

Wordsworth's 'Immortality', 5, 86, 100, 140
  see also Wordsworth, William
Oliphant, Carolina, *see* Nairne, Baroness
Oliphant, Charles, 143, 147
Oliphant, Laurence, Sr, 130
Oliphant, Laurence, Jr, 126, 143, 147
opere buffe, 175
Ossian, 62, 96, 98–9, 114, 163–4
Oswald's Pocket Companion, 139
'Over the Water to Ch—lie (Jacobite stanzas), 138

Paine, Thomas, 24–5, 146
Parliament, 61, 120–1, 150
Paterson, Don, 2, 49
Paton, Elizabeth, 30, 33, 39, 42, 57, 78
Peblis to the Play, 157
Phoebus, 163, 165
  see also Apollo
'Pierre Menard, Author of the Quixote', *see* Borges, Jorge Luis
Pindar, 101
Pittock, Murray, 138
plantations, 3, 30, 33, 36–9, 70, 125
Poems, Chiefly in the Scottish Dialect (1786), 5, 10, 18, 29–30, 40, 56–71
  motifs of farewell and burial in, 26, 60, 72
  Wordsworth's reaction to, 75, 79–80, 83, 95, 98
Poems, Chiefly in the Scottish Dialect (1787), 42, 48, 53, 62, 71, 78
  changes in and additions to, 32, 64, 71, 78
  Hugh Blair's advice and critiques, 16, 63–4
  profits, 36
  subscribers, 24, 126
Poems, Chiefly in the Scottish Dialect (1793), 48, 162
'Poet Burns' persona, 3–5, 13–14, 40, 53, 65, 186
  in *Poems* (1786), 71–4, 77–9
  in songs, 110–11
  in 'Tam o'Shanter', 151, 175
  in 'The Whistle', 163
Poetical Sketches, 75
  see also Wordsworth, William

'Polemo-Middinia', *see* Drummond of Hawthornden, William
Pope, Alexander, 14, 163
   'Eloisa to Abelard', 100
   'Elegy to the Memory of an Unfortunate Lady', 68
   'Messiah, The', 91
   'Rape of the Lock, The', 163, 165
popular songs, 4, 46, 118
postcolonial approaches to Scottish literature, 9, 17–20
predestination, 33, 62, 171
Prelude, The, 80, 88, 106
   see also Wordsworth, William
Purdie, Robert, 126–7

The Rambler, 91
Ramsay, Allan, 11, 18, 59, 63, 91
   The Gentle Shepherd, 11–12
   Scots Proverbs, 186–88
'Rashes, The' (Jacobite-related air), 133
Redgauntlet, 109
   see also Scott, Sir Walter
Regency Bill crisis (1788), 22, 139
Rich, Adrienne, 88
Richmond, John, 14, 39, 50
Ricks, Christopher, 77, 93
Riddell, Maria, 94
Riddell, Robert, 23, 162–6
'Rob Burness' persona, 3–5, 27, 30, 48–50, 57, 186
   in early manuscripts, 29–30, 32, 40–1, 44, 53–5
   in *Poems* (1786), 65, 67, 69, 71–3, 79, 106
Robertson, Margaret, 139
Rogers, Charles, 132, 147
Rodgers, Hugh, 90
Ross, Alexander, 12, 77
Ross, Marlon B., 23

Satan, 62, 64, 66, 168–72
   Milton's Satan in *PL*, 13, 53, 111
   see also 'Address to the Deil', *under* Burns, Robert, poems and songs
'Scotch Poems', *see Kilmarnock Manuscript*
Scots Musical Museum, The, 54, 89, 115, 120–1, 126
   Burns as contributor, coeditor, 27, 128
   Burns's notes in, 112
   'Farewell to the Highlands' in, 109, 112–13, 115, 116
      see also Burns, Robert, poems and songs
   'Hey tutie tatey' in, 141–2
      see also Burns, Robert, poems and songs
   'Highland balou, The' in, 118–19
      see also Burns, Robert, poems and songs
   Law manuscript, 112, 142
   'Tam Lin' in, 47
      see also Burns, Robert, poems and songs
   'Strong Walls of Derry' (traditional) in, 112
      see also Johnson, James
Scott, Sir Walter, 9, 125, 128, 185
   see also Redgauntlet and *Waverley*
Scottish Enlightenment, 18–19
Scottish National Party, 142
Scrutiny, *see* Leavis, F.R. and Queenie D.
Second Commonplace Book (Edinburgh), 142
Seditious Meetings Act (1795), 118
Select Collection, The, *see* Thomson, George
Shakespeare, William, 7, 29, 63, 111, 185
   Julius Caesar, 187–9
'Shawnboy' (air), 139
Scheherazade (*1001 Nights*), 155
Shelley, Percy, 27
Shenstone, William, 6, 40, 82–3, 89
   'The Schoolmistress', 90, 92
Sharpe, Charles, 24
Shiach, Morag, 23
'Sir Andrew Barton' (ballad), 164
'Sir Patrick Spens' (ballad), 101
Skoblow, Jeffrey, 91, 152
slavery, 25, 141, 145, 187, 189, 199
   in Jamaica, 36–8, 70, 111
      see also 'Address to the Deil', *under* Burns, Robert, poems and songs
   see also Douglass, Frederick
   see also 'Scots Wha Hae', *under* Burns, Robert, poems and songs
   see also 'The Slave's Lament', *under* Burns, Robert, poems and songs
Smith, Adam, 9, 19, 41
Smith, Barbara Herrnstein, 10
Smith, G. Gregory, 151–2, 157
Smith, George, 54
Smith, James, 13, 53, 76, 104

Smollett, Tobias, 9, 17–18
Sneddon, David, 50, 52
Sommers, Thomas, 160
sorner (beggar), 119
Spectator, The, 91
   see also Addison, Joseph
Spenserian stanza-form, 47, 51, 56, 59, 90
Speirs, John, 9
Spivak, Gayatri, 15, 17–18
Stair Manuscript, 49
standard Habbie in Burns, 46, 51–4, 61–2, 65, 104
   in Fergusson, 29, 53, 61–2, 158
   in Wordsworth, 80, 88, 104, 106
Stafford, Fiona, 77
Stephen, Leslie, 23
Sterne, Laurence, 60, 69
Stevenson, Robert Louis, 12–13, 160
'Strong Walls of Derry' (trad. song), 113–14, 123
Stuart, Charlotte, Duchess of Albany, 122
Syllepsis in Burns, 62, 153, 163

Talbot, Colonel, 119
   see also Scott, Sir Walter, *Waverley*
Tarbolton, 20, 42, 60, 70, 154–5
Thomson, George, 21–2, 120, 128, 135
   see also Select Collection
Thomson, James, 6, 82, 87, 89–92
Thomson, Margaret, 7, 56, 70, 173–5
To the Lighthouse, see Woolf, Virginia
Treasonable and Seditious Practices Act (1795), 118
Tristram Shandy, see Laurence Sterne
True Loyalist, The, 137–9, 146
Truth, Sojourner, 25

Union of Parliaments, 17

Virgil, 91
   Aeneid, 163, 167–8, 176
Vindication of the Rights of Woman, A, see Wollstonecraft, Mary

Walkinshaw, Clementina, 122
Warton, Thomas, 56, 64, 78
'Waulking Song, A', see Alexander MacDonald
Waverley, 109–10, 118–19, 128, 130, 138
   see also Scott, Sir Walter
Weston, John C., 90
Whitman, Walt, 2, 88
Williams, Helen Maria, 25
Williams, Raymond, 12–13
Wilson, Hugh, 54
Wilson, John (Dr Hornbook), 166
Wilson, John (printer), 30, 32, 56
Wilson, Robert (suitor of Jean Armour), 31-2
Wollstonecraft, Mary, 25
Woolf, Virginia, 15
Wordsworth, Dorothy, 4, 75, 85, 88, 94–5,105
Wordsworth, William, 4, 6, 13, 14, 111, 189
   ambivalence about Burns, 26, 75, 83, 93, 94–5, 98
   Burns poems echoed in Wordsworth
   'A Bard's Epitaph', 5
   'Despondency', 68
   'Lament, The', 99
   'Man Was Made to Mourn', 27, 68
   'Tam o'Shanter', 158–9, 166, 171
   'Tam Samson's Elegy', 97–8
   'The Vision', 5, 77, 80–7, 96, 99–100
   'To a Mountain Daisy', 5, 95–6
   see also under Burns, Robert, poems and songs
   Burnsworth persona, 75–6, 84, 87–8, 104, 107
   diction, 11, 75, 76–7, 89
   elements in Burns admired by, 3, 5–6, 68, 73, 76–7, 83
   first encounter with Burns's *Poems* (1786), 58, 65, 75, 79, 80–1,106
   Leech Gatherer, 85, see also 'Resolution and Independence'
   'Letter to a Friend of Robert Burns', 77, 94, 159
   shorter poems:
   'At the Grave of Burns', 80, 105–6, 107
   'Benjamin the Waggoner', 76, 88
   'Hart Leap Well', 106
   'If thou indeed derive thy light', 77, 80
   'Lines in Early Spring', 87
   'Ode: Intimations of Immortality', 5, 76, 86, 100–2, 140
   'Poet's Epitaph, A', 104–5

'Resolution and Independence', 76, 79, 81, 83–7, 104–5, 107
'Simon Lee, the Old Huntsman', 76, 97–8
'Tintern Abbey', 88, 106
'"There!" said a Stripling', 76, 95
'There was a boy', 106
'Thoughts Suggested the Day Following', 76, 93
'To the Sons of Burns', 76, 88, 96, 100
'Written in a Blank Leaf of Macpherson's Ossian', 98–9
see also The Prelude
poets as stars, 80–4
Rydal Mount, 81
suppresses Burns's social dimension, 87–8
visits Dumfries, 93, 96

Young, Edward, 48, 62, 100